# Quicken 2007

## THE OFFICIAL GUIDE

**Maria LANGER**

**McGraw-Hill**

New York   Chicago   San Francisco
Lisbon   London   Madrid   Mexico City   Milan
New Delhi   San Juan   Seoul   Singapore   Sydney   Toronto

**The *McGraw-Hill* Companies**

McGraw-Hill books are available at special quantity discounts to use as premiums and sales promotions, or for use in corporate training programs. For more information, please write to the Director of Special Sales, Professional Publishing, McGraw-Hill, Two Penn Plaza, New York, NY 10121-2298. Or contact your local bookstore.

### Quicken® 2007 The Official Guide

1234567890 CUS CUS 019876

ISBN-13: 978-0-07-226380-0

ISBN-10:    0-07-226380-6

**Sponsoring Editor**
  Megg Morin

**Editorial Supervisor**
  Janet Walden

**Project Editor**
  LeeAnn Pickrell

**Acquisitions Coordinator**
  Agatha Kim

**Technical Editor**
  Intuit

**Copy Editor**
  William McManus

**Proofreader**
  Susie Elkind

**Indexer**
  Rebecca Plunkett

**Production Supervisor**
  James Kussow

**Composition**
  Apollo Publishing Services

**Art Director, Cover**
  Jeff Weeks

**Cover Designer**
  Pattie Lee

To Mike Barden, for believing in me

# Contents At A Glance

## Part Five   The Planning Center

## Part Six   The Tax Center

## Part Seven   Appendixes

# Contents

## Part Two   The Cash Flow Center

# Part Three    The Investing Center

## Part Seven Appendixes

# Acknowledgments

This book, like any other, is the end product of a lot of imagination and hard work by many people. I'd like to take a moment to thank some of the people who were involved with the creation of this book.

First, a big thanks goes out to Megg Morin, acquisitions editor at McGraw-Hill. Megg worked hard to keep me motivated to work on this project (the sushi really helped!) and, as usual, did her best to make things run smoothly.

Many thanks go out to the folks at Intuit, including Rebecca Fogg and Kjirsten Petersen. Another thanks goes out to the Quicken 2007 development and beta teams for their hard work in fine-tuning Quicken to make it better than ever. But the biggest thanks go out to Mike Barden for his prompt technical editing and response to questions.

More thanks go out to the production and editorial folks at McGraw-Hill—including LeeAnn Pickrell, Bill McManus, Agatha Kim, Susie Elkind, and Rebecca Plunkett—and the production team at Apollo.

The last thanks goes to my husband Mike, for putting up with me for the past 23 years.

# Introduction

Choosing Quicken Personal Finance Software to organize your finances was a great decision. Quicken has all the tools you need to manage your personal finances. Its well-designed, intuitive interface makes it easy to use. And its online and automation features make entering transactions and paying bills a snap. But if that isn't enough, Quicken also offers features that can help you learn more about financial opportunities that can save you time and money—two things there never seems to be enough of.

This introduction tells you a little about the book, so you know what to expect in the chapters to come.

## About This Book

Throughout this book, I tell you how to get the most out of Quicken. I start by explaining the basics—the common everyday tasks that you need to know just to use the program. Then I go beyond the basics to show you how to use Quicken to save time, save money, and make smart financial decisions. Along the way, I show you most of Quicken's features, including many that you probably didn't even know existed. You'll find yourself using Quicken far more than you ever dreamed you would.

### Assumptions

In writing this book, I had to make a few assumptions about your knowledge of your computer, Windows, Quicken, and financial management. These assumptions give me a starting point, making it possible for me to skip over the things that I assume you already know.

#### What You Should Know About Your Computer and Windows

To use this book (or Quicken 2007, for that matter), you should have a general understanding of how to use your computer and Windows. You don't need to be an expert. As you'll see, Quicken uses many standard and intuitive interface elements, making it easy to use—even if you're a complete computer novice.

At a bare minimum, you should know how to turn your computer on and off and how to use your mouse. You should also know how to perform basic Windows tasks, such as starting and exiting programs, using menus and dialog boxes (called just *dialogs* in this book), and entering and editing text.

If you're not sure how to do these things, check the manual that came with your computer or try working through the Windows Tour. These two resources can provide all the information you need to get started.

## What You Should Know About Quicken and Financial Management

You don't need to know much about either Quicken or financial management to get the most out of this book; I assume that both are new to you.

This doesn't mean that this book is just for raw beginners. I provide plenty of useful information for seasoned Quicken users—especially those of you who have used previous versions of Quicken—and for people who have been managing their finances with other tools, such as other software (welcome to Quicken!) or pencil and paper (welcome to the new millennium!).

Because I assume that all this is new to you, I make a special effort to explain Quicken procedures as well as the financial concepts and terms on which they depend. New concepts and terms first appear in italic type. By understanding these things, not only can you better understand how to use Quicken, but you also can communicate more effectively with finance professionals such as bankers, stock brokers, and financial advisors.

## Organization

This book is logically organized into seven parts, each with at least two chapters. Each part covers either general Quicken setup information or one of Quicken's five financial centers. Within each part, the chapters start with the most basic concepts and procedures, most of which involve specific Quicken tasks, and then work their way up to more advanced topics, many of which are based on finance-related concepts that Quicken makes easy to master.

I want to stress one point here: It is not necessary to read this book from beginning to end. Skip around as desired. Although the book is organized for cover-to-cover reading, not all of its information may apply to you. For example, if you're not the least bit interested in investing, skip the chapters in the Investing Center part. It's as simple as that. When you're ready for the information that you skipped, it'll be waiting for you.

Now here's a brief summary of the book's organization and contents.

### Part One: Quicken Setup and Basics

This part of the book introduces Quicken's interface and features and helps you set up Quicken for managing your finances. It also provides the information you need to set up and test Quicken's online features. If you're brand-new to Quicken, I highly recommend reading at least the first three chapters in this part of the book.

Part One has four chapters:

- **Chapter 1:** Getting to Know Quicken
- **Chapter 2:** Using Quicken Express Setup
- **Chapter 3:** Setting Up Accounts, Categories, and Classes
- **Chapter 4:** Going Online with Quicken and Quicken.com

## Part Two: The Cash Flow Center

This part of the book explains how to use Quicken to record financial transactions in bank and credit card accounts. One chapter concentrates on the basics, while another goes beyond the basics to discuss online features available within Quicken and on Quicken.com. This part of the book also explains how to automate many transaction entry tasks, reconcile accounts, and use Quicken's revised reporting features.

There are five chapters in Part Two:

- **Chapter 5:** Recording Bank and Credit Card Transactions
- **Chapter 6:** Using Online Banking Features
- **Chapter 7:** Automating Transactions and Tasks
- **Chapter 8:** Reconciling Your Accounts
- **Chapter 9:** Examining Your Cash Flow

## Part Three: The Investing Center

This part of the book explains how you can use Quicken and Quicken.com to keep track of your investment portfolio and get information to help you make smart investment decisions. The first chapter covers the basics of Quicken's investment tracking features, while the other two chapters provide information about online investment tracking and research tools and the features within Quicken.com that help you evaluate your investment position.

There are three chapters in Part Three:

- **Chapter 10:** Entering Your Investment Transactions
- **Chapter 11:** Using Transaction Download and Research Tools
- **Chapter 12:** Evaluating Your Position

## Part Four: The Property & Debt Center

This part of the book concentrates on assets and liabilities, including your home and car and related loans. It explains how you can track these items in Quicken and provides tips for minimizing related expenses.

There are three chapters in Part Four:

- **Chapter 13:** Monitoring Assets and Loans
- **Chapter 14:** Managing Household Records
- **Chapter 15:** Keeping Tabs on Your Property and Debt

## Part Five: The Planning Center

This part of the book tells you how you can take advantage of Quicken's extensive, built-in planning tools to plan for your retirement and other major events in your life. As you'll learn in this part of the book, whether you want financial security in your retirement years or to save up for the down payment on a house or college education for your children, Quicken can help you. It covers Quicken's Planners as well as its financial calculators. It also provides a wealth of tips for saving money and reducing debt.

There are three chapters in Part Five:

- **Chapter 16:** Planning for the Future
- **Chapter 17:** Using Financial Calculators
- **Chapter 18:** Reducing Debt and Saving Money

## Part Six: The Tax Center

This part of the book explains how you can use Quicken's Tax Center features to simplify tax preparation, plan for tax time, and reduce your tax liability.

Part Six has two chapters:

- **Chapter 19:** Simplifying Tax Preparation
- **Chapter 20:** Planning for Tax Time

## Part Seven: Appendixes

If twenty chapters of information aren't enough for you, two appendixes offer additional information you might find useful when working with Quicken:

- **Appendix A:** Managing Quicken Files
- **Appendix B:** Customizing Quicken

# Conventions

All how-to books—especially computer books—have certain conventions for communicating information. Here's a brief summary of the conventions I use throughout this book.

## Menu Commands

Quicken, like most other Windows programs, makes commands accessible on the menu bar at the top of the application window. Throughout this book, I tell you which menu commands to choose to open a window or dialog or to complete a task. I use the following format to indicate menu commands: Menu | Submenu (if applicable) | Command.

## Keystrokes

Keystrokes are the keys you must press to complete a task. There are two kinds of keystrokes.

**Keyboard Shortcuts**   Keyboard shortcuts are combinations of keys you press to complete a task more quickly. For example, the shortcut for "clicking" a Cancel button may be to press the ESC key. When instructing you to press a key, I provide the name of the key in small caps like this: ESC. If you must press two or more keys simultaneously, I separate them with a hyphen, like this: CTRL-P.

**Literal Text**   Literal text is text that you must type in exactly as it appears in the book. Although this book doesn't contain many instances of literal text, there are a few. I display literal text in boldface type like this: **Checking Acct**. If literal text includes a variable—text you must substitute when you type—I include the variable in bold-italic type like this: *Payee Name*.

## Icons

I use icons to flag two specific types of information.

**New in Quicken 2007**   In addition to interface changes, the folks at Intuit made changes to Quicken's feature set. The New in Quicken 2007 icon identifies many new features.

**Quicken Premier**   This book covers Quicken Deluxe and Quicken Premier. The Quicken Premier icon identifies those features available in the Premier version of Quicken only.

## Sidebars

This book also includes "What Does This Mean to You?" sidebars. These sidebars are my attempt to put a specific Quicken feature into perspective by either telling you how I use it or offering suggestions on how you can use it. I think you'll learn a lot from these sidebars, but like all sidebars, they're not required reading.

# About the Author

Finally, let me tell you a little bit about me.

I graduated from Hofstra University with a BBA in Accounting in—well, you don't really need to know *when*. I worked as an accountant, auditor, and financial analyst over the next eight years. Then I realized that I really didn't like what I was doing every day and took the necessary steps to change careers. I've written more than 60 computer books since the change, many of which are about business and productivity software such as Word, Excel, and FileMaker Pro. In 1998, I wrote *Quicken 99: The Official Guide,* and since then I've been revising it for each update of Quicken.

I use Quicken. I've been using it for years. I use it to manage multiple bank and credit card accounts, track three mortgages and a home equity loan, and pay all of my bills (online, of course). I also use its investment features to track my portfolio and research the companies in which I invest. While I don't use all Quicken features regularly, I've used most of them at least once to keep track of my finances and plot my financial future.

Frankly, I can't imagine not using Quicken. And I'm glad to have the opportunity to show you why you should agree.

# Quicken Setup and Basics

This part of the book introduces Quicken Personal Finance Software's interface and features. It begins by explaining how to install Quicken and showing you the elements of its user interface. It offers an entire chapter with instructions for setting up Quicken for the first time using the Quicken Express Setup feature. Then it tells you all about Quicken's accounts, categories, and classes, and explains how you can modify the default setup to add your own. Finally, it explains why you should be interested in online access and how you can set up Quicken to access the Internet and Quicken.com. The chapters are as follows:

**Part One**

# Getting to Know Quicken

## In This Chapter:

- *An overview of Quicken*
- *Installing Quicken*
- *Starting Quicken*
- *The Quicken interface*
- *Onscreen Help*

If you're brand new to Quicken Personal Finance Software, get your relationship with Quicken off to a good start by properly installing it and learning a little more about how you can interact with it.

In this chapter, I provide a brief overview of Quicken, explain how to install and start it, take you on a tour of its interface, and show you how to use its extensive Onscreen Help features. Although the information I provide in this chapter is especially useful to new Quicken users, some of it also applies to users who are upgrading.

## What Is Quicken?

On the surface, Quicken is a computerized checkbook. It enables you to balance your accounts and organize, manage, and generate reports for your finances. But as you explore Quicken, you'll learn that it's much more. It's a complete personal finance software package—a tool for taking control of your finances. Quicken makes it easy to know what you have, how you are doing financially, and what you should do to strengthen your financial situation.

## What Quicken Can Help You Do

At the least, Quicken can help you manage your bank and credit card accounts. You can enter transactions and have Quicken generate reports and graphs that show where your money went and how much is left.

Quicken can help you manage investment accounts. You can enter transactions and have Quicken tell you the market value of your investments. Quicken can also help you organize other data, such as the purchase price and current worth of your possessions, the outstanding balances on your loans, and vital information you may need in the event of an emergency.

With all financial information stored in Quicken's data file, you can generate net worth reports to see where you stand today. You can also use a variety of financial planners to make financial decisions for the future. And Quicken's tax features, including export into TurboTax and the Deduction Finder, can make tax time easier on you and your bank accounts.

Quicken's online features can automate much of your data entry. Online banking enables you to keep track of bank account transactions and balances and to pay bills without writing checks or sticking on stamps. Online investing enables you to download investment transactions. You can also read news and information about investment opportunities and advice offered by financial experts.

Now tell me, can the paper check register that came with your checks do all that?

## Quicken Basic, Deluxe, Premier, and Premier Home & Business

Intuit offers several versions of Quicken 2007 for Windows for managing personal finances: Basic, Deluxe, Premier, and Premier Home & Business.

Quicken Basic is an entry-level product designed for people who are new to personal finance software. As its name suggests, it includes basic features to track bank accounts, credit cards, investments, budgets, and loans. It also enables you to use online account access and payment, shop for insurance and mortgages, and download investment information for a brokerage account.

Quicken Deluxe is more robust. Designed for people who want to take a more active role in financial management, investments, and planning, it includes all the features in Quicken Basic plus the financial alerts feature, money-saving features for tax time and debt reduction, free access to investment information, and the Emergency Records Organizer and Home Inventory features.

Quicken Premier has all the features of Quicken Deluxe, plus additional features for investing and tax planning and preparation.

This book covers Quicken Premier. Although much of its information also applies to Quicken Basic and Deluxe, this book covers many features that are not included in the Basic version and a handful of features that are not included in the Deluxe version. (I use the Quicken Premier icon to identify those features that are available only in Quicken Premier.) If you're a Quicken Basic or Deluxe user, consider upgrading to Quicken Premier so you can take advantage of the powerful features it has to offer.

One more thing—Intuit also offers a special version of Quicken for small business owners: Quicken Premier Home & Business. This one program can handle all of your personal and basic business financial needs. If you're juggling the financial records for your personal life and a small business, be sure to check out Quicken Premier Home & Business—it can make the task a lot easier.

# Getting Started

Ready to get started? In this section, I explain how to install, start, and register Quicken.

## Installing Quicken

Quicken uses a standard Windows setup program that should be familiar to you if you've installed other Windows programs.

Insert the Quicken 2007 CD into your CD-ROM drive. A dialog should appear, offering to install Quicken 2007 on your hard disk. Click the Install Quicken button to start the Quicken installer.

If this dialog does not appear automatically, you can start the installer by double-clicking the My Computer icon on your desktop and then double-clicking the icon for your CD-ROM drive in the window that appears.

The installer displays a series of dialogs with information and options for installing Quicken. Read the information in the Welcome dialog and click Next to continue. When asked to agree to a software license agreement, select the I Accept The Terms In The License Agreement And Acknowledge Receipt Of The Quicken Privacy Statement option. (If you select the other option, you cannot click Next and cannot install the software.) You can click the Quicken Privacy Statement link to open this important document in a Web browser window and read it; close the browser window when you're finished to return to the installer. Click Next in the Install Wizard window.

In the Destination Folder dialog, the installer tells you where Quicken will be installed—normally, C:\Program Files\Quicken. You can click the Change button and use the dialog that appears to change the installation location. To keep the default location—which is what I recommend—just click Next.

In the Ready To Install The Program dialog, the installer displays a summary of what it will do. If this is a first-time Quicken installation, all it will do is install Quicken 2007. But if you're upgrading from a previous version, the installer will begin by uninstalling whatever version is currently installed. Only the Quicken program files will be deleted; your data files will remain intact so you can use them with Quicken 2007. Click Install.

Wait while the installer uninstalls the previous version of Quicken (if necessary) and copies the Quicken 2007 files to your hard disk. When installation is complete, the installer displays a dialog offering to check for Quicken updates. You have two options:

- **Get Update** uses your Internet connection to access updates on Intuit's Web site. I highly recommend using this feature if you have an Internet connection; then you start out using the very latest version of the Quicken 2007 software and financial institution information. When you click the Get Update button, the Quicken One Step Update Status window appears. Wait while it connects to the Internet, checks for updates, and downloads and installs available updates. The whole process should take less than a minute or so. In the Quicken Update window that appears, click the Use Quicken Now button.
- **Next** skips the update step. Use this option if you don't have an Internet connection or you'd rather update the software another time. When you click Next, another dialog appears, telling you that the Quicken installation is complete. Click Done to dismiss the dialog.

Quicken should start automatically. Skip ahead to the section titled "Preparing a Data File," later in this chapter, to start using Quicken. If Quicken does not start, follow the instructions in the next section to start it.

## Starting Quicken

You can start Quicken in several different ways. Here are the two most common methods.

**Opening the Quicken Shortcut**    An Express installation of Quicken places a Quicken Premier 2007 shortcut icon on your Windows desktop. Double-clicking this shortcut opens Quicken Premier.

**Opening Quicken from the Task Bar**    You can also use the Windows task bar's Start button to start Quicken and other Quicken components. Choose Start | All Programs | Quicken 2007 | Quicken 2007 to start Quicken.

## Preparing a Data File

Quicken stores all of your financial information in a Quicken data file. Before you can use Quicken, you must either create a data file with Quicken Guided Setup or convert an existing data file for use with Quicken 2007.

### New User Startup

If you're a brand-new Quicken user, a Welcome To Quicken 2007 dialog appears. You have two options:

**I Am New To Quicken.**   When you select this option and click Next, Quicken displays a dialog with two options for naming your data file:

- **I Will Use The Default File Name And Location** tells Quicken to name your data file QDATA and save it in C:\Documents and Settings\\*yourname*\\ My Documents\Quicken. Click Next to create the file.
- **I Want To Choose A Different File Name And Location** displays the Create Quicken File dialog when you click Next. Use this dialog to enter a name and select a disk location for your Quicken data file. Click OK in the dialog to create the file.

**I Am Already A Quicken User.**   When you select this option and click Next, Quicken displays the Select Your Data File dialog, which has three options:

- **Open A File Located On This Computer** displays the Open Quicken File dialog, which you can use to select a file on your hard disk. After selecting and opening a file, continue following the instructions in the section titled "Converting a Data File as Part of an Upgrade."
- **Restore A Quicken Data File I've Backed Up To CD Or Disk** enables you to open a backup file for use with Quicken 2007. (This option works only with files you created using Quicken's Backup command, which is discussed in Appendix A.) When you select this option and click Next, Quicken displays the Restore Quicken File dialog to locate and open the file you want to restore. When restoration is complete, Quicken instructs you to open the data file from the File menu. Choose File | Open and use the Open Quicken File dialog to locate and open the data file. If a dialog appears telling you that you have to convert the data file, continue following the instructions in the section titled "Converting a Data File as Part of an Upgrade."
- **Start Over And Create A New Data File** displays the Create Quicken File dialog, which you can use to enter a name for your new Quicken data file. Quicken then displays Quicken Express Setup so you can set up your data file. I explain how to use Quicken Express Setup in Chapter 2.

When you've created your Quicken data file, the Welcome screen of Quicken Express setup appears. It helps you set up your Quicken data file to meet your financial management goals and take advantage of the features Quicken has to offer. I explain how to use Quicken Express Setup in Chapter 2.

If you're following along and would like to set up your data file now, skip ahead to Chapter 2 and follow the instructions there. Then, to learn more about how Quicken works, read the section titled "The Quicken Interface," later in this chapter.

## Converting a Data File As Part of an Upgrade

If you upgraded from a previous version of Quicken, when you first start Quicken, it displays the Convert Your Data dialog (shown next). Clicking OK converts the existing data file named in the dialog to Quicken 2007 format and saves the original file in C:\Documents and Settings\*yourname*\My Documents\Quicken\Q06Files.

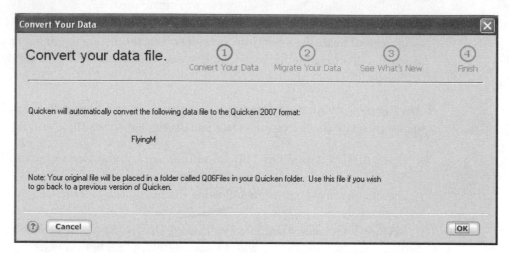

When the conversion is complete, Quicken displays the Upgrading To Quicken 2007 screen. Follow the prompts to learn what's new in Quicken 2007. When you're finished viewing information about new features, the Quicken Home window (see Figure 1-1), which I tell you about in the section titled "The Quicken Interface," appears.

# Registering Quicken

Sooner or later, when you launch Quicken after setting up a Quicken data file, the Product Registration dialog will appear. It tells you about the benefits of registering Quicken and offers buttons for getting more information or beginning the registration process.

The registration process has two parts. The first part is the basic product registration, which enables you to receive online software updates and download online stock quotes for free. The second part enables you to enter your Quicken.com member name, so you can customize certain features of Quicken.com to show your data. (If you don't have a member name, you'll be prompted to create one.) As you'll learn in Chapter 4 and throughout this book, Quicken.com is full of great features to help you manage your finances from any computer with an Internet connection, anywhere in the world. You'll need an Internet connection to complete the registration process and to access features on Quicken.com.

To start the registration process, click the Register Now button. Then follow the instructions that appear on the screen to enter information about yourself and your Quicken.com member name and password. When the registration process is complete, you can continue working with Quicken.

# The Quicken Interface

Quicken's interface is designed to be intuitive and easy to use. It puts the information and tools you need to manage your finances right within mouse pointer reach. You never have to dig through multiple dialogs and menus to get to the commands you need most.

In this section, I tell you about the components of the Quicken interface and explain how you can use them to make your work with Quicken easy.

## Account Bar

The Account Bar lists each of your Quicken accounts, organized by Center, on the left side of all Center and register windows (refer to Figures 1-1 and 1-3). If you can't see all of the accounts in the Account Bar, you can click the arrow button at the top or bottom of the Account Bar to scroll its contents. You can also click the – or + button beside a Center heading to hide or display the list of accounts beneath it. By default, account balances appear in the bar; you can right-click the Account Bar and choose Hide Amounts from the context menu that appears to hide amounts from view. (This also makes the Account Bar narrower so more information appears in the window beside it.)

The Center name headings in the Account Bar are actually buttons you can click to view each Center window. The Quicken Home button, which appears above the Account Bar, displays the Quicken Home window (refer to Figure 1-1). The account names are links; click an account name to view its register (refer to Figure 1-3). You can customize the Account Bar to move accounts from one Center to another or to hide an account from the Account Bar; I explain how in Chapter 3.

## Windows

Quicken displays information in windows. It uses different types of windows for the various types of information it displays.

### Centers

Centers, such as the Cash Flow Center, provide information about your financial status. They also offer clickable links to access related Quicken and Quicken.com features.

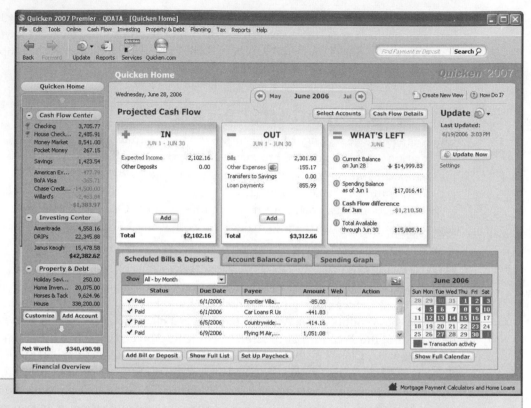

**Figure 1-1 • The Quicken Home window displays a concise summary of your current and projected financial situation.**

A Center exists for each major area of Quicken:

- **Quicken Home** (see Figure 1-1) provides an overview of your finances, including projected cash flow, scheduled bills and deposits, and Online Update status. You can create new views to show the things that interest you most; I tell you how in Appendix B.
- **Cash Flow Center** provides information about your cash, bank, and credit card accounts, as well as alerts and scheduled transactions. I discuss the Cash Flow Center and its options in detail in Part Two of this book.
- **Investing Center** provides information about your investment accounts and individual investments. I cover investing and the Investing Center in Part Three.
- **Property & Debt Center** provides information about asset and liability accounts, including your home, car, related loans, and auto expenses. I discuss the Property & Debt Center and related features in Part Four.

- **Planning Center** gives you access to Quicken's financial planners, as well as the assumptions you need to set up to use the planners effectively. I discuss Quicken's financial planners and the Planning Center in Part Five.
- **Tax Center** provides information related to your taxes, including projected taxes, a tax calendar, and your year-to-date income and tax-related expenses. I cover Quicken's tax features and the Tax Center in Part Six.

## List Windows

A list window (see Figure 1-2) shows a list of information about related things, such as accounts, categories, classes, or scheduled transactions. You can use a list window to perform tasks with items in the list.

## Register Windows

You use a register window (see Figure 1-3) to enter and edit transactions for a specific account. Each account has its own register. Page tabs at the top of the window enable

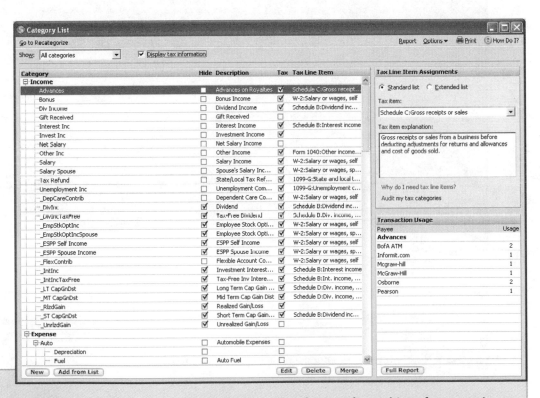

**Figure 1-2 • The Category List window displays a list of categories and transfer accounts.**

you to switch from the register entries to account information. A Bills And Scheduled Transactions list may appear at the bottom of some registers; you can hide this list if you like. I tell you more about using registers throughout this book.

## Report Windows

Quicken's report windows (see Figure 1-4) enable you to create and access subreports based on a main report. A list of all reports appears in the left column of the window. Click a report link to view the report in the main window. To create a subreport, double-click a report line item amount. You can also use options and buttons at the top of the window to work with, customize, and save reports. I explain how to create and customize reports and graphs in Chapter 9.

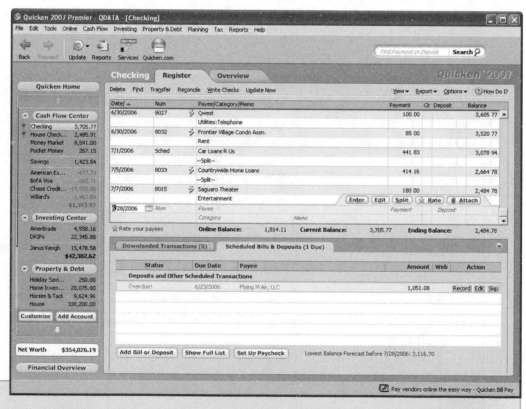

**Figure 1-3 • Here's a register window for a checking account.**

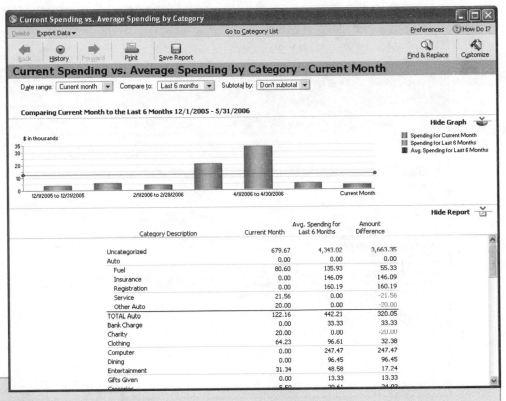

**Figure 1-4 • The report window usually includes a report and a graph.**

## Internet Window

Quicken features a built-in Web browser, which enables you to view information on Quicken.com from within Quicken in an Internet window (see Figure 1-5). I tell you more about Quicken's built-in browser and Quicken.com in Chapter 4.

## Features and Commands

Quicken offers a number of ways to access its features and commands, including standard Microsoft Windows elements such as menus and dialogs, and Quicken elements such as the toolbar, button bar, and links and buttons in Center windows.

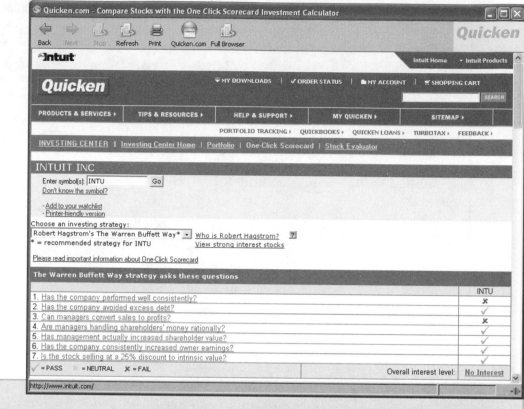

**Figure 1-5 • Quicken.com content appears in an Internet window like this one.**

## Menus

Like all other Windows programs, Quicken displays a number of *menus* in a menu bar at the top of the screen. You can choose commands from the menus in three ways:

- Click the menu name to display the menu. If necessary, click the name of the submenu you want (shown here), and then click the name of the command you want. Press ALT to activate the

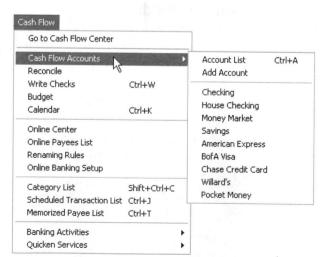

menu bar and press the keyboard key for the underlined letter in the menu that you want to open. If necessary, press the key for the underlined letter in the submenu that you want to open, and then press the key for the underlined letter in the command that you want.

- Press the shortcut key combination for the menu command that you want. A command's shortcut key, if it has one, is displayed to the right of the command name on the menu.

## Shortcut Menus

*Shortcut menus* (which are sometimes referred to as *context* or *context-sensitive* menus) can be displayed throughout Quicken. Point to the item for which you want to display a shortcut menu and click the right mouse button. The menu, which includes only those commands applicable to the item, appears at the mouse pointer, as shown here.

## Dialogs

Like other Windows applications, Quicken uses *dialogs* to communicate with you. Some dialogs display a simple message, while others include text boxes, option buttons, check boxes, and drop-down lists you can use to enter information. Many dialogs also include a Help button that you can use to get additional information about dialog options.

## Toolbar

The *toolbar* is a row of buttons along the top of the application window, just beneath the menu bar (see Figures 1-1 and 1-3), that gives you access to other navigation techniques and features. The toolbar is customizable; I explain how to customize it in Appendix B. Here's a quick look at the buttons that appear by default:

- **Back** displays the previously opened window.
- **Forward** displays the window you were looking at before you clicked the Back button. This button is only available if you clicked the Back button to view a previously viewed window.
- **Update** opens the One Step Update dialog so you can connect to the Internet and update all your online information at once. Clicking the triangle that's part of this button displays a menu of commands related to the One Step Update feature, including Update Settings, Manage My Passwords, and Schedule Updates. I discuss One Step Update in Chapter 7.

- **Reports** displays the main Reports & Graphs window, which you can use to create reports and graphs based on Quicken data. I cover Quicken's reporting feature in detail in Chapter 9.
- **Services** displays the Quicken Services window, which provides information about additional Quicken services.
- **Quicken.com** displays the Quicken.com home page in an Internet window. I introduce Quicken.com in Chapter 4.

## Button Bar

The *button bar* is a row of textual buttons and menus that appears just above the contents of many Quicken windows (refer to Figures 1-2, 1-3, and 1-4). Most items on the button bar, which vary from window to window, are buttons; simply click one to access its option. The items with triangles beside their names are menus that work just like the menu bar menus.

Keep in mind that Quicken's Onscreen Help may refer to the button bar as the *toolbar*. I refer to it as the *button bar* throughout this book to differentiate between it and the graphical toolbar at the top of the Quicken application window.

## Links and Buttons in Center Windows

Center windows, such as the Quicken Home window shown in Figure 1-1, include links and buttons you can click to get more information about using Quicken or to access its features. Although this book tends to concentrate on menu commands for accessing features, you can also access most of Quicken's features through various Center windows.

# Onscreen Help

In addition to the How Do I? menu in the button bar of many Quicken windows and the Help button in dialogs, Quicken includes an extensive Onscreen Help system to provide more information about using Quicken while you work. You can access most Help options from the Help menu, which is shown here.

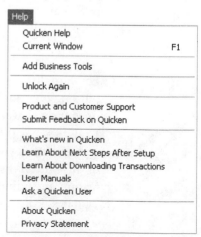

Here's a brief summary of some of the components of Quicken's Onscreen Help system.

## Quicken Help

Quicken's Onscreen Help uses the same Help engine used by most Windows programs. You can use it to browse or search Help topics or display Help information about a specific window.

## What Does This Mean to You? Onscreen Help

These days, any decent software program offers onscreen help. So what's the big deal about Quicken's?

Quicken's Onscreen Help is especially...well, *helpful*. It covers every program feature and provides step-by-step instructions for performing many tasks. Clickable links make it easy to jump right to a topic you want to learn more about. And as you'll discover while using Quicken, Help is available throughout the program—not just in the Quicken Help windows.

Onscreen Help also gives you, a Quicken user, the opportunity to help make Quicken a better software program. At the bottom of most Help windows, you'll find a link labeled "Give Us Feedback." Click this link to tell the folks at Intuit exactly what you need Quicken to do to make it more useful to you.

## Browsing or Searching Help

Start by choosing Help | Quicken Help. A Quicken Help window like the one in Figure 1-6 appears. The left side of the window has three tabs for browsing Help topics:

- **Contents** (see Figure 1-6 on the next page) lists Help topics organized in "books." Clicking a book opens or closes the book. Clicking a topic link displays information and links for accessing additional information in the right side of the window.
- **Index** lists Help topics alphabetically. You can enter a keyword at the top of the index list to narrow down the topics. Double-click a topic to display information about it in the right side of the window.
- **Search** enables you to search for information about a topic. Enter a search word in the top of the tab, and then click the List

Topics button. Double-click the title of a topic in the search results list to display information about it in the right side of the window.

### Getting Help for the Current Window

The Current Window command on Quicken's Help menu displays the Quicken Help window with information about the active window. This is probably the quickest and easiest way to get information about a specific topic or task with which you are working. You can also access this command by pressing F1.

## Product and Customer Support

The Product And Customer Support command on the Help menu opens the Quicken Product And Customer Support window, which offers links you can click to explore support options available on the Intuit Web site. Clicking a link displays related information in the window.

## User Manuals

In addition to the brief printed documentation that comes with the Quicken 2007 Deluxe or Premier CD-ROM, an electronic copy of the *Getting Started With Quicken* manual is available for download from the Intuit Web site. Choose Help | User Manuals, and then click the link labeled "Getting Started With Quicken" in the window that appears. Quicken uses its built-in Web browser to display a documentation page. Click links to download or view the documentation you want to see.

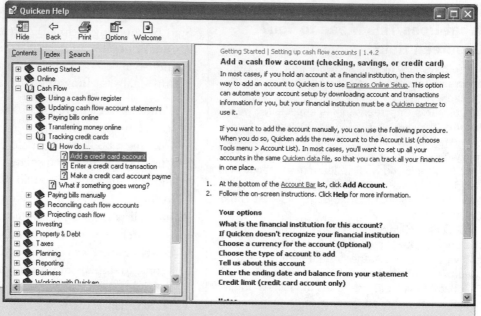

**Figure 1-6 • The Contents tab of Quicken Help makes it easy to browse through Onscreen Help for specific information.**

## Adding Features to Quicken

If you're wondering whether the version of Quicken installed on your computer is the best one for you, be sure to check out Help | Add Business Tools. This command displays a window that provides more information about features in Quicken Premier Home & Business. This window also includes links you can use to purchase unlock codes that will convert your version of Quicken to a more powerful version.

If you have already purchased an unlock code for Quicken, choose Help | Unlock Again to enter it into Quicken and upgrade immediately.

## Exiting Quicken

When you're finished using Quicken, choose File | Exit. This saves your data file and closes the Quicken application.

Sometimes when you exit Quicken, you'll be asked whether you want to back up your Quicken data file. I tell you how to back up data files in Appendix A.

# Using Quicken Express Setup

## In This Chapter:

- *Overview of data files and accounts*
- *Setting up a checking account*
- *Adding income items*
- *Adding credit cards and bill reminders*

To use Quicken Personal Finance Software, you must set up your Quicken data file for your financial situation. This means creating accounts and entering starting balance information.

Quicken's Express Setup makes setting up a Quicken data file easy by prompting you for information about yourself, your checking account, your paychecks or other regular income, and your credit cards and other bills. Quicken Express Setup automatically appears when you first start using Quicken—or when you create a new Quicken data file—to help get you started quickly.

In this chapter, I explain how to use Quicken Express Setup to create a Quicken data file for your financial situation. I also review how you can use information in your Quicken Home window to fine tune your data file to take advantage of all of Quicken's features.

## Chapter 2

# Before You Begin

Before you start the setup process, it's a good idea to understand how data files and accounts work. You should also gather together a few documents to help you set up your accounts properly.

## Data Files

All of the transactions you record with Quicken are stored in a *data file* on your hard disk. This file includes all the information that makes up your Quicken accounting system.

Although it's possible to have more than one Quicken data file, it isn't usually necessary. One file can hold all of your transactions. In fact, it's difficult (if not downright impossible) to use more than one Quicken file to track a single account, such as a checking or credit card account. And splitting your financial records among multiple data files makes it impossible to generate reports that consolidate all of the information.

When would you want more than one data file? Well, you could use two data files if you wanted to use Quicken to organize your personal finances and the finances of your business, which has entirely separate bank, credit, and asset accounts, or if you're using Quicken to track the separate finances of multiple individuals.

Appendix A covers a number of data file management tasks, including creating additional data files and backing up your data files.

## Accounts

An *account* is a record of what you either own or owe. For example, your checking account is a record of cash on deposit in the bank that is available for writing checks. A credit card account is a record of money you owe to the credit card company or bank for the use of your credit card. All transactions either increase or decrease the balance in one or more accounts.

Quicken Express Setup helps you create accounts within Quicken so you can track the activity and balances in your bank, credit card, investment, and other accounts.

## What You Need

To set up accounts properly, you should have balance information for the accounts that you want to monitor with Quicken. You can get this information from your most recent bank, investment, and credit card statements. It's a good idea to gather these documents before you start the setup process so they're on hand when you need them.

If you plan to use Quicken to replace an existing accounting system—whether it's paper-based or prepared with a different computer program—you may also find it helpful to have a *chart of accounts* (a list of account names) or recent financial statements. This way, when you set up Quicken accounts, you can use familiar names.

## Quicken Express Setup

Quicken Express Setup offers an easy-to-use interface for setting up a Quicken data file. It walks you through the setup process, step by step, so you can provide the basic information Quicken needs to help you manage your finances.

Quicken Express Setup—which was known as Quicken Guided Setup in previous versions of Quicken—has been completely overhauled for Quicken 2007. It's now quicker and easier than ever to use. Rather than spend a lot of time going through the process of setting up every aspect of your finances, Quicken Express Setup helps you to create just the accounts, categories, and reminder information you need to get started quickly.

In this part of the chapter, I explain how to use Quicken Express Setup to set up a Quicken data file.

### Getting Started

As discussed in Chapter 1, Quicken Express Setup launches automatically when you start using Quicken as a new user or create a new data file.

The first thing that appears is its Welcome window. It tells you a little about Express Setup and what it helps you do. After reading the information in the window and gathering together the appropriate documents, click the Next Step button at the bottom of the screen.

### Entering Information About You

Quicken Express Setup's Customize Quicken For You window, which is shown in Figure 2-1, prompts you to enter information about yourself, your spouse and dependents, and some of your property. It also asks whether you own a business. Quicken Express Setup uses this information for Quicken's planning and tax features and to determine what categories you'll need to record your transactions. I tell you about Quicken's planners in Part Five of this book, and about Quicken categories in Chapter 3 and throughout this book.

When you are finished entering information in this window, click Next Step.

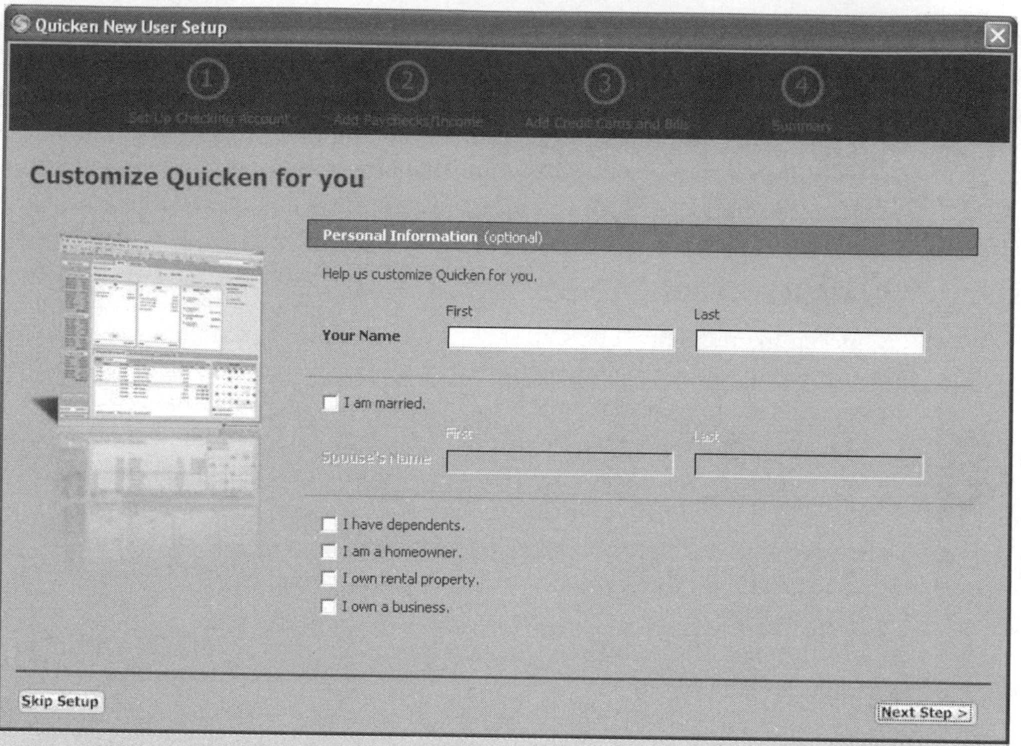

**Figure 2-1 • Enter some personal information Quicken needs to customize the data file for your financial situation.**

## Setting Up Your Primary Checking Account

Quicken Express Setup displays the Set Up Your Primary Checking Account window. Enter the name of your bank in the text box. As you type, Quicken tries to match what you type with a built-in list of financial institutions. If your bank's name appears in the list, you can select it to complete the entry. Click Next Step.

If your bank's branches are organized by location, connection type, or purpose, a dialog like the one shown here may appear. Choose the correct option from the drop-down list and click OK. If you don't know what option to choose, you can call your bank's online technical support department and ask which option to choose for using Quicken.

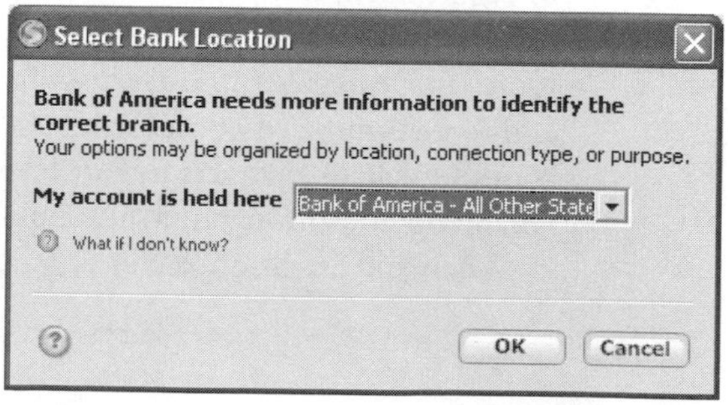

If your bank supports online account access, a window asks if you want to use this feature to connect to your bank. You have two options; the one you choose determines how to complete the account creation process.

## Completing the Account Creation Process by Connecting to Your Bank

Choose the Yes, I Want To Connect option to complete the account creation process automatically by connecting to your bank. This benefits you in two ways. First, information for your account is automatically downloaded into Quicken, saving you the bother of doing a lot of manual data entry. Second, if you have more than one bank account in your primary financial institutions, you can add all of the accounts to your Quicken data file using the Express Setup feature.

If you choose this option, the window expands, as shown in Figure 2-2, to offer text boxes for your username and password. Enter this information and click Next Step.

Quicken uses your Internet connection to connect to your bank. It then displays a list of all of your bank accounts. As you can see in the following illustration, each

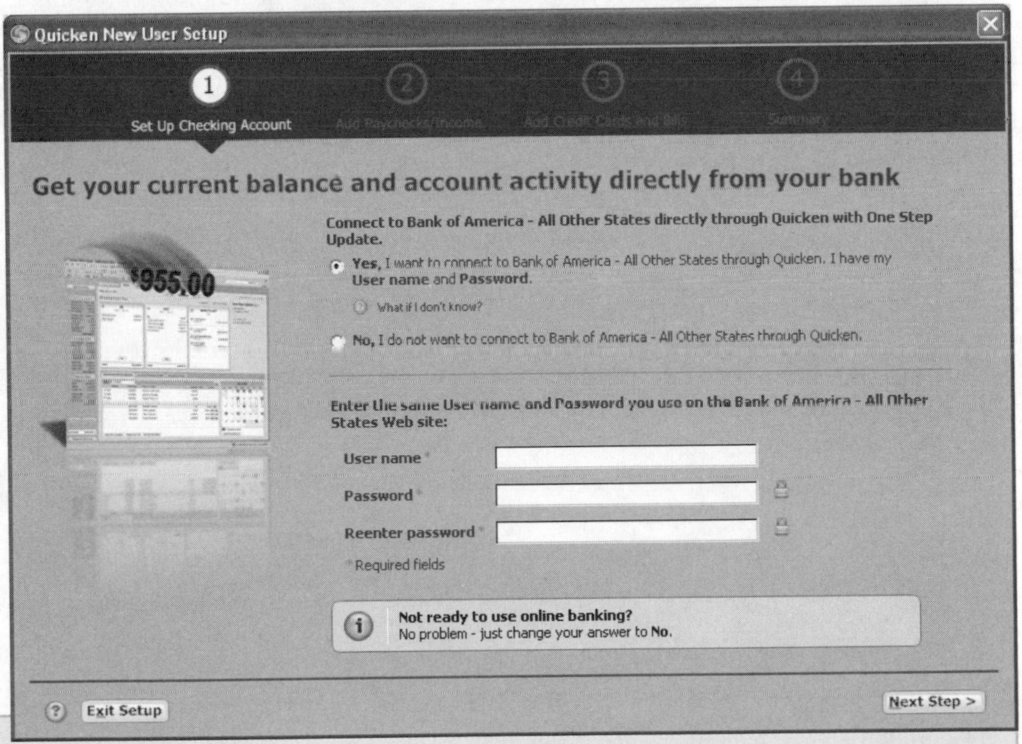

**Figure 2-2** • **Enter bank login information in this window.**

account is identified by its account number. Turn on the check box beside each account you want to track in your Quicken data file. You can also edit the contents of the Quicken Account Name column for each account to give it an easy-to-identify name, such as *My Checking* or *Joint Checking*. Then click Next Step.

| Add | Account Type | Quicken Account Name |
|---|---|---|
| ☑ | Checking | 00467619 Checking |
| ☐ | Checking | 00467615 Checking |
| ☐ | Checking | 00467417 Checking |

## Completing the Account Creation Process Manually

Choose the No, I Do Not Want To Connect option to complete the account creation process manually. The window expands to display fields for entering an account name, statement ending date, and ending date balance (see Figure 2-3).

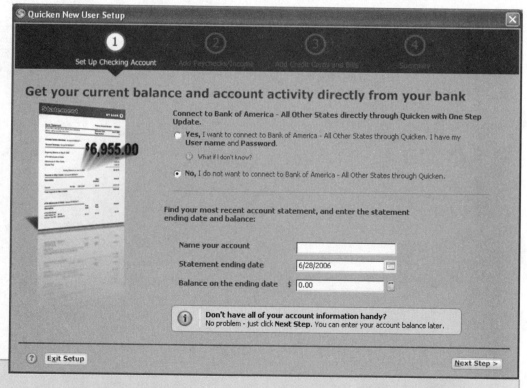

Figure 2-3 • Enter information about your primary checking account in these fields.

Give the account a name that makes sense to you—especially if you have more than one checking account. You can get the statement ending date and ending balance information from the account's most recent bank statement. Then click Next Step.

## Adding Deposits and Other Income

The Add My Deposits And Other Income window of Quicken Express Setup (see Figure 2-4) allows you to enter information into Quicken about the regular sources of income you (and your spouse) receive. This enables Quicken to plan for and remind you about income items.

To add an income item, enter information in the first row of the table in the window. You can press the TAB key to move from one field to the next. To add another item, click the Add Row button and follow the same procedure to enter

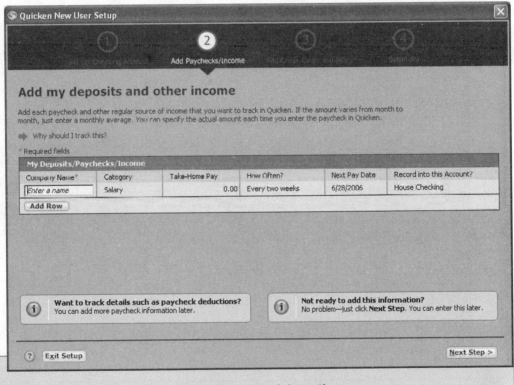

**Figure 2-4 • Use this window to add regular income information.**

information. The following illustration shows what this table might look like with three income items added:

| My Deposits/Paychecks/Income | | | | | |
| --- | --- | --- | --- | --- | --- |
| Company Name* | Category | Take-Home Pay | How Often? | Next Pay Date | Record into this Account? |
| Flying M Air | Salary | 1,235.95 | Every two weeks | 6/30/2006 | Maria's Checking |
| Arizona HVAC | Salary | 1,895.46 | Every two weeks | 7/7/2006 | Mike's Checking |
| Trust Distribution | Other Income | 1,000.00 | Quarterly | 7/1/2006 | Maria's Checking |
| Add Row | | | | | |

When you are finished entering income items, click the Next Step button.

## Adding Bills and Expenses

The Add Regular Bills And Expenses window of Quicken Express Setup (see Figure 2-5) enables you to schedule regular credit card and bill payments, whether the amounts are the same or different each time they're paid. This feature makes it

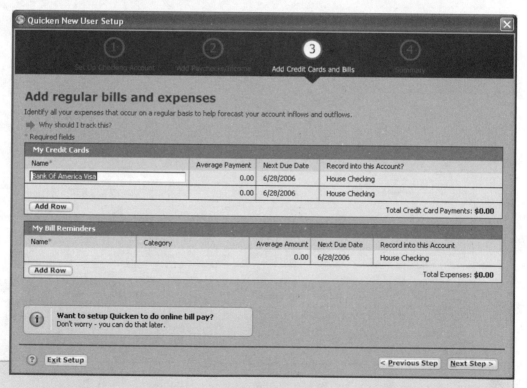

**Figure 2-5 • You can add credit cards and other regular payments to Quicken in this window.**

virtually impossible for you to forget a scheduled payment, while automating most of the bill payment entry tasks.

The Add Regular Bills And Expenses window is split into two parts: My Credit Cards and My Bill Reminders.

## Adding Credit Card Payments

The My Credit Cards part of the Add Regular Bills And Expenses window (refer to Figure 2-5) lists your credit cards, including any that might have been found while connected to your bank to set up your primary checking account.

For each credit card, fill in the information across a row of the table, pressing TAB to move from one field to the next. You can click the Add Row button to add additional credit cards. Here's what it might look like with two credit cards added:

| My Credit Cards | | | |
|---|---|---|---|
| Name* | Average Payment | Next Due Date | Record into this Account? |
| Bank Of America Visa | 250.00 | 7/15/2006 | House Checking |
| MBNA MasterCard | 500.00 | 7/22/2006 | Maria's Checking |
| Add Row | | | Total Credit Card Payments: **$750.00** |

## Adding Bills

The My Bill Reminders part of the window (refer to Figure 2-5) is for entering reminders about the bills you pay regularly. This might include payments for things like rent, electricity or other utilities, or car insurance.

For each bill, fill in the information across a row of the table, pressing TAB to move from one field to the next. Be sure to choose an appropriate category from the Category drop-down list. If a suitable category does not appear, choose one that's close; you can add a better category later. To add another bill, click the Add Row button. Because the My Bill Reminders area can only display two items at a time, if you have more than that, a scroll bar appears along the right side of the table's list, as shown next:

| My Bill Reminders | | | | |
|---|---|---|---|---|
| Name* | Category | Average Amount | Next Due Date | Record into this Account |
| APS | Utilities:Gas & Electric | 100.00 | 7/2/2006 | House Checking |
| Qwest | Utilities:Telephone | 60.00 | 7/1/2006 | House Checking |
| Add Row | | | | Total Expenses: **$194.00** |

When you are finished entering bills, click the Next Step button.

## Reviewing Your Setup Information

The Review Your Information window, which is shown in Figure 2-6, summarizes all of the information you have set up in your Quicken data file. Scroll through the information to see if it's complete. You can always add an income item, credit card payment, or bill reminder by clicking the Add Row button in the appropriate area. You can also modify an item's settings by clicking the item you want to change in the table and making the change, or delete an item by clicking its Delete button.

When you're satisfied with the setup, click Next Step. A Congratulations window appears. Click Finish to dismiss it.

## Finishing Up

Quicken Express Setup may perform a few more tasks before displaying the Quicken Home window for your new data file.

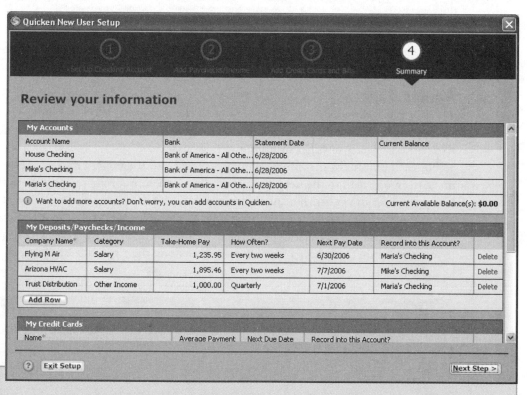

**Figure 2-6 • The Review Your Information window summarizes all setup information.**

If you set up your primary checking account by connecting to your bank, Quicken connects to your bank again to download transactions and balances. It displays the One Step Update window as it works. When the download is complete, it may display the Rename Your Payees dialog. I explain how to download transactions and rename payees in Chapter 6. When the download is complete, it displays the account register window for your checking account so you can review and accept downloaded transactions.

When the Quicken Express Setup process is complete, your Quicken Home window should appear (see Figure 2-7). It displays only the information you've provided manually or through transaction download.

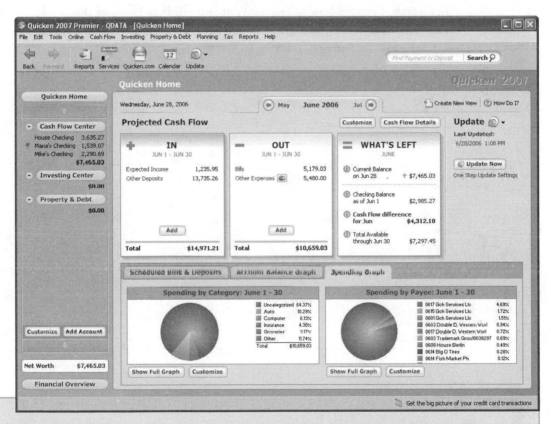

**Figure 2-7 • Here's what the Quicken Home window might look like immediately after using Quicken Express Setup and adding bank accounts via online access.**

## Other Setup Tasks

Quicken Express Setup provides just enough information to get you started using Quicken. Although you can start using Quicken immediately after completing the setup process, you might want to perform the following additional setup tasks to complete the setup of your data file:

- Add other bank or credit card accounts to track balances and net worth. I explain how in Chapter 3.
- Add other categories to categorize your income and expenditures. Chapter 3 explains how to do this, too.
- Add investment accounts, to track investments and include their value in your net worth. I explain how to track investments in Part Three of this book.
- Add asset and liability accounts to track the value of things you own and owe. I cover property and debt tracking in Part Four of this book.

# Setting Up Accounts, Categories, and Classes

**Chapter 3**

## In This Chapter:

- *Overview of setting up accounts*
- *Working with the Account List window*
- *Setting up categories and subcategories*
- *Working with the Category List window*
- *Setting up classes*
- *Working with the Class List window*

When you first set up your Quicken Personal Finance Software data file, it includes a number of default categories based on questions you answered in the Quicken Express Setup process. Don't think you're stuck with just those categories. You can add and remove categories at any time. The same goes for accounts—you can add them as you see fit. Modifying the accounts and categories in your Quicken data file is a great way to customize Quicken to meet your needs.

In this chapter, I explain how to modify and work with the Quicken accounts and categories you'll use to organize your finances. I also explain how to set up an optional categorization feature: classes.

## Accounts

To track your finances with Quicken, you must have created at least one account. While many of your expenditures may come from your checking account, you probably have more than one account that Quicken can track for you. By setting up all of your accounts in Quicken, you can keep track of balances and activity to get a complete picture of your financial situation.

If you used Quicken Express Setup to set up your Quicken data file, as discussed in Chapter 2, you should already have at least one Quicken account—your primary checking account—set up and ready to use. You can follow the instructions later in this chapter to set up other accounts.

This part of the chapter tells you a little more about Quicken's accounts and how you can use the Account List window to create and modify your accounts.

### Types of Accounts

As discussed in Chapter 2, an *account* is a record of what you either own or owe. Quicken offers various kinds of accounts for different purposes. Table 3-1 summarizes the accounts and how they are organized within Quicken.

#### What You Own

In accounting jargon, what you own are *assets*. In Quicken, an asset is one type of account; several other types exist as well:

| Account Type | Center | Center Group | Asset or Liability |
|---|---|---|---|
| Checking | Cash Flow | Spending | Asset |
| Savings | Cash Flow | Savings | Asset |
| Credit Card | Cash Flow | Credit | Liability |
| Cash | Cash Flow | Spending | Asset |
| Brokerage | Investing | Investment | Asset |
| IRA, SEP, Keogh | Investing | Retirement | Asset |
| 401(k), 403(b) | Investing | Retirement | Asset |
| Single Mutual Fund | Investing | Investment | Asset |
| House | Property & Debt | Asset | Asset |
| Vehicle | Property & Debt | Asset | Asset |
| Asset | Property & Debt | Asset | Asset |
| Liability | Property & Debt | Liability | Liability |

**Table 3-1 • Overview of Quicken Account Types**

**Spending**    Spending accounts, which are displayed in the Cash Flow Center, are used primarily for expenditures. Quicken distinguishes between two types of spending accounts: Checking and Cash.

**Savings**    Savings accounts, which are displayed in the Cash Flow Center, are used to record the transactions in savings accounts.

**Investment**    Investment accounts, which are displayed in the Investing Center, are for tracking the stocks, bonds, and mutual funds in your portfolio that are not in retirement accounts. Quicken distinguishes between two types of investment accounts: Brokerage and Single Mutual Fund.

**Retirement**    Retirement accounts, which are also displayed in the Investing Center, are for tracking investments in retirement accounts. Quicken distinguishes between two types of retirement accounts. One type combines IRA, SEP, and Keogh, and the other combines 401(k) and 403(b). Retirement accounts should fall into either of these two broad categories.

**Asset**    Asset accounts, which are displayed in the Property & Debt Center, are used for tracking items that you own. Quicken distinguishes between three different types of asset accounts: House, Vehicle, and Asset.

### What You Owe
The accounting term for what you owe is *liabilities*. Quicken offers two kinds of accounts for amounts you owe:

**Credit**    Credit, which is displayed in the Cash Flow Center, is for tracking credit card transactions and balances.

**Liability**    Liability, which is displayed in the Property & Debt Center, is for tracking loans and other liabilities.

## Setting Up Accounts
You create new accounts with the Account Setup dialog. No matter what type of account you create, Quicken steps you through the creation process, prompting you to enter information about the account, such as its name and balance. In this section, I explain how to use the Account Setup dialog to set up new accounts and tell you what kind of information you'll have to enter for each account type.

## Getting Started

Begin by opening the Account Setup dialog. There are several ways to do this; here are two of them:

- Choose Tools | Account List (or press CTRL-A) to display the Account List window (see Figure 3-1 later in this chapter). Click the Add Account button in its button bar.
- Choose Cash Flow | Cash Flow Accounts | Add Account, Investing | Investing Accounts | Add Account, or Property & Debt | Property & Debt Accounts | Add Account.

The appearance of the Account Setup dialog will vary depending on the method you used to open it. If you used the first method or used the second method to create a Cash Flow or Investing account, the dialog begins by prompting you for the financial institution in which the account is held. If you used the second method to create a Property & Debt account, the dialog begins by prompting you for the type of account you want to create.

## Entering Account Information

Follow the prompts in the Account Setup dialogs to enter required information for the account you are creating. Click the Next button to progress from one dialog to the next. You can click Back at any time to go back and change information. You know you're finished when the Next button is replaced with a Done button; click it to save the account information.

Account information includes the financial institution in which the account is held (if applicable), the account name, an optional description, the account balance, and the date of the account balance. Almost every type of Quicken account requires this information. If you don't know the balance of an account, you may set it to $0.00 and make adjustments later, either when you get a statement or when you reconcile the account. If the account can be accessed online by Quicken, Quicken will automatically download the account balance information, as well as many recent transactions, as part of the account creation process.

I provide details for creating specific types of accounts throughout this book:

- Cash Flow Center accounts are covered in Chapter 5.
- Investing Center accounts are covered in Chapter 10.
- Property & Debt Center accounts are covered in Chapter 13.

## Finishing Up

When you've finished entering information for a new account, click the Done button. You may be prompted to enter more information about the account, depending on the type of account and the financial institution you selected for it. The detailed instructions in Chapters 5, 10, and 13 for creating specific account types review all of the additional information you may have to enter.

## Working with the Account List Window

You can view a list of all of your accounts at any time. Choose Tools | Account List or press CTRL-A. The Account List window, which has two tabs, appears.

### Viewing Accounts

The View Accounts tab (see Figure 3-1) displays a list of all accounts organized by Center and group. For each account, the account's name, online services status, number of transactions, description, and balances appear. The window also provides subtotals for each group of accounts, as well as totals for each Center. The Balance Total at the bottom of the window is the net of all accounts—your net worth.

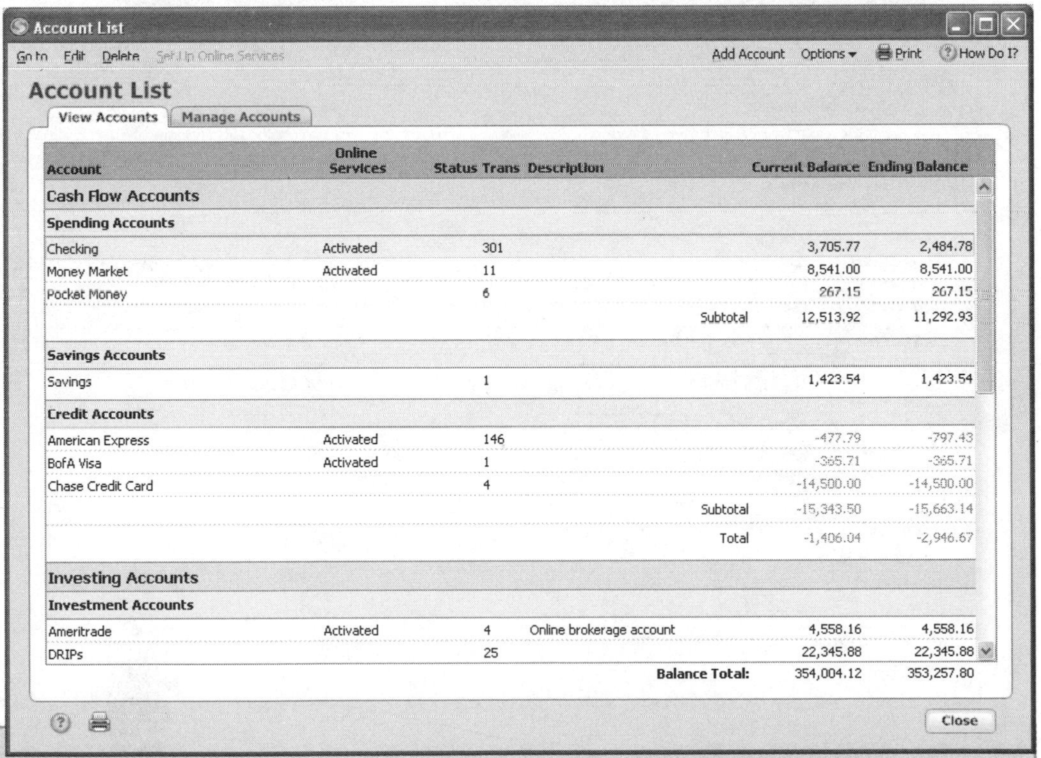

**Figure 3-1 • The View Accounts tab of the Account List window lists all of your accounts.**

## Managing Accounts

The Manage Accounts tab (see Figure 3-2) enables you to work with the accounts you have set up in Quicken. You can use this tab to customize the display of accounts in lists, including the Account Bar. For Quicken 2007, this window has been redesigned to be easier to use.

**Hiding an Account**   To hide an account from view, turn on the check box in the Hide In Quicken column for the account. This disables the other two check boxes and removes the account from view in any list in which it would appear. In fact, the account even disappears from the View Accounts tab of the Account List window (refer to Figure 3-1) unless you choose View Hidden Accounts from the window's Options menu. You may want to use this feature to remove accounts you no longer use or need to see—without removing the transactions they contain. Keep in mind that you cannot use a hidden account in a transaction; to do so, you must first unhide the account by turning off the check box in this window.

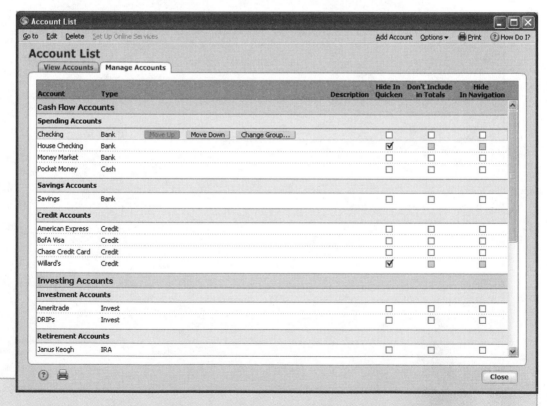

**Figure 3-2 • The Manage Accounts tab of the Account List window enables you to customize the display of accounts.**

**Excluding an Account's Balance in Totals**    To exclude an account's balance in subtotal and total calculations, turn on the check box in the Don't Include In Totals column for the account. This displays the balances for the account in gray in the View Accounts tab and omits the balances from any totals calculated in Quicken.

**Removing an Account from the Account Bar**    To remove an account from the Account Bar, turn on the check box in the Hide In Navigation column for the account. Although the account remains in the View Accounts tab of the Account List window and other lists and menus where it would normally appear, it no longer appears in the Account Bar. You may want to use this feature to keep the Account Bar short by excluding accounts you seldom access.

**Changing the Order of Accounts**    To change the order in which accounts appear in the Account List window and Account Bar, select an account and click the Move Up or Move Down button to move it. You can move an account to any position within its group.

**Changing an Account's Group**    To change the group in which an account appears, select the account and click the Change Group button. A Change Group dialog, like the one shown here, appears:

The options this dialog offers depend on the type of account you select. Select a new group for the account and click the OK button. The account moves to that group in the Account List window and the Account Bar. If you assign a group in a different Center, the account even moves to menus of accounts for that Center—for example, choosing the Asset option in the dialog shown here moves the Money Market account to the Property & Debt Accounts submenu under the Property & Debts menu.

## Other Account Management Tasks

You can use the button bar on either tab of the Account List window to perform a number of other account management tasks. Select the account you want to work with and click a button:

- **Go To** opens the register for the selected account. I explain how to use the various types of account registers throughout this book. (You can also open an account by double-clicking its name in the Account List window or by clicking it in the Account Bar.)

- **Edit** displays the General Information tab of the Account Details dialog for the selected account. As shown next, this dialog includes basic information about the account that you can view or edit. The Online Services tab, when available, tells you whether online services are available for the account and whether they are activated. It also lets you deactivate online services. (I tell you more about online account services in Chapters 6 and 11.)

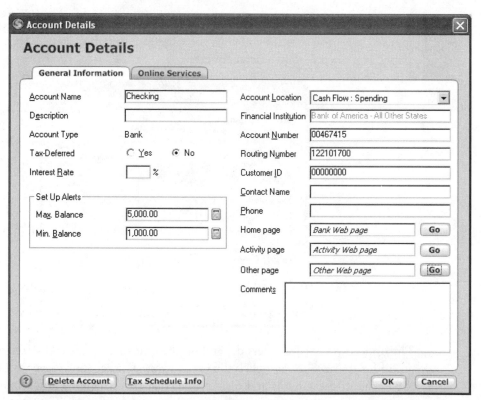

- **Delete** enables you to delete the selected account. It displays a dialog you can use to confirm that you want to delete the account. You must type **yes** into the dialog and click OK to delete the account. Remember that when you delete an account, you permanently remove all of its transactions from your Quicken data file. To get the account out of sight without actually deleting it and its data, consider hiding it instead. I explain how to do this earlier in this chapter in the section titled "Working with the Account List Window."

- **Set Up Online Services**, when available, displays the Quicken Account Setup dialog, which you can use to enable online account access features for the account. This option is available only for certain types of accounts and certain financial institutions. I explain how to use this dialog in Chapters 6 and 11.

- **Add Account** displays the Create New Account dialog so you can create a new account.

- **Options** offers commands for changing the view of the Account List window.

- **Print** prints an account list.

- **How Do I?** displays the Quicken Help window, which lists a variety of common account management tasks. Click a task to view help information onscreen.

## Categories

When you create a data file, Quicken automatically creates dozens of commonly used categories based on information you enter about yourself and other options you set. Although these categories might completely meet your needs, at times you may want to add, remove, or modify a category to fine-tune Quicken for your use.

## Types of Categories

There are basically two types of categories:

- **Income** is incoming money. It includes receipts such as your salary, commissions, interest income, dividend income, child support, gifts received, and tips.

- **Expense** is outgoing money. It includes insurance, groceries, rent, interest expense, bank fees, finance charges, charitable donations, and clothing.

---

### What Does This Mean to You?
### Categories

Categories? Subcategories? Sound confusing? Like a lot of work? Take it from me: it isn't. And it's worth the time you spend doing it.

Here's how it works. When you enter a transaction in Quicken, you'll categorize it using one of your predefined categories. (Sometimes Quicken can even guess the right category the first time you enter a transaction for a payee!) The next time you enter a transaction for the same payee, Quicken automatically assumes the transaction will use the same category, so Quicken enters it for you. I'm willing to bet that nine times out of ten, Quicken's assumption is right. So it really isn't that much work.

Worth the trouble? You bet! By properly categorizing transactions, you can get a true picture of where your money comes from and where it goes. You can create realistic budgets based on accurate spending patterns to help you save money. You can create tax reports that'll save you—or your tax preparer—time. You can even automate much of your tax preparation by exporting all those properly categorized transactions right into Intuit's TurboTax tax preparation software.

So don't leave category fields blank when you enter transactions. Take that extra step. It's worth it.

Besides, there's always the Miscellaneous category if you can't think of a more appropriate one.

## Subcategories

A *subcategory* is a subset or part of a category. It must be the same type of category as its primary category. For example, you may use the Auto category to track expenses to operate your car. Within that category, however, you may want subcategories to record specific expenses, such as auto insurance, fuel, and repairs. Subcategories make it easy to keep income and expenses organized into manageable categories, while providing the transaction detail you might want or need.

## Working with the Category List Window

You can view a list of all of your categories at any time. Choose Tools | Category List, or press SHIFT-CTRL-C. The Category List window appears (see Figure 3-3).

The Category List window lists all categories and transfer accounts under three broad headings: Income, Expense, and Transfers and Payments. Category names appear in an outline view, with subcategories indented beneath them. You can

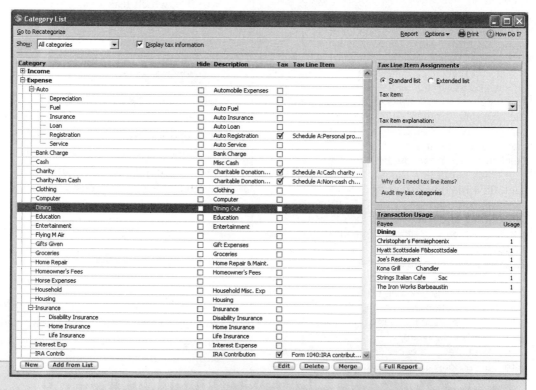

**Figure 3-3 • The Category List window includes all categories and provides information about tax line assignments and transactions.**

click – and + buttons to hide or display categories or subcategories, or choose a predefined group of categories from the Show drop-down list to specify which categories should appear in the window. You can also turn on the Hide Description check box for a category to remove it from lists without actually deleting it from your Quicken data file. And, as shown in Figure 3-3, when you select a category name, Quicken displays a list of the payees with transactions for that category.

In this section, I explain how to use the Category List window to add, modify, delete, and perform other tasks.

## Creating a New Category

To create a new category, click the New button at the bottom of the Category List window (refer to Figure 3-3). The Set Up Category dialog appears. Enter information about the category—the following illustration shows an example—and click OK.

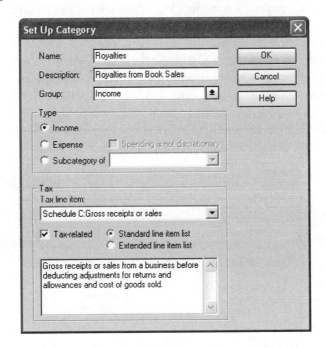

Here's a quick summary of the kind of information you should provide for each category.

**Category Information**    The basic category information includes the category name, which is required, and the description and group, which are optional. Groups are used primarily for budgeting, which I discuss in Chapter 18. For now, you can either leave the Group box empty or choose an existing group from the drop-down list.

**Type**    Use options in the Type area to select the type of category: Income, Expense, or Subcategory. In addition to classifying income and expense items properly, the type of category you specify will determine where the category appears in reports and graphs. For example, income categories always appear before expense categories, and subcategories appear immediately below their parent categories. If you select Subcategory, you must choose a category from the drop-down list beside it. If you do not have complete control over spending for an expense category, you can turn on the Spending Is Not Discretionary check box. This option, which is also used primarily for budgeting, applies to required fixed expenditures such as rent, car insurance, and child care.

**Tax**    You can use the tax area options to specify whether a category is tax-related and, if so, what tax form it appears on. This can be a real timesaver at tax time by enabling you to organize your income and expenditures as they appear on tax forms. I tell you more about using Quicken at tax time in Chapter 19. You are not required to enter anything in this area.

## Adding Multiple Categories at Once

Quicken makes it easy to add multiple related categories all at once. For example, suppose you just bought your first home (congratulations!) and want to add categories for homeowners to your Quicken data file. Click the Add From List button at the bottom of the Category List window (refer to Figure 3-3) to display the Add Categories dialog, which is shown here:

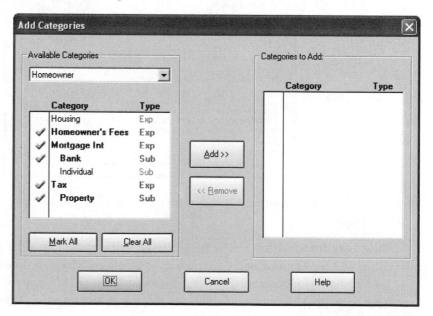

Choose a category group from the Available Categories drop-down list, and then click to add a green check mark beside each category you want to add. When you click Add, the selected categories appear in the Categories To Add list. Click OK to add the categories and dismiss the dialog.

## Editing, Deleting, and Merging Categories

You can also use the Category List window (see Figure 3-3) to edit, delete, or merge categories. Select the name of the category you want to work with, and then click a button at the bottom of the window.

**Edit**   The Edit button displays the Edit Category dialog, which looks and works just like the Set Up Category dialog (shown earlier) for the selected category. You can use this to make just about any change to a category. You can even "promote" a subcategory to a category by changing its type.

**Delete**   The Delete button enables you to delete the selected category. Clicking the Delete button displays different dialogs depending on the category that is selected. Quicken begins by warning you that the category and any subcategories beneath it will be deleted. Then:

- If you selected a category without transactions, when you click OK, the category is deleted.
- If you selected a category or subcategory with transactions, the Delete Category dialog, shown next, appears. You can use this dialog to replace the category with another category throughout your data file. Choose another category from the drop-down list and click OK. If you click OK without choosing a replacement category, any transactions that referenced the category you deleted will be marked as uncategorized. If the category you deleted has subcategories, this dialog appears for each subcategory that has transactions.

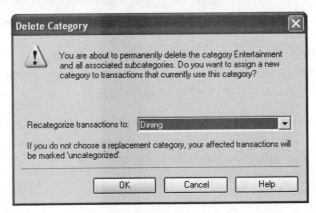

**Merge**   The Merge button lets you merge transactions using the currently selected category with transactions using another category. This, in effect, recategorizes all of the transactions for the selected category. Clicking Merge displays the Merge Category dialog, shown next. Choose another category from the drop-down list. If you want to delete the category you selected, turn on the check box—this makes the dialog work the same way as the Delete Category dialog shown earlier. Click OK to perform the merge. One thing to keep in mind: if the category you selected is not used in any transactions, a dialog will tell you that there's nothing to merge.

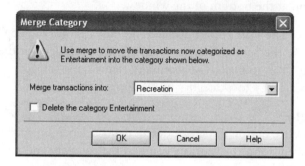

## Displaying Tax Information

Turning on the Display Tax Information check box at the top of the Category List window displays tax-related information for each category. It also splits the Transaction Usage area so its top half can be used to assign a tax line to a selected category (see Figure 3-3). I tell you more about assigning tax lines to categories in Chapter 19.

## Creating a Transaction Usage Report

The Transaction Usage area lists all payees with transactions that reference a selected category. You can click the Full Report button to instantly generate a complete report of all transactions, including amounts, for the selected category.

## Other Category List Window Options

Buttons and menus on the Category List window's button bar (see Figure 3-3) enable you to perform other tasks with list contents:

- **Go To Recategorize** displays the Recategorize dialog, which you can use to change one category to another throughout your data file. I explain how to recategorize transactions in Chapter 5.

- **Report** creates a report of the transactions for the selected category. I tell you more about creating reports in Chapter 9. Clicking this button is the same as clicking the Full Report button at the bottom of the Transaction Usage area of the window.
- **Options** is a menu with additional options for viewing the Category List window, including commands for displaying category descriptions (shown by default), category groups, and category types in the list.
- **Print** prints the category list.
- **How Do I?** displays the Quicken Help window with a list of links for common category-related window tasks. Click a link to display information about that task.

# Classes

A *class* is an optional identifier for specifying what a transaction applies to. For example, if you have two vehicles for which you track expenses, you can create a class for each vehicle, such as "Jeep" and "Chevy Truck." Then, when you record a transaction for one of the vehicles, you can include the appropriate class with the category for the transaction. Because Quicken can produce reports based on categories, classes, or both, classes offer an additional dimension for tracking and reporting information.

I want to stress here that using classes is completely optional. It's not necessary to set them up or use them at all. In fact, many Quicken users—including a few I know at Intuit—don't take advantage of this feature. It's your decision.

## Displaying the Class List Window

Quicken maintains a list of all the classes you create. You can display the Class List window by choosing Tools | Class List or by pressing CTRL-L. This illustration shows an example with some classes I created.

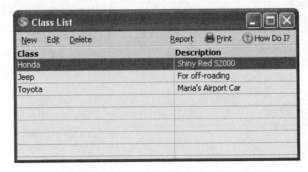

## What Does This Mean to You? Classes

If you were doubtful about the benefit of using categories in transactions, classes will certainly be a hard sell. Fortunately, I don't have to sell it to you because you really don't have to use this feature at all.

That said, let me explain how I use classes. I write books for a living. I've written tons of them. And I use Quicken to track my income and expenses for each book.

Sure, I could use the category feature to set up a separate category for every book I've ever written or revised—there are currently 62 of them!—but why bother when the class feature is available? I simply set up a separate class for each book I've written. Then, when I record an income or expense transaction related to a specific title, I can use the same income and expense categories I always use for writing-related income and expenses. I just add, almost as an afterthought, the class that corresponds to the book.

What's the benefit of doing this? Well, suppose I want to determine which of my titles earns the most money. I can create a Profit and Loss Report within Quicken, with separate columns for each class—in this case, book title. Then, when it's time to revise a title, I know in advance whether it's going to be worth my while.

Maybe this example doesn't apply to you. But here's one that might.

Got kids? Try this. Create a separate class for each child. Then, when you've got expenses for a specific family member, record the transaction with the appropriate class name. (If you've got income related to a specific child, I'm impressed; be sure to include the class name with those transactions, too.) Then, when that partially grown bundle of joy asks for $357.49 to buy a new skateboard, you can show him a report of how much he's cost you so far when you say no.

## Creating a New Class

Click the New button on the button bar in the Class List window. The Set Up Class dialog, which is shown here, appears. Use it to enter information about the class.

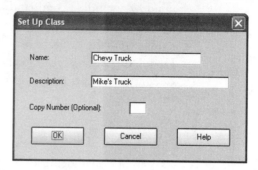

Only one piece of information is necessary: the class name. You may want to make it short so it's easy to remember and enter. The description can be used to provide additional information on the class's use. The copy number enables you to associate classes with different but similar activities. For example, if you have two separate businesses for which you report activity on two Schedule Cs, you can assign Copy 1 to one business's classes and Copy 2 to the other business's classes.

When you click OK, the class is added to the list. You can create as many classes as you like.

## Working with the Class List Window

You can use buttons in the button bar near the top of the Class List window to work with the class list or a selected class:

- **New** enables you to create a new class, as discussed earlier.

- **Edit** enables you to modify the currently selected class name or other information.
- **Delete** enables you to delete the currently selected class. When you delete a class, the class name is removed from all transactions in which it appeared. (The transaction remains properly categorized.)
- **Report** prints a transaction report by class. I tell you more about Quicken's reporting features in Chapter 9.
- **Print** prints the class list.
- **How Do I?** displays the Quicken Help window with a list of links related to working with classes. Click a link to view the help information onscreen.

# Going Online with Quicken and Quicken.com

## In This Chapter:

- *Benefits of going online with Quicken*
- *Getting connected to the Internet*
- *Setting up Quicken for an Internet connection*
- *Testing and troubleshooting your connection*
- *An introduction to Web surfing*
- *Accessing Quicken.com*
- *Quicken financial partners*

Many of Quicken Personal Finance Software's features work seamlessly with the Internet. If you have access to the Internet, either through a connection to an Internet service provider (ISP) or through a connection to an online service such as America Online, you can take advantage of these online features to get up-to-date information, automate data entry, pay bills, and obtain Quicken maintenance updates automatically.

In this chapter, I tell you why you might want to take advantage of Quicken's online features. Then I explain how to set up Quicken to go online. Finally, I tell you a little about surfing the Web and introduce you to Quicken.com, a great source of information and services for Quicken and Quicken users.

## Going Online

If you're already using your computer to access the features of the Internet or online services such as America Online, you probably already know a lot about it. In this part of the chapter, I fill in any gaps in your knowledge by telling you about the benefits of going online with Quicken and addressing any security concerns you might have. Finally, for the folks who aren't already online, I explain what you need to connect to the Internet to use Quicken's online features.

### Why Go Online?

Before I go any further, I want to remind you that you don't *have* to go online to use Quicken. Quicken is a good financial management software package, even without its online features. But Quicken's online features make it a *great* financial management software package. As you'll see in this section and throughout this book, Quicken uses the Internet to help you make better financial decisions. How? By providing you with information and resources that are relevant to your personal financial situation.

The best way to explain the benefits of going online is to list a few of the features online users can take advantage of.

### If You Have a Bank Account, You Can Benefit

Throughout the month, you write checks and mail them to individuals and organizations. You enter these transactions in your checking account register. At month's end, you reconcile the account. You can do all this without going online; I tell you how in Chapters 5 and 8.

But if you register for transaction download with your bank, you can download all bank account activity on a regular basis so you know exactly when the transactions hit your account—even the ATM and debit card transactions you always forget to enter. If you register for online payment, you can pay your bills without licking another envelope or pasting on another stamp. I explain how all this works in Chapter 6.

---

### What Does This Mean to You?
### Online Account Access

Let me get something off my chest here. Online account access and Bill Pay are the reasons I use Quicken to manage my finances.

With five checking accounts, three savings accounts, and a handful of credit card accounts for my personal finances and the finances of three small businesses, I simply can't be bothered manually entering transactions and writing checks. Heck, I'd be spending more time entering transactions than getting work done without Quicken online access.

I depend on Quicken's online features to automate transaction entry and bill payments. As you'll see throughout this book, Quicken has all kinds of timesaving features; in my opinion, the online features are the best of them.

## If You Have Credit Cards, You Can Benefit

Do you have credit cards? If so, you can take advantage of Quicken's credit card tracking features, which I cover in Chapter 5, to keep track of your charges, payments, and balances. You don't need to go online.

But if you sign up for transaction download, all your credit card charges can be downloaded directly into Quicken, eliminating the need for time-consuming data entry, while giving you an up-to-date summary of your debt and how you spent your money. I tell you more about this in Chapter 6.

## If You Invest, You Can Benefit

Quicken can keep track of your investments, whether they are 401(k) accounts, mutual funds, or stocks. You can enter share, price, and transaction information into Quicken, and it will summarize portfolio value, gains, and losses. It'll even keep track of securities by lot. You don't need to go online to track your investments. I explain how in Chapter 10.

But with online investment tracking, Quicken can automatically obtain quotes on all the securities in your portfolio and update your portfolio's market value. Depending on your brokerage firm, you may also be able to download transactions, account balances, and holdings. Quicken can also alert you about news stories that affect your investments and automatically download the headlines so you can learn more with just a click. You can also get valuable up-to-date research information about securities that interest you, so you can make informed investment decisions. I tell you about all this in Chapter 11.

## If You Want to Save Money, You Can Benefit

Mortgages. Car loans. Bank accounts. Insurance. All of these have one thing in common: their rates vary from one provider to another. Shopping for the best deal can be time-consuming work—wading through newspaper and magazine ads, making calls, visiting banks. Quicken can help you understand the basics of loans, banking, and insurance. Its planners can help you evaluate the deals you learn about, and all without going online.

But with the help of Quicken's built-in Internet links, you can shop for the best deal online, without leaving the comfort of your desk, getting newspaper ink all over your hands, or spending an afternoon listening to music while on hold. Up-to-date rates are only a mouse click away with an Internet connection and Quicken to guide you.

### Enough Already!

If all this doesn't convince you that going online with Quicken can help you save time, save money, and get smarter, stop reading and skip ahead to Chapter 6. You'll probably never be convinced. I will say one more thing, however: after using Quicken's online features for more than nine years now, I can't imagine using Quicken any other way.

## Security Features

Perhaps you're already convinced that the online features can benefit you. Maybe you're worried about security, concerned that a stranger will be able to access your accounts or steal your credit card numbers.

You can stop worrying. The folks at Intuit and the participating banks, credit card companies, and brokerage firms have done all the worrying for you. They've come up with a secure system that protects your information and accounts.

### PINs

A *PIN,* or *personal identification number,* is a secret password you must use to access your accounts online. If you have an ATM card or cash advance capabilities through your credit card, you probably already have at least one PIN, so the idea shouldn't be new to you. It simply prevents anyone from accessing the account for any reason without first entering the correct PIN.

An account's PIN is initially assigned by the bank, credit card company, or brokerage firm. Some companies, such as American Express, require that your PIN consist of a mixture of letters and numbers for additional security. You can change your PINs to make them easier to remember—just don't use something obvious like your birthday or telephone number. And don't write it on a sticky note and attach it to your computer's monitor!

If you think someone might have guessed your PIN, you can change it. In fact, it's a good idea to change all your PINs and passwords regularly—not just the ones you use in Quicken.

### Encryption

Once you're online and you've correctly entered your PIN, the instructions that flow from your computer to the bank, credit card company, or brokerage firm are *encrypted.* This means they are encoded in such a way that anyone able to "tap in" to the transmission would "hear" only gibberish. Quicken does the encryption using, at a minimum, the 56-bit single Data Encryption Standard (DES). Quicken is also capable of encrypting data with stronger methods, including the 128-bit RC4 or 168-bit triple DES. Once the encrypted information reaches the computer at the bank, credit card company, or brokerage firm, it is unencrypted and then validated and processed.

Encryption makes it virtually impossible for any unauthorized party to "listen in" to your transmission. It also makes it impossible for someone to alter a transaction from the moment it leaves your computer to the moment it arrives at your bank, credit card company, or brokerage firm for processing.

### Other Security Methods

Quicken also takes advantage of other security methods for online communications, including Secure Sockets Layer (SSL) encryption, digital signatures, and digital certificates. Together, these security methods make online financial transactions secure—even more secure than telephone banking, which you may already use!

## Getting Connected

To take advantage of Quicken's online features, you need a connection to the Internet. You get that through an *ISP* (Internet service provider), an organization that provides access to the Internet, usually for a monthly fee. These days, literally thousands of ISPs can provide the access you need for Quicken's online features.

If you don't already have an account with an ISP, you must set one up before you can configure Quicken to use its online features. Check your local phone book or newspaper to find an ISP near you. Your ISP can explain everything you need to get connected and help you set up your computer to go online.

# Setting Up and Testing an Internet Connection

To use Quicken's online features, you may need to set up Quicken for your Internet connection. This part of the chapter explains how to set up, test, and troubleshoot a Quicken Internet connection.

If you went through the Quicken Express Setup process discussed in Chapter 2 and

created at least one account that utilizes Quicken's online features, chances are that Quicken is already set up to work with your Internet connection. If that is the case, you can skip this section, unless you need to modify or troubleshoot your connection.

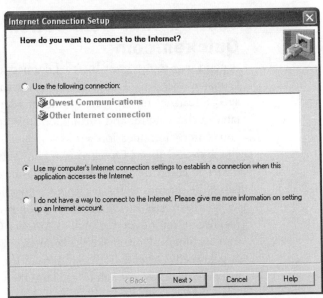

### Internet Connection Setup

Choose Edit | Preferences | Internet Connection Setup. The Internet Connection Setup dialog, shown here, appears.

This dialog offers three options:

- **Use The Following Connection.** This option enables you to select from an existing list of Internet connections. This list is maintained by Windows based on Internet connection profiles you create with the Internet Connection Wizard. If you have only one connection profile (like I do), the only item in this list will be Other Internet Connection. If you select this option, when you click Next, the dialog explains what to do when you need to connect to the Internet.
- **Use My Computer's Internet Connection Settings To Establish A Connection When This Application Accesses The Internet.** This option tells Quicken to use your active Internet connection profile to connect to the Internet from within Quicken. If you select this option, when you click Next, the dialog tells you a little about your connection. Quicken will automatically connect to the Internet using these settings any time it needs to.
- **I Do Not Have A Way To Connect To The Internet. Please Give Me More Information On Setting Up An Internet Account.** Select this option only if you do not already have an Internet connection set up within Windows. When you click Next, Quicken provides additional instructions for getting an ISP and using the Internet Connection Wizard to set up your connection.

Make your selections in the dialog and click Next or Done to get more information or complete the setup process. If you need help setting up an Internet connection, consult Windows Help.

You can change the options for an Internet connection profile at any time. Just follow these instructions again.

## Testing Your Connection with a Visit to Quicken.com

A good way to test your Internet connection is to visit Quicken.com, the official Quicken Web site. This site offers information about Intuit products as well as special features for registered Quicken users. I tell you more about Quicken.com later in this chapter and throughout this book. For now, connect to it to make sure your Internet connection works.

Choose Online | Quicken On The Web | Quicken.com, or just click the Quicken.com button in the toolbar. Quicken attempts to connect to the Internet using the settings in the Internet Connection Setup dialog.

What you see during the connection process will vary depending on your ISP. If you use an online service such as America Online, the service's access software may start automatically to make the connection. You may be prompted to enter a username or password. Other dialogs may appear. It may be necessary to switch from connection software back to Quicken by clicking the Quicken button on the Windows task bar.

When the connection is complete, Quicken requests the Quicken.com home page. It appears in a Quicken Internet window (see Figure 4-1).

If you were already connected to the Internet when you accessed one of Quicken's online features, or if you have a direct connection to the Internet, you won't see the connection happening. Instead, the Quicken.com page will simply appear in a Quicken Internet window (see Figure 4-1).

## Troubleshooting Connection Problems

If you follow the instructions I provided throughout this chapter, you shouldn't have any trouble connecting to the Internet with Quicken. But things aren't always as easy as they should be. Sometimes even the tiniest problems can prevent you from successfully connecting and exchanging data.

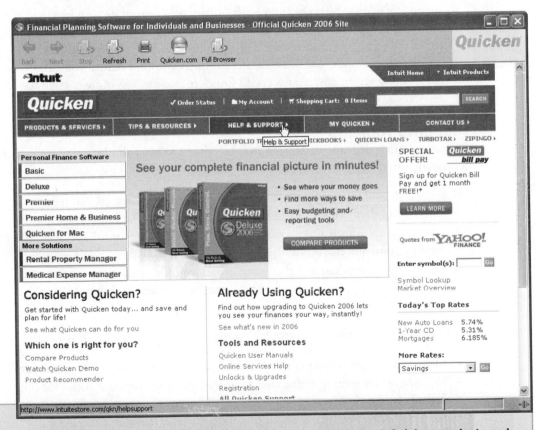

**Figure 4-1 • The Quicken.com home page provides information about Quicken products and services, and links to features for registered users.**

In this section, I provide some troubleshooting advice to help you with connection problems you may experience. Check this section before you start pulling out your hair and cursing the day computers were invented.

## Setup Problems

To determine whether the problem is a Quicken setup problem or a general Internet setup problem, exit Quicken and try connecting to the Internet from another program, such as your regular Web browser or e-mail program.

- If you can connect to the Internet from another program but not from Quicken, the problem may be with Quicken's Internet connection setup. Go back to the section titled "Internet Connection Setup" earlier in this chapter and repeat the setup process. You'll probably want to select the second option in the Internet Connection Setup dialog.
- If you can't connect to the Internet from any other program or with dial-up networking (for dial-up connections), the problem is with your Internet setup for Windows, your modem (for dial-up connections), or your network (for direct connections). You must fix any problem you find before you can successfully set up and connect with Quicken. Consult Windows Help for assistance.

## Modem Problems

Problems with a dial-up connection may be related to your modem. Try each of the following, attempting a connection after each one:

- Check all cables between your computer and your modem (if you have an external modem) and between your modem and the telephone outlet.
- Check the telephone line to make sure it has a dial tone and that it is not being used by someone else or another program.
- Turn off your modem and then turn it back on. Or, if you have an internal modem, restart your computer. This resets the modem and may resolve the problem.

If you can connect but have trouble staying connected, try the following:

- Make sure no one is picking up an extension of the phone line while you are online.
- Make sure call-waiting is disabled by entering the appropriate codes for the dial-up connection.
- Have the phone company check the line for noise. If noise is detected, ask the phone company to fix the problem. (It shouldn't cost you anything if the line noise is the result of a problem outside your premises.)

## Network Problems

Problems with a direct connection may be related to your network. Try these things, attempting a connection after each one:

- Check all cables between your computer and the network hub or router.
- Check to make sure the correct proxy server information was entered into Windows Internet Connection Wizard.
- Restart your computer. Sometimes resetting your computer's system software can clear network problems.
- Ask your system administrator to check your network setup.

# Exploring Quicken.com

Quicken.com, the official Quicken site, supports Quicken users in three different ways:

- Provides information about Quicken and Quicken-compatible software and services that can help you get the most out of Quicken.
- Enables registered Quicken users to store Quicken account balances, reminders, and transactions entered on the Web in a secure environment. These features can make Quicken.com an extremely useful tool, especially to Quicken users who spend much of their time away from home.
- Offers access to basic and advanced financial information, including stock quotes, loan rates, and insurance providers. This helps Quicken users find the financial information they need to make informed decisions.

Quicken.com is a dynamic Web site that changes frequently. The screen illustrations and features I tell you about will probably appear differently when you connect. In addition, brand-new features might be added after the publication of this book. That's why I won't go into too much detail. The best way to learn about the features of Quicken.com is to check them out for yourself.

## An Introduction to Web Surfing

Let me take a moment to explain exactly what you're doing when you connect to Quicken.com and the other Quicken features on the Web. If you're brand new to *Web surfing*—that is, exploring Web sites—be sure to read this section. But if you're a seasoned surfer, you probably already know all this stuff and can skip it.

One more thing: this section is not designed to explain everything you'll ever need to know about browsing the World Wide Web. It provides the basic information you need to use the Web to get the information you need.

## Going Online

When you access Quicken's online features, you do so by connecting to the Internet through your ISP. It doesn't matter whether you connect via a modem or a network, or whether your ISP is America Online, your local cable company, or Joe's Dial-up Internet Service. The main thing is having a connection or a conduit for information.

Think of an Internet connection as some PVC piping running from your computer to your ISP's computer, with a valve to control the flow of information. Once the valve is open (you're connected), any information can flow through the pipe in either direction. You can even exchange information through that pipe in both directions at the same time. This makes it possible to download (or retrieve) a Web page with your Web browser while you upload (or send) e-mail with your e-mail program.

Quicken's online features use the pipe (or connection) in two ways:

- The integrated Web browser enables you to request and receive the information you want. It's live and interactive—click a link, and a moment later your information starts to appear. Quicken can display Web pages in its built-in Internet window (see Figure 4-1) or your default browser's window.
- The transaction download, online payment, and several other features work in the background to communicate with financial institutions with which you have accounts. Quicken sends information you prepared in advance and retrieves the information the financial institution has waiting for you.

This chapter concentrates on Web browsing with Quicken—using Quicken's integrated Web browser to access interactive features on Quicken.com. But it also provides some information to help you find financial institutions that work with Quicken for the transaction download and online payment features.

## Navigating

The main thing to remember about the Web is that it's *interactive*. Every time a Web page appears on your screen, it'll offer a number of options for viewing other information. This is known as navigating the Web.

**Hyperlinks and Forms**    You can move from page to page on the Web in two ways, both of which are illustrated in Figure 4-1:

- **Hyperlinks** (or links) are text or graphics that, when clicked, display another page. Hypertext links are often underlined, colored text. Graphic links sometimes have a colored border around them. You can always identify a link by pointing to it—your mouse pointer will turn into a hand with a pointing finger, and a screen tip may appear to describe the link.
- **Forms** offer options for going to another page or searching for information. Options can appear in pop-up menus, text boxes that you fill in, check boxes

that you turn on, or option buttons that you select. Multiple options often appear. You enter or select the options you want and click a button to send your request to the Web site. The information you requested appears a moment later.

**Other Navigation Techniques**    Several of the buttons on the Quicken browser's toolbar (refer to Figure 4-1) are navigation buttons:

- **Back** displays the previously viewed page.
- **Next** displays the page you viewed after the current page. This button is available only after you have used the Back button.
- **Stop** stops the loading of the current page. This may result in incomplete pages or error messages on the page. You might use this button if you click a link and then realize that you don't really want to view the information you requested.
- **Refresh** loads a new copy of the Web page from the Web site's server. This button is handy for updating stock quotes or news that appears on a page.
- **Print** enables you to print the currently displayed page.
- **Quicken.com** takes you to the Quicken.com home page (refer to Figure 4-1).
- **Full Browser** starts and switches to your default Web browser. Quicken continues to run in the background. You can switch back to Quicken at any time by clicking its icon on the Windows task bar.

## Accessing Quicken on the Web

You can access Quicken's online features using commands on its Online menu. One of these commands, Quicken On The Web, is really a submenu with several options for Quicken Web features.

### Quicken.com

Quicken.com is the official Quicken Web site. Although designed to be of most use to Quicken users, many of its features are accessible to anyone.

### Quicken Support

The Quicken Support command takes you to the Help & Support home page. This is where you can find answers to frequently asked questions, information about solving problems with Quicken, and program updates. Use this command when you can't find the information you need in this book or in Quicken's Onscreen Help.

### Quicken Products

The Quicken Products command takes you to the Products & Services page, where you can learn more about and purchase other Intuit products, including Quicken-compatible checks and supplies, and TurboTax, a tax preparation software product that works with Quicken. Stop by once in a while to check out special offers and new products.

# Participating Financial Institutions

If you're interested in keeping track of your finances with the least amount of data entry, you should be considering Quicken's online features for transaction download and online payment. I explain the benefits of these features near the beginning of this chapter. Chapters 6 and 11 tell you how to use them. But you can't use them until you've set up an account with a participating financial institution and applied for the Online Account Services you want to use.

When you create a bank, credit card, or investment account as discussed in Chapters 2 and 3, Quicken prompts you to enter the name of your financial institution. Quicken can determine whether your financial institution is one of the participating financial institutions and prompt you to set up transaction download and online payment features, if they are available. If you've already set up your accounts for Online Account Services, you can skip this section. But you may find it useful if you're shopping around for another financial institution and want one that works with Quicken.

## Finding a Participating Institution

Finding a Quicken financial partner is easy. Choose Online | Participating Financial Institutions. The Apply For Online Financial Services window appears (see Figure 4-2). This page, which is updated each time a new participating institution comes on board, offers links with information about each of the institutions. To get information about a specific institution, click a link in the Online Financial Services area to narrow down the list of institutions. Then click a link in the Financial Institution Directory area. Information about the financial institution appears in the main part of the window.

Note that if you have not set up Quicken for your Internet connection or registered the Quicken software, a dialog may appear telling you that you need to do one or both of these things to continue. Follow the prompts within the dialog as necessary. Eventually, the Apply For Online Financial Services window (see Figure 4-2) will appear.

Participating financial institutions offer five types of online financial services:

- **401(k) Account Access** enables you to download 401(k) and 403(b) investment account transactions and balances directly into your Quicken data file.
- **Banking Account Access** enables you to download bank account transactions directly into your Quicken data file.
- **Bill Pay** enables you to send payment instructions from within Quicken. This makes it possible to pay bills and send payments to anyone without writing a check.
- **Brokerage Account Access** enables you to download brokerage and other investment account transactions directly into your Quicken data file.
- **Credit/Charge Card Access** enables you to download credit or charge card transactions directly into your Quicken data file.

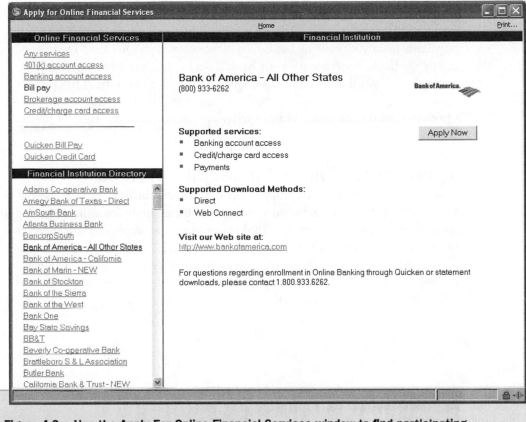

**Figure 4-2 • Use the Apply For Online Financial Services window to find participating financial institutions and apply for online financial services.**

If your bank, credit card company, or brokerage firm is not on the list, you have three options:

**Change financial institutions.**    I know it sounds harsh, but if your bank or credit card company doesn't support online banking services with Quicken and you really want to use this feature, you can find a financial institution that does support it and open an account there.

**Wait until your financial institution appears on the list.**    The list of participating institutions is updated quite often. If your bank or credit card company doesn't appear there today, it may appear next month—or next year. You can hurry things along by asking your financial institution to become a participating institution. It might add this feature if enough customers ask for it.

**Use Quicken Bill Pay and Quicken Credit Card.**    If you're interested only in the Bill Pay feature, you can use Quicken Bill Pay. This enables you to process payments from your existing bank accounts from within Quicken. There's no need to change banks or wait until your bank signs on as a participating financial institution. If you'd like to download credit card transactions into Quicken, sign up for the Quicken Credit Card. You can learn more about Quicken Bill Pay and Quicken Credit Card in the Quicken Services window; choose Tools | Quicken Services to display it.

## Applying for Online Financial Services

The information pane of the window for the financial institution you selected (see Figure 4-2) provides information about how you can apply for online banking. In most cases, you'll either click the Apply Now button to apply or learn more, or call the toll-free number that appears onscreen and speak to a company representative. This gets the wheels turning to put you online. It may take a few days to get the necessary access information, so apply as soon as you're sure you want to take advantage of the online financial services features.

# The Cash Flow Center

# Part Two

This part of the book explains how to use Quicken Personal Finance Software to keep track of the bank and credit card accounts in the Cash Flow Center. It starts by explaining the basics of manually recording bank and credit card transactions, and then tells you how you can take advantage of online transaction entry and payment processing features such as Online Account Services and Bill Pay. It provides details about how you can tap into the power of Quicken to automate many entry tasks, thus saving you time. It also explains how to reconcile accounts and how to use Quicken's upgraded reporting features to learn more about what you have and how you're doing financially. This part has five chapters:

# Recording Bank and Credit Card Transactions

## Chapter 5

## In This Chapter:

- *Creating cash flow accounts*
- *Entering payments and other transactions*
- *Using splits and classes*
- *Writing and printing checks*
- *Entering credit card transactions*
- *Transferring money*
- *Working with existing transactions*
- *Adding notes and attachments*

At Quicken's core is its ability to manage your bank accounts. This is probably Quicken's most used feature. You enter the transactions, and Quicken keeps track of account balances and the source and destination of the money you spend. You can even have Quicken print checks for you.

Using similar transaction entry techniques, Quicken can also help you keep track of credit card accounts. You enter transactions as you make them or at month's end when you receive your statement and pay your bill. Quicken keeps track of balances and offers you an easy way to monitor what you used your credit card to buy. It also enables you to keep an eye on how much your credit cards cost you in terms of finance charges and other fees.

# Getting Started

Before you can use Quicken Personal Finance Software to track bank and credit card transactions, you should prepare by creating the necessary accounts and learning how recording transactions works. In this section, I provide an overview of the account types, along with examples of transactions you might make. I also provide detailed step-by-step instructions for creating cash flow accounts.

## Overview of Accounts and Transactions

Most of the transactions you track with Quicken will involve one or more of its banking and cash accounts. Here's a closer look at each account type, along with some transaction examples. As you read about these accounts, imagine how they might apply to your financial situation.

### Bank Accounts

Quicken offers two types of accounts that you can use to track the money you have in a bank:

- **Checking** accounts include check writing privileges. These accounts usually have a lot of activity, with deposits to increase the account balance and checks that decrease the account balance.
- **Savings** accounts are for your savings. These accounts usually don't have as much activity as checking accounts. You can use a savings account to track the balance in a certificate of deposit (CD), holiday savings club, or similar savings account.

Generally speaking, bank account transactions can be broken down into three broad categories: payments, deposits, and transfers.

**Payments**    Payments are cash outflows. Here are some examples:

- You write a check to pay your electric bill.
- You withdraw money from your savings account to buy a gift for your mother.
- You use your ATM card to withdraw spending money from a bank account.
- You use your debit card to buy groceries.
- You pay a monthly checking account fee.

**Deposits**    Deposits are cash inflows. Here are some examples:

- You deposit your paycheck into your checking account.
- You sell your old computer and deposit the proceeds into your savings account.
- Your paycheck or Social Security check is deposited into your bank account as a direct deposit.
- You earn interest on your savings account.

**Transfers**    A transfer is a movement of funds from one account to another. Here are some examples:

- You transfer money from an interest-bearing savings account to your checking account when you're ready to pay your bills.
- You transfer money from a money market account to your home equity line of credit account to reduce its balance.

## Credit Card Accounts

Credit card accounts track money you owe, not money you own. Some credit cards, such as MasterCard, Visa, American Express, and Discover, can be used in most stores that accept credit cards. Other credit cards, such as Macy's, Dillard's, and Texaco, can be used only in certain stores. But they all have one thing in common: if there's a balance, it's usually because you owe the credit card company money.

Credit card account transactions can also be broken down into two categories: charges and payments.

**Charges**    Charges result when you use your credit card to buy something or the credit card company charges a fee for services. Here are some examples:

- You use your Visa card to buy a new computer.
- You use your Discover card to pay for a hotel stay.
- You use your Texaco card to fill the gas tank on your boat at the marina.
- A finance charge based on your account balance is added to your Macy's bill at month's end.
- A late fee is added to your MasterCard bill because you didn't pay the previous month's bill on time.
- A fee is added to your American Express bill for annual membership dues.

The opposite of a charge is a *credit*. Think of it as a negative charge; don't confuse it with a payment. Here are two examples:

- You return the sweater you bought with your American Express card to the store you bought it from.
- In reviewing your MasterCard bill, you discover that a merchant charged you in error, and you arrange to have the incorrect charge removed.

**Payments**    Payments are amounts you send to a credit card company to reduce your balance. Here are three examples:

- You pay the minimum amount due on your Visa card.
- You pay $150 toward the balance on your Macy's card.
- You pay the balance on your American Express card.

## Cash Accounts

Quicken also offers cash accounts for tracking cash expenditures. For example, you might create an account called My Wallet or Spending Money and use it to keep track of the cash you have on hand. Cash accounts are like bank accounts, but there's no bank. The money is in your wallet, your pocket, or the old coffee can on the windowsill.

Cash accounts have two types of transactions: receive and spend.

**Receive**    When you receive cash, you increase the amount of cash you have on hand. Here are some examples:

- You withdraw cash from the bank for weekly spending money.
- You sell your *National Geographic* magazine collection for cash at a garage sale.
- You get a $20 bill in a birthday card from your grandmother.

**Spend**    When you spend cash, you reduce your cash balance. Here are some examples:

- You buy coffee and a newspaper and pay a bridge toll on your way to work.
- You give your son his allowance.
- You put a $20 bill in the birthday card you send to your granddaughter.

## Creating Cash Flow Accounts

In Chapter 3, I briefly discuss how to use the Account Setup dialog to create new Quicken accounts. Here are the details for creating Cash Flow Center accounts.

Begin by choosing Cash Flow | Cash Flow Accounts | Add Account to display the Quicken Account Setup dialog:

## Entering Financial Institution Information

Quicken's extensive online account access features make it possible to automate data entry and account reconciliations for accounts held in participating financial institutions. (I tell you more about how you can find a participating financial institution in Chapter 4.) To take advantage of these features, Quicken usually starts the account creation process by prompting you to enter the name of your bank. You have two options:

- **This Account Is Held At The Following Institution** enables you to specify the bank in which the account is held. Enter the name of the bank in the text box. As you type, Quicken displays a drop-down list that attempts to match the characters to those in its internal database of supported financial institutions. If your bank appears on the list, click it to select and enter it. Otherwise, finish typing and click Next. If you entered the name of a financial institution Quicken does not recognize, it displays a dialog like the one shown next, enabling you to select one with a similar name or keep the one you entered.

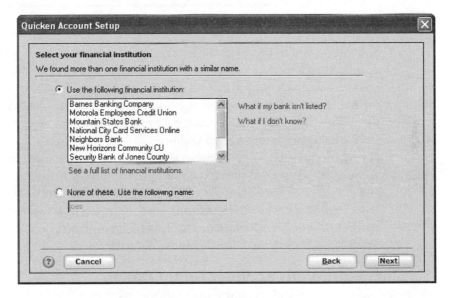

- **This Account Is Not Held At A Financial Institution** tells Quicken that the account you are creating is not held at a financial institution—for example, a cash account.

If the account is held at a financial institution that supports Quicken's online features, a dialog similar to this may appear:

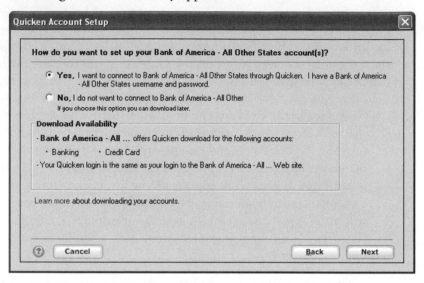

You have two options:

- **Yes** enables you to complete the account setup process by going online and downloading information from your financial institution. This is the recommended method for completing account setup. To do this, you must already have a customer ID and password for accessing your account information via Quicken. If you select this option, click Next and continue following instructions in the section titled "Completing the Account Setup Online."
- **No** enables you to complete the account setup process by manually entering account information. You can use this option if you don't have a customer ID and password or are not interested in setting up the account for online features. You can always enable online features later; I explain how in Chapter 6. If you select this option, click Next and continue following instructions in the section titled "Completing the Account Setup Manually."

## Completing the Account Setup Online

How you complete the account setup online varies depending on how your financial institution enables you to download Quicken data.

**Online Setup for Direct Download**   Financial institutions that support direct download enable you to download bank or credit card account balance and transaction information from within Quicken. For these financial institutions, Quicken displays a dialog like the one shown next, prompting you to enter your customer ID once and password twice. Enter the information provided by your financial institution and click Next.

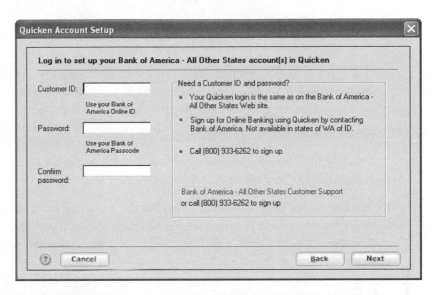

Quicken connects to the Internet to exchange some information with your bank or credit card company. When it's finished, it displays a dialog like this one. As you can see, my husband and I keep Bank of America pretty busy.

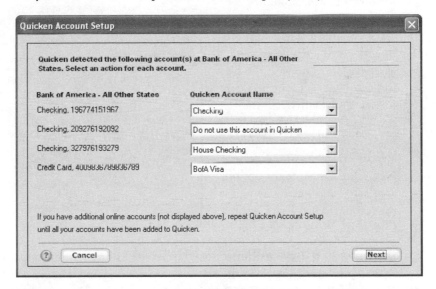

For each account listed, you have three options:

* To match the account to an existing Quicken account, choose the account name from the drop-down list.
* To create a new Quicken account for the account, choose Add A New Account In Quicken from the drop-down list. Then enter a name for the account in the Name Your New Account dialog that appears and click OK.

- To exclude an account from your Quicken data file, choose Do Not Use This Account In Quicken from the drop-down list.

Note that the drop-down lists appear only if you have already set up at least one cash flow account in Quicken but have not yet set up that account for online account access. If you're creating accounts for the first time, edit boxes appear in place of the drop-down lists; simply enter a name in the box beside each account you want to track in Quicken to create the account.

When you're finished setting account options, click Next. Quicken confirms that the account(s) has been set up. Click Done.

**Online Setup for Web Connect Download**   Financial institutions that support Web Connect download require that you use your Web browser to connect to the bank or credit card company's Web site, log in, and manually initiate a download. Although this may seem like a lot of work, it really isn't. For these institutions, Quicken may display a dialog confirming that you have your customer ID and password for accessing your account. It then starts your Web browser and goes to the institution's login page. Enter the information provided by your bank or credit card company and click the Log In button. Then navigate the Web site until you find a button or link

for downloading account information into Quicken via Web Connect and start the download. If a dialog appears asking what to do with the file, indicate that you want to open it with Quicken. When the download is finished, a dialog like the one shown here should appear. Make sure the Create A New Quicken Account option is selected and enter a name for the account. Then click Continue. Quicken creates the account.

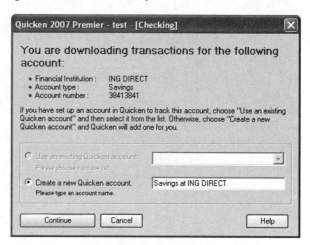

**Downloading Transactions**   As part of the online setup process, Quicken may download transactions into the account you are creating. I explain how to work with downloaded transactions in Chapter 6. For now, click Done in an Online Update Summary dialog if one appears.

## Completing the Account Setup Manually

If the account is not held at a financial institution that supports Quicken's online features, or if you indicated that you want to set up the account manually, Quicken displays a dialog like the one shown next, prompting you for an account type. Select the appropriate option and click Next.

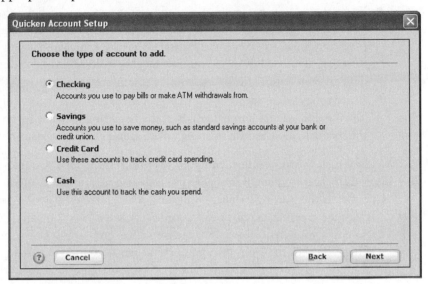

Quicken prompts you to enter a name for the account. Enter a descriptive name and click Next. As shown in the following illustration, Quicken prompts you to enter your account ending statement date and balance.

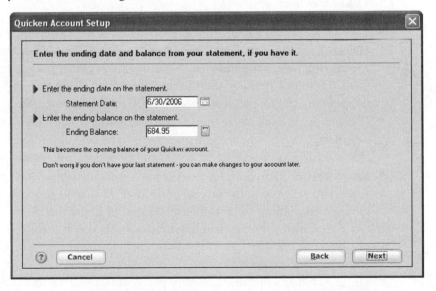

For checking, savings, and credit card accounts, you have three options:

- Enter the ending statement date and balance from your most recent account statement. This is the quickest, most accurate way to create an account. The statement date becomes your account's start date, and you will enter only those transactions that were made after that date or that did not clear that statement.

- Enter the ending statement date and balance from an earlier account statement. This is also an accurate way to create the account, but it will require that you play "catch up" to enter more transactions into Quicken. (If you use Online Account Services, however, you may be able to have several months' worth of data entered automatically for you; I explain how in Chapter 6.)

- Enter today's date and **0** in the dialog. This is fast, but it certainly isn't accurate. You'll eventually have to either adjust the beginning balance for the account or use the reconciliation feature to create an adjusting entry after your first reconciliation.

For a cash account, unless you plan to enter transactions you made before you created the account, you'll probably use today's date and the contents of your wallet or pocket as the starting balance information.

If you are creating a credit card account, click the Next button. Quicken prompts you to enter your credit limit. If the account has one—most do—enter it.

When you click the Done button, the Quicken Account Setup dialog disappears and the account register for the account appears (refer to Figure 5-1 later in this chapter).

## Tips for Creating Cash Flow Accounts

Here are a few additional things to keep in mind when creating accounts for the Cash Flow Center:

- Give each account a name that clearly identifies it. For example, if you have two checking accounts, don't name them "Checking 1" and "Checking 2." Instead, include the bank name (such as "USA Bank Checking") or account purpose (such as "Joint Checking") in the account name. This prevents you from accidentally entering a transaction in the wrong account register.

- If you create a bank or credit card account with a balance date and amount from a bank statement—the recommended way—be careful not to enter transactions that already appear on that statement or in previous statements.

- Entering your credit limit for a credit card account enables Quicken to alert you when you get close to (or exceed) your limit. If a credit card account doesn't have a credit limit—for example, an American Express card—you may want to enter your own personal spending limit. This makes it possible to take advantage of Quicken's alerts feature to prevent overspending in that account. I tell you about alerts in Chapter 9.

- Using a cash account to track every penny you spend, from the cup of coffee you buy at work in the morning to the quart of milk you pick up on your way home that evening, isn't for everyone. You may prefer to track only large cash inflows or outflows and record the rest as miscellaneous expenses.

# Entering Transactions

To make the most of Quicken, you must enter transactions for the accounts you want to track. You can do this manually, as discussed in this chapter, or, if the account is enabled for Online Account Services, you can track your account activity automatically via download, as discussed in Chapter 6. Either way, you'll need to know how to enter transactions for cash flow accounts.

You can enter transactions in several ways, based on the type of transaction:

- Use *registers* to record virtually any type of transaction, including manual checks, bank account payments and deposits, credit card charges and payments, and cash receipts and spending.
- Use the *Write Checks window* to record checks to be printed by Quicken.
- Enter *transfers* to transfer money from one account to another.

## Using Account Registers

Quicken's account registers offer a standard way to enter all kinds of transactions. As the name suggests, these electronic account registers are similar to the paper checking account register that comes with your checks.

To open a register, click its name in the Account Bar or choose its name from the Cash Flow Accounts submenu under the Cash Flow menu. The account window appears. If necessary, click the Register tab to display the account register window (see Figure 5-1). Use it to enter and record transactions.

### Overview of the Account Register

Before I begin my discussion of entry techniques, let's take a closer look at the account register window in Figure 5-1.

**Downloaded and Scheduled Transactions**     The bottom half of the window may display one of two tabs of information:

- **Download Transactions** displays a setup form for enabling Online Account Services or a list of transactions that have already been downloaded but not yet accepted into the account. I explain how to set up online account access features and work with downloaded transactions in Chapter 6.
- **Scheduled Bills & Deposits** (see Figure 5-1) displays a list of upcoming, due, and overdue scheduled transactions. I tell you more about scheduled transactions in Chapter 7.

You can show or hide this information in the bottom half of the register window by clicking the small arrow button on the right end of the bar on which the tabs appear.

**Figure 5-1 • Here's the account register window for a checking account.**

**The Button Bar**   This window's button bar includes a number of buttons and menus you can use for working with transactions and changing the window's view:

- **Delete** deletes the selected transaction. When you click this button, a dialog appears to confirm that you really do want to delete the transaction.
- **Find** displays the Quicken Find dialog, which you can use to search for transactions based on a variety of criteria. I explain how to search for transactions later in this chapter in the section titled "Searching for Transactions."
- **Transfer** displays the Transfer dialog, which I tell you about later in this chapter in the section titled "Transferring Money," so you can create a transfer transaction.
- **Reconcile** enables you to reconcile the account. I tell you how to reconcile accounts in Chapter 8.
- **Write Checks** displays the Write Checks window, which you can use to write checks to be printed from Quicken. I explain how to write checks later in this chapter in the section titled "Writing Checks."

- **Set Up Online** displays the Quicken Account Setup dialog (shown earlier) so you can enable Online Account Services, if they are available for the account.
- **View** displays a menu of options for filtering, sorting, and viewing the list of transactions. The One-Line Display command collapses register entries so only one line per transaction shows.
- **Report** displays a menu of reports that are available for the selected transaction. Use commands to generate reports from within the account register window. I tell you more about Quicken's reporting features in Chapter 9.
- **Options** displays a menu with options for setting register preferences and for toggling the display of the Download/Scheduled Bills & Transactions tabs. I tell you more about customizing Quicken's registers in Appendix B.
- **How Do I?** displays the Quicken Help window, with a list of topics related to using a cash flow account register.

## Basic Entry Techniques

To enter a transaction, begin by clicking in the first empty line at the end of the account register window (refer to Figure 5-1). This activates a new, blank transaction. You can then enter transaction information into each field and press ENTER to complete the transaction.

Although the entry process is pretty straightforward, here are a few things to keep in mind when entering transactions.

**Advancing from Field to Field**    To move from one text box, or *field,* to another when entering transactions, you can either click in the next field's text box or press the TAB key. Pressing TAB is usually quicker.

**Using Buttons**    Buttons appear when certain fields are active:

- When the Date field is active, a calendar icon appears. You can click it to display a calendar and then click calendar buttons to view and enter a date.
- When one of the two Amount fields is active, a calculator icon appears. You can click it to use a calculator and enter calculated results.
- When the Payee or Category field is active, a Report button appears. You can click this button to display a pop-up report of transactions for that payee or in that category, like the one shown here.

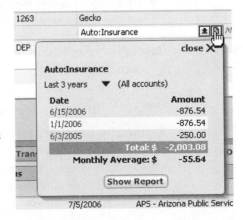

**Using the Num Field**    The Num field is where you enter a transaction number or type. You can enter any number you like or use the drop-down list (shown next) to display a list of standard entries; click an option to enter it for the transaction. You can also press the + or − key on the keyboard to increment or decrement the check number while the Num field is active.

- **Next Check Num** automatically increments the most recently entered check number and enters the resulting number in the Num field.
- **ATM** is for ATM transactions. You may also want to use it for debit or check card transactions.
- **Deposit** is for deposits.
- **Print Check** is for transactions for which you want Quicken to print a check. Quicken automatically enters the check number when the check is printed.
- **Send Online Payment** is for online payments. This option appears only when Online Payment is enabled for the account. I tell you about paying bills online in Chapter 6.
- **Online Transfer** is for online transfers of funds from one account to another. This option appears only when Online Payment is enabled for the account. I tell you about online banking in Chapter 6.
- **Transfer** is for a transfer of funds from one account to another.
- **EFT**, which stands for Electronic Funds Transfer, is for direct deposits and similar transactions.

**QuickFill**    As you start to enter the name of a payee or payer that is already in your Quicken data file, Quicken may fill in the entire name and details from the most recent transaction for you. This is Quicken's QuickFill feature, which I tell you more about in Chapter 7.

**Automatic Categorization**    After entering a payee for the first time, Quicken may fill in the category for you. This is Quicken's automatic categorization feature, which enters categories based on thousands of payee names programmed into it. You'll find that in most cases, Quicken assigns an appropriate category. But you can change the category if you like and, from that point on, Quicken's QuickFill feature will use the category you assign for future transactions to that payee. Chapter 7 provides more information about QuickFill.

**Entering New Categories**    If you enter a category that does not exist in the Category List, Quicken displays the New Category dialog, offering to create a new category with that name. Click Yes to use the Set Up Category dialog to create a new category, or click No to return to the register and enter a different category. If you turn off the Prompt Before Creating New Categories check box in the New Category dialog, Quicken automatically displays the Set Up Category dialog every time you enter a category that does not exist in the Category List. I explain how to create categories in Chapter 3.

**Entering Multiple Categories**    To enter more than one category for a transaction, click the Split button. I explain how to enter transactions with splits a little later in this chapter in the section titled "Using Splits."

**Entering Subcategories**    When you choose a subcategory from the Category field's drop-down list, Quicken automatically enters the subcategory's parent category name, followed by a colon character (:) and the subcategory name. To type in a subcategory, use the same notation. Here's what it might look like in a register entry:

| 6/15/2006 | 1263 | Gecko | | 876 54 | | | 1,082 11 |
| | | Auto:Insurance | | | | | |

**Entering Memos**    You can enter a brief memo about the transaction in the field to the right of the Category field. This memo can help you remember what a transaction is for.

**Using Transaction Buttons**    As shown in Figure 5-1, five buttons appear on the second line for the active transaction. You can use these buttons to work with the transaction:

- **Enter** enters the transaction into the account register. If Quicken's sound option is turned on, you should hear a cash register *ch-ching* sound when you click it. (You can turn Quicken sounds on or off in the Quicken Preferences dialog, which I discuss in Appendix B.)
- **Edit** displays a menu of editing options for the transactions. I discuss some of the Edit menu's commands later in this chapter in the section titled "Changing Transactions."
- **Split** opens the Split Transaction window for the transaction. I explain how to enter a transaction with splits in the next section.
- **Rate** enables you to enter a rating for the business referred to in the transaction on Zipingo.com. If you have never used Zipingo, follow the instructions that appear onscreen to create a Zipingo account and enter your rating.

- **Attach** displays a menu that enables you to add a follow-up flag, note, or electronic image attachment to the transaction. I explain how to attach items to transactions later in this chapter in the section titled "Adding Notes and Attachments."

## Using Splits

A *split* is a transaction with more than one category. For example, suppose you pay one utility bill for two categories of utilities—electricity and water. If you want to track each of these two expenses separately, you can use a split to record each category's portion of the payment you make. This enables you to keep good records without writing multiple checks to the same payee.

To record a transaction with a split, click the Split button in the account register or Write Checks window when entering the transaction. The Split Transaction window, which is shown next, appears. Click in the first blank line and select a category. If desired, enter a memo for the category in the Memo field. Then enter the amount for that category in the Amount field. Repeat this process for each category you want to include in the transaction. Here's what the Split Transaction window might look like with two categories entered:

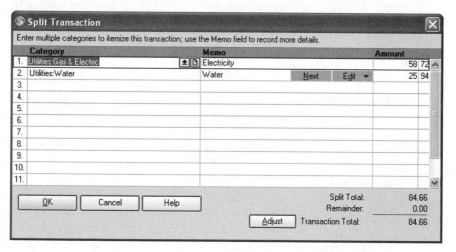

If you entered a transaction amount before clicking the Split button, you can monitor the Remainder and Transaction Total values in the Split Transaction window to make sure you've accounted for the entire transaction amount. If you entered an incorrect amount, you can click the Adjust button to adjust the transaction amount to match the Split Total.

When you're finished entering transaction categories, click OK or press ENTER. If you left the transaction amount empty before clicking the Split button, a dialog appears, asking if you want to record the transaction as a payment or deposit. Select the appropriate option and click OK.

As shown next, the word *Split* appears in the Category field for the transaction in the account register window:

Two buttons appear beside the Category field when you activate a transaction with a split:

- The green check mark displays the Split Transaction window so you can review and edit the transaction.
- The red *X* clears all lines from the split. Use this option with care—it permanently removes all category information from the transaction.

## Using Classes

As discussed in Chapter 3, a class is an optional identifier for specifying what a transaction applies to. To include a class in a transaction, enter a slash (/) followed by the class name after the category. Here's an example in the register window:

| 6/25/2006 | 1265 | Bonanza Leasing | | 304 60 | | 1,743 93 |
| | | Rent/Honda | Garage Rent | | | |

If you enter a class name that is not on the Class List, Quicken displays the Set Up Class window so you can create the class on the fly. I explain how to create classes in Chapter 3.

## Tracking Credit Cards with Quicken

Tracking bank account transactions and balances is just one part of using Quicken. It's also a great tool for tracking credit cards. Knowing how much you owe on your credit cards helps you maintain a clear picture of your financial situation.

How you use Quicken to track your credit cards depends on how accurate you want your financial records to be and how much effort you're willing to spend to keep Quicken up-to-date.

## Credit Card Tracking Techniques

You can use either of two techniques for paying credit card bills and monitoring credit card balances with Quicken:

- Use your checking account register or the Write Checks window to record amounts paid to each credit card company for your credit card bill. Although this does track the amounts you pay, it doesn't track how much you owe or the individual charges.

- Use a credit card account register to record credit card expenditures and payments. This takes a bit more effort on your part, but it tracks how much you owe and what you bought.

In my opinion, it's worth the extra effort to track your credit card expenditures and balances in individual credit card accounts. And if you utilize Quicken's Transaction Download feature for your credit card accounts, as I discuss in Chapter 6, it won't take much time or effort to get the job done.

## Recording Strategies

You can use two strategies for recording transactions in credit card accounts. Choosing the strategy that's right for you makes the job easier to handle.

**Enter as You Spend**   One strategy is to enter transactions as you spend. To do this, you must collect your credit card receipts—which might be something you already do. Don't forget to jot down the totals for any telephone and online shopping you do. Then, every day or every few days, sit down with Quicken and enter the transactions.

While this strategy requires you to stay on top of things, it offers two main benefits:

- Your Quicken credit card registers always indicate what you owe to credit card companies. This prevents unpleasant surprises at month-end or at the checkout counter when you're told you've reached your limit. It also enables you to use the alerts feature to track credit card balances; I tell you about that in Chapter 9.
- At month-end, you don't have to spend a lot of time entering big batches of transactions. All (or at least most) of them should already be entered.

I'll be the first to admit that I've never been able to use this strategy. I just don't like holding on to all those pieces of paper. (Of course, since signing up for Transaction Download, all this information is entered automatically for me. You can learn more about Transaction Download in Chapter 6.)

**Enter When You Pay**   The other strategy, which you may find better for you, is to enter transactions when you get your monthly statement. With this strategy, when you open your credit card statement, you'll spend some time sitting in front of your computer with Quicken to enter each transaction. If there aren't many, this isn't a big deal. But it could take some time if there are many transactions to enter.

Of course, the main benefit of this strategy is that you don't have to collect credit card receipts and spend time throughout the month entering your transactions. But you still have to enter them! This is the method I use for the one credit card I have that I cannot access online yet.

| Credit: Visa | Register | Overview | | | | | Quicken 2007 |
|---|---|---|---|---|---|---|---|

Delete  Find  Transfer  Reconcile · · · · · · · · · · · · · · · · · · View ▼  Report ▼  Options ▼  (?) How Do I?

| Date/▲ | Ref | Payee/Category/Memo | | Charge | Clr | Payment | Balance |
|---|---|---|---|---|---|---|---|
| 6/10/2006 | | Shell Oil | | 64 85 | | | 2,528 69 |
| | | Auto:Fuel | | | | | |
| 6/12/2006 | | ABC Bank Visa | | | | 500 00 | 2,028 69 |
| | | [Checking] | | | | | |
| 6/13/2006 | | Big Mama's Restaurant | | 35 94 | | | 2,064 63 |
| | | Dining | Dinner w/Mike | | | | |
| 6/14/2006 | | Triple D Western World | | 138 74 | | | 2,203 37 |
| | | Clothing | | | | | |
| 6/15/2006 | | ABC Bank Visa | | 29 57 | | | 2,232 94 |
| | | Interest Exp | Finance Charges | | | | |
| 6/20/2006 | | Triple D Western World | | | | 45 19 | 2,187 75 |
| | | Clothing | Return Shirt | Enter  Edit  Split  ☆ Rate  📎 Attach | | | |
| 6/20/2006 | Ref | | | Charge | | Payment | |
| | | Category | Memo | | | | |

☆ Rate your payees · · · · · · · · Credit Remaining:   7,812.25   **Ending Balance:**   2,187.75

**Figure 5-2 • This example shows some typical transactions in a credit card register.**

## Entering Credit Card Transactions

Entering credit card transactions isn't very different from entering checking account or savings account transactions. Here are a few examples, all of which are illustrated in Figure 5-2.

**Entering Individual Charges**  Open the account register for the credit card account. Then enter the charge transaction, using the name of the merchant that accepted the charge as the payee name. You can leave the Ref box empty.

**Entering Credits**  Enter the transaction just as if it were a charge, but put the amount of the credit in the Payment box. This subtracts it from your account balance.

**Entering Finance Charges**  In the credit card account register, enter the name of the credit card company as the payee and the amount of the finance charge as a charge. You can use the Interest Exp category for the transaction.

**Entering Payments**  In the account register for your checking account or in the Write Checks window, enter a payment transaction with the credit card company name in the Payee box. Enter the credit card account name in the Category text box; you should find it as a transfer account at the bottom of the Category drop-down list that appears when you activate the field. The checking account register transaction should look like the one shown next. Figure 5-2 shows what this transaction looks like in the credit card account register.

| 6/12/2006 | 8038 | ABC Bank Visa | | 500 00 | | | 7,152 19 |
|---|---|---|---|---|---|---|---|
| | | [Visa] | | | | | |

**Recording Credit Card Rebates**    Some credit card companies offer rebates for purchases. How you record a rebate depends on how the rebate is received:

- To record a rebate received as a check, deposit the check as usual and enter the amount of the rebate as a deposit in that account.
- To record a rebate received as a reduction in the credit card account balance, enter the amount of the rebate in the credit card account as a payment. (Just remember that a rebate is not a payment that counts toward your monthly obligation to the credit card company.)

What you use as a category for this transaction is completely up to you. You may want to use the Interest Exp account, thus recording the rebate as a reduction in your interest expense. Or, perhaps, if the rebate applies to a certain purchase only, you'd use the category you originally used for that purchase. For example, I have an AOPA MasterCard, which gives me a 5 percent rebate on aircraft fuel purchases. I record the rebate using the Fuel category I created to track fuel expenses. If you have a lot of credit cards that offer rebates, you may want to create a Rebate income account and use that as the category for all rebate transactions. These are just suggestions. There is no right or wrong way to do it.

## Entering Cash Transactions

Although Quicken enables you to keep track of cash transactions through the use of a cash account, not everyone does this. The reason: most people make many small cash transactions every day. Is it worth tracking every penny you spend? That's something you need to decide.

Personally, I don't track all cash transactions. I track only expenditures that are large or tax deductible. You may want to do the same. If so, you still need to set up a cash account, but you don't need to record every transaction. That's what I do; Figure 5-3 shows an example.

**Cash Receipts**    Cash receipts may come from using your ATM card, cashing a check, or getting cash from some other source. If the cash comes from one of your other accounts through an ATM or check transaction, when you record that transaction, use your cash account as the transfer in the Category field. That increases your cash balance. Here's what the transaction might look like in your checking account:

| 6/10/2006 | ATM | Withdrawal | | 40 00 | | | | 2,349 74 |
| | | [Pocket Money] | | | | | | |

**Important Cash Expenditures**    In your cash account, record large, tax-deductible, or other important cash expenditures like any other transaction. Be sure to assign the correct category.

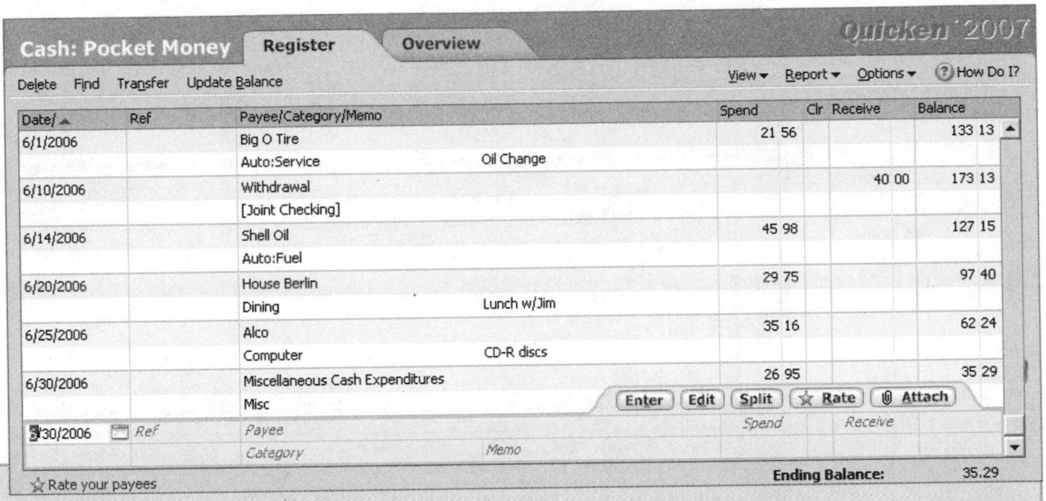

| Cash: Pocket Money | **Register** | Overview | | | | *Quicken* 2007 |
|---|---|---|---|---|---|---|

Delete   Find   Transfer   Update Balance     View ▾   Report ▾   Options ▾   ? How Do I?

| Date/▲ | Ref | Payee/Category/Memo | | Spend | Clr | Receive | Balance |
|---|---|---|---|---|---|---|---|
| 6/1/2006 | | Big O Tire | | 21 56 | | | 133 13 |
| | | Auto:Service | Oil Change | | | | |
| 6/10/2006 | | Withdrawal | | | | 40 00 | 173 13 |
| | | [Joint Checking] | | | | | |
| 6/14/2006 | | Shell Oil | | 45 98 | | | 127 15 |
| | | Auto:Fuel | | | | | |
| 6/20/2006 | | House Berlin | | 29 75 | | | 97 40 |
| | | Dining | Lunch w/Jim | | | | |
| 6/25/2006 | | Alco | | 35 16 | | | 62 24 |
| | | Computer | CD-R discs | | | | |
| 6/30/2006 | | Miscellaneous Cash Expenditures | | 26 95 | | | 35 29 |
| | | Misc | | ( Enter ) ( Edit ) ( Split ) ( ☆ Rate ) ( 🔗 Attach ) | | | |
| 6/30/2006 | Ref | Payee | | Spend | | Receive | |
| | | Category | Memo | | | | |

☆ Rate your payees                                           **Ending Balance:**        35.29

**Figure 5-3 • Here are a few typical transactions in a cash account.**

**Other Cash Expenditures**   Throughout the week, you may spend 50¢ for a newspaper, a dollar for a cup of coffee, and about $12 for lunch at your favorite hamburger joint. Recording transactions like these can be tedious, so don't bother if you don't want to. Instead, at the end of the week, compare your cash on hand to the balance in your cash account register. Then, enter a transaction to record the difference as an expenditure. You can use the Misc category and enter anything you like in the Payee field.

# Writing Checks

Quicken's Write Checks window uses a basic check-like interface to record checks. You enter the same information that you would write on an actual check. You then tell Quicken to print the check based on the information you entered. (I explain how to print checks later in this chapter in the section titled "Printing Checks.")

   To open the Write Checks window, choose Cash Flow | Write Checks or press CTRL-W. The Write Checks window, which is shown in Figure 5-4, appears. If necessary, choose the name of the account for which you want to write checks from the drop-down list near the top of the window. Then enter the necessary information for a check and record the transaction.

## Overview of the Write Checks Window

The Write Checks window is a busy place, with a lot of information and options. Before I explain how to use it to enter transactions, let's take a look at its options.

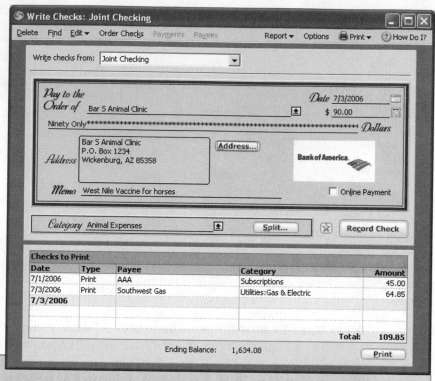

**Figure 5-4 • Here's the Write Checks window, with a few checks already created.**

**The Button Bar** The Write Checks window's button bar includes a number of buttons and menus for working with transactions and changing the window's view:

- **Delete** deletes the selected transaction. When you click this button, a dialog appears to confirm that you really do want to delete the transaction.
- **Find** displays the Quicken Find dialog, which you can use to search for transactions based on a variety of criteria. I explain how to search for transactions later in this chapter in the section titled "Searching for Transactions."
- **Edit** is a menu full of commands for creating, editing, and working with transactions. I discuss many of these commands later in this chapter in the section titled "Working with Existing Transactions."
- **Order Checks** displays the Checks & Supplies page of the Quicken Services window, with information on how you can order check stock that is compatible with Quicken.
- **Payments** displays the Bills & Deposits list, which I discuss in Chapter 7.
- **Payees** displays the Online Payee List window, which I cover in Chapter 6.

- **Report** displays a menu of reports that are available for the selected transaction. Use commands to generate reports from within the Write Checks window. I tell you more about Quicken's reporting features in Chapter 9.
- **Options** displays the Quicken Preferences dialog, which you can use to customize the way the Write Checks window looks and works; I tell you more about customizing Quicken in Appendix B.
- **Print** enables you to print checks. I tell you more about that later in this chapter in the section titled "Printing Checks."
- **How Do I?** displays the Quicken Help window, with a list of topics related to the Write Checks window.

**Account List**   The Write Checks From drop-down list near the top of the window displays a list of accounts from which you can write checks. Be sure to choose the correct account from the list before entering check information.

**Check Form**   The middle of the window displays a form that looks and works a lot like a paper check. This is where you enter transaction information.

**Checks To Print**   The Checks To Print area of the window lists all of the checks that have been entered in the Write Checks window that have not yet been printed. When you enter a transaction in the Write Checks window, it is added to this list.

## Entering Transactions in the Write Checks Window

The Write Checks window (refer to Figure 5-4) is like a cross between a paper check and Quicken's account register window. You fill in the check form like you would fill in the blanks on a paper check. Quicken's QuickFill feature makes data entry quicker and easier by recalling entry information from similar transactions to the same payee, and its automatic categorization feature can automatically "guess" the category for many new transactions. You must enter a valid Quicken category in the Category field, just as you would when entering a transaction in the account register. Clicking the Record Check button completes the transaction and adds it to the Checks To Print list (see Figure 5-4), as well as the account register, as shown here:

| Date/ ▲ | Num | Payee/Category/Memo | | Payment | Clr | Deposit | Balance |
|---|---|---|---|---|---|---|---|
| 7/1/2006 | Print | AAA | | 45 00 | | | 1,698 93 |
| | | Subscriptions | | | | | |
| 7/3/2006 | Print | Southwest Gas | | 64 85 | | | 1,634 08 |
| | | Utilities:Gas & Electric | | | | | |
| 7/3/2006 | Print | Bar S Animal Clinic | | 90 00 | | | 1,544 08 |
| | | Animal Expenses | West Nile Vaccine for horses | | | | |

Consult the earlier section "Using Account Registers" for details about the information that should be entered into most fields. Here are a few additional things to consider when entering transactions in the Write Checks window:

**Addresses on Checks**   If you enter an address on the check, you can mail the check using a window envelope. The address is automatically added to the Quicken Address Book. You can click the Address button in the Write Checks window to display the Edit Address Book Record dialog, which you can use to modify an address in the Address Book.

**Check Memos**   If you enter a note on the memo line of a check, it might be visible if you mail the check in a window envelope.

**Online Payments**   An Online Payment check box appears in the Write Check window if Online Payment is enabled for the account for which you are writing a check. Turning on this check box creates an online payment instruction for your bank. I tell you about online payments in Chapter 6.

## Transferring Money

You can also record the transfer of funds from one account to another. You might find this feature especially useful for recording telephone or ATM transfers.

### Using the Transfer Dialog

One way to record a transfer is with the Transfer dialog. Open the account register window for one of the accounts involved in the transfer transaction and click the Transfer button on the button bar. The Record A Transfer Between Quicken Accounts dialog, which is illustrated next, appears. Choose the source and destination accounts from the drop-down lists, enter a transaction date and amount, and click OK.

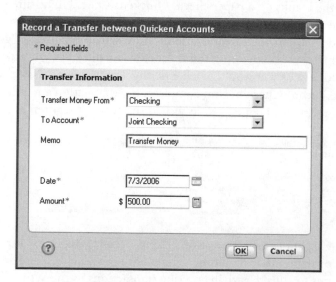

## Recording a Transfer in the Account Register Window

The Transfer dialog isn't the only way to record a transfer. You can also record a transfer in the account register window of either the source or destination account. When you choose Transfer (TXFR) from the Num drop-down list, the Category drop-down list displays only transfer accounts. Choose the other transfer account from the list and complete the transaction.

The following illustrations show a transfer from one checking account to another. Here's what the source (Checking) account transaction looks like:

| 7/3/2006 | TXFR | Transfer Money | | 500 00 | | | 4,258 94 |
|---|---|---|---|---|---|---|---|
| | | [Joint Checking] | | | | | |

And here's what the corresponding destination (Joint Checking) account transaction looks like:

| 7/3/2006 | | Transfer Money | | | 500 00 | 2,198 93 |
|---|---|---|---|---|---|---|
| | | [Checking] | | | | |

# Working with Existing Transactions

So far, this chapter has concentrated on entering transactions. What do you do when you need to modify a transaction you already recorded? That's what this section is all about.

## Searching for Transactions

Quicken includes four commands to help you locate and work with transactions:

- **Find** enables you to search for transactions in the active account based on any field.
- **Find Next** searches for transactions matching the previously entered Find criteria.
- **Find/Replace** enables you to find transactions based on any field and replace any field of the found transactions.
- **Recategorize** enables you to find transactions for a specific category and replace the category.

The following sections take a closer look at each of these commands. They also explain how you can use the new Find Payment or Deposit field on the toolbar to find transactions quickly.

### Using the Find and Find Next Commands

To use the Find command, begin by opening the account register or Write Checks window for the account you want to search. Then choose Edit | Find & Replace | Find, click the Find button on the window's button bar, or press CTRL-F. The Quicken Find dialog, which is illustrated here, appears.

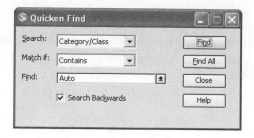

Start by choosing an option from the Search drop-down list, which includes all register fields for a transaction. Then choose a Match If option to indicate how the search criteria should be matched. Enter the search criteria in the Find box. If you enter a space in the Find box, Quicken searches for entries for which the Search field is blank; this is a great way to find uncategorized transactions. To search backward (relative to the currently selected transaction), turn on the Search Backwards check box.

After setting up the search, if you click the Find button, Quicken selects the first match found in the window. You can then click the Find button again to find the next match. If you click the Find All button, Quicken displays the Search Results window, which lists all the matches it found. You can double-click a match to view it in the account register window.

The Find Next command uses the criteria set up in the Quicken Find dialog, which Quicken remembers throughout your Quicken session. Later, to conduct the same search, you can choose Edit | Find & Replace | Find Next or press SHIFT-CTRL-F.

## Using the Find/Replace Command

The Find/Replace command works throughout Quicken, not just with the active account register or Write Checks window. To use it, choose Edit | Find & Replace | Find/Replace. The Find And Replace dialog appears. The top part of the dialog looks and works much like the Quicken Find dialog. You can turn on the Show Matches In Split check box at the bottom of the dialog if you want Quicken to find all matches, including those that appear in splits.

Once you set up the search and click the Find All button, a list of matches appears in the bottom half of the dialog, as shown next. Click beside each found item you want to change to place a green check mark there. Then set options in the Replace and With boxes. Click Replace to replace all checked items with the replacement option you specified. A dialog confirms that the replacement has been made.

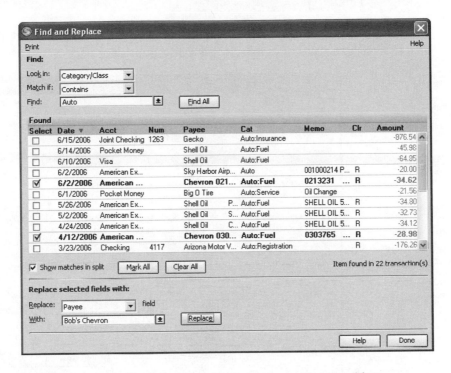

Note that if you use this feature to rename Payees as illustrated here, you may automatically set up renaming rules. I tell you about Quicken's Renaming Rules feature in Chapter 6.

## Using the Recategorize Command

The Recategorize command works like the Find/Replace command, but it finds and replaces only categories. For example, suppose you were using the Misc category a little more often than you should, and you know that some transactions could be recategorized. You can use the Recategorize command to find transactions with the Misc category and then change some or all of them to a more appropriate category.

Choose Edit | Find & Replace | Recategorize to display the Recategorize dialog. Start by using the Look In drop-down list to choose the type of transaction you want to find: Transactions (entered transactions), Memorized Payees, or Scheduled Transactions. Then choose a category from the Find Category drop-down list and click Find All. A list of matches appears in the Recategorize dialog, as shown next. Select the transactions for which you want to change the category, choose a new category from the drop-down list at the bottom of the dialog, and click Recategorize to replace the categories for selected transactions all at once.

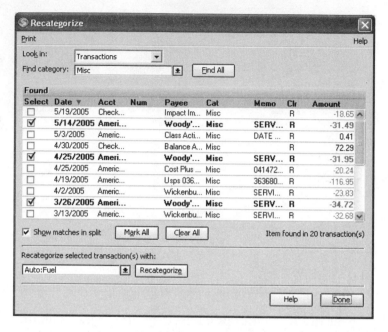

## Using the Find Payment or Deposit Field

Quicken's Find Payment or Deposit field, which appears in the toolbar, makes it quick and easy to find transactions. Simply enter a search word or phrase in the field—it can be all or part of a payee name, category, or even memo—and click Find All. Quicken displays a Search Results window, like the one shown next:

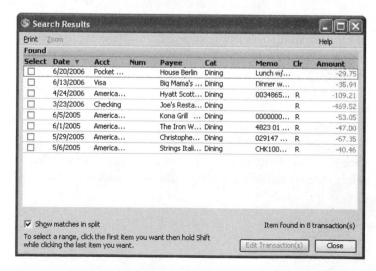

You can turn on the check box beside any transaction(s) you want to edit and click the Edit Transaction(s) button. The Find And Replace dialog (shown earlier) appears, with just those transactions listed. You can then use the replace options at the bottom of the dialog to modify the transactions.

## Sorting Transactions

You might also find it helpful to click a register's column heading or use the Sort options (under the View menu in the account register window's button bar) to change the sort order of transactions. For example, sorting by check number groups the transactions by the Num field, making it easy to find transactions by type. You can quickly move to a specific date or transaction number by dragging the scroll box on the scroll bar. The QuickScroll feature, shown here, displays the date of the transaction that will appear when you release the scroll box.

## Changing Transactions

Quicken enables you to change a transaction at any time—even after it has been cleared. This makes it possible to correct errors in any transaction you have entered.

**Making Simple Changes**    If all you want to do is change one of the fields in the transaction—such as the category, date, or number—simply find the transaction in the appropriate account register, make changes as desired, and click the Enter button to record them.

**Using the Edit Menu**    The Edit menu, shown here, appears when you click the Edit button in the account register window for the currently selected transaction. It offers other options for working with a selected transaction:

- **Enter** enters the transaction in the register. Choosing this command is the same as clicking the Enter button or pressing ENTER.
- **Restore Transaction** enables you to change a transaction back to the way it was before you started changing it. This option is available only if you have made changes to the selected transaction.
- **Split** opens the Split window for the transaction. Choosing this command is the same as clicking the Split button. I explain how to use the Split feature earlier in this chapter in the section titled "Using Splits."

- **Notes And Flags** displays the Transaction Notes And Flags dialog (which is shown later in this chapter in the section titled "Adding Notes, Flags, and Alerts") so you can add transaction notes, flag the transaction in a specific color, or create an alert for follow-up.

- **Attachments** displays the Transaction Attachment dialog (shown later in this chapter in the section titled "Attaching Checks, Receipts, or Other Images") so you can attach checks, receipts, and other images to the transaction.

- **Cut Transaction(s)** copies the selected transaction and removes it from the account register.

- **Copy Transaction(s)** copies the selected transaction without removing it from the account register.

- **Paste Transaction(s)** pastes the last-copied transaction into the current account register. This option is available only after a transaction has been copied. You might want to cut a transaction to paste it into another register if you realize that you entered it in the wrong register.

- **Edit Transaction(s)** displays the Find And Replace dialog (shown earlier in this chapter in the section titled "Searching for Transactions") so you can use the Replace feature to modify the selected transaction(s).

- **New** enables you to create a new transaction for the account. This does not affect the currently selected transaction.

- **Delete** deletes the selected transaction. This is the same as clicking the Delete button in the button bar. Remember that deleting a transaction removes the transaction from the Quicken data file, thus changing the account balance and category activity.

- **Undo Delete** restores the transaction you just deleted. You must use this command immediately after deleting a transaction to restore the transaction.

- **Insert Transaction** enables you to insert a transaction before the selected transaction in the account register. This does not affect the currently selected transaction.

- **Move Transaction(s)** displays the Move Transactions(s) dialog (shown here), which you can use to move a transaction from the current account register to a different account register. Simply choose an account name from the drop-down list and click OK to complete the move.

- **Undo Accept All Transactions** restores accepted transactions to unaccepted status. This command is available only if the last thing you did was accept transactions. I tell you more about accepting transactions in Chapter 6.

- **Memorize Payee** tells Quicken to add the selected transaction to its list of memorized payees. Memorized payees are used for the QuickFill feature, which I discuss in Chapter 7.
- **Schedule Bill Or Deposit** enables you to schedule the transaction for a future date or to set up the transaction as a recurring transaction. I tell you more about scheduling transactions in Chapter 7.
- **Void Transaction(s)** marks the selected transaction as void. This reverses the effect of the transaction on the account balance and category activity without actually deleting the transaction.
- **Reconcile** enables you to indicate whether the transaction should be marked as Not Reconciled, Cleared, or Reconciled. I explain how to reconcile accounts in Chapter 8.
- **Find** displays the Find dialog, which I discuss earlier in this chapter in the section titled "Searching for Transactions."
- **Find Next** searches for transactions matching the previously entered Find criteria. I explain how to use the Find Next command earlier in this chapter in the section titled "Searching for Transactions."
- **Go To Matching Transfer** displays the selected transaction in the account register for the other part of a transfer. For example, if the selected transaction involves the checking and savings accounts and you are viewing it in the checking account register, choosing the Go To Transfer command displays the same transaction in the savings account register. This command is available only if the selected transaction includes a transfer.
- **Go To Specific Date** enables you to move to a different date within the register. This does not affect the currently selected transaction.
- **Cancel Payment** sends a cancel payment instruction to your bank to stop an online payment. This option is available only for online payments that have not yet been made.
- **Payment Inquiry** enables you to contact your bank to inquire about the transaction. This option is available only for online payments.
- **Properties** displays the View Posting Date dialog, which you can use to view information about an online payment. This option is available only for online payments.

**Selecting More Than One Transaction**   You may have noticed that several of the Edit menu commands enable you to work with more than one transaction at a time. To do this, you need to select multiple transactions. Here's how:

- To select several individual transactions in an account register, hold down CTRL and click each transaction you want to include. The transactions change color to indicate they are selected.

- To select a range of transactions, click to select the first transaction in the range. Then hold down SHIFT and click the last transaction in the range. All transactions between the first and the last transaction change color to indicate they have been selected.

## Adding Notes and Attachments

Quicken's attachment feature enables you to add notes, flags, reminders, and image files to a transaction or account. This makes it possible to store all kinds of digital information in your Quicken data file, including cancelled checks, receipts, or photographs.

### What Does This Mean to You? Transaction Attachments

If there's such a thing as a "Paperwork Reduction Act," then why do I seem to keep accumulating more and more paper? Bank statements, cancelled checks, receipts. It never seems to end. But I know that the moment I throw away an important tax-related document, that's the day I'll get a letter from Uncle Sam, asking to see it.

That's where Quicken's new transaction attachment feature can help. If you have a scanner, you can digitize important papers and attach their image files to the transactions or accounts they relate to. Then, when you need to consult the document, you can quickly and easily find it in Quicken and view it onscreen. You can even print a copy, with the click of a button!

Sure beats dealing with all those file boxes I just bought at the office supply store.

### Adding Notes, Flags, and Alerts

You can add a note, color-coded flag, or follow-up alert—or all three—to any Quicken transaction. You do this in the account register window.

First, select the transaction you want to add the item to. Then click the Attach button for the transaction and choose Add Follow-Up Flag or Add Note, choose Edit | Transaction | Notes And Flags, or choose Notes And Flags from the menu that appears when you click the Edit button for the transaction. The Transaction Notes And Flags dialog, shown next, appears.

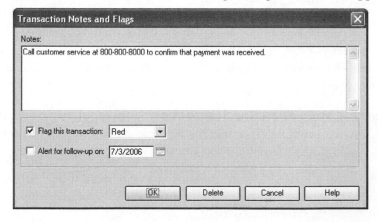

Add items to the transaction as follows:

- To add a note, type the text of the note into the Notes box. This adds a note icon to the transaction, beneath the date. Pointing to the icon displays the note in a screen tip box.
- To flag the transaction, turn on the Flag This Transaction check box. Then choose a color from the drop-down list. This adds a flag icon, in the color you indicated, to the transaction, beneath the date. (The flag icon replaces the note icon if the transaction also has a note.)
- To create a follow-up alert, turn on the Alert For Follow Up On check box and enter a date in the box beside it. (You can add a follow-up alert only if the transaction is already flagged.) This adds an alert to the Alerts Center window, which I discuss in Chapter 9.

Click OK to save your settings.

## Attaching Checks, Receipts, or Other Images

Quicken 2006 added the ability to attach image files to transactions or accounts. You can use this feature to file digital copies of important documents with the transactions or accounts they relate to.

In Quicken 2007, the attachment feature has been improved. You can now add images from a file on disk, scan images directly into Quicken from your scanner, or paste in images from the clipboard.

### Attaching Images to Transactions

You attach an image to a transaction in the account register window. Begin by selecting the transaction you want to attach the item to. Then click the Attach button for the transaction and choose an option from the Attach Electronic Image submenu that appears, choose Edit | Transaction | Attachments, or choose Attachments from the menu that appears when you click the Edit button for the transaction.

In the Transaction Attachments dialog that appears (shown next), use the Attach New or Attach Another drop-down list to choose the type of attachment you want to add: Check, Receipt/Bill, Invoice, Warranty, or Other. Then click one of the Image From buttons:

- **File** displays the Select Attachment File dialog, which you can use to locate, select, and open a file on disk. The file must be in a format readable by Internet Explorer, such as JPG, GIF, TXT, HTML, PDF, and PNG. When you click Open, the file's content appears in the Transaction Attachment dialog.
- **Scanner** may display the Select Source dialog, which you can use to select your scanner. It then displays your scanner's standard scanning interface, which you can use to scan an image. When the scan is complete, the image appears in the Transaction Attachment dialog.

- **Clipboard** pastes the contents of the clipboard into the Transaction Attachments dialog. (To use this option, you should select and copy an image *before* opening the Transaction Attachment dialog.)

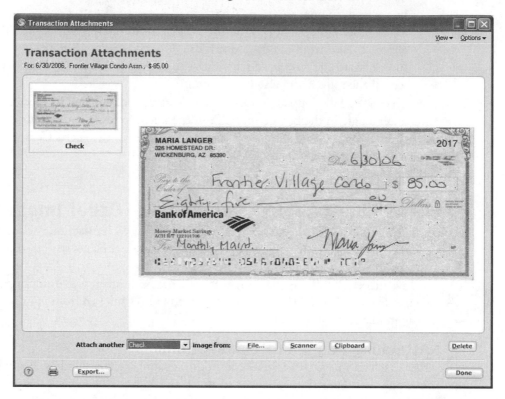

 Quicken 2007 enables you to add as many attachments as you like to a transaction. To add other attachments, just repeat the process to attach another item. When you're finished, click Done to close the Transaction Attachments dialog. An Attachment icon appears beneath the transaction date to indicate that items are attached.

## Attaching Transactions to Accounts

You can also attach images and other files to an account. You might find this useful for storing bank statements or other documents that relate to the entire account rather than just one attachment.

You attach items to an account in the Account Attachments snapshot of the account's Overview window. Open the account you want to work with and click the Overview tab. Then scroll down to the bottom of the window to see the Account Attachments snapshot. For investment accounts, you'll find this snapshot in the account's Summary tab.

To attach a file, click the Add button in the Account Attachments snapshot. The Add Attachment dialog, which is shown next, appears.

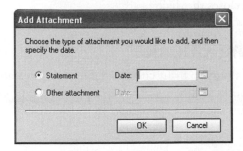

Select the option button for the type of file you want to attach and enter a date in the corresponding Date box. When you click OK, the Account Attachments dialog, which looks and works exactly like the Transaction Attachments dialog shown earlier, appears. Use this dialog to attach one or more items to the account. When you're finished, click Done. The attachments appear in a list in the Account Attachments snapshot, as shown next:

| Account Attachments | | |
|---|---|---|
| Date | Statements | Other Attachments |
| 7/1/2006 | 2 | |
| 6/30/2006 | 1 | 2 |
| Add | | View |

## Working with Attachments

Once a file has been attached to a transaction or account, you can view, remove, replace, or print it at any time.

To work with a transaction attachment, click the Attachment icon for the transaction. The Transaction Attachments dialog (shown earlier) opens. Click the thumbnail image or icon for the attached item to work with it.

To work with an account attachment, select the attachment in the Account Attachments snapshot and click the View button. The Account Attachments dialog, which looks like the Transaction Attachments dialog, appears. Click the thumbnail image or icon for the attached item to work with it.

You can use buttons in the Transaction Attachments or Account Attachments dialog to work with attachments:

- **Help** (which appears as a question mark) displays the Quicken Help window, with links to topics about attaching digital images to transactions and accounts. Click a link to view the help information.
- **Print** (which appears as a small printer icon) prints the attachment.

- **Export** saves the attachment as a file on your disk.
- **Delete** removes the attachment.
- **Done** closes the dialog.

# Printing Checks

Quicken's ability to print checks enables you to create accurate, legible, professional-looking checks without picking up a pen (or a typewriter). In this section, I explain how to print the checks you enter in the Write Checks window, discussed earlier in this chapter.

## Getting the Right Checks

Before you can print checks from Quicken, you must obtain compatible check stock. Quicken supports checks in a number of different styles:

- **Standard checks** print just checks. There's no voucher or stub.
- **Voucher checks** pair each check with a similarly sized voucher form. When you print on a voucher check, the transaction category information, including splits and classes, can be printed on the voucher part.
- **Wallet checks** pair each check with a stub. When you print on a wallet check, the transaction information is printed on the stub.

In addition to these styles, you can get the checks in two different formats for your printer:

- **Page-oriented** checks are for laser and inkjet printers.
- **Continuous** checks are for pin-feed printers.

A catalog and order form for checks may have been included with your copy of Quicken. You can use it to order checks. If you have an Internet connection, you can order checks online from within Quicken by choosing Cash Flow | Quicken Services | Order Checks & Supplies or by clicking the Order Checks button in the button bar of the Write Checks window (see Figure 5-4).

## Setting Up

Quicken must also be set up to print the kind of checks you purchased. You do this once, and Quicken remembers the settings.

Choose File | Printer Setup | For Printing Checks to display the Check Printer Setup dialog, as shown next. Use the drop-down lists and option buttons to specify settings for your printer and check stock. Following are a few things to keep in mind when changing settings in this dialog.

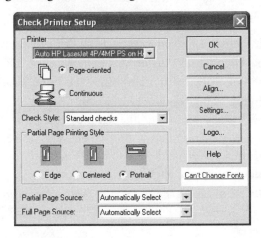

## Partial Page Printing Options

If you select the Page-Oriented option and either Standard or Wallet checks in the Check Printer Setup dialog, you can also set options for Partial Page Printing Style. This enables you to set up the printer for situations when you're not printing an entire page of checks:

- **Edge** is for inserting the page against one side of the feeder. The left or right edge of the checks enters the feeder first.
- **Centered** is for centering the page in the feeder. The left or right edge of the checks enters the feeder first.
- **Portrait** is also for centering the page in the feeder, but in this case, the top edge of each check enters the feeder first.

If your printer supports multiple feed trays, you can also set the source tray for partial and full pages by choosing options from the Partial Page Source and Full Page Source drop-down lists.

## Continuous Printing Options

If you select the Continuous option and either Standard or Wallet checks in the Check Printer Setup dialog, the dialog changes to offer two Continuous options:

- **Bypass The Driver** should be turned on for a continuous printer that skips checks or prints nothing.
- **Use Low Starting Position** should be turned on for a continuous printer that cuts the date or logo off your checks.

## Checking the Settings for Page-Oriented Checks

If you're using page-oriented checks, you can check your settings by printing a sample page on plain paper. Here's how:

1. Click the Align button in the Check Printer Setup dialog.
2. In the Align Checks dialog that appears, click the Full Page Of Checks button.
3. In the Fine Alignment dialog, click the Print Sample button.
4. When the sample emerges from your printer, hold it up to the light with a sheet of check stock behind it. The sample should line up with the check.
5. If the sample does not line up properly with the check stock, set Vertical and/or Horizontal adjustment values in the Fine Alignment dialog. Then repeat steps 3 through 5 until the alignment is correct.
6. Click OK in each dialog to accept your settings and close it.

# Printing

Once setup is complete, you're ready to print checks.

Open the account register for the account you want to print checks for. Then insert the check stock in your printer and choose File | Print Checks, or click the Print button in the Write Checks window. The Select Checks To Print dialog, which is shown next, appears. Enter the number of the first check that will be printed in the First Check Number box. Then set other options as desired. If you select the Selected Checks option, you can click the Choose button to display a list of checks and check off the ones you want to print. Click Done in that window to return to the Select Checks To Print dialog.

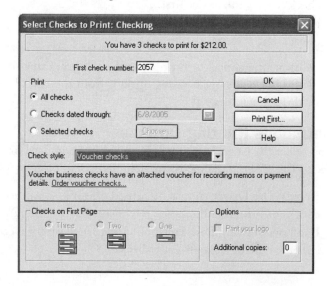

When you click Print First or OK, Quicken sends the print job to your printer. It then displays a dialog asking if the checks printed correctly. You have two options:

- If all checks printed fine, just click OK.
- If a problem occurred while printing the checks, enter the number of the first check that was misprinted and then click OK. You can then go back to the Select Checks To Print dialog and try again.

# Using Online Banking Features

## Chapter 6

## In This Chapter:

- *Benefits and costs of online banking*
- *Setting up Online Account Services*
- *Downloading and comparing transactions*
- *Setting up payees*
- *Processing online payments and transfers*
- *Entering transactions on the Web*
- *Updating your Quicken accounts on Quicken.com*

Life can be pretty hectic sometimes—too hectic to keep track of your bank accounts, pay bills before they're overdue, and buy stamps to mail your bills. Quicken Personal Finance Software's Online Account Services enable you to do most (if not all) of your banking from the comfort of your own home so banking can be a lot less of a chore. Several features can be used separately or together:

- **Transaction Download** enables you to download bank and credit card account activity, and transfer money online between accounts.
- **Online Payment** enables you to pay bills online, without manually writing or mailing a check. (Quicken Bill Pay offers the features of Online Payment, even if your bank does not support it.)

In addition, two banking-related features work in conjunction with Quicken.com:

- **WebEntry** enables you to enter Quicken transactions on the Web. This makes it possible to record Quicken transactions from any computer, anywhere in the world.
- **Bank Account Update** enables you to upload your account balances to Quicken.com so you can view them from any computer with Internet access.

In this chapter, I explain how these features work and how you can use them to save time while keeping track of your finances.

The instructions in this chapter assume that you have already configured Quicken for an Internet connection. If you have not done so, do it now. Chapter 4 provides the instructions you need to set up and test an Internet connection. This chapter also assumes that you understand the topics and procedures discussed in Chapters 3 and 5. This chapter builds on many of the basic concepts discussed in those chapters.

# Online Account Services

Here's a closer look at Quicken's Online Account Services, including what the services are, how they work, and how you can expect to benefit from them.

## Transaction Download

Quicken's Transaction Download feature can perform several tasks, depending on your financial institution. Here's the scoop.

### How It Works

Generally speaking, financial institutions can support Transaction Download three ways.

**Direct Connect**    Many financial institutions support direct communication between Quicken and the financial institution's server. This so-called *Direct Connect* method is the most powerful way to use the Transaction Download feature. To download transactions, you simply click a button in Quicken's Online Center window, provide brief instructions and a PIN, and wait while Quicken gets the information you want. Quicken does all the work.

**Web Connect**    Many financial institutions that don't support Direct Connect enable you to download specially formatted *Web Connect* files. To do this, you must log in to your financial institution's Web site using the information your financial institution supplies, navigate to a download page, and indicate what data you want to download. Once the Web Connect file has been downloaded, Quicken reads it and knows exactly which Quicken account it applies to.

**Express Web Connect**     Quicken 2007's new Express Web Connect feature makes it possible to use One Step Update to download Web Connect transactions from your bank without accessing its Web site. This more fully integrates Web Connect downloads into the Quicken interface, making it quicker and easier to get transactions into Quicken.

## Downloaded Transactions

Bank account transaction downloads include all deposits, checks, interest payments, bank fees, transfers, ATM transactions, and debit card transactions. Credit card transaction downloads include all charges, credits (for returns or adjustments), payments, fees, and finance charges. Quicken displays all of the transactions, including those you have not yet entered in your account register, as well as the current balance of the account. A few clicks and keystrokes is all it takes to enter the transactions you missed. This feature makes it virtually impossible to omit entries, while telling you exactly how much money is available in a bank account or how much money you owe on your credit card account—no more surprises in that monthly statement.

## Additional Features of Direct Connect

If your financial institution supports Direct Connect, you may also be able to take advantage of the following two features:

**Transfer Money Between Accounts**     If you have more than one bank account at the same financial institution, you can use Online Account Access to transfer money between accounts. Although many banks offer this feature by phone, it usually requires dialing a phone number and entering an account number and PIN while navigating through voice prompts. Even if you get a real person on the phone, you still have to provide the same litany of personal identification information every time you call. With Direct Connect, you merely enter a transfer transaction and let Quicken do the rest.

**Send E-Mail Messages to Your Financial Institution**     Ever call the customer service center at your bank or credit card company to ask a question? If you're lucky, real people are waiting to answer the phone. But if you're like most people, your financial institution uses a call routing system that requires you to listen to voice prompts and press telephone keypad keys to communicate with a machine. Either way, when a real person gets on the line, you have to provide all kinds of information about yourself just to prove that you are who you say you are. *Then* you can ask your question. The e-mail feature that's part of Direct Connect enables you to exchange e-mail messages with your bank or credit card company's customer service department. You normally get a response within one business day.

## Online Payment and Quicken Bill Pay

Online Payment enables you to send a check to anyone without physically writing, printing, or mailing a check. You enter and store information about the payee within Quicken. You then create a transaction for the payee that includes the payment date and amount. You can enter the transaction weeks or months in advance if desired— the payee receives payment on the date you specify.

Online Payment is one of the least understood Quicken features. Many folks think it can be used to pay only big companies like the phone company or credit card companies. That just isn't true. You can use Online Payment to pay any bill, fund your IRA, donate money to a charity, or send your brother a birthday gift.

### How It Works

Suppose you use Quicken to send online payment instructions to pay your monthly bill at Joe's Hardware Store. You've already set up Joe as a payee by entering the name, address, and phone number of his store, as well as your account number there. Quicken sends your payment instructions to your bank, which stores it in its computer with a bunch of other online payment instructions. When the payment date nears, the bank's computer looks through its big database of payees that it can pay by wire transfer. It sees phone companies and credit card companies and other banks. But because Joe's store is small, it's probably not one of the wire transfer payees. So the bank's computer prepares a check using all the information you provided. It mails the check along with thousands of others due to be paid that day.

Joe's wife, who does the accounting for the store (with Quicken Premier Home & Business, in case you're wondering), gets the check a few days later. Although it looks different than a handwritten check, when she deposits it with the other checks she gets that day, it clears just like any other check. The amount of the check is deducted from your bank account and your account balance at Joe's. If you use Transaction Download, the check appears as a transaction. It also appears on your bank statement. If your bank returns canceled checks to you, you may get the check along with all your others.

### When the Money Leaves Your Account

The date the money is actually withdrawn from your account to cover the payment varies depending on your bank. There are four possibilities:

- One to four days before the payment is processed for delivery
- The day the payment is processed for delivery
- The day the payment is delivered
- The day the paper check or electronic funds transfer clears your bank

To find out when funds are withdrawn from your account for online payments, ask your bank.

## The Benefits of Online Payment

Online Payment can benefit you in several ways. You can pay your bills as they arrive, without paying them early—the payee never receives payment before the payment date you specify. You don't have to buy stamps, and the bank never forgets to mail the checks.

## Quicken Bill Pay

If your bank does not support Online Payment, you can still take advantage of this feature by signing up for Quicken Bill Pay. This service works with your checking account like Online Payment does.

### What Does This Mean to You? Online Payment Costs

If you think Online Payment sounds expensive, do the math. Here's an example. I get 20 payments per month for $5. If I had to mail 20 checks, it would cost me $7.80 in postage. So I'd actually save $2.80 per month if I made 20 online payments. Even if I don't make 20 payments a month, I also don't have to stuff envelopes, apply return address labels, or stick on stamps. My bills get paid on time, I earn more interest income, and I haven't bounced a check in more than eight years.

Does it sound like I'm sold on this feature? You bet I am!

## Costs

The cost of Quicken's online account services varies from bank to bank. Check with your bank to determine the exact fees. Here's what you can expect:

- Transaction Download is often free to all customers or to customers who maintain a certain minimum account balance. Otherwise, you could pay up to $5 for this service.

- Online Payment is sometimes free, but more often it costs from $5 to $10 per month for 20 to 25 payments per month. Each additional payment usually costs 40¢ to 60¢. Again, some banks waive this fee if you maintain a certain minimum balance.

- Quicken Bill Pay is $9.95 for up to 20 payments and $2.49 for each set of five payments after that. (These prices are subject to change.)

## Security

If you're worried about security, you must have skipped over the security information in Chapter 4. Go back and read that now. It explains how Quicken and financial institution security works to make Online Account Services safe.

# Setting Up Online Account Services

To use the Online Account Services supported by Quicken, you must configure the appropriate Quicken accounts. This requires that you enter information about your financial institution and the account with which you want to use these features.

## Applying for Online Account Services

Before you can use one of the online account services, you must apply for it. I tell you how at the end of Chapter 4. Normally, all it takes is a phone call, although some banks and credit card companies allow you to apply online. Another way to apply or get application information is to click the Sign Up Now button that appears in the Quicken Account Setup dialog shown later in this chapter.

To learn more about and apply for Quicken Bill Pay, choose Online | Quicken Bill Pay | Learn About Quicken Bill Pay. After reading the information in the Quicken Services window that appears, click the Enroll Now link to connect to the Internet and fill out the Quicken Bill Pay Application form.

The application process for these services usually takes a week but may take less. You'll know that you're ready to go online when you get a letter with setup information. The setup information usually consists of the following:

**PIN (Personal Identification Number)**    You'll have to enter this code into Quicken when you access your account online. This is a security feature, so don't write down your PIN on a sticky note and attach it to your computer monitor. There is a chance that your financial institution may send this information separately for additional security. Quicken refers to this information as a password.

**Customer ID Number**    This is often your Social Security number or taxpayer identification number.

**Bank Routing Number**    Although your bank might send routing number information, Quicken won't need it. It knows what financial institution you're using based on the information you provide when you create the account. That's why it's so important to choose the correct financial institution when you create an account.

**Account Number for Each Online Access–Enabled Account**    This tells your financial institution which account you want to work with. In many instances, Quicken may not need this information either.

## Setting Up Online Account Services

With customer ID and PIN in hand, you're ready to set up your account (or accounts) for Online Account Services. You can set up the account in a number of ways; rather than cover them all, I cover the most straightforward method.

Keep in mind that if you set up an account using the online method, as discussed in Chapter 4, and you already have online account access enabled at your bank, your account may already be set up for online access. You can tell if it is by following the instructions in the "Checking Online Account Service Status" section later in this chapter.

## Setting Up for Direct Connect and Quicken Bill Pay

Begin by creating an account as instructed in Chapter 5. Be sure to enter the correct financial institution in the Quicken Account Setup dialog when prompted. Quicken should display a dialog asking whether you want to set up your account online or manually. Select the Online option and click Next to display a login dialog like this:

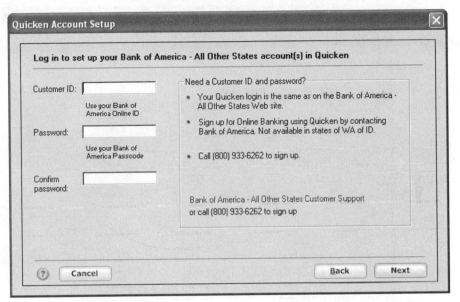

If the account has already been set up but has not been activated for Online Account Services, you can display the login dialog by switching to the account register for the account and clicking the Set Up Online button in the register's button bar.

Enter your customer ID and PIN or password in the appropriate boxes and click Next. Quicken connects to the Internet and downloads information about your accounts from your financial institution. If it prompts you to change your password, use the dialog that appears to do so.

What Quicken does next depends on your financial institution's Quicken server and what method you used to initiate the setup process.

**Entering Account and Routing Information**     For some banks, Quicken may display a dialog that prompts you to select an account type, enter your account number, and enter a bank routing number. It may also offer check boxes to indicate the services you want to use. Provide the requested information and click Next. Quicken displays a dialog telling you that you have successfully set up the account(s). Click Next in that dialog to download your first batch of transactions. Then skip ahead to the section titled "More About Transaction Download."

**Matching Accounts**   For other banks, if you are setting up online services for an existing Quicken account, Quicken may display a dialog like the one shown next, which includes a drop-down list of all the accounts at the financial institution that has Online Account Services enabled. Choose the correct account from the drop-down list and click Next.

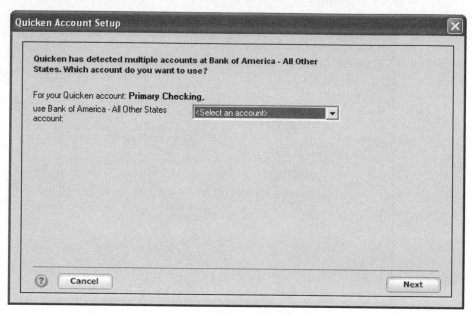

Quicken may offer to set up other accounts at that financial institution; follow the instructions in the dialog that appears (shown next) to do so if you wish. Then Quicken displays a dialog telling you that you have successfully set up the account(s). Click Done in that dialog to download your first batch of transactions, and skip ahead to the section titled "More About Transaction Download."

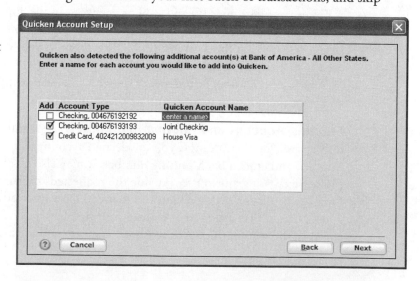

## Setting Up for Web Connect and Express Web Connect

Begin by creating an account as instructed in Chapter 5. Be sure to enter the correct financial institution in the Quicken Account Setup dialog when prompted. Quicken should display a dialog asking whether you want to set up your account online or manually. Select the Online option and click Next.

Or, if the account has already been set up but has not been activated for Online Account Services, you can display the previously illustrated dialog by switching to the account register for the account and clicking the Set Up Online button in the register's button bar.

Quicken may display one or more dialogs to collect additional login information for your account. For example, for my ING Direct savings account, Quicken asked some of the same questions ING asks when I log into its Web site: the last three digits of my Social Security number, my ZIP code, my year of birth, etc. Quicken gathers this information for use with the Express Web Connect feature.

For Web Connect access, Quicken launches your Web browser, connects to the Internet, and displays a login screen for your financial institution (refer to Figure 6-1). Log in to your account, navigate to the page where you can download your account statement, and download it. If several formats are offered, it's vital that you choose Quicken or Quicken Web Connect. During the download, if your Web browser prompts you to save or open the file, indicate that you want to open it with Quicken or Quicken Launcher.

When the download is complete, if necessary, switch back to Quicken. A dialog like the one shown next should appear:

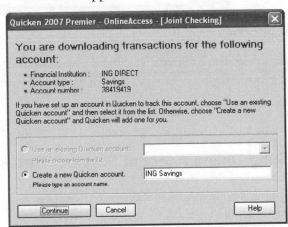

You have two options:

- **Use An Existing Quicken Account** enables you to choose an existing Quicken account from the drop-down list. Make sure you choose the correct account!
- **Create A New Quicken Account** enables you to enter a name for a new Quicken account.

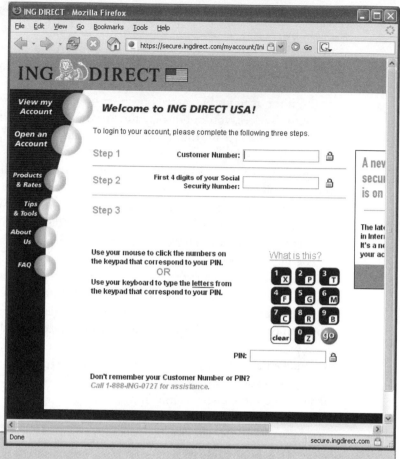

**Figure 6-1 • Quicken displays the login screen for your financial institution's Web site.**

Click Continue. Quicken downloads your first batch of transactions. Skip ahead to the section titled "More About Transaction Download."

## Checking Online Account Service Status

You can confirm that an account has been set up for Online Account Services. Open the account's register and click the Overview tab. The Account Attributes area should indicate whether services are available or activated. Here's an example.

Clicking the Change Online Services button in the Account Attributes area

| Account Attributes | Options ▼ |
|---|---|
| Account Name | Joint Checking |
| Tax-Deferred | No |
| Description | |
| Financial Institution | Bank of America - All Other States |
| Account Number | 327976193279 |
| Routing Number | 117061706 |
| Customer ID | 165841784 |
| Transaction Download | Activated |
| Online Payment through... | Activated |
| View on Quicken.com | Available |
| Web Page(s): | |

**Edit Account Details** | **Change Online Services**

displays the Online Services tab of the Account Details dialog. You can use this dialog to activate or, in this case, deactivate Online Account Services.

## More About Transaction Download

Quicken makes a distinction between two types of downloaded transactions:

- **Online transaction instructions** are those transactions that have been sent to your financial institution but have not yet cleared your account. For example, suppose you used your bank's Web site to pay one of your bills. This transaction is in your bank's computer server, but it hasn't been completed or cleared. When you download transactions for that account, Quicken downloads the payment instruction so you can record it as an upcoming payment in your account.
- **Cleared transactions** are those transactions that have cleared your account and are included in your current account balance. For example, suppose you made a deposit at the bank. As soon as the bank accepts the deposit, the deposit is said to have "cleared" and is included in your current bank account balance. Cleared transactions can include deposits, checks, online payments, ATM transactions, debit card transactions, bank or interest fees, and interest earnings.

### How Quicken Downloads Transactions

When you instruct Quicken to download transactions, it actually performs two tasks while "talking" to your financial institution's server. First, it asks for all of the online transaction instructions the financial institution has received since the last time Quicken connected. Then it asks for all of the transactions that have cleared since the last time Quicken connected. If transactions exist in both groups, Quicken displays them for review and approval separately.

### First-Time Transaction Download

The first time you download transactions from your financial institution to Quicken—normally, when you set up the account for online account access—Quicken performs some special tasks to make setup quicker and easier:

- If your first transaction download includes only cleared transactions, Quicken automatically accepts them into the account register, using its automatic categorization feature to assign categories whenever possible. (You may want to review the transactions to modify categories or assign categories to transactions Quicken did not categorize.) At the same time, Quicken automatically calculates (or, in some instances, recalculates) the account's opening balance so your account register will have a recent history of transactions as well as a balance that matches the financial institution's.

- If your first transaction download includes both online payment instructions and cleared transactions, Quicken displays both types of transactions for you to review separately. (You can tell that the download includes online payment instructions because links labeled "Online Payments" and "Cleared" appear in the Downloaded Transactions tab, as shown in the following illustration.) You must review the online payment instructions before you review the cleared payments. Although you can review them each individually, the best way to review them all quickly is to click the Accept All button at the bottom of the window. You can then review and accept downloaded transactions, as I discuss in the section titled "Comparing Downloaded Transactions to Register Transactions" later in this chapter.

# The Online Center

When you enable Online Account Services, you can use the Online Center to work with Quicken's online features. This window gives you access to all the lists and commands you need to download transactions, create payments, transfer money, and exchange e-mail with your financial institution.

## Using the Online Center Window

To open the Online Center window, choose Online I Online Center. Figure 6-2 shows what the Transactions tab of this window looks like with one of my financial institutions selected.

A number of button bar buttons and menus enable you to work with the window's contents:

- **Delete** removes the selected item. This button is not available in all tabs of the Online Center window.
- **Payees** displays the Online Payee List window, which I discuss later in this chapter in the section titled "Entering Online Payee Information."
- **Repeating** displays the Repeating Online tab of the Bills & Deposits list window. I tell you more about using this feature later in this chapter in the section titled "Scheduling Repeating Online Payments."

- **Contact Info** displays the Contact Information dialog for the currently selected financial institution. You can use the information in the dialog to contact the bank or credit card company by phone, Web site, or e-mail.
- **Password Vault** gives you access to Quicken's Password Vault feature, which I discuss in Chapter 7. (This option may appear only if you have online banking features enabled for accounts at more than one financial institution.)
- **Renaming Rules** displays some information about Quicken's Renaming feature, which enables you to automatically change the downloaded name of a payee to a more familiar name. Clicking OK in this dialog displays the Renaming Rules For Downloaded Transactions dialog. I explain how to use this feature later in the section titled "Renaming Downloaded Payees."
- **Print** prints the transactions that appear in the window.
- **Options** displays a menu of commands for working with the current account or window.

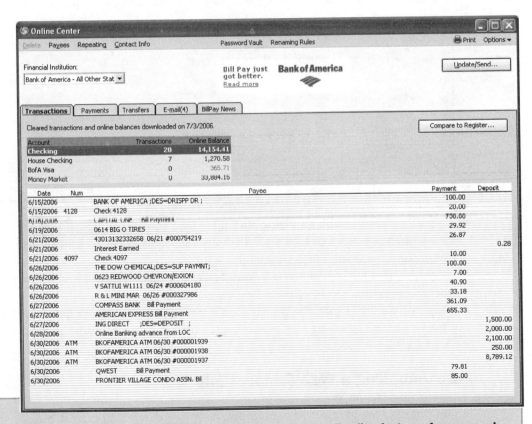

**Figure 6-2 • The Online Center window gives you access to all online features for your cash flow accounts.**

## Downloading and Reviewing Transactions

One of the main features of Online Account Services is the ability to download transactions from your financial institution into Quicken. You do this with the Transactions tab of the Online Center window (refer to Figure 6-2). Here's how you can take advantage of this feature.

### Connecting to the Financial Institution with Direct Connect or Express Web Connect

If your financial institution supports Direct Connect or Express Web Connect, you can download all transactions from within Quicken.

In the Online Center window, choose the name of your bank or credit card company from the Financial Institution drop-down list. If necessary, click the Transactions tab. Then click the Update/Send button. The Online Update For This Account dialog, which is shown next, appears. Click to toggle the check marks beside the instructions you want to send, enter your password, and click Update Now.

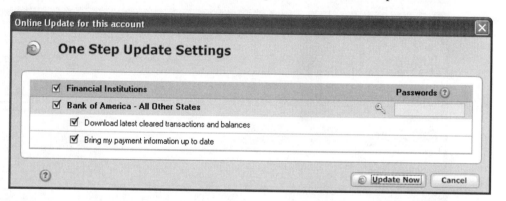

Quicken might display a dialog offering to save your passwords. If you click Yes, follow the instructions in Chapter 7 to set up the Password Vault feature. You may then need to reinitiate the download procedure.

Wait while Quicken connects to your bank. A status dialog appears while it works. When Quicken has finished exchanging information, the status dialog disappears and the One Step Update Summary window (see Figure 6-3) takes its place. Continue following the instructions later in the chapter in the section titled "Viewing Downloaded Transactions."

### Downloading a Web Connect File

If your financial institution supports Web Connect but not Express Web Connect, you'll have to log in to your financial institution's Web site and manually download the statement information just as you did when you first set up the account for Online Account Services.

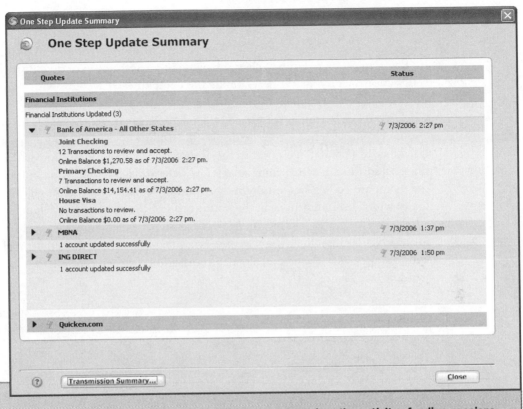

**Figure 6-3 • The One Step Update Summary window summarizes the activity of online sessions.**

In the Online Center window, choose the name of your bank or credit card company from the Financial Institution drop-down list. If necessary, click the Transactions tab. Then click the Update/Send button. Quicken connects to the Internet and displays your financial institution's login page. Log in, navigate to the page where you can download statements, and download the statement or transactions you want. If necessary, switch back to Quicken. It should automatically import the transactions you downloaded into the correct account and display an Online Update Summary window like the one in Figure 6-3. Continue following the instructions in the next section.

## Viewing Downloaded Transactions

After transactions have been imported into Quicken, the One Step Update Summary window appears. As shown in Figure 6-3, it summarizes the activity that took place while you waited.

There are three ways to continue:

- Click the Close button in the One Step Update Summary window to dismiss it. Then, in the Account bar, click the name of an account with downloaded transactions. (A red flag appears beside the name of each account with downloaded transactions.)
- Click the Close button in the One Step Update Summary window. If necessary, choose Online | Online Center to display the Online Center window again. The downloaded transactions appear in the Transactions tab of the window when the financial institution and account are selected (refer to Figure 6-2). You can then click the Compare To Register button in that window to view the account register with the downloaded transactions in the bottom half of the window (see Figure 6-4).
- Click the Go To Register button in the One Step Update Summary window for an account for which you want to review transactions. The account register window appears with the downloaded transactions in the bottom half of the window (see Figure 6-4).

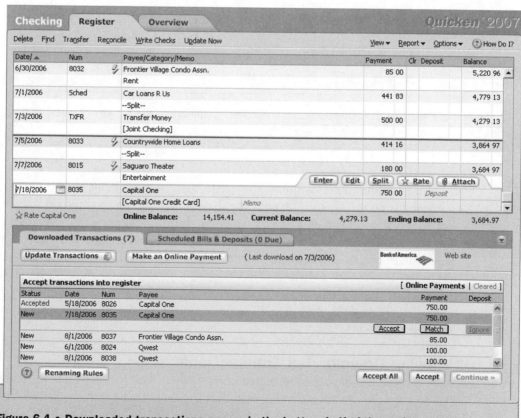

**Figure 6-4 • Downloaded transactions appear in the bottom half of the register window.**

If downloaded transactions do not appear in the account register, click the Downloaded Transactions tab at the bottom of the register window to display them.

Keep in mind that the first time you connect via Direct Connect, the bank normally sends all transactions from the past 60 or more days. After that, only new transactions will be downloaded. For Web Connect downloads, you can often specify the transaction period when you set up the download.

## Comparing Downloaded Transactions to Register Transactions

Your job is to compare the downloaded transactions to the transactions already entered in your account register. This enables you to identify transactions that you neglected to enter or that you entered incorrectly. In addition, because Quicken will automatically enter a date, transaction number, and amount—and in the case of some transactions, the payee and category (based on previously memorized transactions)—using this method to enter a transaction can be much faster than entering it manually in the account register window.

The Status column in the bottom half of the account register window (refer to Figure 6-4) identifies three types of transactions:

- **Match** identifies transactions that match those in the register. This will happen if the transaction has already been entered in the Quicken register.
- **New** identifies transactions that do not appear to be in the register.
- **Accepted** identifies matched transactions that you have accepted. When a downloaded transaction has been accepted, a small c appears in the Clr column of the account register to indicate that the item has cleared the bank but has not yet been reconciled.

When you select a transaction in the bottom half of the window, the transactions below it shift down to make room for a blank line with three buttons. You can use these to work with the selected transaction.

**Accepting a Matched Transaction**    If a transaction matches one in the register, you can accept it by selecting it in the list at the bottom of the window and clicking the Accept button.

**Entering and Accepting a New Transaction**    To enter and accept a new transaction, select the transaction in the bottom half of the window. Quicken begins preparing a register transaction entry for it, as you can see in Figure 6-4. Fill in the missing details, including the payee, category, and memo. Then click Enter in the top half of the window or Accept in the bottom half. Quicken enters and accepts the transaction.

**Unmatching a Matched Transaction**   If a matched transaction really shouldn't be matched, select it in the bottom half of the window and choose Unmatch or Make New from the Edit pop-up menu beneath it. There's a subtle difference between these two commands:

- **Unmatch** tells Quicken that it got the match wrong, but this command lets Quicken attempt to match it to another transaction. As a result, it may come up with another match. It's your job to determine whether the new match is correct. If it can't find a match, the status changes to New.
- **Make New** tells Quicken that the transaction shouldn't match any existing transaction. The status changes to New and Quicken can then treat it as a new transaction.

**Manually Matching a Transaction**   If a downloaded transaction identified as New should match one in the register, or if a single transaction corresponds to multiple transactions in your account register, you can manually match them up. In the bottom half of the window, select the transaction that you want to match manually, and click the Match button. The Manually Match Transactions dialog, which is shown next, appears. Turn on the check box(es) for the transaction(s) you want to include in the match. When you click Accept, Quicken creates an entry for the transaction that includes each of the register transactions on a separate split line. You can click the Split button for the transaction to edit it as desired.

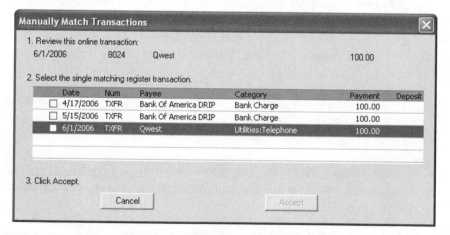

**Deleting a New Transaction**   To delete a new transaction, select the transaction in the bottom half of the account register window and choose Delete from the Edit pop-up menu beneath it. A confirmation dialog appears; click Yes to remove the transaction from the list.

**Comparing Transactions from Different Sources**   If an account has
downloaded transactions from different sources, textual links for each source appear
near the top of the Downloaded Transactions tab in the account register window. The
following illustration shows an example with Online Payments, WebEntry (discussed
later in this chapter in the section titled "WebEntry"), and Cleared transactions. If
Online Payments appears, you must review and accept those transactions first. To
review transactions from a specific source, click the link for that source. When there
is only one source of transactions, the links do not appear.

| Accept transactions into register | | | | [ **Online Payments** \| WebEntry \| Cleared ] | |
|---|---|---|---|---|---|
| Status | Date | Num | Payee | Payment | Deposit |
| New | 7/5/2005 | 5216 | CableAmerica | 69.95 | |
| New | 7/5/2005 | 5215 | Countrywide Home Loans | 714.16 | |

**Accepting All Downloaded Transactions**   Accept All accepts all transactions
into your account register without reviewing them one by one. Keep in mind that
some transactions may not be properly categorized.

## Renaming Downloaded Payees

One of the potentially annoying things about entering transactions by accepting
downloaded activity information is the way your bank identifies payees. For
example, my bank identifies the payee for my cable television company as
"CableAmerica{026-144710}" instead of plain old "CableAmerica." Fortunately,
Quicken can automatically rename bank-assigned payee names with names you
prefer. You do this in the Renaming Rules For Downloaded Transactions dialog,
which is shown here:

To open this dialog, click the Renaming Rules button at the bottom of the Downloaded Transactions tab of the register window (refer to Figure 6-4) or choose Online | Renaming Rules. The top half of the dialog lists all the renaming rules that have already been created. The bottom half of the dialog has options you can select to enable the Renaming feature and let Quicken automatically create renaming rules for you. (I recommend selecting On for both options.)

You can use buttons to the right of the list to add, modify, or remove renaming rules.

**New**    Clicking the New button displays the Create Renaming Rule dialog. Enter the name you want to see as the payee name in the Change Payee To box. Then choose an option from the first drop-down list to determine which field Quicken should match, choose a match option from the middle drop-down list, and enter match text in the text box. For example, if I wanted to change every downloaded item containing the text *CableAmerica{026-144710}* to *CableAmerica,* I'd set the dialog as shown here. You can click the Add New Item link to add another line of matching criteria; doing so tells Quicken to match *all* criteria you enter. When you click OK in the dialog, the renaming rule is added to the list.

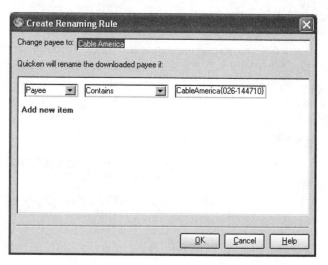

**Edit**    Clicking the Edit button displays the Edit Renaming Rule dialog, which looks and works just like the Create Renaming Rule dialog just shown. This dialog enables you to modify settings for the selected renaming rule.

**Delete**    Clicking the Delete button removes the selected renaming rule from the list. You'll have to click OK in the confirmation dialog that appears to remove the rule.

## Paying Your Credit Card Bill

If payment on your credit card bill is due, you may be notified in the Online Update Summary window when you successfully download transactions via Direct Connect. When you've finished reviewing, comparing, and accepting downloaded transactions, you can use Quicken to review your bill and enter a payment transaction.

If necessary, choose Online | Online Center to display the Online Center window. Click the Payment Information button in the Transactions tab. A dialog appears, providing information about the statement date, minimum payment due, and account balance. If you click the Make Payment button, the Make Credit Card Payment dialog appears. Begin by selecting an Amount To Pay option. If you select Other Amount, enter the amount in the text box. Then select a payment method option and choose a payment account.

The option you select in the Payment Will Be area determines what happens when you click OK:

- **Printed Check** displays the Write Checks window, with the payment transaction already filled in. Edit the transaction as necessary and click the Record Check button to complete it. The check can be printed the next time you use the Print Checks command. I explain how to use the Write Checks window in Chapter 5.
- **Hand-Written Check** displays the account register window, with the payment transaction already filled in. Edit the transaction as necessary and click the Enter button to complete it. You must then write the check by hand. I explain how to use an account register window to enter transactions in Chapter 5.
- **Online Payment** displays the Payments tab of the Online Center window with the payment transaction already filled in. Edit the transaction as necessary and click the Enter button to complete it. The payment instruction will be sent to your bank the next time you click the Update/Send button. To use the Online Payment option, one of your bank accounts must be set up for Online Payment through your bank or Quicken Bill Pay. In addition, the credit card company must be set up as an online payee. I tell you more about making online payments in the next section.

## Making Online Payments

The Payments tab of the Online Center window enables you to enter payment instructions for accounts for which you have enabled the Online Payment feature. Figure 6-5 shows what it looks like.

In the rest of this section, I explain how to set up online payees, enter payment information for one-time and repeating payments, and work with payment instructions.

**Figure 6-5 • Use the Payments tab of the Online Center window to make online payments.**

## Entering Online Payee Information

To send payments from your account, your bank must know who and where each payee is. To ensure that your account with the payee is properly credited, you must also provide account information. You do this by setting up online payees.

Click the Payees button in the Online Center window, or choose Online | Online Payee List. The Online Payee List window shown in Figure 6-6 lists all the individuals and organizations you pay using the financial institution indicated in the drop-down list with Quicken's Online Payment feature.

You can use options on the button bar to work with selected items in the window:

- **New** enables you to create a new online payee.
- **Edit** enables you to modify the information for the selected online payee.
- **Delete** removes the selected online payee. Deleting a payee simply deletes the payee's information from the Online Payee List window. It does not change any transactions for a payee. You cannot delete a payee for which unsent payment instructions exist in the Online Center window.

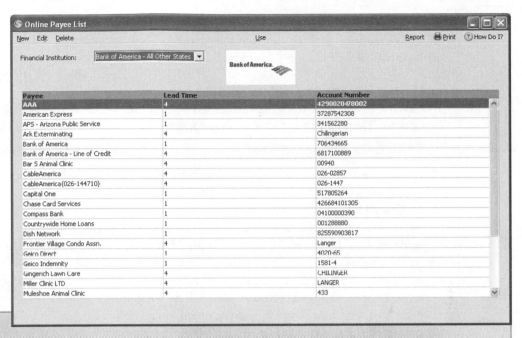

**Figure 6-6 • The Online Payee List window lists all of the online payees set up with your financial institution.**

- **Use** switches you back to the Payments tab of the Online Center window (see Figure 6-5) and inserts the selected payee into the payment form.
- **Report** displays a report of all payments made to the selected online payee.
- **Print** prints a list of online payees.
- **How Do I?** provides instructions for performing specific tasks with the Online Payee List window.

To create a new online payee, click New to display the Set Up Online Payee dialog, shown here. Fill in the boxes by entering the payee name and address, your account number on the payee's records, and the payee's phone number.

When you click OK, a dialog containing the information you just entered appears. Check the information in this box carefully. If there is an error, your payment might not reach the payee or it might not be properly credited to your account. Remember, your bank will not be sending a billing stub with the payment—just the payment. When you're satisfied that the information is correct, click Accept. The payee is added to the list.

## Entering Payment Instructions

If necessary, switch back to the Payments tab of the Online Center window (see Figure 6-5). Then fill in the fields in the middle of the window with the payment information:

- **Processing Date** is the date the bank should begin processing the payment. For some banks, this date is fixed based on the Delivery Date field and can't be changed.
- **Delivery Date** is the date you want the payee to receive payment. This is the date the bank will either write on the check or make the electronic funds transfer. The check may be received before that date, depending on the mail (if the check is mailed). The date you enter, however, must be at least the same number of business days in advance as the lead time for the payee—usually four days. That means if you want to pay a bill on Wednesday, June 29, you must enter and send its instructions to your bank on or before Friday, June 24. To process payment as soon as possible, just enter today's date and Quicken will adjust the date for you. For some banks, the delivery date cannot be changed; instead, specify a Processing Date that allows enough time for the payment to be made on a timely basis.
- **Payee** is the online payee to receive payment. Quicken's QuickFill feature fills in the payee's name as you type it. If desired, you can choose it from the drop-down list of online payees. If you enter a payee that is not in the Online Payee List window, Quicken displays the Set Up Online Payee dialog so you can add the new payee's information. This enables you to create online payees as you enter payment instructions.
- **$** is the amount of the payment.
- **Category** is the category for the transaction. You can either enter a category, choose one from the drop-down list, or click the Split button to enter multiple categories.
- **Memo**, which is optional, is for entering a note about the transaction.

When you've finished entering information for the transaction, click Enter. The transaction appears in the list in the bottom half of the window with the words "Payment request ready to send" in the Status column beside it. You can repeat this process for as many payments as you want to make.

## What Does This Mean to You? Payment and Delivery Dates

Don't let the Processing Date and Delivery Date options confuse you. The Delivery Date is the important date. It determines whether your payment will make it to the payee on time. Whenever possible, I give the bank an extra two days. So, for example, if a bill is due on June 29, I'd instruct the bank to pay on June 27. This isn't because I don't have confidence in Quicken or my bank. It's because I have less confidence in the postal service.

If the Delivery Date field on your form can't be changed, don't panic. Just enter a Processing Date at least four days (or six, if you're extra cautious like me) before the date you want the payment to arrive. That should give your bank enough time to get the payment to the payee without getting you in trouble.

## Entering Online Payments in the Account Register

Another way to enter an online payment instruction is to simply enter the transaction in the appropriate account register. Enter **SEND** in the Num field, enter the remaining transaction information as usual, and click Enter. You may find this method quicker, especially if you've worked with Quicken for a while and are familiar with the account register window.

## Scheduling Repeating Online Payments

Some payments are exactly the same every month, such as your rent, a car loan, or your monthly cable television bill. You can set these payments up as repeating online payments.

Here's how it works. You schedule the online payment once, indicating the payee, amount, and frequency. Quicken sends the instructions to your bank. Thirty days before the payment is due, your bank creates a new postdated payment based on your instructions and notifies you that it has created the payment. Quicken automatically enters the payment information in your account register with the appropriate payment date. The payment is delivered on the payment date. This happens regularly, at the interval you specify, until you tell it to stop. Because you don't have to do a thing to continue paying regularly, the more payments you make with this feature, the more time you save.

(Using this feature to pay an amortized loan such as a mortgage works a little differently. I tell you about it later in this chapter in the section titled "Linking a Repeating Online Payment to an Amortized Loan.")

In the Online Center window's button bar, click the Repeating button. The Repeating Online tab of the Bills & Deposits window, which is shown in Figure 6-7, appears.

Choose Scheduled Transaction from the Create New menu in the window's button bar. The Add Scheduled Transaction dialog, which is shown next, appears.

I explain how to create a transaction with this dialog in Chapter 7, so you can get details there.

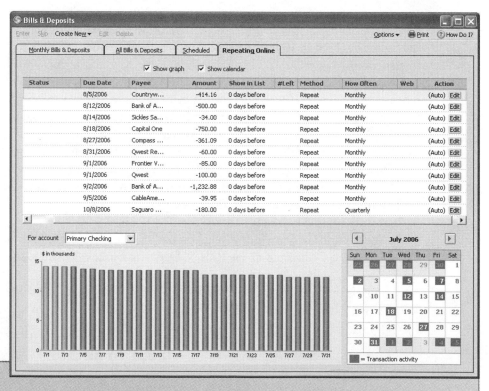

**Figure 6-7 • The Repeating Online tab of the Bills & Deposits window lists all repeating online payments.**

There are two very important things to remember when using the Add Scheduled Transaction form to create a repeating online payment:

- Choose Online Payment From Quicken from the Method drop-down list. This tells Quicken that the payment will be made online.
- Turn on the This Is A Repeating Online Payment check box. This tells Quicken to send one instruction for multiple repeating payments.

When you click OK to save the payment instruction, it appears in the Repeating Online tab of the Bills & Deposits list window.

You can use button bar options to work with items listed in the Bills & Deposits list window:

- **Enter** records the selected repeating online payment in the register.
- **Skip** skips payment of the selected repeating online payment.
- **Create New** enables you to create a new scheduled transaction or paycheck. I tell you more about this menu in Chapter 7.
- **Edit** displays the Edit Repeating Online Payment dialog, shown here, so you can modify the details of the repeating online payment.

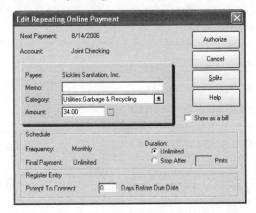

- **Delete** removes the repeating online payment from the list, thus canceling future payments. You must click Delete in the confirmation dialog that appears to remove the transaction.
- **Options** offers commands for changing the sort order of payments in the list.
- **Print** prints a list of repeating online payments.
- **How Do I?** provides instructions for completing tasks with the Bills & Deposits list.

## Linking a Repeating Online Payment to an Amortized Loan

Repeating online payments are perfect for paying off loans. After all, loan payments are the same every month and must be paid by a certain date. You can set up a repeating online payment instruction, send it to your financial institution, and let Quicken and your bank make the payments automatically every month for you.

Set up the repeating online payment instruction for the loan payment as instructed in the earlier section "Scheduling Repeating Online Payments." Don't worry about all the categories that are part of a loan payment transaction. Just choose the loan account as the category. You don't even have to get the date or amount right. When you link the transaction to the loan, Quicken will make the necessary adjustments. Be sure to click Authorize to save the payment instruction.

Choose Property & Debt | Loans or press CTRL-H to display the Loans window. If necessary, choose the loan account's name from the Choose Loan menu in the button bar to display the information for the loan for which you want to use the payment instruction.

Click the Edit Payment button to display the Edit Loan Payment dialog. Then click the Payment Method button. In the Select Payment Method dialog, select Repeating Online Payment. Then choose the repeating online payment instruction you created from the Repeating Payment drop-down list. When you are finished, the Select Payment Method dialog might look something like the dialog shown here.

## What Does This Mean to You?
## Repeating Online Loan Payments

Setting up a loan payment as a repeating online payment has got to be one of the best timesaving features available in Quicken. It does all kinds of neat things for you.

First, it ensures that your loan payment is made regularly, on a timely basis, with no monthly effort on your part. Second, it automatically adjusts the balance of your loan principal account (a liability account) by accurately calculating interest and principal paid for every entry. (You know these amounts change every month, right? Can you imagine doing the entries manually? Egads!) And since the loan account balance is updated with every payment, your net worth is always up-to-date.

Just set it and forget it. That should be this feature's slogan. And if you're in a fog about how to set up a loan in Quicken, don't fret. I explain all in lucky Chapter 13.

Click OK in each dialog to dismiss it. Quicken links the loan payment to the repeating online payment instruction. It makes changes to the payment instruction, if necessary, to match the payment categories and split information. The next time you connect to your financial institution, the instruction will be sent and payments will begin.

## Sending Payment Instructions

Once your payment instructions have been completed, you must connect to your bank to send the instructions. In the Online Center window, click the Update/Send button. Quicken displays the Online Update window, which lists all of the payment instructions, including any repeating payment instructions. Enter your password and click the Update Now button.

Wait while Quicken establishes an Internet connection with your bank and sends your payment (or payment cancellation) instructions. When it has finished, it displays the Online Update Summary window. Click Done.

In the Payments tab of the Online Center window, the words "Scheduled for delivery on" followed by the payment date appear in the Status column beside the payment instructions that have been sent to your bank.

## Canceling a Payment

Occasionally, you may change your mind about making a payment. Perhaps you found out that your spouse already sent a check, or that you set up the payment for the wrong amount. For whatever reason, you can cancel an online payment that you have sent to your bank—as long as there's enough time to cancel it.

Here's how it works. When you send a payment instruction to your bank, it waits in the bank's computer. When the processing date (determined by the number of days in the payee's lead time and the payment date) arrives, the bank makes the payment. Before the processing date, however, the payment instructions can be canceled. If you send a cancel payment instruction to the bank before the processing date, the bank removes the instruction from its computer without sending payment to the payee. Quicken won't let you cancel a payment if the processing date has already passed. If you wait too long, the only way to cancel the payment is to call the bank directly and stop the check.

Keep in mind that canceling a payment instruction isn't the same as stopping a check. If you send the cancel payment instruction in time, the bank should not charge a fee for stopping the payment.

**Canceling a Regular Online Payment**    In the Online Center window, select the payment that you want to cancel and click the Cancel Payment button. Click Yes in the confirmation dialog that appears. Use the Update/Send button to send the cancel payment instruction.

**Stopping a Single Repeating Online Payment**    In the Online Center window, select the payment you want to stop and click the Cancel Payment button. Click Yes in the confirmation dialog that appears. Use the Update/Send button to send the cancel payment instruction. Note that the payment may not appear in the Online Center window unless you have reviewed and approved all downloaded payment transactions, as instructed earlier in this chapter.

**Stopping All Future Payments for a Repeating Online Payment**    In the Repeating tab of the Bills & Deposits window, select the payment you want to stop and click Delete. Click Delete in the confirmation dialog that appears. The transaction is removed from the list. Then use the Update/Send button in the Online Center window to send the cancel payment instruction.

## Transferring Money Between Accounts

If you have more than one account enabled for Online Account Services via Direct Connect at the same financial institution, you can use the Transfers tab of the Online Center window, shown in Figure 6-8, to transfer money from one account to another.

Enter the transfer information—source account, destination account, and amount—in the fields in the middle of the window. When you click Enter, the information is added to the list of transfers at the bottom of the window.

Like payment instructions, you must send transfer instructions to your bank in order for the transaction to take place. Click the Update/Send button, enter your password, and click the Update Now button to send the instructions.

## Exchanging E-Mail with Your Financial Institution

You can use the E-mail tab of the Online Center window to exchange e-mail messages with financial institutions for which you have enabled Online Account Services via Direct Connect. Keep in mind that not all financial institutions support this feature. Also, remember that this communication is between you and your financial institution, not Intuit (makers of Quicken). It is intended primarily for exchanging information about your account, not technical support for using Quicken.

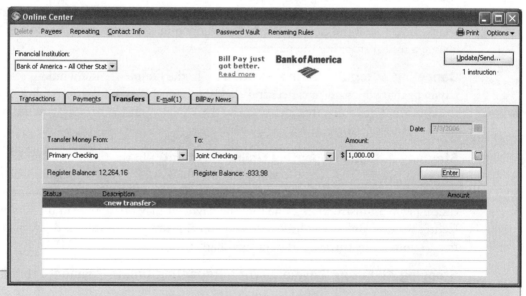

**Figure 6-8 • Use the Transfers tab of the Online Center window to transfer funds from one account to another at the same financial institution.**

## Creating an E-Mail Message

In the E-mail tab of the Online Center window, click Create. If a Create dialog like the one shown here appears, use it to set general options for your e-mail message. If your message is about an online payment, choose the account from the Account drop-down list and select the payment from the Payments scrolling list.

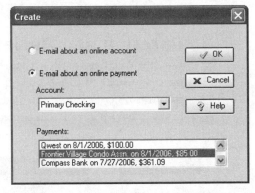

When you click OK, a Message window appears. Use it to compose your e-mail message. When you click OK, the message is saved. It appears in the bottom half of the E-mail tab of the Online Center window, ready to be sent to your financial institution.

## Exchanging E-Mail Messages

Using e-mail is a lot like having a box at the post office. When you write a letter, you have to get it to the post office to send it to the recipient. When you receive a letter, you have to go to the post office and check your box to retrieve it. E-mail works the same way. Connecting is a lot like going to the post office to send and retrieve messages.

In the Online Center window, click the Update/Send button. Quicken displays the Online Update window, which includes any e-mail messages you may have created that need to be sent. Enter your password and click the Update Now button. Then wait while Quicken establishes an Internet connection with your bank and exchanges e-mail.

## Reading an E-Mail Message

When your bank sends you an e-mail message, it appears in the E-mail tab of the Online Center window. To read the message, select it and click Read. The message appears in a message window. If desired, you can click the Print button to print the message for future reference.

# WebEntry

Quicken's WebEntry feature enables you to enter transactions for your Quicken accounts via the Web. You use a Web browser to navigate to a specific Web page on the Quicken.com site, enter your user ID and password if prompted, and enter transactions. Then, when you're back at your desk with Quicken running, you can use the One Step Update command to download transactions stored on the Web into your Quicken data file.

You must register Quicken before you use this feature. Registering Quicken sets up a Quicken.com account for you to store your transaction information.

## Entering and Reviewing Transactions

Use any Web browser to navigate to http://www.quicken.com/webentry/, the WebEntry page on Quicken.com. You may have to enter your user ID and password to log in to Quicken.com before the page appears. Figure 6-9 shows an example of what it looks like with a transaction ready to be entered.

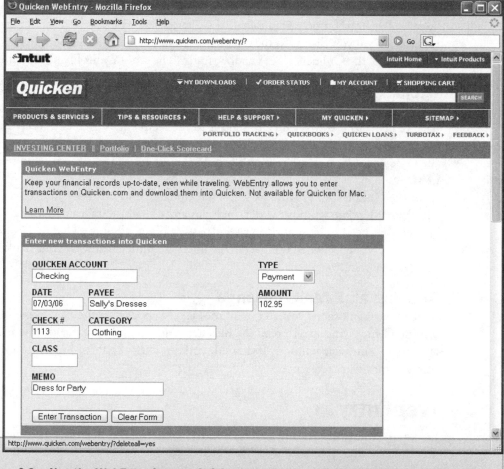

**Figure 6-9 • Use the WebEntry form on Quicken.com to enter transactions for your Quicken data file from anywhere in the world.**

Enter transaction information into the form and click Enter Transaction to enter the transaction into the Web database. Repeat this process for as many transactions as you like. Don't worry if you don't know the exact name of an account or category; you can correct any errors when you download the transactions into Quicken.

You can review the transactions you enter by scrolling down in the window after entering any transaction. The Review WebEntry Transactions area lists each transaction stored in the database on Quicken.com, as shown here:

| Review WebEntry transactions | | | | |
|---|---|---|---|---|
| 07/03/06 | **Checking** | **Sally's Dresses** | | $102.95 |
| | 1113 | Clothing | Dress for Party | Payment |
| STATUS: Not Downloaded | | Delete   Edit | | |
| 07/2/06 | **Checking** | **Quicken Press** | | $2000.00 |
| | | Advances | | Deposit |
| STATUS: Not Downloaded | | Delete   Edit | | |
| 07/03/06 | **House Checking** | **Home Depot** | | $234.97 |
| | 1114 | Home Repair | Irrigation Supplies | Payment |
| STATUS: Not Downloaded | | Delete   Edit | | |

## Downloading Transactions into Quicken

When you're ready to download WebEntry transactions into Quicken, click the Update button on Quicken's toolbar. The One Step Update dialog, which I tell you more about in Chapter 7 and elsewhere throughout this book, appears. Make sure the check mark beside Download WebEntry Transactions From Quicken.com is turned on. Then click Update Now. If a Quicken.com login dialog appears, enter your username and password in the appropriate boxes and click OK.

Quicken establishes a connection to the Internet and displays a status dialog while it updates information. When it's finished, it displays the Online Update Summary window, which informs you that your Web transactions were downloaded. Click Done.

## Accepting Transactions

You're not done yet. The downloaded transactions must be accepted into the Quicken accounts. Open the account register for an account for which you have downloaded a WebEntry transaction. If necessary, click the Downloaded Transactions tab to display the downloaded transactions, as shown next:

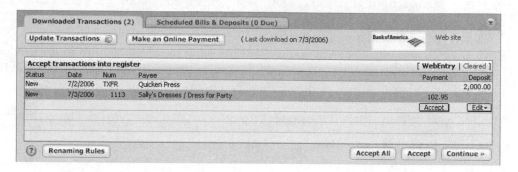

If you have downloaded transactions from other sources such as Online Account Services, you may need to click the WebEntry link near the top of the Downloaded Transactions tab to view WebEntry transactions. This link appears only if you have downloaded data from multiple sources.

Does this transaction list look familiar? It should! It's almost identical to the one in Figure 6-4. It works the same, too. You can learn more in the section titled "Comparing Downloaded Transactions to Register Transactions" earlier in this chapter.

## Using WebEntry Again

The next time you use WebEntry, you should notice two things:

- Drop-down lists appear for the Quicken Account and Category fields. These drop-down lists are updated each time you download WebEntry transactions. This makes it easier to enter transactions accurately in the future.
- The transactions you entered on the Web and then imported into Quicken have the status Sent To Quicken. These transactions will not be sent again.

# Updating Your Bank Accounts on Quicken.com

Quicken enables you to upload your account balances to Quicken.com, where you can view them from any computer in the world.

Why would you want to do that? Well, suppose you're traveling for business and one of the local shops has an incredible hand-woven Navajo rug that you really want to buy. You're not sure how much money is in your checking account, and you don't want to write a check for the purchase unless you know for sure that you can cover it. So while you're at work checking your portfolio on Quicken.com (as discussed in Chapter 11), you take a peek at your account balance, which your spouse has been updating with Quicken while you're away. Fortunately, you have enough in the account, and you can make the purchase. You can even use WebEntry to enter that big check in your account (as discussed in the previous section).

Think this might be helpful? Here's how you set it up and make it happen.

## Enabling Account Update

Choose Edit | Preferences | Customize Online Updates to display the Customize Online Updates dialog. Click the Accounts tab to display a list of the Quicken accounts that can be displayed on the Web, as shown next. Click to place a check mark beside each account you want to view on the Web. Then click OK to save your settings.

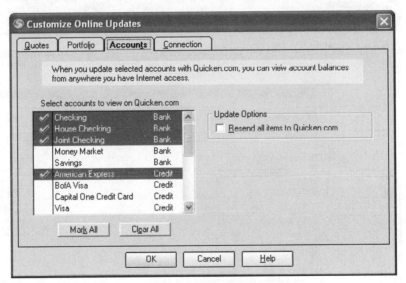

## Updating Account Information

Click the Update button on Quicken's toolbar to display the One Step Update dialog. Turn on the Update My Banking Accounts On Quicken.com check box and click Update Now. Wait while Quicken connects to the Internet and sends your data. (You may have to log in to Quicken.com; if so, a dialog will appear.)

## Checking Account Balances on Quicken.com

You can view your account balances on Quicken.com by using a Web browser to visit http://www.quicken.com/myaccounts/. Figure 6-10 shows what this page might look like; as you can see, it includes not only your bank accounts, but Portfolio Export information as well. (I tell you more about Portfolio Export in Chapter 11.)

Keep in mind that you must be logged in to Quicken.com for your account information to appear. If you are not logged in, Quicken will prompt you to log in.

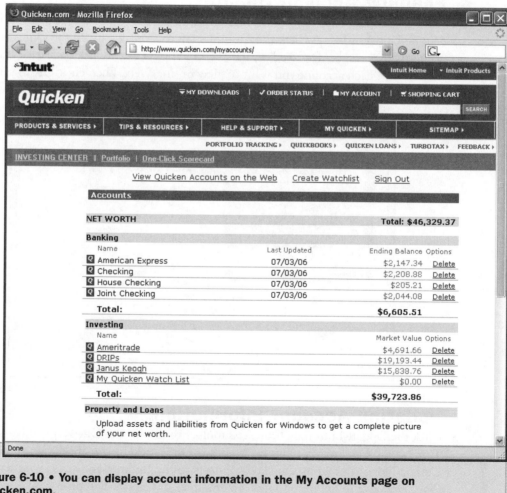

**Figure 6-10 • You can display account information in the My Accounts page on Quicken.com.**

# Automating Transactions and Tasks

## Chapter 7

## In This Chapter:

- *QuickFill and memorized payees*

- *Scheduled transactions*

- *Calendar*

- *Paycheck Setup*

- *Address Book*

- *One Step Update and the Password Vault*

- *Scheduling updates*

Quicken Personal Finance Software includes a number of features to automate the entry of transactions. You got a glimpse of one of them, QuickFill, in Chapter 5. In this chapter, I tell you about QuickFill and the other features you can use to automate transaction entries or remind yourself when a transaction is due. I also explain how you can use Quicken's One Step Update feature to handle all of your online tasks at once. I'm sure you'll agree that these features can make data entry and other Quicken tasks quicker and easier.

Before you read this chapter, make sure you have a good understanding of the data entry techniques covered in Chapter 5. This chapter builds upon many of the basic concepts discussed there.

## QuickFill and Memorized Payees

As you enter transactions, Quicken is quietly working in the background, memorizing transaction information for each payee. It creates a database of memorized payees. It then uses the memorized payees for its QuickFill feature.

### How It Works

QuickFill works in two ways:

- When you enter the first few characters of a payee name in the Write Checks or account register window, Quicken immediately fills in the rest of the name. When you advance to the next text box or field of the entry form, Quicken fills in the rest of the transaction information based on the last transaction for that payee.
- You can select a memorized payee from the drop-down list in the Payee field of the Write Checks or account register window. Quicken then fills in the rest of the transaction information based on the last transaction for that payee.

QuickFill entries include amounts, categories, and memos. They can also include splits and classes. For example, you might pay the cable or satellite company for television service every month. The bill is usually the same amount each month. The second time you create an entry with the company's name, Quicken fills in the rest of the transaction automatically. You can make adjustments to the amount or other information as desired and save the transaction. It may have taken a minute or so to enter the transaction the first time, but it'll take only seconds to enter it every time after that.

By default, the QuickFill feature is set up to work as discussed here. If it does not, check the QuickFill options to make sure they are set properly. I tell you how in Appendix B.

### Working with the Memorized Payee List

If desired, you can view a list of memorized payees, as shown in Figure 7-1. Just choose Cash Flow | Memorized Payee List or press CTRL-T.

### Button Bar Buttons

You can use buttons on the button bar to add, modify, or delete memorized payees or work with the Memorized Payee List:

- **Go To Find And Replace** displays the Find And Replace dialog, which you can use to replace payee names. I explain how to use the Find And Replace dialog in Chapter 5.

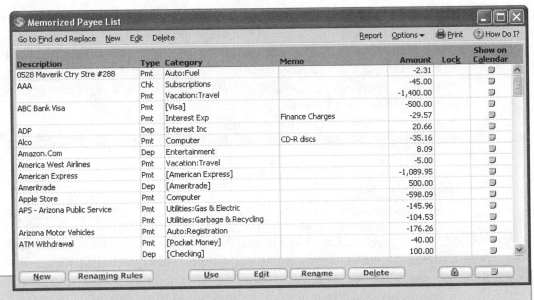

Figure 7-1 • Each line in the Memorized Payee List represents the last transaction recorded for a payee.

- **New** displays the Create Memorized Payee dialog, shown next, which you can use to create brand-new transactions without actually entering them into any register of your Quicken data file. Just fill in the fields to enter transaction information and click OK. The new transaction appears in the Memorized Payee List window.

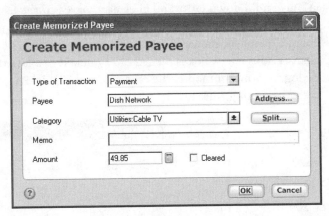

- **Edit** displays the Edit Memorized Payee dialog for the currently selected transaction. This dialog looks and works like the Create Memorized Payee dialog.

- **Delete** displays a dialog asking you to confirm that you really do want to delete the selected memorized payee. If you delete the transaction, it is removed from the Memorized Payee List only—not from any register in the Quicken data file.
- **Report** displays a Payee Report for the currently selected transaction's payee.
- **Options** offers commands for changing the sort order and other view options for the Memorized Payee List.
- **Print** prints a list of memorized payees.
- **How Do I?** provides additional information for completing tasks with the Memorized Payee List window.

## Other Options

You can also use buttons at the bottom of the window to work with a selected payee:

- **New** displays the Create Memorized Payee dialog, discussed and shown earlier.
- **Renaming Rules** displays the Renaming Rules For Downloaded Transactions dialog, which you can use to set automatic payee renaming options for transactions downloaded from your financial institutions. I explain how to set up renaming rules in Chapter 6.
- **Use** displays the appropriate register for entering the transaction and fills in the transaction's information for you. You must click the Enter button to accept the entry.
- **Edit** displays the Edit Memorized Payee dialog for the currently selected transaction. This dialog looks and works like the Create Memorized Payee dialog.
- **Rename** displays the Merge And Rename Payees dialog, shown next, which you can use to enter a new name for the selected payee. (To rename multiple payees at once, hold down CTRL and click each payee in the list to select them all before clicking the Rename button.) Enter a new name in the dialog and click OK to change the payee name. If the Create Renaming Rules For Future Downloaded Transactions check box is turned on, Quicken displays the Edit Renaming Rule dialog, so you can modify the renaming rule Quicken suggests. I explain how to create renaming rules in Chapter 6.

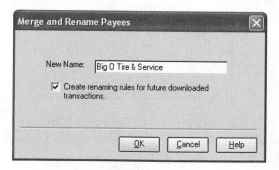

- **Delete** enables you to delete the selected memorized payee. This does not remove any transactions from Quicken registers.
- **Lock** (an icon) toggles the locked setting for the selected transaction. When locked, the payee's transaction will not be rememorized if you make any changes to it when you use it.
- **Calendar** (an icon) toggles the calendar setting for the selected transaction. When enabled, the transaction will appear on the Calendar (refer to Figure 7-5).

# Bills, Deposits, and Scheduled Transactions

One of my favorite Quicken features is the ability to tell Quicken about the bills, deposits, and other transactions that need to be made in the future—especially the ones that happen on a regular basis. This Scheduled Transactions feature, when fully utilized, doesn't just prevent you from forgetting to pay bills; it can completely automate the transaction entry process.

In this part of the chapter, I tell you more about scheduled transactions, including how to set up and use them.

## Overview of Scheduled Transactions

Generally speaking, you can use two types of scheduled transactions:

- **One-time transactions** are future transactions that you expect to record only once. For example, suppose you are arranging to purchase some furniture. You have already paid a deposit for the furniture and you know that the balance will be due at month-end, when the furniture is delivered. You can schedule that month-end payment in advance.
- **Recurring transactions** are transactions that occur periodically, on a regular basis. Many of your monthly bills are good examples: rent or mortgage payments, car payments, utility bills—unfortunately, there are too many to list!

Scheduled transactions aren't only for payments. You could schedule transactions for incoming funds, too, such as an expected bonus or a monthly child-support check you receive. You can even schedule your paycheck—but I recommend using Quicken's Paycheck Setup feature, which I discuss later in this chapter, to do that.

## Making the Most of Scheduled Transactions

Quicken's Scheduled Transactions feature is one of the best timesaving features Quicken offers. By taking full advantage of this feature, you can minimize the time you spend entering transactions into Quicken. That's a good thing, right? After all, you have better things to do with your time than punch numbers into a computer.

Here are a few suggestions from a seasoned Quicken user (yours truly) about how you can make the most of the Scheduled Transactions feature. See how many you can use—and how much time they can save you.

**Set up all recurring transactions as scheduled transactions.** Recurring payments are things like monthly and quarterly bills for rent, mortgage, insurance, utilities, and other regular bills. Recurring deposits are things like your paycheck, commissions, and other regular income. Set them all up, even if the amounts vary from one payment or deposit to the next. The quickest way to set these up is with Quicken Express Setup, as discussed in Chapter 2, but the Add Scheduled Transaction dialog, covered in this chapter, offers more flexibility. Not only does having these transactions set up in advance make them quick and easy to enter, but it enables you to take advantage of Quicken's budgeting and forecasting features, which I cover in Chapter 18.

**Use Paycheck Setup to track gross pay and deductions.** Paycheck Setup may take a bit of time to set up, but it can save you a lot of time and effort while keeping close track of your gross pay and all deductions. This enables you to utilize Quicken's tax planning and reporting features without spending a lot of time to enter data. Be sure to set up all paychecks for the people included in your Quicken data file—normally you and, if you're married, your spouse.

**Let Quicken automatically enter transactions whenever possible.** If Quicken automatically enters transactions for you, entering recurring transactions is a real no-brainer. Quicken does all the entry work; all you do is make the payment or deposit. The only unfortunate thing about this option is that it works best with transactions that have the same amount each time they are made. Still, I'm sure you'll find enough transactions to take advantage of this.

**Use the Online Payment or check printing feature.** Scheduled transactions seem to work best when coupled with either Quicken's Online Payment feature, which is covered in Chapter 6, or its check printing feature, which is covered in Chapter 5. (Of the two, I prefer online payments, for reasons I expound in Chapter 6.) Once the transaction is entered, Quicken can either automatically send payment instructions when you connect to your financial institution or automatically print checks for payments when you print all checks. So not only is Quicken entering the transaction details for you, but it's making the payments, too! (Ah, if only it could go out, get a job, and earn the money you spend so you don't have to.)

**Record transactions several days in advance.** You don't have to wait until you make a payment or deposit to record the associated transaction. You can enter transactions in advance so your account register reflects both the current and future balances. Just be sure to enter the transaction due dates rather than entry dates when entering them into Quicken. I especially like doing this for payments, because Quicken can clearly show me that even if I have a nice fat balance today, transactions due over the next few days may leave considerably less to work with. I use this, in effect, as a very short-term forecasting tool. (Quicken's *Cash Flow Forecast* feature, which I cover in Chapter 18, does a better job of predicting the future.)

**Set up reminders based on how often you use Quicken.**    When you schedule a transaction and indicate that Quicken should prompt you to enter it, you can specify the number of days in advance that you should be reminded. Set this value based on how often you use Quicken. For example, if you use Quicken only once a week, set this value to 10. If you use Quicken every other day, set it to 4. This way, you're sure to be reminded in time to enter a scheduled transaction and make the payment or deposit associated with it.

**Remember that scheduling a transaction is not the same as recording it.** You must record a transaction to have it appear in the appropriate register, print a check for it, or send an online payment instruction for it. Scheduling the transaction is only part of the job—the big part. You still have to make sure those transactions are entered in a timely manner. That's why I recommend using automatic entry and reminders whenever possible—so you don't forget to finish the transaction entry job.

## Creating a Scheduled Transaction
Quicken offers several ways to schedule transactions. I cover two of them in this chapter.

### Using Quicken Express Setup
Quicken Express Setup makes it quick and easy to schedule bills and other transactions by enabling you to set up multiple recurring bills at once. I explain how this works in Chapter 2.

### Using the Add Scheduled Transaction Dialog
Another way to create a scheduled transaction is with commands in the Bills & Deposits window. Choose Cash Flow | Bills & Deposits or press CTRL-J. The Bills & Deposits window, which is shown in Figure 7-2, appears.

Choose Scheduled Transaction from the Create New menu on the button bar. The Add Scheduled Transaction dialog appears, as shown in Figure 7-3. Use it to enter information about the transaction, including the account, payee, category or transfer account, memo, and scheduling information. You can click the Split button to enter more than one category for the transaction. When you're finished setting up the transaction, click OK to save it.

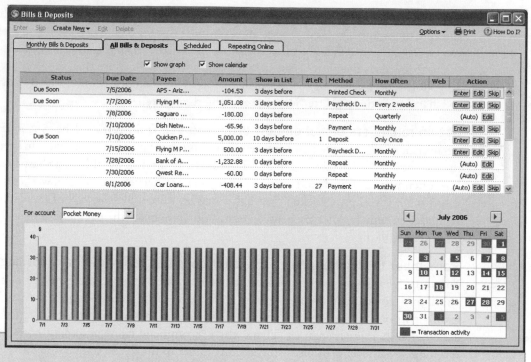

**Figure 7-2 • The Bills & Deposits window lists all recurring and one-time bills, deposits, and other scheduled transactions.**

The Add Scheduled Transaction dialog has quite a few options that don't appear elsewhere in Quicken. Here's a closer look at each of them.

**Method**   The type of transaction you choose determines how the transaction will appear in your account register when it is entered, and it may trigger other Quicken features. You can choose from five options on the Method drop-down list in the Payment Information area:

- **Payment** records the transaction as a payment, which decreases the balance in a cash flow account. The Num field in the account register for the transaction remains blank; you can always fill it in later if desired. Use this option for handwritten checks or cash payments.

- **Online Payment From Quicken** records the transaction as an online payment, which decreases the balance in a cash flow account. The Num field in the account register is set to SEND, which signals Quicken to send the transaction with other payment instructions. If you choose this option, you can turn on the This Is A Repeating Online Payment check box to set up the payment as a

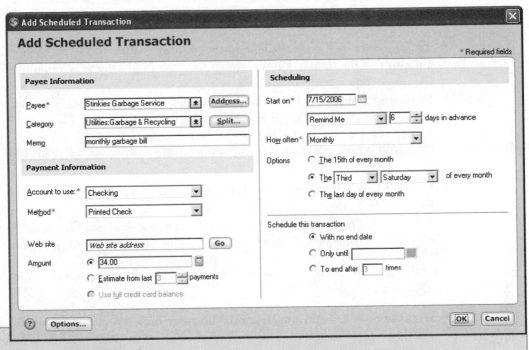

**Figure 7-3 •** Use the Add Scheduled Transaction dialog to add transactions for bills, deposits, and other items.

repeating online payment. I tell you more about repeating online payments in Chapter 6.

- **Printed Check** records the transaction as a payment using a check to be printed. This decreases the balance in a cash flow account. The Num field in the account register is set to PRINT, which signals Quicken to include the transaction with other checks to be printed. Use this option for scheduling transactions using Quicken's check printing feature.

- **Deposit** records the transaction as a deposit, which increases the balance in a cash flow account. The Num field in the account register is set to DEP. Use this option for deposits.

- **Transfer** sets up a transfer between two accounts. You might use this option to record regular transfers from your checking account to a holiday savings account.

**Web Site** This option, which is new in Quicken 2007, enables you to enter the URL for the payee's Web site. You can then click the Go button beside the Web address to open the payee's site in your default Web browser.

**Amount**    The Amount area offers three options for setting the transaction amount:

- The amount box (beside the first option button) enables you to enter a dollar amount that the transaction will always use. You can change the amount when the transaction is entered, if necessary.
- **Estimate From Last *N* Payments** enables you to specify how many previous transactions Quicken should average to calculate an amount. This is a rolling average; Quicken's calculation will change every time the payment is made. If you select this option, be sure to enter the number of transactions Quicken should include.
- **Use Full Credit Card Balance** tells Quicken to use the credit card account's balance when calculating a payment. This is especially useful for credit card accounts that must be paid in full when due, such as American Express. This option is available only if the transaction is to make a credit card payment.

**Scheduling**    The Scheduling area enables you to set scheduling options. You have several options:

- **Start On** is the transaction date or the first date for a repeating transaction. You can then use the drop-down list beneath the date to indicate whether Quicken should remind you to enter the transaction or enter it automatically. Enter the number of days in advance that you should be reminded or that the transaction should automatically be entered.
- **How Often** enables you to set options for a recurring transaction. Choose an option from the drop-down list. Your options are Only Once, Weekly, Every Two Weeks, Twice A Month, Every Four Weeks, Monthly, Every Two Months, Quarterly, Twice A Year, Yearly, and Estimated Tax (which follows the IRS estimated tax payment schedule).
- **Options** enables you to set the exact payment date. Select an option for a specific day of the month or a time of the month (such as the fourth Friday).
- **Schedule This Transaction** offers options so you can specify how long recurring payments should be made. Select an option and enter values as necessary. With No End Date repeats the transaction until you delete it from the Bills & Deposits window. Only Until enables you to set a specific ending date. To End After *N* Times enables you to specify a number of transactions. (You can use this last option for loan or lease payments—although they may seem to go on forever, they do eventually end.)

**Options**    Clicking the Options button at the bottom of the Add Scheduled Transaction window displays a dialog like the one shown next, which you can use to set additional options for the transaction.

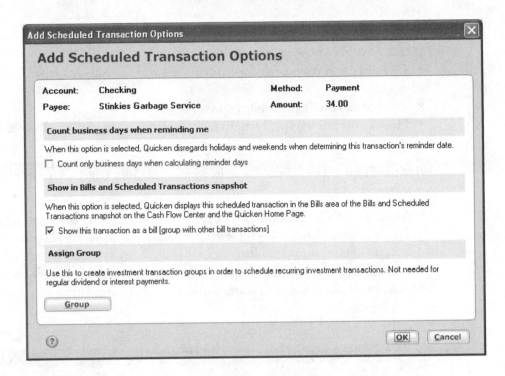

## Viewing Scheduled Transactions

Quicken displays scheduled transactions in three places: the Bills & Deposits window, the Scheduled Bills & Deposits lists that appear in various places throughout Quicken, and the Calendar. Here's a quick look at each.

### The Bills & Deposits Window

The Bills & Deposits window (refer back to Figure 7-2) displays a list of all future transactions. To view and work with the list, choose Cash Flow | Scheduled Transaction List or press CTRL-J.

**Button Bar Options**     You can use button bar options to create, modify, delete, or enter scheduled transactions:

- **Enter** immediately enters the selected transaction into the appropriate register.
- **Skip** enables you to skip the payment (or next payment) of that transaction.
- **Create New** enables you to create a new scheduled transaction or paycheck. I explain how to add a scheduled transaction earlier in this chapter and how to add a paycheck later in this chapter.
- **Edit** displays an Edit dialog that you can use to modify the selected transaction. The dialog that appears varies depending on the type of transaction that is selected when you click Edit.

- **Delete** removes the scheduled transaction. It does not remove any transactions that have already been entered in a register.
- **Options** offers commands for changing the way the Bills & Deposits window is sorted.
- **Print** prints a list of scheduled transactions.
- **How Do I?** provides instructions for completing tasks with the Bills & Deposits window.

**Window Tabs**    The Bills & Deposits window has four tabs that organize the transactions:

- **Monthly Bills & Deposits** (see Figure 7-4) displays all scheduled transactions for the month. You can click the arrows beside the name of the month to view transactions for other months.
- **All Bills & Deposits** (refer to Figure 7-2) displays all types of scheduled transactions.
- **Scheduled** displays all scheduled transactions that are not repeating online payments.

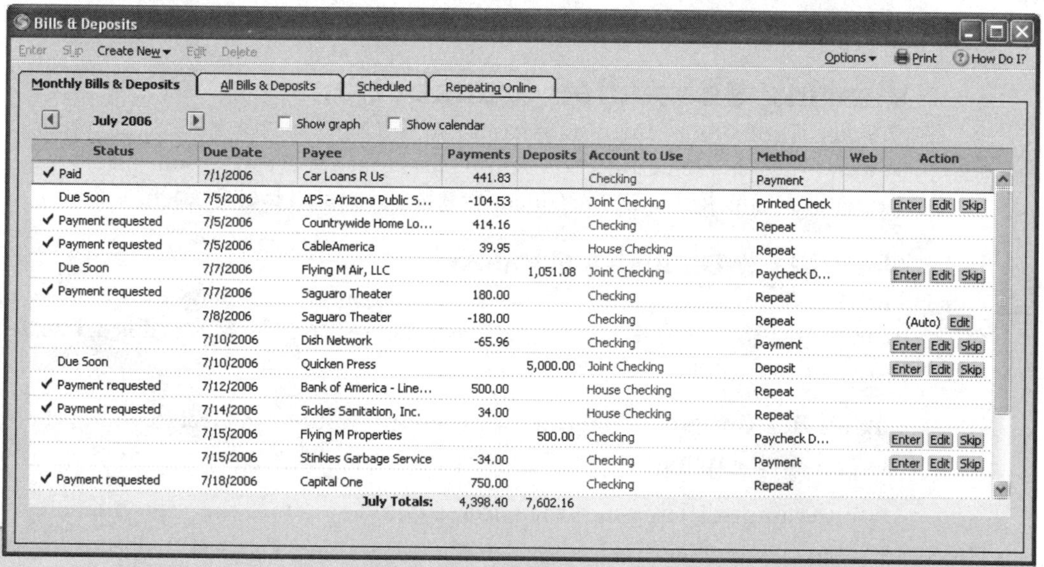

**Figure 7-4 • The Monthly Bills & Deposits tab of the Bills & Deposits window shows you the scheduled bills and deposits for the month.**

- **Repeating Online** displays only repeating online payments. I discuss repeating online payments in Chapter 6.

**Display Check Boxes**    Two check boxes enable you to display additional information in the window, as shown in Figure 7-2.

- **Show Graph** displays a column chart showing cash flow for a selected account for the month.
- **Show Calendar** displays one or two calendars that indicate dates on which transactions will be made.

**Status Column**    The Status column in the Bills & Deposits window provides information about the current status of the transaction.

**Action Column**    The Action column of the Bills & Deposits window may include buttons for working with a transaction. If a transaction has not yet been processed, you can click a button beside the transaction to enter, edit, or skip it. The buttons that appear beside an item vary depending on the window tab the item appears on and the item's status. I explain how to use these buttons to enter, edit, and skip transactions in the section titled "Working with Scheduled Transactions" later in this chapter.

## Scheduled Bills & Deposits Lists

Scheduled Bills & Deposits lists appear in a number of places throughout Quicken. For example:

- The Quicken Home window includes a Scheduled Bills & Deposits list, shown next. It lists overdue and upcoming bills, and can display a small calendar that indicates days on which transactions are due.

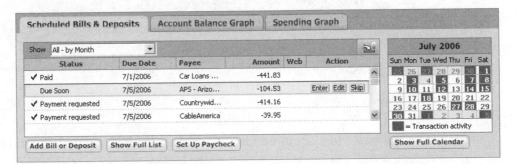

- The My Data tab of the Cash Flow Center window displays a complete list of Scheduled Bills & Deposits, shown next. You can click a button beside each transaction to enter, edit, or skip it.

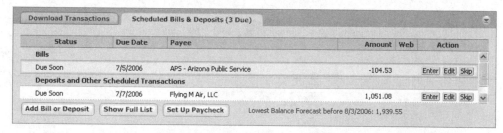

| Scheduled Bills & Deposits | | | | | Options ▼ |
|---|---|---|---|---|---|

Show [ All - by Month ▼ ]  ☐ Show graph   ☐ Show calendar

◀   **July 2006**   ▶

| Status | Due Date | Payee | Amount | Web | Action |
|---|---|---|---|---|---|
| ✔ Paid | 7/1/2006 | Car Loans R Us | -441.83 | | |
| Due Soon | 7/5/2006 | APS - Arizona Public... | -104.53 | | Enter Edit Skip |
| ✔ Payment requested | 7/5/2006 | Countrywide Home ... | -414.16 | | |
| ✔ Payment requested | 7/5/2006 | CableAmerica | -39.95 | | |
| Due Soon | 7/7/2006 | Flying M Air, LLC | 1,051.08 | | Enter Edit Skip |
| ✔ Payment requested | 7/7/2006 | Saguaro Theater | -180.00 | | |
| | 7/8/2006 | Saguaro Theater | -180.00 | | (Auto) Edit |
| | 7/10/2006 | Dish Network | -65.96 | | Enter Edit Skip |
| Due Soon | 7/10/2006 | Quicken Press | 5,000.00 | | Enter Edit Skip |
| ✔ Payment requested | 7/12/2006 | Bank of America - Li... | -500.00 | | |
| ✔ Payment requested | 7/14/2006 | Sickles Sanitation, Inc. | -34.00 | | |
| | 7/15/2006 | Flying M Properties | 500.00 | | Enter Edit Skip |
| | 7/15/2006 | Stinkies Garbage Se... | -45.00 | | Enter Edit Skip |
| ✔ Payment requested | 7/18/2006 | Capital One | -750.00 | | |
| | 7/21/2006 | Flying M Air, LLC | 1,051.08 | | Enter Edit Skip |
| ✔ Payment requested | 7/27/2006 | Compass Bank | -361.09 | | |
| | 7/28/2006 | Bank of America | -1,232.88 | | (Auto) Edit |
| | 7/30/2006 | Qwest Residential | -60.00 | | (Auto) Edit |

[ Add Bill or Deposit ]  [ Show Full List ]  [ Set Up Paycheck ]   Lowest Balance Forecast before 8/3/2006: -1

- Each account register window can include a Scheduled Bills & Deposits list, like the one shown next. The list includes only the transactions scheduled for that account. You can click a button beside each transaction to enter, edit, or skip it. If this list does not appear in the bottom of a register window, click the Scheduled Bills & Deposits tab to display it.

| Download Transactions | Scheduled Bills & Deposits (3 Due) | | | | |
|---|---|---|---|---|---|
| **Status** | **Due Date** | **Payee** | **Amount** | **Web** | **Action** |
| **Bills** | | | | | |
| Due Soon | 7/5/2006 | APS - Arizona Public Service | -104.53 | | Enter Edit Skip |
| **Deposits and Other Scheduled Transactions** | | | | | |
| Due Soon | 7/7/2006 | Flying M Air, LLC | 1,051.08 | | Enter Edit Skip |

[ Add Bill or Deposit ]  [ Show Full List ]  [ Set Up Paycheck ]   Lowest Balance Forecast before 8/3/2006: 1,939.55

**Buttons and Menu Commands**   The Scheduled Bills & Deposits lists often include several buttons at the bottom of the list and may include an Options menu at the top of the list. You can use these buttons and menu commands to get more information about transactions, display the Bills & Deposits List window (refer to Figures 7-2 and 7-4), add scheduled transactions, or set up a paycheck. The options that appear vary depending on where the list appears within Quicken.

**Schedule These?**   The Schedule These? list in the Scheduled Bills & Deposits list of the Cash Flow Center's My Data tab, when present, displays transactions that Quicken "thinks" you might want to schedule for the future. It builds this list based on categories used in the transactions or transactions you have entered more than once. Here are a few things you can do to work with this list:

- To instruct Quicken to look for more items for the list, choose Scan For Recurring Transactions from the Options pop-up menu at the top of the Scheduled Bills & Deposits list. If Quicken finds any more candidates for the list, it adds them.
- To schedule a transaction in the list, click the Yes button beside it. Quicken displays the Edit All Future Transactions dialog, which I discuss a little later in this chapter, so you can turn the transaction into a scheduled transaction.
- To remove a transaction from the list, click the No button beside it.
- To remove all transactions from the list, choose Reject All Candidate Transactions from the Options pop-up menu at the top of the Scheduled Bills & Deposits list. If you change your mind, you can choose Reconsider Rejected Scheduled Transactions from the Options menu to redisplay them.

## Calendar

Quicken's Calendar keeps track of all your transactions—past and future—by date. To open the Calendar, choose Tools | Calendar or press CTRL-K. The Calendar window, which is shown in Figure 7-5, appears.

**Button Bar Options**   You can use button bar options to work with the window's contents:

- **Go To Date** enables you to go to a specific calendar date. Click the calendar icon and use the tiny calendar that appears to locate and select the date you want. Or enter the date in the edit box and click the Go button.
- Arrow buttons on either side of the month name enable you to move from one month to another.
- **Add Note** enables you to enter a note for the selected date. The note you enter appears on the calendar (refer to the July 13 box in Figure 7-5). To view a note, click it.
- **Options** offers additional commands for viewing and working with the Calendar window.
- **Print** prints the Calendar.
- **Help** displays the Quicken Help window with information about using the Calendar.

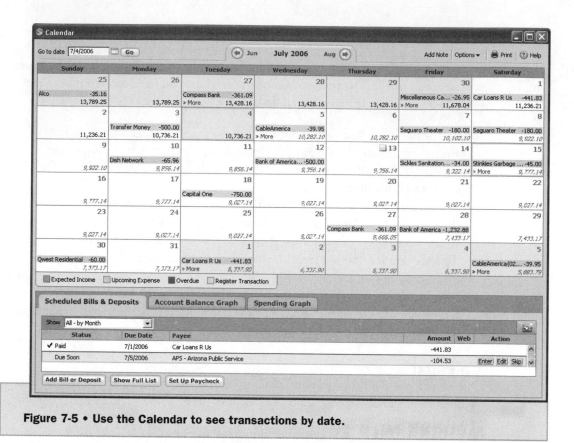

**Figure 7-5 • Use the Calendar to see transactions by date.**

**The Transactions Window** When you double-click a calendar date (or single-click a selected date), the Transactions window, which lists all the transactions for that date, appears:

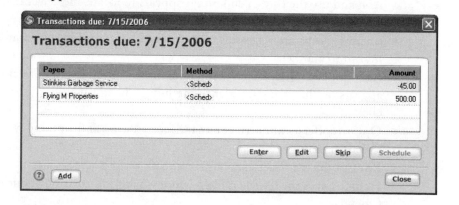

You can use buttons in the window to work with transactions:

- **Add** enables you to enter a new transaction or create a new scheduled transaction. The dialog that appears when you click this button offers all the options of the Add Scheduled Transaction dialog shown earlier.
- **Enter** enables you to enter the currently selected transaction in the appropriate account register. This option is only available if the transaction has not already been entered.
- **Edit** enables you to modify the currently selected transaction.
- **Delete** removes the selected transaction. This option is only available for transactions that have already been entered.
- **Skip** enables you to skip the payment (or next payment) of that transaction. This option is available only for transactions scheduled for future dates.
- **Schedule** enables you to create a new scheduled transaction based on the selected transaction. This option is only available if the currently selected transaction is not a scheduled transaction.

**Account Balances**    The dollar amounts that appear in the bottom of each calendar date box show the total account balances for the accounts displayed in the window, taking all payments into consideration. (You can specify which accounts to include by choosing Select Calendar Accounts from the Options menu in the button bar.) This feature works, in effect, like a simplified forecasting tool. I explain how to use Quicken's more powerful Cash Flow Forecast feature in Chapter 18.

## Working with Scheduled Transactions

Scheduling a transaction was the hard part. (Not very hard, though, was it?) Entering, editing, and skipping a scheduled transaction is easy. Here's one way—in my opinion, the quickest and easiest—to work with scheduled transactions.

Choose Tools | Scheduled Transaction List or press CTRL-J to display the Bills & Deposits window. Click the tab for the list you want to work with (see Figures 7-2 and 7-4). Then click one of the buttons beside a transaction to work with it.

**Enter** The Enter button displays the Enter Transaction dialog, which is shown next. Use this dialog to finalize settings for a transaction. When you click Enter Transaction, the transaction is entered into the account register.

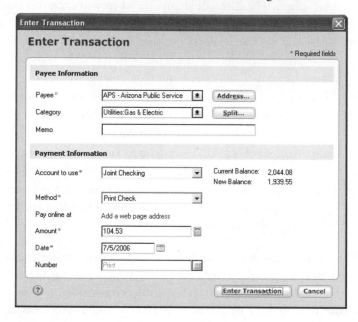

**Edit** The Edit button displays the Edit All Future Transactions dialog, which looks and works very much like the Add Scheduled Transaction dialog, shown earlier in Figure 7-3. Use this dialog to modify settings for the transaction's future entries. This is the same dialog you'd use to create a scheduled transaction based on Schedule These? candidates, as discussed earlier.

**Skip** The Skip button skips the next entry for the transaction. When you click this button, a confirmation dialog appears, asking if you want to skip the transaction that is due and telling you when the next transaction will be due. Click Yes to skip it. The transaction moves down in the list and its due date changes to the next due date.

## Using Paycheck Setup

The Paycheck Setup feature offers yet another way to automate transactions. You use it to enter information about your regular payroll check and its deductions. Then, when payday comes along, Quicken automatically enters the payroll deposit information based on the Paycheck Setup transaction.

Although you can use Paycheck Setup to record payroll checks with varying amounts and deductions—such as a check with varying hourly wages or overtime pay—it can be a real timesaver if your paycheck is the same (or almost the same) every payday. If your paycheck does vary, be sure to include all possible deductions, even if their values are often zero. Then it'll be easy to just plug in different values when you need to.

## Getting Started

Start by choosing Cash Flow | Banking Activities | Set Up Paycheck or click the Set Up Paycheck button in any Scheduled Bills & Deposits list. The Paycheck Setup dialog appears. The first screen provides general information about Paycheck Setup and how it works. Click Next to begin.

Note that if you have already set up a paycheck, following these instructions displays the Manage Paychecks dialog, which I discuss later in the section titled "Managing Paychecks." Click New in that dialog to display the Paycheck Setup dialog and create a new paycheck. If you entered net payroll information for a paycheck when you created your Quicken data file with Quicken Express Setup, you can use this dialog to access and modify the paycheck you created to add detailed payroll information.

The first thing Quicken wants to know is whether the paycheck is yours or your spouse's (if applicable) and what the company name is. It uses this information to properly categorize the payroll deductions in each paycheck and to give the paycheck a name. After entering this information, click Next.

Next, Quicken asks what you want to track. You have two options:

- **I Want To Track All Earnings, Taxes, And Deductions** tells Quicken you want to keep track of all payroll deductions when recording a paycheck. This option makes it possible to take advantage of Quicken's tax planning features, which I discuss in Part Six of this book. If you select this option, continue following the instructions in the next section, "Tracking All Earnings and Deductions," after clicking Next.
- **I Want To Track Net Deposits Only** tells Quicken that you just want to track the net take-home pay, not the gross pay and deductions. This option makes setting up a paycheck a bit quicker, but it doesn't tap into Quicken's full power for automatically recording detailed information. If you select this option, continue following the instructions in the section titled "Tracking Net Deposits Only" after clicking Next.

## Tracking All Earnings and Deductions

When you indicate that you want to track all earnings and deductions, Quicken displays the Set Up Paycheck dialog (see Figure 7-6). Use this dialog to enter detailed information about the paycheck. It's a good idea to have a recent pay stub on hand when entering information because you'll want it to be as accurate as possible.

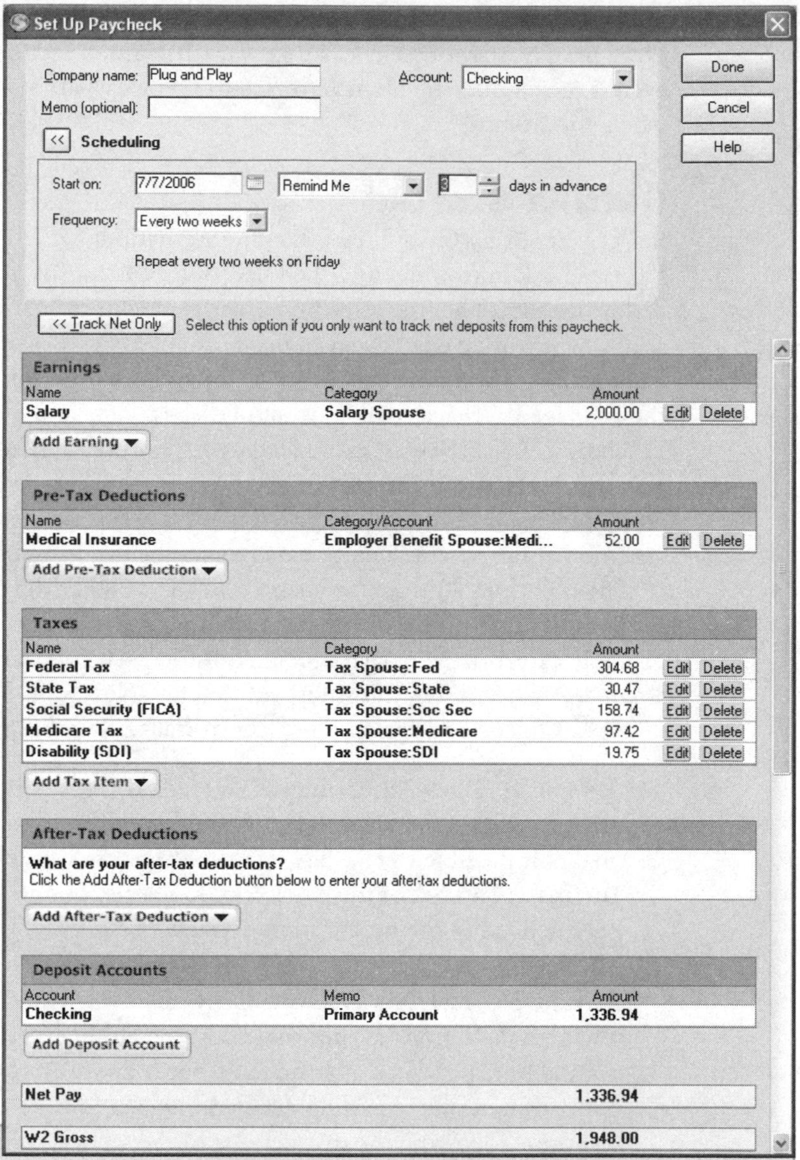

**Figure 7-6 •** You can use the big Set Up Paycheck dialog to enter all details for your paycheck.

## Entering Amounts

You can enter an amount by clicking the default amount (0.00) and typing in a replacement value. Or, if you prefer, you can click the Edit button beside an item to display an Edit dialog, which you can use to enter information.

To add another type of item to the dialog, use the Add pop-up menu in the appropriate section. (You can see some examples of the pop-up menus in the next illustration.) For example, to add a pretax deduction, display the Add Pre-Tax Deduction pop-up menu and choose an option. Then enter the details for that item in the dialog that appears. This may seem like a lot of work, but once the paycheck is set up properly, Quicken will take over and do all the hard work for you.

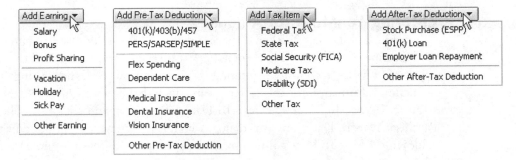

Go through the entire pay stub and enter all deductions into the dialog. Figure 7-6 shows an example; your check will probably have some different earnings and deductions. When you're finished, the Net Pay amount at the bottom of the dialog should match your take-home pay amount.

## Setting Other Options

Before you click Done, make sure you set four very important options:

**Start On**    Enter the date of the next paycheck (or the current paycheck, if you plan to enter this one after setting it up) in the Start On field.

**Frequency**    Use the Frequency drop-down list to indicate how often you receive the paycheck.

**Account**    Use the Account drop-down list to choose the account to which the net pay will be deposited. If the check will be deposited to more than one account—for example, if part of the paycheck is deposited to a company credit union savings account—make sure you add the other account and indicate how much is deposited to each account in the Deposit Accounts area near the bottom of the dialog (refer to Figure 7-6).

**Entry Options**    Select one of the two entry options in the Scheduling area and set the number of days in advance to enter the transaction. The entry options on the drop-down list are

- **Remind Me** includes the paycheck in Scheduled Bills & Deposits lists as a reminder to enter the transaction. You may want to use this option if the

paycheck's amounts vary each payday or if you have the nasty habit of not
depositing your paycheck on the day you get it.

- **Automatically Enter** automatically enters the paycheck in the appropriate
  account register when it's due. This is the best option to select if the paycheck
  is the same each payday, especially if you're lucky enough to have direct deposit
  and you know the funds will be deposited on time.

## Entering Year-to-Date Amounts

When you click Done, Quicken displays a dialog asking if you want to enter year-to-
date information. If year-to-date totals appear on the pay stub you used to set up the
paycheck, I highly recommend entering this information so all the earnings and
deduction information for the current year is included in your Quicken data file.

Select I Want To Enter The Year-To-Date Information and click OK. The
Paycheck Year-To-Date Amounts dialog, which is shown next, appears. Edit the
values in the Year To Date column by clicking each one to select it and entering
a replacement value. When you're finished, click Enter.

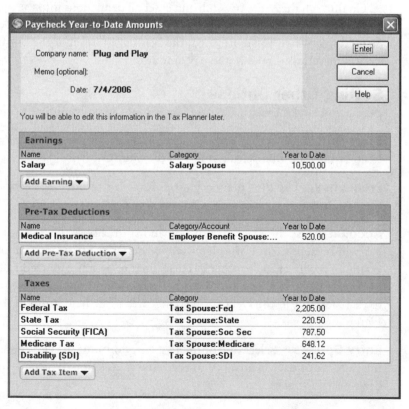

# Tracking Net Deposits Only

When you indicate that you want to track just the net payroll deposits, Quicken displays a Set Up Paycheck dialog like the one shown next. Use this dialog to enter information about the amount you expect to deposit. If you're not sure what the amount will be—like my royalty checks, which vary from one quarter to the next—you can leave the Amount field set to 0.00; if you do so, don't tell Quicken to enter the paycheck without prompting you, or it will enter 0 each payday!

Be sure to set the correct options throughout the dialog, especially in the Scheduling area. These options are discussed earlier in this chapter in the section titled "Setting Other Options." When you're finished, click Done.

# Managing Paychecks

Once you have at least one paycheck set up, you can use the Manage Paychecks dialog to modify it, delete it, or add another. Choose Cash Flow | Banking Activities | Set Up Paycheck or click the Set Up Paycheck button in any Scheduled Bills & Deposits list. The Manage Paychecks dialog, which is shown next, appears. It lists all paychecks that have been set up in Quicken. You can use the buttons on the bottom of the dialog to work with paychecks.

**New**   The New button displays the Paycheck Setup dialog, discussed earlier in this chapter, so you can set up a paycheck.

**Edit**    The Edit button displays the Edit Future Paychecks dialog for the currently selected paycheck. This dialog looks and works much like the Set Up Paycheck dialogs shown earlier. Use it to modify the paycheck setup for all future paychecks. Making changes in this dialog does not modify recorded paycheck transactions.

**Delete**    The Delete button deletes the selected paycheck. This does not delete any paycheck transactions already recorded—just the scheduled paycheck transaction. You'll have to click Yes in a confirmation dialog to remove the paycheck from Quicken.

## Entering Paycheck Transactions

Entering a paycheck transaction is just as easy as entering a scheduled transaction. Display a Scheduled Bills & Deposits list in which the paycheck appears, then click the Enter button beside the paycheck. The Edit Current Paycheck And Enter Into Register dialog appears. It displays all of the information you entered when you set up the paycheck. Modify values and options as necessary and click Enter. The paycheck's information is recorded.

# Address Book

Quicken's Address Book feature automatically stores the address information you enter when using the Write Checks window. You can also use this feature to modify or delete existing information or add new records. Keeping track of addresses with the Address Book makes it easy to insert addresses when writing checks and to look up contact information when you need to follow up on transactions.

## Displaying the Address Book Window

Choose Tools | Address Book to display the Address Book window (see Figure 7-7). It lists all the records in the Address Book.

You can use button bar buttons and menus to work with Address Book window contents:

- **New** enables you to create a new Address Book record.
- **Edit** enables you to edit the selected record.
- **Delete** removes the Address Book record. It does not affect transactions in which the record was used.
- **Modify** offers several commands for modifying the selected record or selecting multiple records.
- **Sort** enables you to change the order of records in the window.
- **Print** offers commands for printing Address Book record information.
- **How Do I?** displays the Quicken Help window with instructions for working with the Address Book.

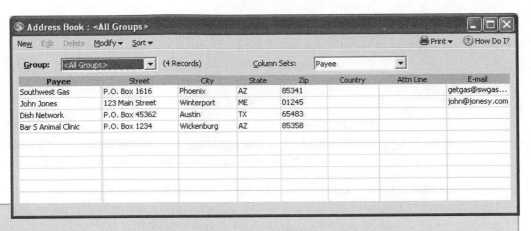

**Figure 7-7 •** Use the Address Book to keep track of the organizations and individuals you do business with.

## Adding or Modifying Address Book Records

To add a new Address Book record, click New on the button bar of the Address Book window. The Edit Address Book Record dialog, which is shown here, appears.

You can also use the Edit Address Book Record dialog to edit an existing record. Simply select the record in the Address Book window and click the Edit button in the button bar.

The Edit Address Book Record dialog has five tabs for record information. Click a tab to display its options and then enter the information you want to store. Here's what you can enter in each of the five tabs:

- **Payee** is for the information that would normally appear in a Write Check window, as well as some additional contact information.
- **Contact** is for the name, title, phone numbers, and Web site of a specific person.
- **Secondary** is for a secondary mailing address and e-mail address.
- **Personal** is for personal information, such as spouse and children's names, birthday and anniversary, and still more phone numbers.
- **Miscellaneous** is for additional information, such as user-defined fields and notes.

## Printing Entry Information

You can print the information in the list in three formats: list, labels, and envelopes.

Start by selecting a record or using the Group drop-down list at the top of the Address Book window to display the records that you want to print. Then choose one of the options on the Print menu on the button bar:

**List**   Choosing List displays a Print dialog just like the one that appears when printing Quicken reports. Use it to enter printing options, and then click OK to print the list. Consult Chapter 9 for more information about printing lists and reports.

**Labels**   Choosing Labels displays the Print Labels dialog. It includes a list of commonly used Avery label products; be sure to select the right one before you click the Print button to print. To print a sheet of return address labels, choose an address from the drop-down list in the Return Address area and select the Return Address (Whole Sheet) option in the Print Selection area.

**Envelopes**   Choosing Envelopes displays the Print Envelope dialog. Use it to print #10 envelopes for Address Book records. Just set options in the dialog, put envelope stock into your printer, and click the Print button.

# One Step Update and the Password Vault

As discussed in Chapters 6 and 10, the Bank Account Update, Portfolio Export, and WebEntry features use One Step Update to update information on the Web and download transactions entered on the Web. But that's not all One Step Update can do. This feature makes it possible to handle many of your connection chores at once. When used in conjunction with the Password Vault feature, you can click a few buttons, enter a single password, and take a break while Quicken updates portfolio and account information for you. You can even schedule updates to occur automatically when Quicken isn't running.

## Using One Step Update

The idea behind One Step Update is to use one command to handle multiple online activities. This eliminates the need to use update commands in a variety of locations throughout Quicken. One command does it all.

### Setting Up the Update

Choose Online | One Step Update or click the Update button in the toolbar. If a dialog appears, asking if you want to set up the Password Vault, click No for now; I explain how to use this feature later in this chapter in the section titled "The Password Vault." The One Step Update dialog, which is shown in Figure 7-8, appears. It lists all of the items that can be updated. Green check marks appear to the left of each

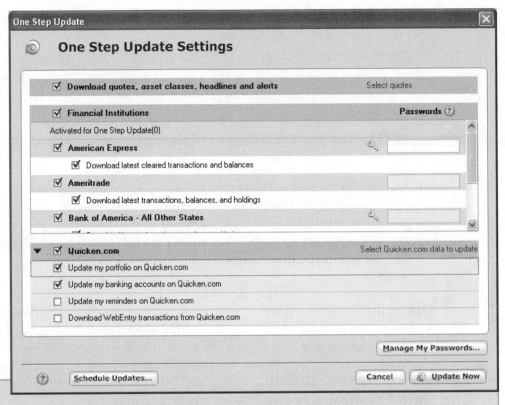

**Figure 7-8 •** Use the One Step Update dialog to set up and start a One Step Update online session.

item that will be updated when you connect. You can click in the first column to toggle the check marks there.

The dialog is split into three areas:

**Download Quotes, Asset Classes, Headlines, and Alerts**    This area offers one option to download security quotes, asset classes, financial headlines, and security-related alerts. You can select which quotes should be downloaded by clicking the Select Quotes link. I tell you more about downloading quotes in Chapter 11.

**Financial Institutions**    The Financial Institutions area lists all the financial institutions for which online account services have been enabled. Your list will differ from the one shown here—unless you have the same financial institutions I have! You can enter your password in a box to the right of each institution name when you're ready to update your data. Note that this part of the dialog scrolls; be sure to scroll down if necessary to set options for financial institutions at the bottom of the list.

**Quicken.com**   The Quicken.com area lists activities for uploading or exporting your Quicken data with Quicken.com. You can customize these options by clicking the Select Quicken.com Data To Update link. The options include:

- **Update My Portfolio On Quicken.com**, which I discuss in Chapter 11, copies information from the portfolio in your Quicken data file to the Web so you can view it on Quicken.com.
- **Update My Banking Accounts On Quicken.com** copies banking account information from your Quicken data file to the Web so you can view it on Quicken.com. I discuss this feature in Chapter 6.
- **Update My Reminders On Quicken.com** copies the information from your Quicken data file's alerts to the Web so you can view it on Quicken.com. I tell you about alerts in Chapter 9 and elsewhere in this book.
- **Download WebEntry Transactions From Quicken.com**, which I discuss in Chapter 6, downloads transactions you enter on Quicken.com to your Quicken data file.

## Updating Information

Make sure check marks appear beside the items you want to update in the One Step Update dialog. If necessary, enter passwords in the text boxes beside financial institutions for which you want to update data. Then click Update Now. Quicken establishes a connection to the Internet and begins transferring data. A Quicken One Step Update Status dialog may appear as it works. You can also monitor progress in the Update snapshot of the Quicken Home window, as shown here.

When the update is complete, the One Step Update Summary dialog appears. As shown in Figure 7-9, it summarizes the activity for the update. You can click one of the buttons in the window to go to your portfolio or a specific register, or click the Done button at the bottom of the window to dismiss it.

## The Password Vault

You might find it a nuisance to have to type in each password when you use the One Step Update feature—especially if you connect to more than one or two financial institutions. This is when the Password Vault can help.

Quicken's Password Vault feature enables you to store all your financial institution passwords in one central location. The passwords are then protected with a single password. When you use One Step Update, you enter just one password to access all

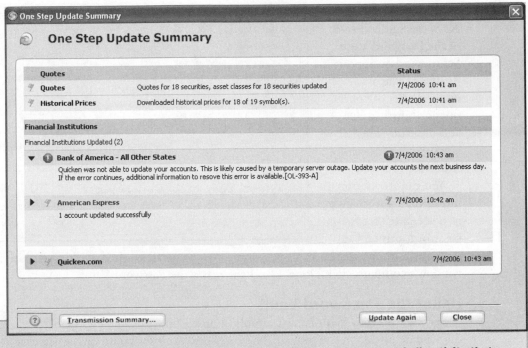

**Figure 7-9 • The One Step Update Summary dialog displays a summary of all activity that occurred during the One Step Update process. As shown here, this session had a problem communicating with one of my financial institutions.**

financial institutions. You must have Online Account Access or Online Payment set up with two or more institutions to use the Password Vault feature.

## Setting Up the Password Vault

Choose Online | Password Vault | Set Up. The Password Vault Setup dialog appears. It provides some introductory information. Click Next to display the first window of the EasyStep tab.

Follow the instructions in each EasyStep tab to choose financial institutions and enter corresponding passwords. You'll enter each password twice because the characters you type do not appear onscreen; this is a secure way of making sure you enter the same thing both times. You can do this for any combination of financial institutions for which you have set up online access.

When you've finished, select the No option when asked whether you want to enter additional passwords. The Password Vault Setup dialog appears. Use it to enter a master password to protect the Password Vault.

When you click Next, the Summary tab of the Password Vault Setup window appears. As shown here, it displays a list of your financial institutions and indicates whether a password has been stored for each one.

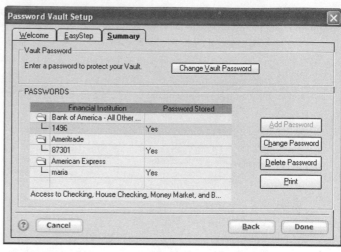

You can use buttons in this dialog to change or delete a selected password, print all passwords, or change the Vault password. When you've finished working with the window's contents, click Done. Quicken creates the Password Vault.

## Using the Password Vault

Using the Password Vault is easy. Simply choose Online | One Step Update or click the Update button in the toolbar. The Password Vault Password dialog appears. Enter your password and click OK. Then continue using One Step Update in the usual way with one difference: you don't have to enter passwords for any of the financial institutions for which a password has been entered in the Password Vault.

You can also use the Password Vault in conjunction with the Update/Send button in the Online Center window, which is discussed in Chapters 6 and 11. Clicking that button automatically displays the Password Vault Password dialog. Enter your password and click OK; Quicken performs the update.

## Editing the Password Vault

Once you've created a Password Vault, you can modify it to change passwords or add passwords for other financial institutions. Choose Online | Password Vault | Edit. In the Password Vault Password dialog that appears, enter the password that protects the Password Vault and click OK.

The Modify Password Vault dialog appears. It looks and works much like the Summary tab of the Password Vault Setup dialog. Use it to make changes to the Password Vault as desired. When you've finished, click Done.

## Deleting the Password Vault

You can delete the Password Vault if you decide you no longer want to use it. Choose Online | Password Vault | Delete. Then click Yes in the confirmation dialog that appears. Quicken deletes the Password Vault. From then on, you'll have to enter passwords for each financial institution when you use One Step Update.

## Scheduling Updates

You can schedule updates to occur when you're not using Quicken. Then, when you start Quicken, your data file is already updated with information from your financial institutions, ready to review and accept into your account registers. Your Quicken.com information can also be automatically updated based on information in your Quicken data file.

### Setting Up the Schedule

To set up a schedule, begin by choosing Online | Schedule Updates. The Schedule Updates dialog, which is shown next, appears. Set options in each area of the dialog and click OK.

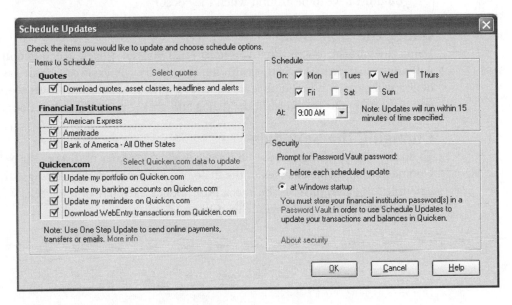

Here's a look at each of the options:

**Items To Schedule**   The Items To Schedule area lists all of the items in the One Step Update dialog I discussed earlier in this chapter. Click to toggle check marks beside each item you want to include in the schedule.

**Schedule**   The Schedule area determines when the updates will occur. Turn on check boxes for each day of the week you want the updates to occur, and then choose a time from the At drop-down list. Since your computer must be running for the updates to take place, set options for when you know your computer will be turned on. Updates will not occur, however, if Quicken is running; this ensures that the automated feature does not interrupt your work with Quicken.

**Security**    Security options enable you to indicate when your computer should prompt you for the Password Vault password. (The Password Vault feature must be set up and used in conjunction with scheduled updates.) You have two options:

- **Before Each Scheduled Update** displays the Password Vault Password dialog just before each update. You may want to select this option if the update is scheduled for a time when you expect to be at work on your computer. This is a more secure option, since it requires you to be present just before the update takes place. If you're not around, however, the update will not take place as scheduled.
- **At Windows Startup** displays the Password Vault Password dialog when you start Windows. This option can make scheduled updates more convenient, since you don't have to be around when they occur.

## Using the Schedule

Using the schedule is easy. First you must exit Quicken, since a scheduled update will not occur when Quicken is running. Eventually, the Password Vault Password dialog will appear. When it appears depends on the schedule and security options you set. Enter your password in the dialog and click Update. Quicken does the rest.

## Changing the Schedule

To change the schedule, choose Online | Schedule Updates to display the Schedule Updates dialog. Make changes in the dialog as desired to modify settings. To cancel scheduled updates, turn off the check boxes beside each day of the week. When you're finished making changes, click OK.

# Reconciling Your Accounts

## Chapter 8

## In This Chapter:

- *Starting a reconciliation*
- *Comparing transactions*
- *Making adjustments*
- *Reconciling credit card accounts*
- *Printing a reconciliation report*
- *Identifying reconciled items*

One of the least pleasant tasks of manually maintaining a bank account is balancing or reconciling it monthly. If you're good about it, you faithfully turn over your bank statement each month and use the form your bank provides to balance the account. There's a lot of adding when it comes to totaling the outstanding checks and deposits, and the longer you wait to do the job, the more adding you'll need to do. And for some reason, it hardly ever comes out right the first time you try. Maybe you've even failed so many times that you've given up. I knew someone who'd open a new checking account once a year just so she could start fresh after 12 months of not being able to balance her account. That's *not* something I recommend.

In this chapter, I explain why you should reconcile your bank statements and how you can do it—quickly and easily—with Quicken Personal Finance Software.

## Reconciling Bank Accounts

*Reconciling* an account refers to the process of comparing transactions in your account register to transactions on the account statement sent to you by your bank. Transactions that match are simply checked off. Transactions that appear only in one place—your account register or the bank's account statement—need to be accounted for.

In this section, I cover the basics of reconciling a bank account with Quicken: comparing transactions, making adjustments, and finishing up.

### What Does This Mean to You?
### Reconciling Accounts

Stop right there! Read this!

I know you were about to skip this chapter. But don't do it. Here's why.

Reconciling your checking account is important. It helps you locate differences between what you think you have in the account and what the bank says you have. It can help you track down bank errors (which do happen once in a while) or personal errors (which, unfortunately, seem to happen more frequently). Completely balancing your checking account and making adjustments as necessary can prevent you from accidentally bouncing checks when you think you have more money than you really do. That can save you the cost of bank fees and a lot of embarrassment.

If you keep track of all bank account activity with Quicken, reconciling your bank accounts is easy. You don't need to use the form on the back of the bank statement. You don't even need a calculator. Just use Quicken's reconciliation feature to enter beginning and ending balances, check off cleared transactions, and enter the transactions you missed. You'll find you're successful a lot more often with Quicken helping you out.

You can use Quicken's reconciliation feature to balance any Quicken cash flow account—including credit card accounts. Although this chapter concentrates on checking accounts, I provide additional information for reconciling credit card accounts, too.

So stifle that yawn and keep reading!

### Getting Started

To reconcile a bank account, you must have the statement for the account. Bank statements usually come monthly, so you won't have to wait long.

With statement in hand, open the account register for the account you want to reconcile. Then click the Reconcile button on the button bar. What happens next depends on whether the account is enabled for online access.

### Accounts Without Online Account Access

If the account is not enabled for online access, the Statement Summary dialog, which is shown next, appears. It gathers basic statement information prior to reconciling the account. Enter information from your bank statement in the appropriate boxes. (Enter service charge and interest earned information only if you have not already entered it in the account register.) Then click OK to continue.

## Accounts with Online Account Access

If the account is enabled for online account access, Quicken may begin by displaying a dialog that reminds you to download recent transactions or compare downloaded transactions to transactions in your register. If so, be sure to do this; it's the only way you can be sure that all transactions recorded by the bank are included in your account register.

Quicken displays the Reconcile Online Account dialog:

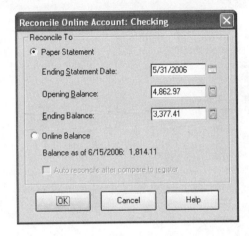

As you can see, this dialog offers two options for reconciling the account:

- **Paper Statement** enables you to reconcile the information in your Quicken account register to your bank statement. It is a traditional account reconciliation, and it works just like the account reconciliation you perform for an account without online account access. If you select this option, you must enter the bank statement ending date and ending balance in the appropriate boxes.
- **Online Balance** enables you to reconcile the account to the balance that was last downloaded for the account. If you select this option, you don't have to enter anything in the boxes. Turning on the Auto Reconcile After Compare To Register check box tells Quicken to reconcile the account to your financial institution's online balance automatically each time you download and accept transactions. With this Auto Reconcile feature enabled, you never have to reconcile the account again.

After setting options in this dialog, click OK to continue.

## Comparing Transactions

The next step in reconciling the account is to compare transactions that have cleared on the statement with transactions in your account register. For this, Quicken displays the Statement Summary window (shown in Figure 8-1), which displays all payments, checks, and deposits.

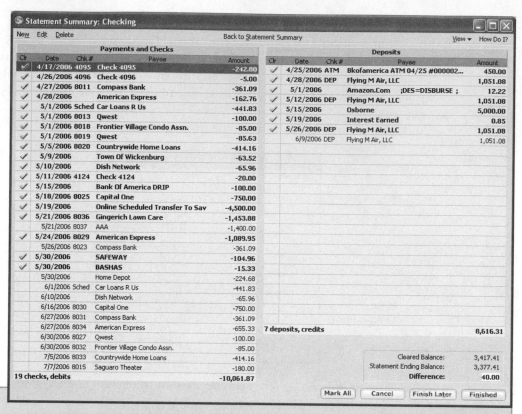

**Figure 8-1 • Use the Statement Summary window to compare your register transactions to your bank statement transactions.**

You can use button bar buttons within this window to work with its contents:

- **New** switches you to the account register window for the account you are reconciling so you can enter a new transaction.
- **Edit** switches you to the selected transaction in its account register window so you can modify it.
- **Delete** removes the selected transaction from the account register.
- **Back To Statement Summary** displays the Statement Summary dialog shown earlier or the Reconcile Paper Statement dialog (which is similar to the top half of the Reconcile Online Account dialog shown earlier) so you can check or change entries there.
- **View** offers options to change the sort order of the window's contents.
- **How Do I?** provides instructions for completing specific tasks with the window.

## Reconciling to a Bank Statement

Your job is to check off the items in the window that also appear on your bank statement. While you're checking off items, be sure to check off the same items with a pen or pencil on your bank statement.

If the account is enabled for online account access and you have been downloading and comparing transactions regularly to accept them into your account register, many of the transactions in the Reconcile Bank Statement window may already be checked off. This speeds up the reconciliation process.

While you're checking off transactions in Quicken and on your bank statement, look for differences between them. Here are some of the differences you might encounter:

- An item that appears on the bank statement but not in your account register is an item that you did not enter. You may have omitted the transaction for a number of reasons. Perhaps it was a bank adjustment that you were not informed about. Or maybe you simply forgot to enter a check. In Figure 8-1, the $40 difference between the Cleared Balance and the Statement Ending Balance is due to the failure to enter an ATM transaction—something many of us forget to do! To enter an omitted transaction, click New on the button bar to switch to the register window. Enter the transaction in the register as shown next and click the Return To Reconcile button to continue the reconciliation. Then click to place a check mark in the Clr column beside the item to mark it cleared.

- An item that appears on both your account register and bank statement but has a different amount or date could be due to an error—yours or the bank's. If the error is yours, you can edit the transaction by double-clicking it in the Reconcile Bank Statement window. This displays the account register window with the transaction selected. Edit the transaction and click the Enter button. Then click the Return To Reconcile button to continue the reconciliation.

- Items that appear in your account register but not on the bank statement are items that have not yet cleared the bank. These are usually transactions prepared just before the bank's closing date, but they can be older. Do not check them off. Chances are, you'll check them off the next time you complete a reconciliation. If, during a bank reconciliation, you discover any uncleared items that are older than two or three months, you should investigate why they have not cleared the bank. You may discover that a check (or worse yet, a deposit) was lost in transit.

## Reconciling to an Online Balance

If you've recently downloaded and accepted transactions for the account, reconciling to an online balance shouldn't take much effort. Items you've already reviewed and accepted will be checked off. Some more recent transactions may not be checked off because they haven't cleared your bank yet. Your job is to look for older transactions that appear in your Quicken account register that aren't checked off. These could represent stale payments that may have been lost in transit to the payee or errors (or duplications) you made when manually entering information into your Quicken account register. Follow up on all transactions more than 60 days old to see why they haven't been included with your downloaded transactions.

# Finishing Up

When you reconcile a bank account with Quicken, your goal is to make the difference between the Cleared Balance and the Statement Ending Balance zero. You can monitor this progress at the bottom of the Statement Summary window, as shown in Figure 8-1.

## When the Difference Is Zero

If you correctly checked off all bank statement items and the difference is zero, you've successfully reconciled the account. Congratulations. Click the Finished button.

## If You Can't Get the Difference to Zero

Sometimes, try as you might, you just can't get the difference to zero. Here are a few last things to check before you give up:

- Make sure all the amounts you checked off in your account register are the same as the amounts on the bank statement.
- Make sure you included any bank charges or earned interest.
- Make sure the beginning and ending balances you entered are the same as those on the bank statement.

If you checked and rechecked all these things and still can't get the difference to zero, click Finished. Quicken displays a dialog like the one shown here that indicates the amount of the difference and offers to make an adjustment to your account register for the amount. Click Adjust to accept the adjustment. The amount of the adjustment will be recorded without a category.

But next month, don't give up!

## First-Time Reconciliations

A while back, I was contacted by a reader who was having difficulties understanding how to reconcile an account for the first time. He seemed to think he needed to come up with some kind of "plug figure" to get the reconciliation to work. He hadn't even *tried* performing the reconciliation, too worried about what *might* happen. Oddly enough, he was an accountant. I suspect that he was over-thinking the situation, but I understand what he was concerned about and decided to address it in the book.

Suppose you have a checking account that you've been using for several years. Recently, you purchased and installed Quicken. You followed my instructions in Chapter 2 (and Chapter 5) to set up your checking account as a Quicken account, using the ending balance on your most recent bank statement—say it was dated 5/11/06—as the beginning balance in the account. After setting up the account, you entered all transactions dated after 5/11/06 into the account register.

June rolls along and you receive your 6/12/06 bank statement. Following the instructions in this chapter, you reconcile the account for the first time. But you discover that the 6/12/06 bank statement includes checks you wrote *before* 5/11/06 that were outstanding (had not cleared the bank) as of the 5/11/06 bank statement. If you don't consider these transactions in your reconciliation, there is a difference between the cleared balance and the statement ending balance. What do you do about these transactions?

This is what was confusing my accountant friend. He thought he needed to make some kind of adjusting entry in Quicken *before* starting the reconciliation. Instead, consider the following two options:

- If you want to record the transactions in your Quicken data file—perhaps to make charges to categories more complete—record them. You can do this during the reconciliation by clicking the New button on the Statement Summary window's button bar (refer to Figure 8-1). I explain how earlier in this chapter. Once the transactions have been entered, be sure to check them off in the Statement Summary window. The difference should go away.
- If you don't want to record the transactions—perhaps you don't care about the categories that would be affected—let Quicken make an adjusting entry for you at the end of the reconciliation. That's the "plug figure" my accountant friend was looking for. He didn't realize that Quicken would take care of it for him.

Once that first reconciliation is complete, you should have no further problems—unless, of course, the 7/12/06 bank statement includes one or more very old checks from before 5/11/06. Then the same situation results, with the same options and resolution.

The moral of this story: Trust Quicken. Even if you can't figure out the accounting procedures behind your finances, Quicken can.

## Other Reconciliation Tasks and Features

Quicken offers a number of other reconciliation features that you might find useful. Here's a quick look at them.

### Reconciling Credit Card Accounts

You can reconcile a credit card account the same way you reconcile a bank account. If you try to enter all credit card transactions as you make them throughout the month, it's a good idea to use the reconciliation feature to compare your entries to the credit card statement, just to make sure you didn't miss any. If you simply enter all credit card transactions when you get your statement, reconciling to the statement really isn't necessary.

When you begin the reconciliation process, Quicken displays either the Statement Summary dialog or the Reconcile Online Account dialog, depending on whether the credit card account has online account access features enabled. Both of these dialogs are shown next; they're similar to the ones that appear when you reconcile a bank account.

Enter information in the appropriate text boxes and click OK to move on to the Statement Summary window, which looks and works almost exactly like the Statement Summary window that was shown in Figure 8-1.

If you can't successfully get the credit card reconciliation to work, Quicken offers to make adjustments. The following illustration shows the Adjusting Register To Agree With Statement dialog for a hopelessly messed-up account that needs adjustments to opening balance, payments, and charges. Choose a category for each adjustment and click Adjust to make the adjusting entries.

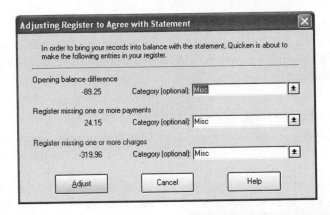

At the conclusion of a credit card reconciliation, Quicken may display the Make Credit Card Payment dialog (shown here), offering to prepare a credit card payment for you. This is particularly handy if you like to pay your credit card bill after reconciling your statement to your entries. Select an account and payment method and click Yes. Quicken prepares the transaction for you.

## Printing a Reconciliation Report

At the end of a reconciliation, Quicken displays a dialog that offers to create a reconciliation report. If you click Yes, the Reconciliation Report Setup dialog, shown here, appears. Set report options in the dialog and click Print to print the report.

I don't usually create reconciliation reports. I have enough paper filed away! But if your reconciliation required an adjusting entry, it might be a good idea to document it by printing a reconciliation report. You can then file the report with your bank statement and canceled checks.

## Identifying Reconciled Items

As shown in the next illustration, Quicken uses the Clr column in an account register to identify items that either have cleared the bank or have been reconciled:

- c indicates that the item has cleared the bank. You'll see a c in the Clr column beside items that you have checked off during a reconciliation if you have not completed the reconciliation. You'll also see a c beside items downloaded and accepted using Quicken's online account access feature, which I discuss in Chapter 6.
- R indicates that the item has been reconciled.

To make it even more obvious that a transaction either has cleared your financial institution or has been reconciled, reconciled transactions appear in gray print rather than black. You can see this in the next illustration, too.

| Checking | Register | Overview | | | | | | | Quicken 2007 |
|---|---|---|---|---|---|---|---|---|---|
| Delete Find | Transfer | Reconcile | Write Checks | Update Now | | | View ▾ | Report ▾ Options ▾ | How Do I? |
| Date/ ▲ | Num | Payee/Category/Memo | | | Payment | Clr | Deposit | | Balance |
| 5/30/2006 | | SAFEWAY | | | 104 96 | R | | | 1,671 65 |
| | | Groceries | | | | | | | |
| 5/30/2006 | | BASHAS | | | 15 33 | R | | | 1,656 32 |
| | | Medical:Medicine | | | | | | | |
| 5/30/2006 | | Home Depot | | | 224 68 | | | | 1,431 64 |
| | | Household | | | | | | | |
| 6/1/2006 | Sched | Car Loans R Us | | | 441 83 | | | | 989 81 |
| | | --Split-- | | | | | | | |
| 6/1/2006 | 4125 | Meals On Wheels | | | 20 00 | c | | | 969 81 |
| | | Charity | | | | | | | |
| 6/1/2006 | 8022 | Frontier Village Condo Assn. | | | 85 00 | c | | | 884 81 |
| | | Rent | | | | | | | |

To prevent errors in your account registers, do not edit transactions that have been reconciled.

# Examining Your Cash Flow

## Chapter 9

## In This Chapter:

- *Cash Flow Center overview*
- *Using alerts*
- *Types of reports and graphs*
- *Creating reports and graphs*
- *Customizing and saving reports and graphs*
- *Printing reports and graphs*

At this point, you'll probably agree that entering financial information into Quicken Personal Finance Software is a great way to organize it. But sometimes organizing information isn't enough. Sometimes you need to see concise summaries of the information you entered, in the form of balances, activity reports, and graphs.

Quicken's Centers provide the kind of information you're looking for, in the form of snapshots, reports, and graphs. In this chapter, I conclude my discussion of Quicken's Cash Flow Center by telling you about the snapshots of information it offers and how you can take advantage of its Cash Flow alerts. I also explain how you can create, modify, and save standard and custom reports and graphs for all Quicken Centers.

# A Closer Look at the Cash Flow Center

The previous chapters in this part of the book have explored many aspects of Quicken's Cash Flow Center, including accounts, transaction entry, Online Account Services, automation features, and reconciliations. But it's the Cash Flow Center window itself that offers a centralized place for examining the results of your work with Cash Flow Center accounts and features.

In this part of the chapter, I take you on a guided tour of the Cash Flow Center's two tabs so you can learn about the information you can find there. To follow along with your data file, click the Cash Flow button on the Account Bar or choose Cash Flow | Go To Cash Flow Center to display the Cash Flow Center window.

## The My Data Tab

The Cash Flow Center's My Data tab (see Figure 9-1) displays a number of snapshots with useful information about your cash flow accounts. Most snapshots include buttons, an Options menu, or both that you can use to work with the snapshot. For example, the Cash Flow Alerts snapshot at the top of the My Data tab has buttons and Options menu commands for showing, setting up, and deleting alerts. I discuss many of these options throughout this part of the book; you can explore the others on your own.

Here's a brief summary of each snapshot you'll find in the My Data tab of the Cash Flow Center.

**Cash Flow Alerts**    The Cash Flow Alerts snapshot lists alerts related to cash flow accounts. You can click underlined links to go to the account or other items the alert applies to. I tell you how to set up and use Cash Flow Center alerts later in this chapter in the section titled "Cash Flow Center Alerts."

**Spending & Savings Accounts**    The Spending & Savings Accounts snapshot lists all of your checking, savings, and cash accounts, along with their current and ending balances. You can click links to view the account register, set up balance alerts, and set interest rates.

**Credit Card Accounts**    The Credit Card Accounts snapshot lists all of your credit card accounts along with their current and ending balances. You can click links to view the account register, set the credit limit, and specify the interest rate.

**Scheduled Bills & Deposits**    The Scheduled Bills & Deposits snapshot lists all of your bills, deposits, and other scheduled transactions. It may also display a list of transactions that Quicken thinks you may want to schedule. Buttons beside each item enable you to enter, edit, or skip a scheduled transaction or to schedule or ignore a suggested transaction. I tell you more about working with scheduled transactions in Chapter 7.

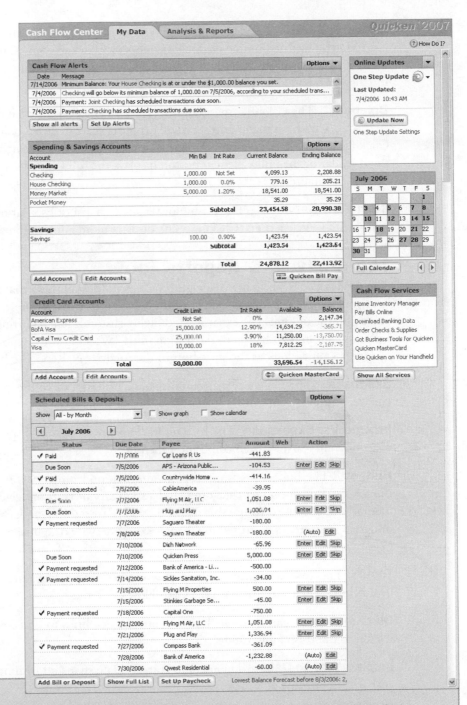

**Figure 9-1** • The My Data tab of the Cash Flow Center includes many useful snapshots related to your cash flow accounts.

**Online Updates**    The Online Updates snapshot provides information about the last time you updated online-enabled accounts or Quicken.com. You can use the Update Now button to initiate an update. I cover Quicken's online banking features in Chapter 6 and One Step Update in Chapter 7.

**Calendar**    The Calendar snapshot displays a small calendar. Each day for which a transaction has been made or is scheduled appears shaded with a bold date number. Clicking arrow buttons beneath the calendar scrolls through different months. Clicking the calendar or the Full Calendar button displays the full Calendar window, which I discuss in Chapter 7.

**Cash Flow Services**    The Cash Flow Services snapshot lists various services available to Quicken users. Clicking a link displays more information about the service.

## The Analysis & Reports Tab

The Analysis & Reports tab (see Figure 9-2) includes snapshots that summarize and help you analyze entries into your cash flow accounts. Most of these snapshots give you a glimpse of Quicken's extensive and highly customizable reporting features, which I discuss later in this chapter in the section titled "Working with Reports and Graphs."

Here's a quick look at the snapshots in the Analysis & Reports tab.

**Expenses**    The Expenses snapshot displays a pie chart of your expenses for the current or previous month.

**Income Vs. Expenses**    The Income Vs. Expenses snapshot displays a column chart of your year-to-date income and expenses.

**Budget**    The Budget snapshot displays information from your budget, including the top five out-of-budget categories, and a summary of your budgeted and actual income and expenses. To use this snapshot, you must set up a budget using Quicken's budgeting feature, as discussed in Chapter 18. Otherwise, the image in this area will be a sample.

**Tools**    The Tools area provides links to a number of Quicken features that you may find helpful when working with the Cash Flow Center.

**Quicken Tips**    The Quicken Tips area offers quick links to Quicken features related to the Cash Flow Center.

**Income Year-To-Date**    The Income Year-To-Date snapshot summarizes your year-to-date income by category.

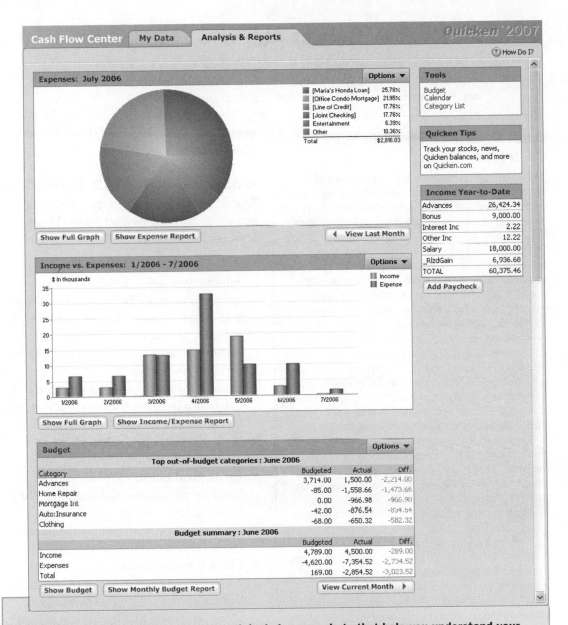

**Figure 9-2 •** The Analysis & Reports tab includes snapshots that help you understand your finances.

## Cash Flow Center Alerts

The Cash Flow Alerts snapshot in the Cash Flow Center's My Data tab (refer to Figure 9-1) lists alerts about your cash flow accounts. Having them at the top of the window helps to make sure that you don't miss them.

In this section, I tell you about the kinds of alerts Quicken offers for the Cash Flow Center and explain how to set them up.

### Cash Flow Alerts Overview

Quicken offers seven different alerts that you can set up for cash flow accounts. Here's a look at each of them:

- **Account Min. Balances** enables you to set minimum balances for your checking and savings accounts. You can set a minimum amount and a reminder amount for each account. Quicken can alert you when the account balance falls below the reminder amount you specify.

- **Account Max. Balances** enables you to set maximum balances for your checking and savings accounts. Quicken alerts you when the account balance climbs above the amount you specify.

- **Credit Card Limits** enables you to set limits for your credit card accounts. You can set a limit amount and a reminder amount. Quicken alerts you if the balance exceeds the reminder amount.

- **Check Reorder Notice** tells Quicken to alert you when you reach a certain check number. You can set this option for checking and savings accounts. This feature can be used whether you use checks provided by your bank or another printer or checks you purchase exclusively for use with Quicken.

- **Monthly Expenses** enables you to specify maximum monthly spending amounts for any Quicken expense category. If you exceed the limit you specified, Quicken alerts you.

---

### What Does This Mean to You?
### Cash Flow Alerts

If you're juggling multiple bank and credit card accounts, Quicken's Cash Flow alerts can really help you keep your sanity. After all, who can keep track of all those balances and keep them where they should be?

For example, suppose you have a checking account and a money market account. The checking account may be free, but only if the balance is at least $1,000. The money market account earns interest, but you're allowed to make only a limited number of monthly expenditures, so it can't replace the checking account. This kind of situation is perfect for Quicken's Alerts feature. Set it up so Quicken tells you when your checking account balance is getting too low—so you can transfer money in from your money market account and avoid paying fees—or too high—so you can transfer money out to your money market account and earn interest on it.

The Alerts feature can also prevent embarrassment at a checkout counter by warning you when a credit card balance is getting dangerously close to its limit. Likewise, it can remind you to pay your credit card bill, so even if your balance is relatively low, you won't forget to make that monthly payment on time.

If you're trying to keep spending under control, Quicken can be a good friend. You can use its Alerts feature to set up maximum spending amounts for specific categories. Find yourself dining out too often? Set the maximum Dining category expenditure for the month. Just can't resist another pair of shoes in the mall? Set the maximum Clothing category expenditure. Then, when you enter the expenditure that puts you over the maximum for the month, Quicken firmly informs you that it's time to stop.

It's like having an impartial financial manager looking over your shoulder.

- **Savings Goals** tells Quicken to alert you when you fall behind on a savings goal. This option works directly with Quicken's Savings Goals feature, which I cover in Chapter 18.
- **Online Services Available** tells Quicken to alert you when one of your financial institutions supports Online Account Services. Quicken can learn about new financial partners when you connect to the Internet to utilize other features. I tell you more about Online Account Services in Chapter 6.

In addition, Quicken offers three other General category reminders that appear in the Cash Flow Center:

- **Online Transactions** tells Quicken to remind you to download transactions from your financial institution if you haven't done so for 30 days or more.
- **Scheduled Transactions Due Soon** tells Quicken to remind you in advance of any scheduled transactions that are due.
- **Send To With Quicken.com** tells Quicken to remind you to export your portfolio, account balances, and reminders to Quicken.com when balances change.

## Setting Up Alerts

You set up alerts with the Setup tab of the Alerts Center window. To display this window, click the Set Up Alerts button in the Cash Flow Alerts snapshot (refer to Figure 9-1) or choose Tools | Set Up Alerts. If necessary, click the plus sign (+) to the left of Cash Flow to display the Cash Flow Center alerts. You can then click the name of one of the alerts to view and set it. Figure 9-3 shows the Account Min. Balances alert being edited.

### Setting Basic Options

To set an alert, begin by selecting the name of the alert on the left side of the window. If necessary, click the check box to place a check mark within it. Then click the value you want to change on the right side of the window and enter a new value. Not all alerts have values you can change; for example, the Online Services Available alert is a simple on or off setting made with the check mark.

### Setting Other Options

You can set two additional options in the bottom half of the window.

**Show Me The Alert As**    Choose from two options for showing the alert:

- **Text In The Alert List** displays the alert as an item in the Cash Flow Alerts snapshot only.
- **Urgent (Pop Up Dialog Box)** displays the alert in a dialog. You must dismiss this in-your-face alert by clicking the OK button in the dialog before continuing to work with Quicken.

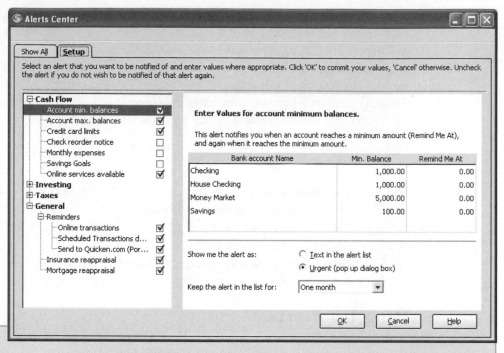

**Figure 9-3 • Use the Setup tab of the Alerts Center to set alerts for Cash Flow and other accounts.**

**Keep The Alert In The List For** You can set the amount of time the alert should remain in the Cash Flow Alerts snapshot. The default setting is One Month, but you can use the drop-down list to choose from One Day, One Week, One Month, One Quarter, or One Year.

## Finishing Up

When you're completely finished setting alerts, click OK to dismiss the Alerts Center window. The alerts will work quietly in the background, watching your finances. When it's time to go to work, they appear as you specified.

## Working with Alerts

Once you've set up alerts, you can view, modify, or delete them as desired. Here's how.

### Viewing Alerts

As shown in Figure 9-1, Cash Flow alerts appear in a snapshot at the top of the Cash Flow Center window.

You can also view alerts in the Show All tab of the Alerts Center window (see Figure 9-4). Click the Show All Alerts button in any Alerts snapshot or choose Tools | Show All Alerts to display them.

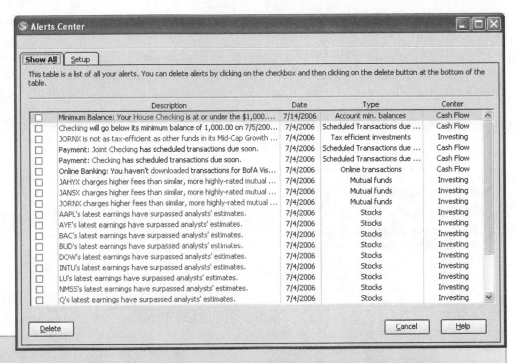

**Figure 9-4 • The Show All tab of the Alerts Center window enables you to view and delete specific alerts.**

## Modifying Alerts

You can change the way an alert works at any time. Choose Tools | Set Up Alerts to display the Setup tab of the Alerts Center (refer to Figure 9-3). Then follow the instructions in the earlier section titled "Setting Up Alerts" to change alert settings.

## Deleting Alerts

To delete an alert, choose Tools | Show All Alerts to display the Show All tab of the Alerts Center (refer to Figure 9-4). Turn on the check box beside each alert you want to delete and click the Delete button. A confirmation dialog appears. Click OK to delete the alert.

To prevent a deleted alert from appearing again in the future, use the Setup Tab of the Alerts Center window (refer to Figure 9-3) to turn off the check box for the alert in the list on the left side of the window.

# Quicken Reporting Overview

Quicken offers a variety of reports and graphs, each of which can be customized to meet your needs. I like to think of reports and graphs as the "fruits of my labor." I spend time entering data into Quicken so Quicken can crunch the numbers for me. I use the reports and graphs it creates to analyze my spending habits, find ways to save money, and submit information to financial institutions when I apply for loans or credit cards.

In this section, I tell you about the types of reports and graphs Quicken offers. Then I explain how you can use a variety of techniques to quickly create reports and graphs based on the information in your Quicken data file. Although I'll concentrate on reports and graphs for the Cash Flow Center, the techniques in this part of the chapter apply to the reports and graphs you create for any Quicken data, regardless of the Center in which it appears.

## What Does This Mean to You? Reporting

Okay, so you're not a corporation with stockholders and SEC reporting requirements. And maybe you're not even involved in any kind of business where reports could help you maximize profits. But that doesn't mean you won't find Quicken's reporting features useful.

I found Quicken extremely useful a few years ago when I applied for a mortgage for a rental property I wanted to buy. I'd been faithfully entering my transactions into Quicken for years and had a complete record of everything I owned and owed. Rather than manually filling out the lengthy forms required by the lender, I created Quicken reports that provided the same information. I also whipped up reports that summarized my current net worth, detailed my investment portfolio, and totaled my year-to-date income and expenses. I sent all these reports to the bank with copies of my recent tax returns. I got a positive answer within a few days. And I didn't even need to take out a calculator!

A friend of mine has a tax preparer do his returns every year. (I guess he hasn't learned about the benefits of TurboTax yet.) In the old days, before he started using Quicken, he'd spend hours with his tax guy, answering questions and shuffling through piles of paper and handwritten notes. Now he uses Quicken to create reports of his income and expenses, including detailed reports for things like charity contributions and medical expenditures. He spends less than an hour with his tax guy and, because they both save time, his tax preparation bill is half what it used to be.

As you can see, reports aren't just for businesses. They're for people like you and me, too.

## Types of Reports and Graphs

Within Quicken are essentially two kinds of reports and graphs: standard and saved. Here's an overview of each one.

### Standard

Quicken includes a number of standard reports and graphs that are organized by topic: Banking, Spending, Comparison, Investing, Tax, Net Worth & Balances, Business, and EasyAnswer. For example, the Banking topic includes Banking Summary, Cash Flow, Missing Checks, Reconciliation, and Transaction reports. These reports and graphs clearly show banking-related information. EasyAnswer reports and graphs answer specific, predefined questions such as, "Where did I spend my money during the period…?" and "How much did I spend on…?"

You select a question and then provide optional information such as a date range, payee, or account. Quicken gathers the information and generates the report or graph.

### Saved

You can create custom reports and graphs by customizing the standard reports and graphs. This multiplies your reporting capabilities, enabling you to create reports or graphs that show exactly what you need to show. When you save your custom reports and graphs, they can be created quickly, with just a few mouse clicks, to display current information.

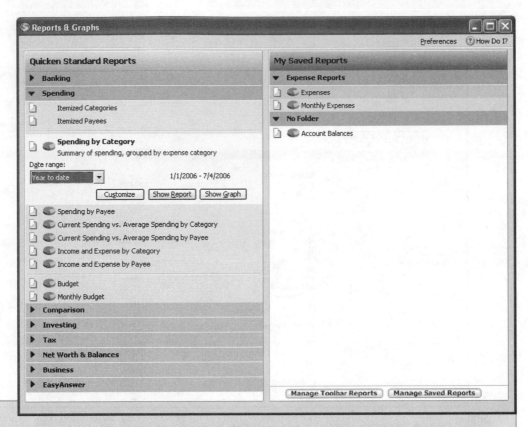

**Figure 9-5 • You can use the Reports & Graphs center window to create reports or graphs.**

## Creating Reports and Graphs

With Quicken, creating a report or graph is as simple as clicking a few buttons. You can use several techniques: choosing a report or graph from the Reports menu, setting options in the Reports & Graphs center window, using the Report button or menu on button bars, and choosing commands from contextual menus. In this section, I explain how to use all of these techniques.

### Reports & Graphs Center

The Reports & Graphs center window (see Figure 9-5) offers one way to create reports and graphs. Choose Reports | Reports & Graphs Center to display it. Click one of the topics on the left side of the window to display a list of the available reports and graphs. The icon that appears to the left of the report name indicates whether you can create a report, a graph, or both.

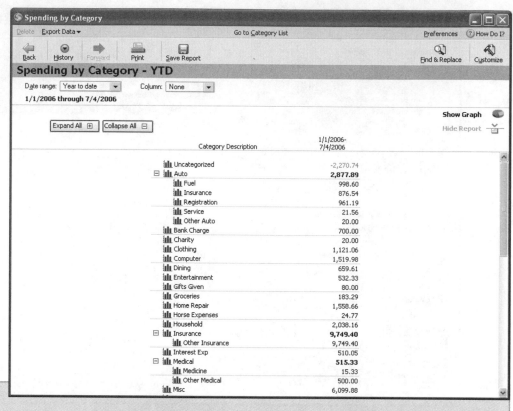

**Figure 9-6 • A Spending By Category report lists expenses by category.**

To create a report or graph, click its name on the left side of the window and then set the Date Range option in the settings area that appears beneath it. You can click the Customize button to further customize the report or graph, as I explain later, in the section titled "Customizing Reports and Graphs." Then click Show Report or Show Graph to display the report or graph. Figure 9-6 shows an example of a report.

## The Reports Menu

Quicken's Reports menu, which is shown here, includes a number of submenus, each of which corresponds to a report topic. To create a report or graph with the Reports menu, click a topic submenu, and then click a report name. Quicken creates the report with default date settings. Figure 9-7 shows an example of a report created directly from the Reports menu.

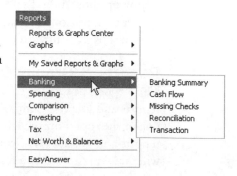

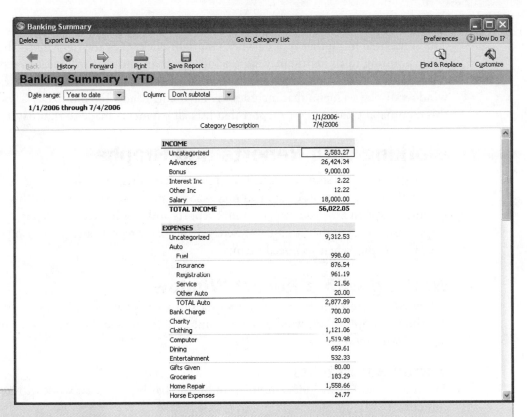

**Figure 9-7 • A Banking Summary report summarizes income and expenses.**

## Report Buttons

You can also create a report by using the Report button or menu on the button bar in some windows. This normally creates a report based on information selected within the window.

In a window that includes a Report button on the button bar, select one of the items in the window. Then click the Report button. A report appears in its own window. For example, you could create a Transaction report for a specific category by selecting a category in the Category List window and then clicking the Report button.

A Report button also appears in an account register window when you activate the Payee or Category field. Clicking this button displays a pop-up *mini report* of recent activity for the payee or category, as illustrated and discussed briefly in Chapter 5. Clicking the Show Report button in the mini report opens a report window with the information.

## Contextual Menus

The contextual menu that appears when you right-click (click the right mouse button) while pointing to an item sometimes includes a command that will create a report for the item. For example, right-clicking the name of a payee in the account register window displays a menu that includes the Payments Made To command. Choosing this command creates a Payee report that lists all payments made to that payee.

# Working with Reports and Graphs

Although Quicken's standard reports and graphs can often provide just the information you need onscreen, you may want to do more with them. In this section, I explain how you can customize reports and graphs, save the reports and graphs you create so they're easy to re-create, and print reports and graphs so you have hard copies when you need them.

## Working with a Report Window

When you create a report or graph, it appears in a report window. Figures 9-6 and 9-7 show examples. This window has a number of features and options you can use to work with reports.

### Button Bar Buttons

The report window includes a number of button bar buttons that work with report contents:

- **Delete** deletes the report from the report list. This button is gray if the report has not been added to the report list. I tell you more about the report list in the section titled "Saving Reports and Graphs" later in this chapter.
- **Export Data** is a menu that includes commands for exporting the report's contents in up to four formats: Export To Excel Compatible format, Copy Report To Clipboard, Report To PDF Format, and Graph To PDF Format. The options that appear on this menu vary depending on the type of report or graph displayed.
- **Go To Category List** displays the Category List window.
- **Preferences** displays the Quicken Preferences dialog for Reports And Graphs so you can set preferences for all reports and graphs you create. I tell you about Reports And Graphs preferences in Appendix B.
- **How Do I?** displays the Quicken Help window with information about creating reports and graphs.

### Toolbar Buttons

The report window also includes a number of toolbar buttons:

- **Back,** which is available only if you are viewing a subreport (see Figure 9-8), returns to the parent report. I explain how to create subreports later in this chapter.

- **History** displays a list of the parent report and all subreports you have created. Choose the name of a report to display it. If you choose the Show Report List command, a Report History navigation bar appears, listing all reports related to the window (see Figure 9-8). You can click the Hide Report List button to hide the list.
- **Forward**, which is available only if you have clicked the Back button, displays the previously viewed report in the window.
- **Print** sends the report or graph to the printer.
- **Save Report** saves the report. I tell you more about saving reports in the section titled "Saving Reports and Graphs" later in this chapter.
- **Find & Replace** displays the Find And Replace dialog, which you can use to modify transactions that make up the report. I explain how to use the Find And Replace feature of Quicken in Chapter 5.
- **Customize** displays the Customize dialog, which you can use to customize the currently displayed report. I explain how to use the Customize dialog later in this chapter in the section titled "Customizing Reports and Graphs."

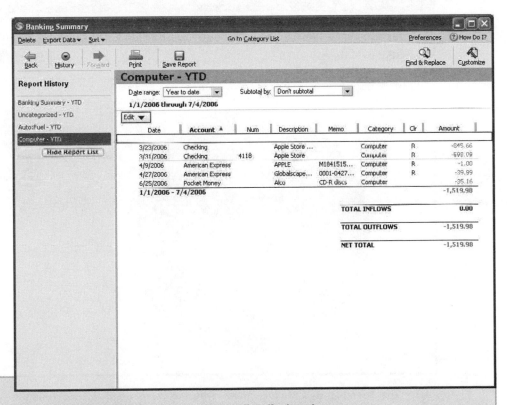

**Figure 9-8 • A subreport with the Report History list displayed**

## Hide/Display Graph/Report

If a report includes a graph, either the graph or a Show Graph button will appear at the top of the report window. Clicking the Show Graph button will display the graph. The button will then turn into a Hide Graph button; clicking it hides the graph. Similarly, the report window may include a Hide Report or Show Report button, depending on whether the report is displayed or hidden.

You can display a large graph instead of a report, as shown in Figure 9-9, by clicking the Show Graph button and then clicking the Hide Report button.

## Hiding or Displaying Report Detail

You can show or hide the details for some reports by clicking a + or − button beside a report line. For example, clicking the − button beside Auto in Figure 9-6 collapses the subcategories beneath Auto to show just the main category totals. The button then turns into a + button, which you click to display the hidden detail. The Expand All or Collapse All buttons do the same thing but for all categories and subcategories.

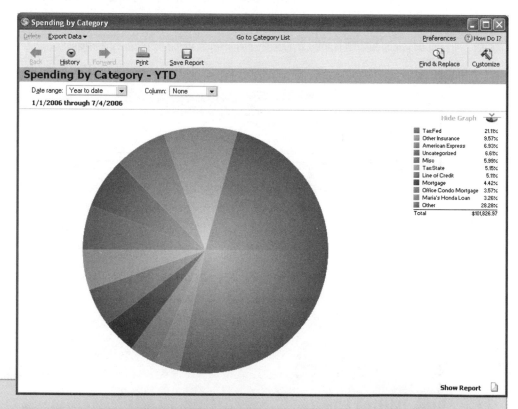

**Figure 9-9 • The Spending By Category graph, with the corresponding report hidden**

## Customizing Reports and Graphs

You can customize just about any report or graph you create so it shows only the information you want to display. When you can customize it, however, depends on how you create it:

- When you create a report or graph using the Reports & Graphs center window (refer to Figure 9-5), you can customize it before or after you create it.
- When you create a report using commands under the Reports menu, the Report button in the button bar, or a command on a contextual menu, you can customize it only after you create it.

Customization options vary from one type of report or graph to another. It's impossible to cover all variables in this chapter. I will, however, tell you about the most common options so you know what to expect. I'm sure you'll agree that Quicken's reporting feature is very flexible when you go beyond the basics.

### Using the Customize Dialog

To customize a report or graph, click the Customize button in the options area for the report or graph in the Reports And Graphs Center window (refer to Figure 9-5) or the Customize button at the top of the report window (refer to Figures 9-6 through 9-9). The Customize dialog, which is shown next, appears. The dialog's full name includes the name of the report or graph.

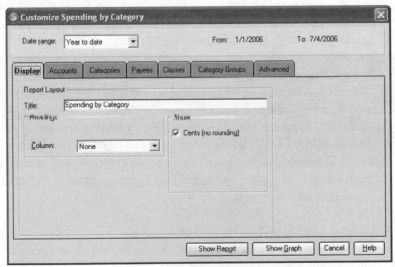

The Customize dialog includes up to seven tabs of options that you can set to customize the report:

- **Display** (shown in the previous illustration) enables you to set display options for the report, such as the title, row and column headings, organization, number formatting, and columns.

- **Accounts** enables you to select the accounts that should be included in the report. Quicken will include transactions or balances in only the accounts you specify in the report.
- **Categories** enables you to select the categories to include in the report. If desired, you can use this tab to include only transactions for which the payee, category, or memo contains certain text.
- **Payees** makes it possible to select the payees to include in the report. If desired, you can use this tab to include only transactions for which the category, payee, or memo contains certain text.
- **Classes** enables you to select the classes to include in the report. If desired, you can use this tab to include only transactions for which the payee, class, or memo contains certain text. This tab, which appears only if you have at least one class defined, makes it possible to generate reports by class. I tell you about classes in Chapter 3.
- **Category Groups** enables you to select the category groups to include in the report. I tell you about category groups in Chapters 3 and 18.
- **Advanced** enables you to set additional criteria for transactions to be included in the report, such as amount, status, and transaction type.

No matter which tab is selected, you also have access to the Date Range area, which you can use to specify a date or range of dates for the report.

Once you have set options as desired, click the Show Report, Show Graph, or OK button. (The button that appears varies depending on whether you can create a report, a graph, or both from within the dialog and how you opened the dialog.) If you are creating the report or graph from the Reports & Graphs center window (refer to Figure 9-5), Quicken creates the report or graph to your specifications. If you are customizing an existing report or graph, Quicken creates a subreport of the original report or graph and displays it in the same report window.

If the custom report or graph isn't exactly what you want, that's okay. Just click the Customize button in the report or graph window and change settings in the Customize dialog to fine-tune the report or graph. When you click OK, Quicken creates a new subreport. You can repeat this process until the report or graph is exactly the way you want it.

## Using the Customize Bar

The Customize bar near the top of a report window (see Figures 9-6 through 9-9) offers another way to customize a report or graph. Use it to change date ranges, modify subtotal settings, or set columns for the report. Quicken immediately creates a subreport based on your revised settings and displays it in the same report window.

## Using QuickZoom

The QuickZoom feature enables you to create a report or graph on the fly. Simply double-click a report line item or a graph bar or legend item. Quicken generates a new subreport for the item you double-clicked and displays it in the same report window.

## Working with Subreports

Quicken creates a subreport each time you customize an existing report or graph or create a QuickZoom report. As you can imagine, it's easy to accumulate quite a few of these subreports when experimenting with Quicken's reporting features.

To view a specific subreport, choose its name from the History menu in the report window's toolbar. The view changes to switch to the report.

You can also choose Show Report List from the History menu in the toolbar to display the Report History list, shown in Figure 9-8. Click the name of the report you want to view to display it.

You can click the Back or Forward button at the top of the navigation bar to move among subreports you have already viewed.

To delete a subreport, display the subreport and then click the Delete button in the button bar.

## Saving Reports and Graphs

You'll often create a predefined report and customize it to create a report you want to be able to see again and again. Rather than creating and customizing the report from scratch each time you want to see it, you can save the report's settings. Then, when you want to view the report again, just select it from a list and it appears. You can do the same for graphs.

### Saving a Report or Graph

To save a report or graph, start by creating, customizing, and displaying it. When it looks just the way you want, click the Save Report button in the report window's toolbar. The Save Report dialog, which is shown here, appears.

Enter a name and description for the report or graph in the appropriate boxes. To save the report or graph in a specific folder, choose the folder name from the Save In drop-down list. You can create a new folder by clicking the Create Folder button, entering a name for the folder in the dialog that appears, and clicking OK. To save all versions of the report that you create, turn on the Save Report History check box. When you're finished setting options, click OK to save the report.

## Viewing a Saved Report or Graph

When you save a report or graph, it appears a number of places throughout Quicken, organized by folder if you have saved them into specific folders.

**The Reports & Graphs Center Window**   Saved reports and graphs appear in the My Saved Reports area of the Reports & Graphs center window (refer to Figure 9-5). Double-click the name of the report or graph to display it.

**The My Saved Reports & Graphs Submenu**   Saved reports and graphs also appear on the My Saved Reports & Graphs submenu under the Reports menu. (This submenu appears only if at least one report has been saved.) Choose a report name to display it.

**The Quicken Toolbar**   If you used the Manage Toolbar Reports dialog to add saved reports to the toolbar, as discussed in the section titled "Managing Toolbar Reports" later in this chapter, they appear as toolbar buttons. Click the button to display the report. If you display a saved report folder on the toolbar, it appears as a pop-up menu button that lists the reports within it.

## Managing Saved Reports

Quicken offers two tools for managing saved reports: the Manage Saved Reports and Manage Toolbar Reports dialogs. You can open both of these dialogs by clicking the appropriate button within the Reports & Graphs center window (refer to Figure 9-5).

### Managing Saved Reports

The Manage Saved Reports dialog, shown here, enables you to organize saved reports by folder, edit report settings, or delete reports. Select the item you want to work with in the report list and click a button.

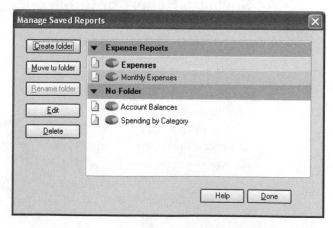

- **Create Folder** displays the Create New Report Folder. Enter a name for the folder in the Name box and click OK. The folder appears in the list.
- **Move To Folder** displays the Move To Report Folder dialog. Choose a different folder from the Name drop-down list and click OK. The item moves to that folder.
- **Rename Folder** displays the Rename Report Folder dialog. Enter a new name for the folder in the Name box and click OK. The folder's name changes.
- **Edit** displays the Edit Saved Report dialog, which enables you to enter a new name and description for the report. Click OK to save your changes.
- **Delete** removes the selected item. When you click this button, a confirmation dialog appears. You must click OK to permanently delete the item.

**Managing Toolbar Reports**    The Manage Toolbar Reports dialog, shown next, enables you to specify which saved reports should appear on the toolbar. Turn on the check box beside each folder or report you want to appear. Then click OK to save your settings.

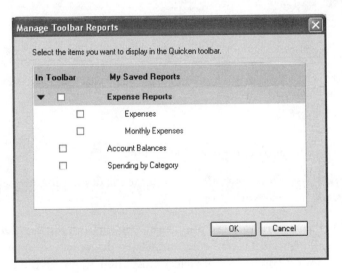

## Printing Reports and Graphs

You can print reports and graphs. This enables you to create hard copies for your paper files or for use when applying for loans or completing your tax returns.

To print a report, subreport, or graph, begin by displaying it in the report window. Then click the Print button in the window's toolbar. The Print dialog, which has been revised and expanded for Quicken 2007, appears (see Figure 9-10). Set options as desired and click Print.

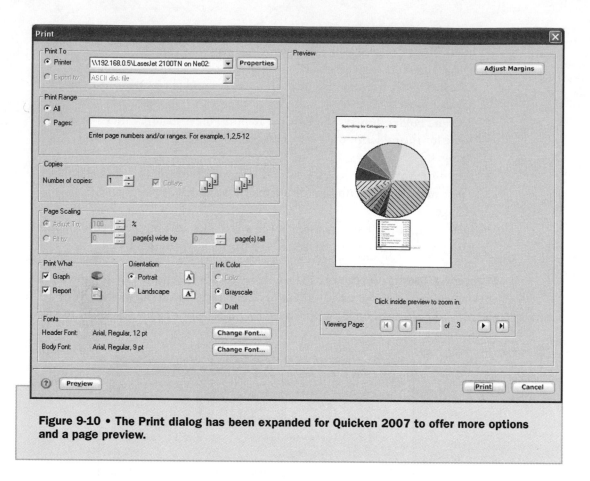

**Figure 9-10 • The Print dialog has been expanded for Quicken 2007 to offer more options and a page preview.**

Here's a look at the available options:

**Print To**   Print To options determine the destination of the printed report or graph. You have two choices:

- **Printer** prints to the printer you choose from the drop-down list, which includes all printers, fax modems, and related devices set up in Windows. This is the option you'll probably select most often. Clicking the Properties button displays the Properties dialog for the currently selected printer.
- **Export To** makes it possible to export the report information in one of three formats you choose from the drop-down list: ASCII Disk File, Tab-Delimited

(Excel-Compatible) Disk File, or PRN (123-Compatible) Disk File. This option is only available if you are printing a report without a graph.

**Print Range**    The print range determines which pages will print. You can use this if the printout is expected to be more than one page. The default setting is All, which prints all pages of the report. To print a range of pages, select Pages, and then enter the page numbers for the page range you want to print.

**Number Of Copies**    The Number Of Copies box determines how many copies of the report will print. If you enter a value greater than 1, you can turn on the Collate check box to collate the copies as they are printed.

**Scaling**    Scaling options enable you to resize a report or graph to a specific percentage or to fit on a certain number of pages. These options are only available for certain printers.

**Print What**    You can toggle two check boxes to determine whether Quicken should print a graph or report or both. The options that are available depend on what's in the report window.

**Orientation**    Orientation determines how the printed report will be viewed. The options are Portrait or Landscape. These are standard options offered by all programs. The icon beside each orientation option illustrates the option.

**Ink Color**    Select one of three options to determine the ink color and quality of the printout: Color (available only if a color printer is selected from the Printer drop-down list), Grayscale, or Draft.

**Fonts**    Use the two Change Font buttons to change the header and body typefaces of the report or graph. Clicking the button displays the Font dialog, which you can use to set standard font options such as font, size, and style.

**Preview**    The Preview area shows a thumbnail preview of the document. You can click the buttons in the Viewing Page area to scroll through all pages of the report. To change the margins for the document, click the Adjust Margins button. The Preview area changes, as shown next, to offer boxes for entering margin values. To view a full-size preview, click the thumbnail in this area or click the Preview button at the bottom of the dialog.

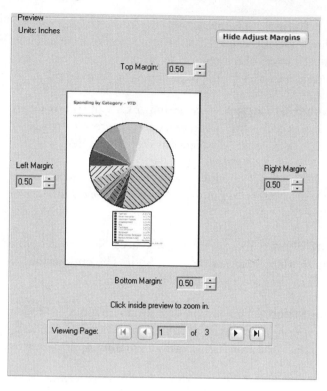

# The Investing Center

This part of the book explains how you can use Quicken Personal Finance Software to track your investments. It begins by explaining the basics of tracking investments in Quicken and then goes on to explain how you can use Quicken's online investment tracking features to download investment information from your brokerage firm and exchange information with Quicken.com. Along the way, it provides a wealth of information you can use to invest wisely and maximize your investment returns. Finally, it explains how you can use Quicken's Investing Center and reporting features to keep an eye on your portfolio and investment returns. This part has three chapters:

# Entering Your Investment Transactions

## Chapter 10

## In This Chapter:

- *Setting up investment accounts*
- *Recording investment transactions*
- *Adding and editing securities*
- *Using the Security Detail View window*

Investments offer individuals a way to make their money grow. Although more risky than deposits made to an FDIC-insured bank, stocks, bonds, mutual funds, and other types of investments have the potential to earn more. That's why many people build investment portfolios as a way to save for future goals or retirement.

In this chapter, I tell you a little about investments and portfolio management and then explain how you can use Quicken Personal Finance Software to keep track of the money you invest.

## Quicken Investment Basics

An *investment* is a security or asset that you expect to increase in value and/ or generate income. There are many types of investments— Table 10-1 lists some of them. This chapter concentrates on the investments you can track with the features in Quicken's Investing Center.

| Type of Investment | Type of Account |
|---|---|
| CD | Savings account or standard brokerage account |
| Money market fund | Savings account or standard brokerage account |
| Stocks in your possession | Standard brokerage account |
| Brokerage account with one or more securities, with or without an associated cash, checking, or interest-earning account | Standard brokerage account |
| Employee stock options | Standard brokerage account |
| Employee Stock Purchase Plan (ESPP) | Standard brokerage account |
| Dividend Reinvestment Program (DRIP) | Standard brokerage account |
| Bonds, including U.S. Savings Bonds | Standard brokerage account |
| Treasury bills | Standard brokerage account |
| Single mutual fund with no cash balance | Single mutual fund account |
| Variable or fixed annuities | Standard brokerage account |
| 401(k) or 403(b) plan | 401(k) or 403(b) account |
| Traditional IRA, Roth IRA, Education IRA, Keogh Plan, SEP-IRA, or SIMPLE-IRA | IRA or Keogh account |
| Real estate | Asset account |
| Real estate investment trusts (REITs) or partnerships | Standard brokerage account |

**Table 10-1 • Quicken Accounts for Various Investment Types**

Before you learn how to use Quicken to track your investments, here's a review of Quicken's investment accounts and a more detailed explanation of why investment tracking is so important.

## Your Quicken Portfolio

The term *portfolio* refers to the total of all of your investments. For example, if you have shares of one company's stock, shares in two mutual funds, and a 401(k) plan account, these are the items that make up your portfolio.

### Types of Investment Accounts

Your Quicken portfolio can include four types of investment accounts. You can have as many investment accounts as you need to properly represent the investments that make up your portfolio.

**Standard Brokerage**   A standard brokerage account is for tracking a wide variety of investments handled through a brokerage firm, including stocks, bonds, mutual funds, and annuities. Like the account at your brokerage firm, it can track income, capital gains, performance, market values, shares, and cash balances for multiple securities.

**IRA or Keogh**   An IRA or a Keogh account is for tracking a variety of retirement accounts, including standard IRA, Roth IRA, Education IRA, SEP-IRA, SIMPLE-IRA, and Keogh plans.

**401(k) or 403(b)**   A 401(k) or 403(b) account is for tracking 401(k), 403(b), or 457 plans, in which you make regularly scheduled, pretax contributions toward investments for your retirement. This type of account can track performance, market value, and distribution among investment choices. If you (and your spouse) have more than one plan, you should set up a separate account for each.

**Single Mutual Fund**   As the name implies, a single mutual fund account is for tracking one mutual fund. It can track the share balance, market value, income, capital gains, and performance of the fund. It can't, however, track interest, cash balances, or miscellaneous income or expenses.

## Choosing the Right Type of Account
Sometimes it's not clear which kind of account is best for a specific type of investment. Table 10-1 offers some guidance.

Keep in mind that you can also track many types of investments in asset accounts. But Quicken's investment accounts enable you to better track and report on the income, capital gains, and performance of your investments.

This chapter concentrates on investment accounts tracked in standard brokerage, IRA or Keogh, 401(k) or 403(b), and single mutual fund accounts.

# The Importance of Portfolio Management
At this point, you may be wondering why you should bother including investment information in your Quicken data file. After all, you may already get quarterly (or even monthly) statements from your broker or investment firm. What you may not realize, however, is how you can benefit from keeping a close eye on your investments. Take a look at what portfolio management with Quicken can do for you.

## Centralizing Your Investment Records
Unless you have only one brokerage account for all your investments, you probably get multiple statements for the stocks, bonds, mutual funds, and other investments in your portfolio. No single statement can provide a complete picture of your portfolio's worth. Quicken can, however. By entering the transactions and values

on each statement within Quicken, you can see the details of your entire portfolio in one place.

### Knowing the Value of Your Portfolio on Any Day

Brokerage statements can tell you the value of your investments on the statement's ending date, but not what they're worth today—or what they were worth on July 1, 2004. Quicken, however, can tell you what your portfolio is worth on any day for which you have entered—or, better yet, downloaded—security prices, and it can estimate values for dates without exact pricing information. If you like to keep your portfolio's value up-to-date with the latest security prices, you can retrieve prices online. I show you how to take advantage of this feature in Chapter 11.

### Keeping Track of Performance History

Manually compiling a complete pricing and performance history for an investment is no small task, especially for periods spanning multiple statements. If you consistently enter investment information in your Quicken data file, however, preparing performance charts and reports is as easy as choosing a menu command or clicking a button.

### Calculating Capital Gains Quickly and Easily

Calculating the gain on the sale of an investment isn't always easy. Considerations include not only the purchase and selling prices, but commissions, fees, stock splits, and purchase lots. Quicken can take all the work out of calculating capital gains, even if you're just considering the sale and want to know what its impact will be. This is extremely helpful at tax time, as I discuss in Chapter 19.

## Creating Investing Center Accounts

Before you can begin tracking your investments with Quicken, you must set up the investment accounts you'll need. I provide basic information about setting up accounts in Chapter 3. In this section, I provide the specifics for creating Investing Center accounts. As you'll see on the following pages, when you create an investment account, Quicken not only prompts you for basic account information but also gathers information about your security holdings. When you're finished creating an account, it's all ready to use for entering transactions and creating reports.

Begin by choosing Investing | Investing Accounts | Add Account to display the Quicken Account Setup dialog shown next:

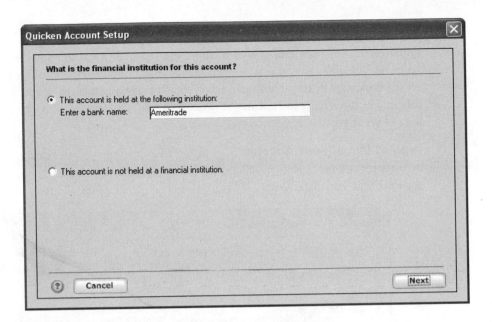

## Entering Financial Institution Information

Quicken's extensive online account access features make it possible to automate data entry for accounts held in participating financial institutions, including many brokerage firms. (I tell you more about how you can find a participating financial institution in Chapter 4.) To take advantage of these features, Quicken starts the account creation process by prompting you to enter the name of your brokerage firm. You have two options:

- **This Account Is Held At The Following Institution** enables you to specify the brokerage firm in which the account is held. Enter the name of the firm in the text box. As you type, Quicken displays a drop-down list that attempts to match the characters to those in its internal database of supported financial institutions. If your brokerage firm appears on the list, click it to select and enter it. Otherwise, finish typing and click Next. If you entered the name of a financial institution Quicken does not recognize, it displays a dialog that enables you to select one with a similar name or keep the one you entered.

- **This Account Is Not Held At A Financial Institution** tells Quicken that the account you are creating is not held at a financial institution—for example, an account to track the value of securities in a safe deposit box.

## Entering Other Basic Information

Quicken may display dialogs that prompt you for additional information about the account. The dialogs that appear and the order in which they appear vary depending on the brokerage firm you indicated when you first began creating the account. Although this makes it difficult to explain the process in a linear manner, I can give you a good idea of what you can expect to see.

**Type of Investment Account**   Quicken may prompt you to select a type of investment account, using a dialog like the one shown here. Select the appropriate account type and click Next.

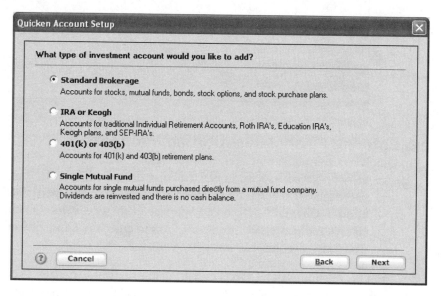

**Account Name**   Quicken may prompt you to enter a name for the account. This is the name that appears in the Quicken account list and reports; it can be the same as or different from the brokerage firm name.

**Setup Options**   If the account is held at a brokerage firm that supports Quicken's online features, a dialog with two setup options appears:

- **Online** enables you to complete the account setup process by going online and downloading information from your brokerage firm. This is the recommended method for completing account setup. To do this, you must already have a customer ID and PIN for accessing your account information via Quicken. If you select this option, click Next and continue following instructions in the section titled "Completing the Account Setup Online."

- **Manual** enables you to complete the account setup process by manually entering account information. You can use this option if you don't have a customer ID and PIN or are not interested in setting up the account for online features. You can always enable online features later; I explain how in Chapter 11. If you select this option, click Next and continue following instructions in the section titled "Completing the Account Setup Manually."

## Completing the Account Setup Online

If you indicated that you want to complete the account setup process online, Quicken displays a dialog like the one shown next, prompting you to enter your customer ID and password. Enter the information provided by your brokerage firm and click Next.

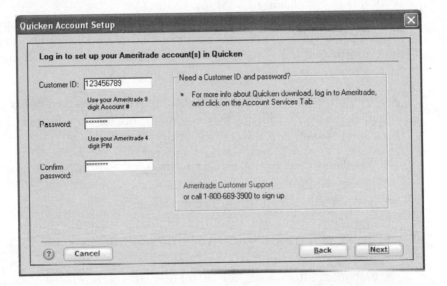

Quicken connects to the Internet to exchange some information with your brokerage firm. When it's finished, it may display a dialog prompting you to enter the account number for your account. Do so and click Next. Another dialog may prompt you for a Quicken account name; turn on the check box in the Add column, enter the name you want to use for the account in Quicken, and click Next. A confirmation dialog should appear, telling you that you are setting up your account. Click Done to dismiss it.

Quicken goes online again and downloads transactions, account balances, and updated quotes and news information for all securities in the account. Click Close in the One Step Update Summary dialog that appears. A Cash Balance Adjustment dialog may appear, offering you an opportunity to adjust the cash balance in the account as of a certain date. Make changes as necessary and click Done. When Quicken is finished, it displays the Summary tab for the account (see Figure 10-2 later in this chapter). You may have to review and accept all downloaded transactions for Quicken to display account balance and holding information; I explain how to do this in Chapter 11.

## Completing the Account Setup Manually

If the account is not held at a brokerage firm that supports Quicken's online features, or if you indicated that you want to set up the account manually, Quicken displays a dialog like the one shown earlier, prompting you to select an account type. Select the appropriate option and click Next.

What Quicken does next depends on the type of investment account you are creating. The following illustrations show some of the dialogs Quicken may display and information it may prompt you for. Click the Next or Done button in each dialog to move through the account creation process.

**Account Name and Other Basic Information**   Quicken displays a dialog that prompts you to enter a name for the account and, for certain types of accounts, other basic information, including the following:

- Tax-deferred status (for a single mutual fund account)
- IRA owner (for an IRA or Keogh account)
- Type of IRA (for an IRA or Keogh account)
- Statement ending date (for 401(k) or 403(b) account)
- Employer name and status (for 401(k) or 403(b) account)
- Account owner (for 401(k) or 403(b) account)
- Statement information (for 401(k) or 403(b) account)

**Loan Tracking**   For 401(k) or 403(b) accounts, Quicken displays a dialog that asks whether you want to track loans against the account. If you have any loans against the account, be sure to indicate how many you have. Quicken will then display one or more dialogs prompting you for information about your loan(s).

**Account Balances**   Quicken may display a dialog like the one shown next, prompting you for the account ending statement date and cash and money market balances.

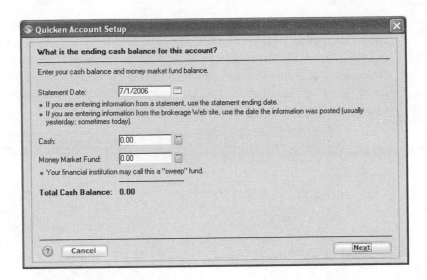

**Securities Held**   A dialog like the one shown next prompts you to enter security ticker symbols and names. Enter one security per line, using the TAB key to move from one box to the next. If you don't know the ticker symbol for a security, you can click the Ticker Symbol Lookup button to look it up online. If you need to enter more than ten securities in the dialog, click the Add More button to add more lines. Don't enter bonds in this dialog; you can add them later.

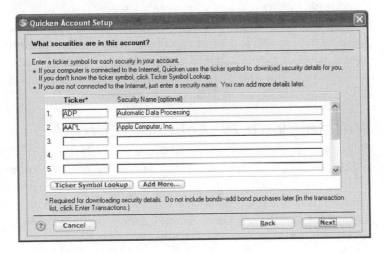

**Current Holdings**   After going online briefly to check the ticker symbols you entered, Quicken displays a dialog like the one shown next. Enter the total number of shares for each security. (You can enter information only for one security if you are creating a single mutual fund type account.) If the type of security—Stock, Mutual Fund, or Other—is incorrect, select the correct option. When you click Next, Quicken displays a dialog that confirms your entries.

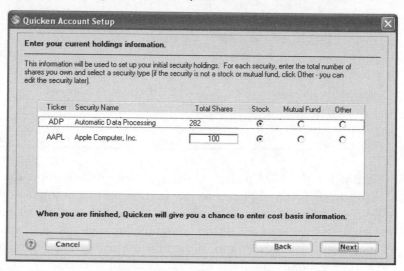

**Paycheck Setup**   When you create a 401(k) or 403(b) account, Quicken displays a dialog that asks whether you want to set up your paycheck. Quicken's Paycheck Setup feature is great for automatically entering 401(k) contributions and loan payments. I tell you more about this feature in Chapter 7.

When you click Done in the last dialog, Quicken displays the Summary tab for the account (see Figure 10-2 later in the chapter).

## Working with Placeholder Entries

Quicken automatically creates special transactions called *placeholder entries* in investment accounts when you enter—either manually or via online account access—current holding information for securities as part of the account setup process. These transactions make it possible to get up and running quickly with Quicken's investment tracking features, but they lack the information Quicken needs to create accurate investment reports.

Here's how it works. When you create an investment account, you tell Quicken what securities are in the account and how many shares of each security you currently own. But Quicken doesn't know when you bought those shares or what you paid for them. Without this historical cost information, Quicken can't calculate your return on investment or your capital gains (or losses) when you sell the security.

Although you can work with a Quicken investment account as soon as it's created, to get the most out of Quicken's investment tracking feature, you should replace the placeholder entries it creates with investment cost information. In this section, I explain how.

## Viewing Placeholder Entries for an Account

You can find an account's placeholder entries with the rest of the transactions for that account. In the Account Bar, click the name of the account to display its window. Then click the Transactions tab. Figure 10-1 shows an example of an investment account that includes two placeholder entries, one of which is selected.

| Date ▲ | Action | Security | Description | Inv Amt | Cash Amt | Cash Bal |
|---|---|---|---|---|---|---|
| 7/1/2006 | Withdraw | Opening Cas... | Opening Cash Balance | | | 0.00 |
| 7/1/2006 | Entry | AUTOMATIC DATA PROCE... | +282 shares | Enter Cost | | |
| | | | Placeholder Entry for holdings amount of 282 shares as of 7/1/2006 | | | |
| | | | | | | Edit Delete |
| 7/1/2006 | Entry | APPLE COMPUTER INC COM | +100 shares | Enter Cost | | |
| | | | Placeholder Entry for holdings amount of 100 shares as of 7/1/2006 | | | |
| 7/5/2006 | | | | | | |

Securities Value: $18,452.14   Cash Balance:   $0.00
Total Market Value:   $18,452.14

Quicken has entered Placeholder Entries for missing transactions
To get complete performance and tax information, enter the missing cost information for these securities.

**Figure 10-1 • Placeholder entries provide share balance information, but not investment cost.**

## Entering Cost Information for Placeholder Entries

To enter security cost information, begin by selecting the placeholder entry you want to work with. Click the Enter Cost link to display the Enter Missing Transactions dialog. Here's what it might look like with some cost information already entered:

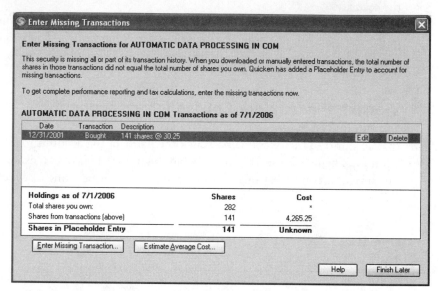

Two buttons at the bottom of the dialog offer methods for entering historical cost information for a security: Enter Missing Transaction and Estimate Average Cost.

**Enter Missing Transaction** This option enables you to enter the individual transactions that make up the total number of shares you hold. In most cases, these transactions would include purchases and stock dividends. This option gives you the most accurate records, but if you have many transactions, entering them all could be time-consuming. When you click this button, Quicken displays the Shares Bought dialog, which enables you to enter transaction details for a security acquisition. I explain how to enter transactions such as purchases and stock dividends later in this chapter in the section titled "Recording Investment Transactions."

**Estimate Average Cost** This option enables you to enter an average estimated cost for all of the shares you hold. Although this method is less accurate than entering individual transactions, it's a lot quicker and may be sufficient if you don't need detailed records of stock costs. You can always go back later and use the Enter Missing Transaction button to record more accurate acquisition details. When you click this button, a dialog like the one shown next appears. Enter either the total cost of the shares in the Cost box or the average price per share in the Price/Share box. Quicken makes any necessary calculations. Click OK to save the entry.

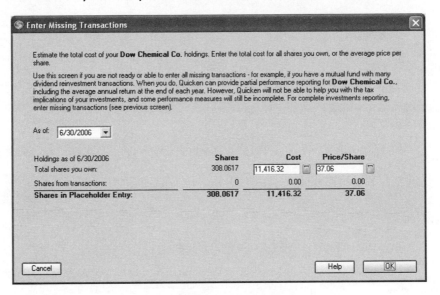

## Viewing Investment Accounts

To view an account's information, begin by clicking the name of the account in the Account Bar. Then click one of the three tabs at the top of the account window: Summary, Performance & Analysis, or Transactions. This part of the chapter takes a quick look at each of these views.

### Summary View

An investment account's Summary view (see Figure 10-2) displays a number of snapshots full of information about the account.

**Holdings**   The Holdings area lists each of the securities held in the account, along with information about each one. You can use various buttons and menus in the Holdings area to work with this information:

- **Options** offers commands to change the view preferences, include sold security lots in the display, get quotes online, or display a complete portfolio. I tell you more about these options throughout this chapter and in Chapter 11.
- **Show** enables you to display a variety of information about the securities, including Value (the default selection), Recent Performance, Historic Performance, or Tax Implications.

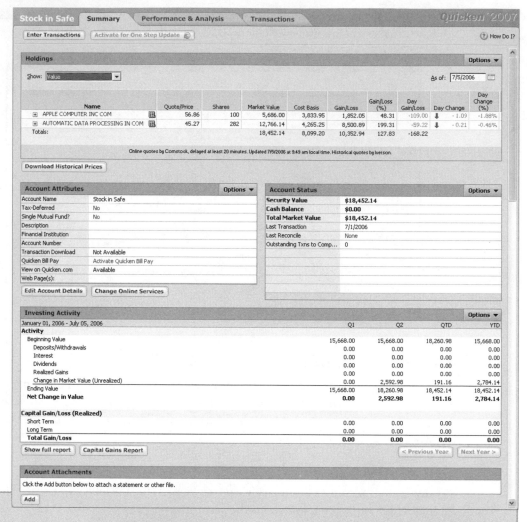

**Figure 10-2 •** Here's an example of Summary view for a standard brokerage account with holdings in two different securities.

- **As Of** enables you to see the account's status on a certain date. Change the date in this box and Quicken recalculates the information as of that date.
- **Download Historical Prices** displays the Get Historical Prices dialog, which you can use to get price history for securities you own or watch. I tell you more about downloading stock prices in Chapter 11.

**Account Attributes**   The Account Attributes area displays basic information about the account. Menus and buttons in this area enable you to modify this information:

- **Options** offers commands to create a new account, view or edit comments, set tax attributes, set or browse Web pages for the account, and store transaction fees.
- **Edit Account Details** displays the General Information tab of the Account Details dialog, which you can use to enter or edit basic information about the account, including its name, tax-deferred status, account number, and contact information.
- **Change Online Services** displays the Online Services tab of the Account Details dialog, which you can use to enable, disable, or change online services for the account. I tell you more about online services in Chapter 11.

**Account Status**   The Account Status area provides information about the status of the account, including the account's value and transactions and download dates. The Options menu in this area offers commands to reconcile the account or view all accounts in the Account List window.

**Investing Activity**   The Investing Activity area summarizes the activity in the account by quarter and provides capital gain (or loss) information. Menus and buttons in this area enable you to view various investment reports or your entire portfolio and to scroll through each year's recorded data. I discuss investing reports and Portfolio view in Chapter 12.

**Account Attachments**   The Account Attachments area enables you to attach statements or other files to the account. This makes these documents easy to find when you need them. I explain how to attach files in Chapter 5.

## Performance & Analysis View

An investment account's Performance & Analysis view (see Figure 10-3) displays three graphical representations of the account's performance. Each snapshot includes an Options menu and one or more buttons to view other graphs or reports.

**Account Value Vs. Cost Basis**   The Account Value Vs. Cost Basis graph uses bars to represent the account's value and a line to represent the cost of the securities. Ideally, the line should be below the tops of the bars, indicating that the securities cost less than they're worth.

**Asset Allocation**   The Asset Allocation chart displays the distribution of your investment among various types of investments, such as large cap stocks, small cap stocks, international stocks, bonds, and cash.

**Allocation By Security**   The Allocation By Security chart displays the distribution of your investment among the securities in the account.

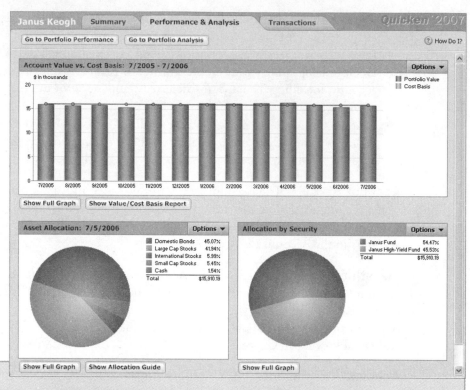

**Figure 10-3 • Here's an example of the Performance & Analysis tab for a brokerage account containing two mutual funds.**

## Transactions View

An investment account's Transaction List (see Figures 10-1 and 10-4) displays the transactions that have been entered for the account, along with the current cash balance. You can click a transaction to display Edit and Delete buttons for it; Edit enables you to modify the transaction, and Delete enables you to delete it. You can also use buttons at the top of the window to enter transactions and, if the account is set up for online account access, to download transactions from your financial institution. I tell you more about online access in Chapter 11.

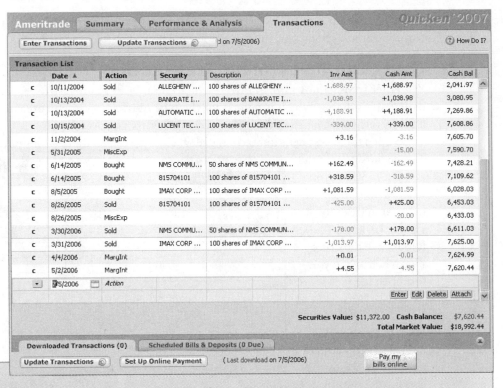

**Figure 10-4 •** **An investment account's Transaction List shows all of the transactions that have been entered into the account.**

## Recording Investment Transactions

The most important part of properly tracking investments is recording all investment transactions. This includes purchases, sales, dividends, and other activity affecting your portfolio's value.

Before you enter a transaction, you must have all of its details. In most cases, you can find the information you need on a confirmation form or receipt you receive from your broker or investment firm. The information varies depending on the transaction, but it generally should include the security name, transaction date, number of shares, price per share, and any commissions or fees.

In this section, I provide some information and advice for entering the most common transactions into investment accounts.

## Using the Investment Transaction Dialog

You enter transactions into an investment account with the investment transaction dialog. This dialog, which is named for the type of transaction you are entering, is a fill-in form with all the fields you need to enter transaction details.

To open the investment transaction dialog, click the Enter Transactions button in the Transactions tab for the account in which you want to enter the transaction (refer to Figures 10-1 and 10-4). It looks like the dialog shown here when you first open it.

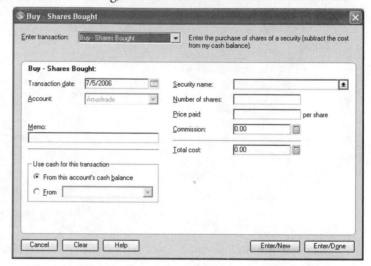

### Investment Actions

To use the investment transaction dialog, you must begin by choosing a transaction type (or *action*) from the Enter Transaction drop-down list. There are dozens of action types organized into two categories: Investment Transactions and Cash Transactions.

**Investment Transactions**   Investment transactions directly affect your security or investment account balances:

- **Buy - Shares Bought** (shown earlier) enables you to add shares to an investment account. The cost of the shares (plus any commissions) is deducted from the account's cash balance (or another account's cash balance).

- **Sell - Shares Sold** enables you to remove shares from an investment account. The proceeds from the sale (net of any commissions) is added to the account's cash balance (or another account's cash balance).

- **Div - Stock Dividend (Non-Cash)** enables you to add shares of a security paid as a dividend.

- **Reinvest - Income Reinvested** enables you to account for investment income (such as dividends) that are reinvested in the security. This is common with dividend reinvestment plans and mutual funds.

- **Inc - Income (Div, Int, Etc.)** enables you to record income from interest, dividends, and capital gain distributions.

- **Add - Shares Added** enables you to add shares to an investment account without an exchange of cash. You might use this option to add shares received as a gift.
- **Remove - Shares Removed** enables you to remove shares from an investment account without an exchange of cash. You might use this option to remove shares you have given to someone else as a gift.
- **Adjust Share Balance** enables you to create a placeholder entry transaction to make your share balance agree with your brokerage statement. You can enter cost information later, as discussed earlier in this chapter in the section titled "Working with Placeholder Entries."
- **Stock Split** enables you to record additional shares received as a result of a stock split.
- **Return Of Capital** enables you to record the return of part of your investment capital.
- **Miscellaneous Expense** enables you to record investment expenses other than commissions.
- **Margin Interest Expense** enables you to record the amount of interest paid as a result of purchasing securities on margin.
- **Bonds Bought** enables you to record the purchase of bonds.
- **Grant Employee Stock Option** enables you to record the receipt of an employee stock option.
- **Exercise Employee Stock Option** enables you to use an employee stock option to buy stock.
- **Reprice Employee Stock Option** enables you to change pricing information for stock options.
- **Bought ESPP Shares** enables you to buy shares in an employee stock purchase program.
- **Sold ESPP Shares** enables you to sell shares purchased through an employee stock purchase program.
- **Short Sale** enables you to record a short sale of a security.
- **Cover Short Sale** enables you to record the purchase of stock to cover a short sale.
- **Corporate Name Change** enables you to record the change of the name of a company for which you own stock. This preserves the old name information; simply editing the security name in the Edit Security dialog does not.
- **Corporate Securities Spin-Off** enables you to record securities obtained through a spin-off of a smaller company from one of the companies in which you own securities.
- **Corporate Acquisition (Stock For Stock)** enables you to record securities obtained in exchange for other securities you own, normally as a result of a corporate acquisition.
- **Cash Transferred Into Account** enables you to record the transfer of cash into the investment account.

- **Cash Transferred Out Of Account** enables you to record the transfer of cash out of the investment account.
- **Shares Transferred Between Accounts** enables you to move shares from one Quicken investment account to another.
- **Reminder Transaction** enables you to enter an investment reminder that will appear each time you start Quicken. You may find this option useful if you want to conduct a transaction at a future date and are worried that you may forget to do it.

**Cash Transactions**    Cash transactions affect the cash balance in an investment account. These actions make it possible to track an investment account's cash balance without using a linked cash account.

- **Write Check** enables you to record a check written from an investment account.
- **Deposit** enables you to record a cash deposit to an investment account.
- **Withdraw** enables you to record the withdrawal of cash from an investment account.
- **Online Payment** enables you to record an online payment from the investment account's cash balance. To use this feature, the account must be enabled for Online Payment or Quicken Bill Pay. I discuss Online Payment in Chapter 6.
- **Other Cash Transaction** enables you to record any type of transaction that affects the investment account's cash balance.

## Completing the Transaction

Investment transaction dialogs and forms are generally self-explanatory and easy to use. Simply fill out the fields in the form and click one of the Enter buttons:

- **Enter/New** enters the current transaction and redisplays the investment transaction dialog so you can enter another transaction.
- **Enter/Done** enters the current transaction and dismisses the investment transaction dialog.

# Entering Common Transactions

Although page count limitations make it impossible to review every kind of investment transaction in this book, here's a look at a few common transactions. They should give you a solid understanding of how the investment transaction dialogs work so you can enter your transactions.

## Buying Shares

A security purchase normally involves the exchange of cash for security shares. In some cases, you may already own shares of the security or have it listed on your

Watch List. In other cases, the security may not already exist in your Quicken data file, so you'll need to set up the security when you make the purchase.

Start by choosing Buy - Shares Bought in the investment transaction dialog to display the Buy - Shares Bought dialog, shown earlier. Enter information about the shares you have purchased:

- **Transaction Date** is the date of the transaction.
- **Account** is the name of the account in which the transaction should be recorded. You cannot change the option chosen from this drop-down list if you are entering a transaction from within the account's Transaction View window; if it's wrong, click Cancel, open the correct account register, and start over.
- **Security Name** is the name of the security. If you enter the name of a security that doesn't already exist in Quicken, the Add Security To Quicken dialog, which I discuss later in the section titled "Adding a New Security," appears so you can add the security to Quicken.
- **Number Of Shares** is the number of shares purchased.
- **Price Paid** is the per share price.
- **Commission** is the amount of commissions you paid to your brokerage or investment firm.
- **Total Cost** is calculated by Quicken. If you're recording the purchase of a fractional number of shares and this amount is off by a penny or two, use the Commission field to adjust the Total Cost. The net effect of tiny adjustments like this is negligible.
- **Use Cash For This Transaction** enables you to specify an account from which the Total Cost should be deducted. By default, this option is set to use cash from the same investment account.

When you're finished entering information about the transaction, click one of the Enter buttons. The transaction appears in the Transactions tab for the account.

If you want to add security shares to an account without an exchange of cash, use the Add - Shares Added action. Its form asks for most of the same information but does not affect any cash balances.

## Selling

A security sale also involves the exchange of cash for security shares. Normally, you dispose of shares you already own, but in some instances, you may sell shares you don't own. This is called *selling short,* and it is a risky investment technique sometimes used by experienced investors. (To record short sale transactions, use the Short Sale or Cover Short Sale action.)

To sell shares, choose Sell - Shares Sold in the investment transaction dialog to display the Sell - Shares Sold dialog. Enter information about the shares you have sold:

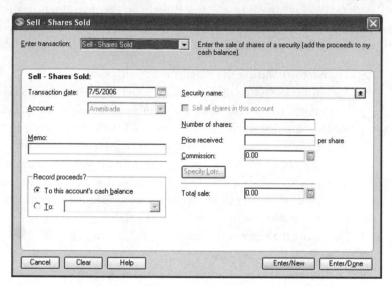

- **Transaction Date** is the date of the transaction.
- **Account** is the name of the account in which the transaction should be recorded. You cannot change the option chosen from this drop-down list if you are entering a transaction from within the account's Transaction View window; if it's wrong, click Cancel, open the correct account register, and start over.
- **Security Name** is the name of the security. You can choose an option from the drop-down list.
- **Sell All Shares In This Account** tells Quicken to automatically enter the total number of shares you own in the Number Of Shares box.
- **Number Of Shares** is the number of shares sold.
- **Price Received** is the per share price.
- **Commission** is the amount of commissions you paid to your brokerage or investment firm.
- **Specify Lots** enables you to specify which shares you are selling when you have multiple purchase lots. You can use this option for additional control over capital gains. For example, if you want to take advantage of long-term capital gains tax breaks, you could sell shares that have been in your possession for more than 12 months. If you want to record a loss, you could sell shares that cost more than the selling price. Obviously, your options will vary depending on the lots, their

acquisition prices, and your selling price. If you select this option, click the Specify Lots button to display a dialog like the one shown here. (This dialog may include an Enter Missing Transactions button if placeholder entries exist for the security.) Use the dialog to enter shares in each lot you are selling or select one of the Auto Select options and click OK. If you don't use the Specify Lots button to select lots, Quicken automatically sells the oldest shares (First In, First Out method).

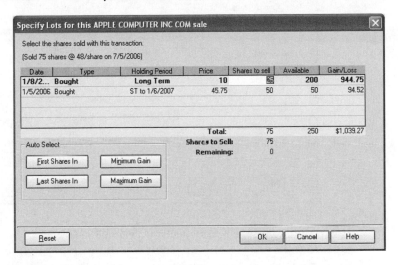

- **Total Sale** is calculated by Quicken by multiplying the per share price by the number of shares and deducting the commission. This is the proceeds from the sale.
- **Record Proceeds?** enables you to specify an account to which the net proceeds should be added.

When you click one of the Enter buttons, Quicken records the transaction.

## Dividend Payments and Other Income

Many investments pay dividends, interest, or other income in cash. (That's why they're so attractive to an investor!) Recording this activity in the appropriate account register enables Quicken to calculate performance accurately, while keeping account balances up-to-date.

Keep in mind that many mutual funds are set up to reinvest income, rather than pay it in cash. Do not use the steps in this section to record a reinvestment of income. Instead, use the Reinvest Income action to enter transaction information.

To record dividend or interest income, choose Inc - Income (Div, Int, Etc.) from the drop-down list in the investment transaction dialog to display the

Inc - Income dialog, shown next. Enter information about a cash payment on an investment:

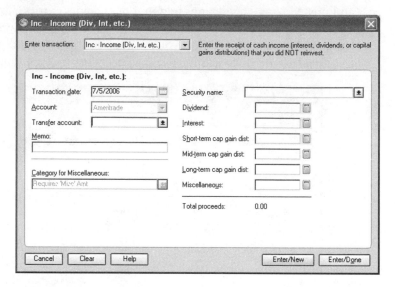

- **Transaction Date** is the date of the transaction.
- **Account** is the name of the account in which the transaction should be recorded. You cannot change the option chosen from this drop-down list if you are entering a transaction from within the account's Transaction View window; if it's wrong, click Cancel, open the correct account register, and start over.
- **Transfer Account** enables you to specify an account into which the income is deposited. Leave this blank if the cash is deposited directly into the investment account.
- **Memo** enables you to enter a brief note about the transaction.
- **Security Name** is the name of the security. You can choose an option from the drop-down list. If the transaction isn't related to a specific security—for example, interest paid on a cash balance in a brokerage account—you can leave this field blank.
- **Dividend, Interest, Short-Term Cap Gain Dist, Mid-Term Cap Gain Dist, Long-Term Cap Gain Dist**, and **Miscellaneous** are fields for entering various types of income. In most cases, you'll use only one or two of these boxes.
- **Total Proceeds** is the total of all income amounts, calculated by Quicken.
- **Category For Miscellaneous** is the category you want to use to record miscellaneous income. This field is available only if you enter a value in the Miscellaneous field.

When you click one of the Enter buttons to record the transaction, it appears in the Transactions tab for the account.

## Other Transactions

Other transactions are just as easy to enter as purchases, sales, and income. Simply choose the appropriate option from the drop-down list in the investment transaction dialog and enter the transaction information in the form that appears. If you have the transaction confirmation or brokerage statement in front of you when you enter the transaction, you have all the information you need to record it.

If you need additional guidance while entering a transaction, click the Help button in the Record Transaction dialog to learn more about the options that must be entered.

# Entering Transactions in the Transaction List

Quicken 2007 now enables you to enter investment transactions directly into the Transaction List window. This feature makes entering transactions quicker for experienced Quicken users.

To begin, scroll down to the blank line at the bottom of the Transaction List. Click the line to activate it and enter the transaction date in the Date column. Then choose an action from the pop-up menu in the Action column and press TAB. The two lines for the transactions fill in with italicized reminders of the information you should enter into each field, as shown next. Fill in the fields with transaction details and click Enter.

| ▾ | 7/5/2006 | Bought | Security ▾ | Shares | Price | Comm... | Amount | | | | |
|---|---|---|---|---|---|---|---|---|---|---|---|
| | | | Memo | | | | | Enter | Edit | Delete | Attach |

# Editing Transactions

Quicken offers two ways to edit transactions: with the investment transaction dialog and in the Transaction List.

## Editing Transactions with the Investment Transaction Dialog

In the Transactions tab for the account (refer to Figure 10-4), select the transaction you want to edit and click the Edit button beneath it. Edit the transaction in the dialog that appears and click Enter/Done to save your changes.

## Editing Transactions in the Transaction List

In the Transactions tab for the account (refer to Figure 10-4), select the transaction you want to edit. Click in the field you want to modify and make the desired change. When you're finished, click Enter.

Keep in mind that to use this technique successfully, you must have a complete understanding of the components of the investment transaction you're trying to change. If you're not sure how to edit the transaction directly as discussed here, I highly recommend that you use the investment transaction dialog to make changes to transactions.

## Adjusting Balances

Occasionally, you may need to adjust the cash balance or number of shares in an investment account or update the balance in a 401(k) account. Here's how.

### Updating an Account's Cash Balance

You can adjust the balance in an investment account with a cash balance. In the Account Bar, click the name of the account you want to adjust. Then choose Investing | Investing Activities | Update Cash Balance. The Update Cash Balance

dialog, which is shown here, appears. (Note that this dialog will not display downloaded cash balance information if the account is not enabled for online access.) Enter the date and the correct balance in the text boxes and click Done. Quicken creates an adjusting entry.

### Updating an Account's Share Balance

You can adjust the number of shares in an investment account. In the Account Bar, click the name of the account you want to adjust. Then choose Investing | Investing Activities | Update Share Balance to display the Adjust Share Balance dialog, shown here. (This is the same as choosing the Adjust Share Balance action in the investment transaction

dialog.) Enter the adjustment date, security, and correct number of shares in the dialog. When you click Enter/ Done, Quicken creates a placeholder entry that adjusts the share balance. I tell you more about placeholder entries in the section titled "Working with Placeholder Entries" earlier in this chapter.

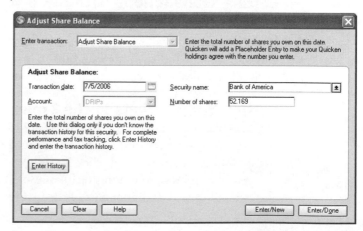

## Updating 401(k) or 403(b) Balances

401(k) or 403(b) account balances change every time you make a contribution through your paycheck. To adjust the balance, click the name of the 401(k) or 403(b) account in the Account Bar to open it. If necessary, click its Summary tab. Click the Update 401(k) Holdings button on the button bar. Then follow the prompts in the Update 401(k)/403(b) Account dialog that appear to update the information. When you're finished, click Done to record the adjustment.

Remember, if you set up your paycheck as discussed in Chapter 7, Quicken will automatically record contributions to your 401(k) or 403(b) account every payday.

# Working with Securities

This chapter talks a lot about securities. But exactly what are they?

In Quicken, a *security* is a single investment that has a share price. Examples of securities include stock shares for a specific company, bonds for a specific company, and mutual funds offered by investment firms. Normally, when you own a security, you own a certain number of shares. To calculate the total value of the security, you'd multiply the number of shares you own by the most recent per share price.

This part of the chapter explains how you can use the Security List, Add Security To Quicken, Edit Security Details, Security Type List, Investing Goal List, and Security Detail View windows to view, add, and work with securities.

## Security List

The Security List window (see Figure 10-5) simply lists the securities in Quicken's data file. You can use this window to add, edit, delete, or hide securities, including *watch list securities*—securities you don't own but want to monitor. To open this window, choose Investing | Security List or press CTRL-Y.

### Using the Button Bar

Button bar options enable you to work with the list's items:

- **New** enables you to create a new security.
- **Edit** enables you to modify the currently selected security.
- **Delete** removes the currently selected security from your Quicken data file. You cannot delete a security that has been used in a transaction.
- **Choose Market Indexes** enables you to add common market indexes, such as the Dow Jones Industrial Average and the S&P 500 Index, to the Security List. This enables you to download quotes for these indexes when you download security prices as discussed in Chapter 11.
- **Hide (x)** removes the currently selected security from all lists without actually deleting it. To view a hidden security, choose View Hidden Securities from the

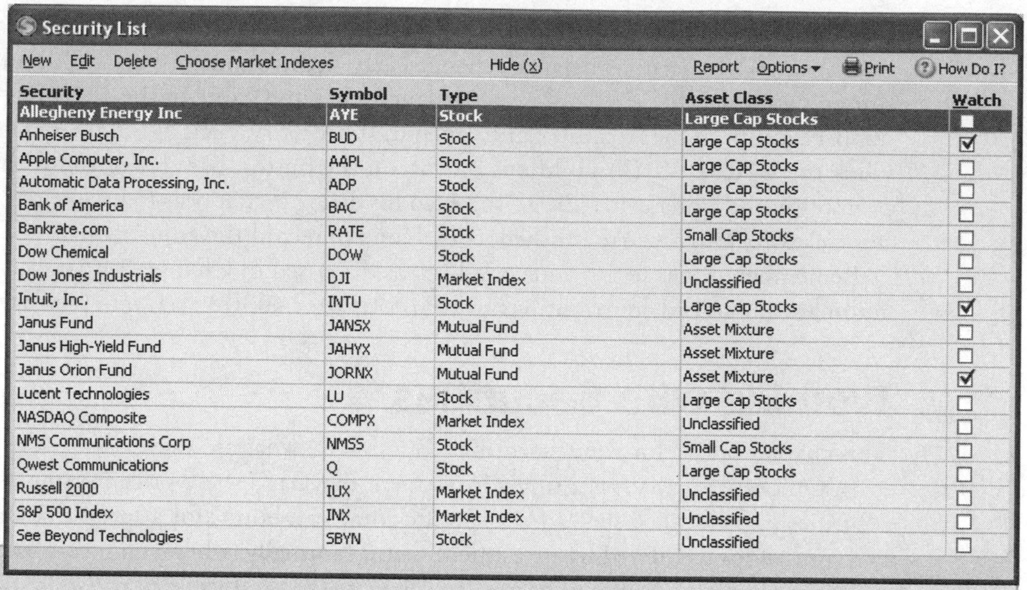

Security List

New Edit Delete Choose Market Indexes Hide (x) Report Options Print How Do I?

| Security | Symbol | Type | Asset Class | Watch |
|---|---|---|---|---|
| Allegheny Energy Inc | AYE | Stock | Large Cap Stocks | ☐ |
| Anheiser Busch | BUD | Stock | Large Cap Stocks | ☑ |
| Apple Computer, Inc. | AAPL | Stock | Large Cap Stocks | ☐ |
| Automatic Data Processing, Inc. | ADP | Stock | Large Cap Stocks | ☐ |
| Bank of America | BAC | Stock | Large Cap Stocks | ☐ |
| Bankrate.com | RATE | Stock | Small Cap Stocks | ☐ |
| Dow Chemical | DOW | Stock | Large Cap Stocks | ☐ |
| Dow Jones Industrials | DJI | Market Index | Unclassified | ☐ |
| Intuit, Inc. | INTU | Stock | Large Cap Stocks | ☑ |
| Janus Fund | JANSX | Mutual Fund | Asset Mixture | ☐ |
| Janus High-Yield Fund | JAHYX | Mutual Fund | Asset Mixture | ☐ |
| Janus Orion Fund | JORNX | Mutual Fund | Asset Mixture | ☑ |
| Lucent Technologies | LU | Stock | Large Cap Stocks | ☐ |
| NASDAQ Composite | COMPX | Market Index | Unclassified | ☐ |
| NMS Communications Corp | NMSS | Stock | Small Cap Stocks | ☐ |
| Qwest Communications | Q | Stock | Large Cap Stocks | ☐ |
| Russell 2000 | IUX | Market Index | Unclassified | ☐ |
| S&P 500 Index | INX | Market Index | Unclassified | ☐ |
| See Beyond Technologies | SBYN | Stock | Unclassified | ☐ |

**Figure 10-5 • Use the Security List window to view, add, edit, or remove securities that you own or watch.**

Options menu on the button bar. To unhide a security, view and select it, and then click the Hide button on the button bar.

- **Report** displays a Security Report for the selected security.
- **Options** displays a menu that enables you to toggle the view of hidden securities.
- **Print** prints a list of securities.
- **How Do I?** displays the Quicken Help window with additional information about using the Security List window.

## Adding a New Security

To add a new security to your Quicken data file—either as a holding or a Watch List item—click the New button in the button bar of the Security List window (refer to Figure 10-5). The Add Security To Quicken dialog appears, displaying screens that prompt you for information about a security.

As shown next, Quicken starts by prompting you for the security's ticker symbol and name. Although the ticker symbol is required if you want to use Quicken's online features to download security values (as I discuss in Chapter 11), entering the correct ticker symbol when you have an Internet connection can automate much of the security setup process. If you don't know the ticker symbol and have an Internet connection, you can click the Look Up button to connect to the Internet and look up the symbol.

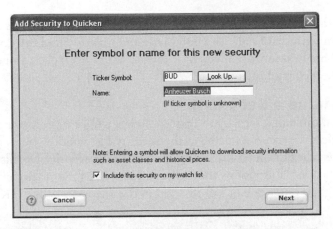

The first screen also offers a check box labeled Include This Security On My Watch List. Turning on this check box tells Quicken to track the security, even if you don't own any shares.

When you click Next, Quicken connects to the Internet to obtain information about the security based on its ticker symbol. If it finds the ticker symbol, it displays the information it has downloaded in the Add Security To Quicken dialog, as shown here. Click Done to add the security to the Security List.

If Quicken can't find information about the security on the Internet, it displays a dialog like the one shown here, enabling you to correct the ticker symbol or add the security manually. If you made an error when entering the ticker symbol, you can enter the correct symbol in the Ticker Symbol text box and click Next to try looking it up on the Internet again.

If you select the Add Manually option, select a security type—Bond, CD, Emp. Stock Option, ESPP, Market Index, Mutual Fund, Other, Stock, or U.S. Savings Bond—and click Next. Another dialog appears, prompting you for additional information about the security, such as its asset class (for a stock), asset class mixture (for a mutual fund), and bond type and maturity and call dates (for a bond). Enter whatever information you have for the security and click Done to add the security to the Security List.

## Editing a Security

You can edit a security to correct or clarify information you previously entered for it. Select the security's name in the Security List window (refer to Figure 10-5) and click the Edit button on the button bar. The Edit Security Details dialog appears; the following illustrations show what it looks like for a stock (left) and for a mutual fund (right). Enter or edit information in the dialog and click OK to save your changes.

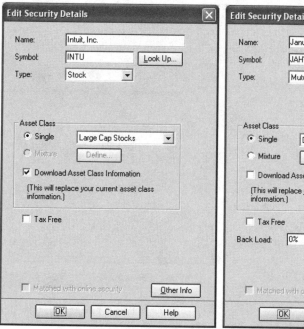

## Security Type List

The Security Type List, which is shown here, displays a list of security types. To display this list, choose Investing | Security Type List.

You can use button bar buttons to modify the list:

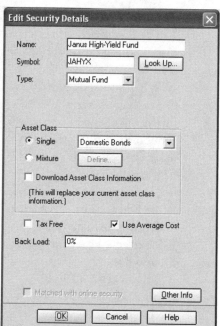

- **New** enables you to create a new security type. Clicking this button displays the Set Up Security Type dialog, which you can use to enter a name for the security type.

- **Edit** enables you to change the name of the currently selected security type.
- **Delete** enables you to remove the currently selected security type from the list.
- **Print** prints the Security Type List.
- **How Do I?** displays the Quicken Help window with instructions for working with the Security Type List.

Adding or removing security types does not affect the drop-down list in the Add Security To Quicken dialog, which lists standard security types.

## Investing Goal List

As illustrated next, the Investing Goal List window displays a list of all investment goals. You may find investment goals useful for organizing your investments based on what you expect them to do for you. You can assign a goal to a security by clicking the Other Info button in the Edit Security Details dialog for the security.

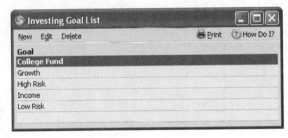

To show the Investing Goal List window, choose Investing | Investing Goal List. You can use button bar buttons to modify the list if desired:

- **New** enables you to create a new investment goal. Clicking this button displays the Set Up Investing Goal dialog, which you can use to enter a name for the goal.
- **Edit** enables you to change the name of the currently selected investment goal.
- **Delete** enables you to remove the currently selected investment goal from the list.
- **Print** prints the Investing Goal List.
- **How Do I?** displays the Quicken Help window with instructions for working with the Investing Goal List.

## Security Detail View

The Security Detail View window (see Figure 10-6) provides a wealth of information about a specific security, including value and performance information, transactions, and price or market value history. You can use this window to enter transactions, update prices, edit a security, or open the Portfolio or account register windows.

To open the Security Detail View window, choose Investing | Security Detail View or click the name or ticker symbol for a security in an account's Summary tab (refer to Figure 10-2). To switch from one security to another, use the drop-down list in the upper-left corner of the window.

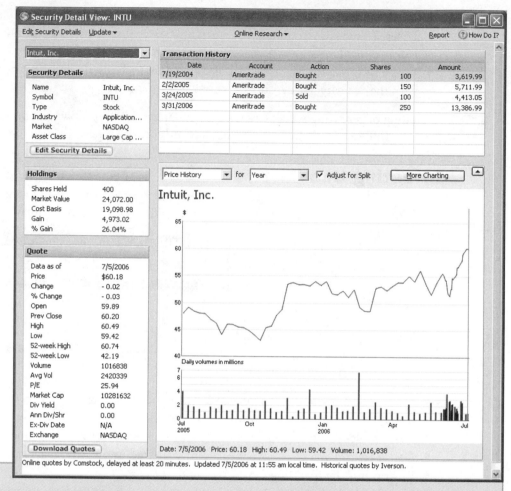

**Figure 10-6 • The Security Detail View window displays all kinds of information about a security you own or watch.**

## Button Bar Buttons

The button bar buttons in the Security Detail View window enable you to edit and update security information:

- **Edit Security Details** displays the Edit Security Details dialog, which I discuss earlier in this chapter in the section titled "Editing a Security."
- **Update** is a menu full of options for using an Internet connection to update current and historical price information for securities you own or watch. These options can be a real timesaver, as I discuss in Chapter 11.

- **Online Research** is a menu full of options for using an Internet connection to research a security. I discuss these options in Chapters 11 and 12.
- **Report** displays a Security Report, which summarizes all activity for the security.
- **How Do I?** displays the Quicken Help window with additional information about using the Security Detail View window and its options.

## Snapshots

The Security Detail View window is organized into snapshots of information about the currently selected security:

- **Security Details** displays general information about the security. You can click the Edit Security Details button to edit the information in this snapshot.
- **Holdings** provides information about your holdings of the security.
- **Quote** provides information from the most recently downloaded quote. (I explain how to download quotes in Chapter 11.)
- **Transaction History** lists all transactions involving that security.
- **Price History** or **Market Value Chart** displays either the price history or the market value for the security as a chart. You can specify which chart to display by choosing an option from the pop-up menu at the top-left corner of the chart. Clicking the More Charting button displays the Multiple Security Charting window, which I discuss in Chapter 11.

# Using Transaction Download and Research Tools

## In This Chapter:

- *Setting up Transaction Download*
- *Downloading transactions*
- *Comparing downloaded transactions to register transactions*
- *Reviewing account balance details*
- *Comparing downloaded holdings to recorded holdings*
- *Downloading stock quotes and news headlines*
- *Exporting your portfolio to Quicken.com*
- *Using online research tools*

Quicken Personal Finance Software offers three separate features for tracking investments online:

- **Transaction Download** enables you to download transactions and balances for your investment accounts. This helps automate the entry of investment transactions and keeps your Quicken records in sync with your brokerage firm's records.
- **Quotes, News, And Alerts Download** enables you to obtain current and historical quotes, asset allocation information, and news headlines about individual stocks, mutual funds, and other investments. This automates the tracking of market values and provides valuable information you can use to make better investment decisions. This feature can also alert you to important information about securities you own or watch.

- **Portfolio Export** enables you to put a copy of your investment portfolio on the Quicken.com Web site, where you can track its value from any computer connected to the Internet—without Quicken.

In this chapter, I tell you about each of these features and explain how they can help you save time and stay informed about your investments. I also tell you about some of the features on Quicken.com that can help you research investments.

The instructions in this chapter assume that you have already configured your computer for an Internet connection. If you have not done so, do it now. Chapter 4 provides the information you need to set up and test an Internet connection for Quicken. This chapter also assumes that you understand the topics and procedures discussed in Chapters 3 and 7, and it builds on many of the basic concepts discussed in those chapters.

# Transaction Download

Transaction Download enables you to download transactions, balance details, and holdings information directly from the financial institutions with which you maintain investment accounts. Each transaction can then be entered into your Quicken investment account with the click of a mouse button. You can also review downloaded account balance details and compare downloaded holdings information to the information recorded in your portfolio.

Many brokerage and investment firms support Transaction Download. You can

| Account Attributes | Options ▼ |
| --- | --- |
| Account Name | Ameritrade |
| Tax-Deferred | No |
| Single Mutual Fund? | No |
| Description | Online brokerage account |
| Financial Institution | Ameritrade |
| Account Number | 873012298 |
| Transaction Download | Available |
| Quicken Bill Pay | Activate Quicken Bill Pay |
| View on Quicken.com | Activated |
| Web Page(s): | www.ameritrade.com |
| Edit Account Details | Change Online Services |

learn whether your brokerage firm supports this feature by checking the Account Attributes area in the Overview tab for the account. Click the name of the brokerage account in the Account Bar and, if necessary, click the Summary tab. As shown here, the word *Available* appears beside Transaction Download in the Account Attributes area if your brokerage firm supports this feature.

## Setting Up Transaction Download

To use Transaction Download, you must first configure the appropriate Quicken accounts. This requires that you enter additional information for the account(s) you want to track, including the account number, your user ID, and a password.

### Applying for Transaction Download

Before you can use Transaction Download, you may need to apply for it. I tell you how at the end of Chapter 4. Normally, all it takes is a phone call, although many brokerage and investment firms allow you to apply online. Another way to apply or get application information is to click the link that appears in the Quicken Account Setup login dialog.

Not all brokerage firms have an application process. Some brokers simply provide Quicken access information on their Web sites. To access your account with Quicken, you simply configure Quicken with your account number and the same password you use to access your account via the Web. There's no need to wait for an application to be processed and additional information to be sent. Check your brokerage firm's Web site to see if these instructions apply to you.

If you do need to apply for Quicken access to your account, it may take up to a week for the application to be processed. You'll know that you're ready to go online when you get a letter with setup information. The setup information consists of the following:

**Customer ID**    This may be your account number, Social Security number, or some other ID the brokerage firm provides.

**Password or PIN**    You'll have to enter your password or PIN into Quicken when you download transactions. If your brokerage firm sends this information, they may send it separately for additional security.

## Setting Up the Account

Setting up Transaction Download is similar to setting up Online Account Services for a bank account or credit card account. In the Account Bar, click the name of the account you want to set up Transaction Download for. Then click the Activate For One Step Update button on the button bar of the Summary or Transactions tab to display the Quicken Account Setup login window, shown next. Enter your customer ID and password in the appropriate boxes and click Next.

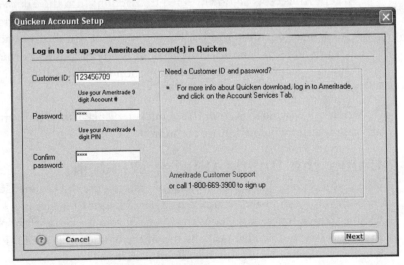

Quicken may connect to the Internet to get more information about your brokerage firm and account. After a moment, it may display a dialog asking for your account number. Enter the number—normally without dashes or spaces—and click Next. Another dialog confirms that you are setting up your account in Quicken.

## Completing Your First Download

When you click Done, Quicken connects to the Internet and downloads transactions

from the past 30 days or more. A New Data Download dialog like the one shown here may appear. It offers two options for handling downloaded transactions:

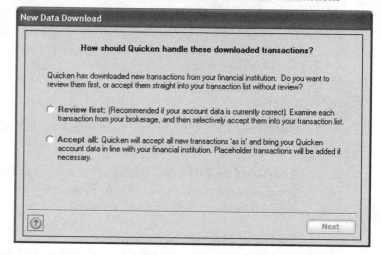

- **Review First** enables you to review each downloaded transaction before accepting it into the Transaction List. When you select this option and click Next, the downloaded transactions appear in the bottom half of the Transaction List, as shown in Figure 11-2 a little later in this chapter. I explain how to review and accept downloaded transactions later in this chapter, in the section titled "Reviewing Transactions."

- **Accept All** accepts all downloaded transactions into the Transaction List without giving you a chance to review them. When you select this option and click Next, Quicken automatically adds all new transactions to the Transaction List for that account and synchronizes your account balances so the information in your Quicken account matches the information for your account at your brokerage or investment firm.

When the download is complete, Quicken displays the Transactions tab of the account register window for the account.

## Using the Online Center Window

When you enable Transaction Download, you can use the Online Center to download account information and compare it to data in your Quicken file. Choose Investing | Online Center. If necessary, choose the name of your brokerage firm from the Financial Institution drop-down list near the top of the window. Figure 11-1 shows what this window looks like for an Ameritrade investment account.

The button bar offers a number of options you can use for working with the Online Center window:

- **Delete** deletes a selected item.
- **Payees** displays the Online Payee List, which I discuss in detail in Chapter 6. (This option is available only if the account can be enabled for online payments.)
- **Repeating** displays the Repeating Online tab of the Scheduled Transaction List window, which I also discuss in Chapter 6. (This option is available only if the account can be enabled for online payments.)
- **Contact Info** displays the Contact Information dialog for the currently selected financial institution. You can use the information in the dialog to contact the bank or credit card company by phone, Web site, or e-mail.
- **Password Vault** gives you access to Quicken's Password Vault feature, which I discuss in Chapter 7. (This option may appear only if you have enabled Online Account Services for accounts at more than one financial institution and have not yet set up the Password Vault feature.)
- **Renaming Rules** displays the Renaming Rules For Downloaded Transactions dialog, which I discuss in Chapter 6.
- **Trade** connects to the Internet and displays your brokerage firm's home page in an Internet window. You can then log in to make online trades.
- **Print** prints the transactions listed in the window.
- **Options** displays a menu of commands for working with the current window.

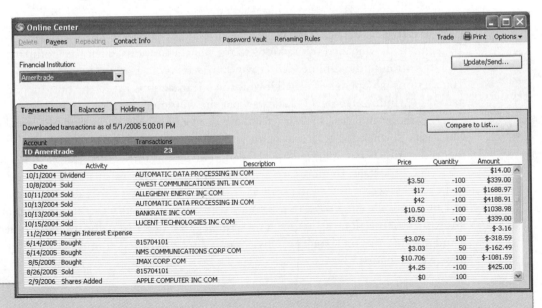

**Figure 11-1 •** Use the Online Center window to download investment transactions and check balances and holdings.

## Downloading Transactions

To download transactions, you must connect to your financial institution. Make sure the brokerage firm is selected in the Online Center window (see Figure 11-1), and then click the Update/Send button. The Online Update For This Account window appears:

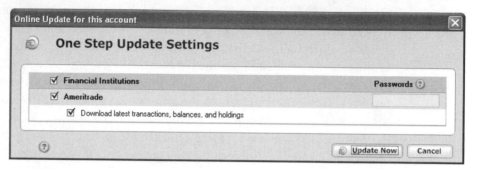

Enter your password and click Update Now. Wait while Quicken connects to your financial institution. A Quicken One Step Update Status window appears during the connection.

When Quicken is finished exchanging information, a One Step Update Summary window appears to summarize the activity that took place while you waited. Click Close. If you display the Online Center window again, you'll see the transactions you downloaded in the bottom half of the window's Transactions tab, as shown in Figure 11-1.

## Reviewing Transactions

To compare downloaded transactions to register transactions, click the Compare To List button in the Online Center window (see Figure 11-1). The account's Transactions tab opens with the Downloaded Transactions list in the bottom half of its window. Figure 11-2 shows what the window might look like.

The window in Figure 11-2 looks and works a lot like the window that appears when you accept downloaded bank and credit card account transactions into Quicken. Consult the section titled "Comparing Downloaded Transactions to Register Transactions" in Chapter 6 for details. In most cases, you'll simply select a new or matched transaction and click the Accept button to accept it or to enter and accept it. Because Quicken will automatically enter most transaction information, using this method to enter an investment transaction can be much faster than entering it manually. If Quicken needs additional information about the transaction, it displays a dialog prompting you for the information it doesn't have.

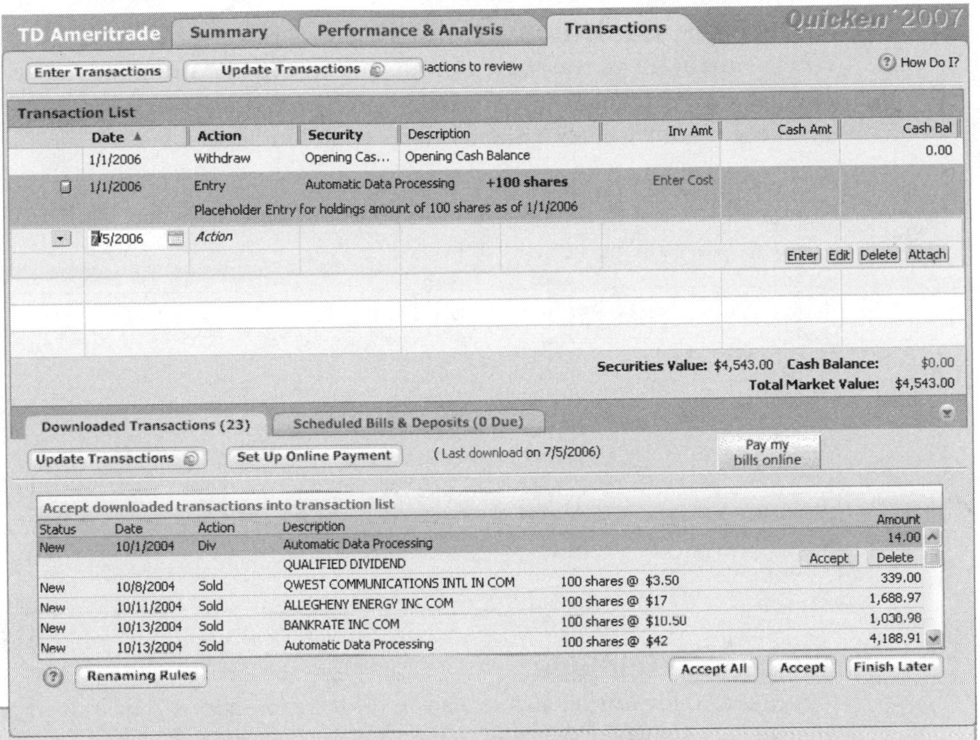

**Figure 11-2 •** Use this window to compare downloaded transactions to those in your Transactions List.

When you're finished working with transactions, click the Done button in the bottom half of the window. If you haven't accepted all transactions, you'll see a Finish Later button instead. Remember that downloaded transactions that have not been accepted may not be entered in your investment register. Thus, your register and portfolio balances may be misstated until you accept all downloaded transactions.

## Adjusting the Cash Balance

If the cash balance in your Quicken account doesn't match the cash balance at your brokerage firm, a Cash Balance Adjustment dialog appears, prompting you to enter the correct balance. I explain how to use this dialog to adjust cash balances in Chapter 10.

## Reviewing Balances

When you download transactions from your financial institution, you also receive detailed account balance information. To review this information, click the Balances tab in the Online Center window. Here's what it might look like:

| Transactions | **Balances** | Holdings |
| --- | --- | --- |

Ameritrade ▼

Balances at Ameritrade as of 6/14/2006 5:00:00 AM

| Balance | Amount | Description |
| --- | --- | --- |
| Cash | $124.95 | Available Cash |
| Margin | $0.00 | Margin Balance |
| Short | $0.00 | Market Value of Securities Held Short |
| Buying Power | $124.95 | Buying Power |
| EquityBalance | $592.45 | EquityBalance |
| AvailableFunds | $124.95 | AvailableFunds |
| TotalMaintReq | $375.00 | TotalMaintReq |
| TotalMarginableLong | $467.50 | TotalMarginableLong |
| MargAcctEquityBal | $592.45 | MargAcctEquityBal |
| EquityPercent | 100% | EquityPercent |
| LiquidationValue | $592.45 | LiquidationValue |
| SMAValue | $6014.55 | SMAValue |
| MoneyMarketBalance | $0.00 | MoneyMarketBalance |
| HouseMaintenanceCall | $0.00 | HouseMaintenanceCall |
| RegulationTCall | $0.00 | RegulationTCall |

## Reviewing Holdings

Your financial institution also sends you information about your individual holdings. You can review this information in the Online Center window and compare it to the information in your portfolio.

To review holdings, click the Holdings tab in the Online Center window. Here's the Holdings tab for the same account shown in the previous illustration:

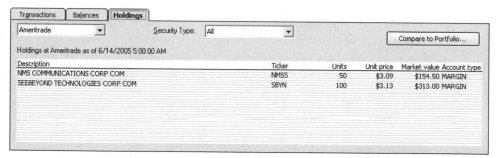

To compare downloaded holdings to holdings in your portfolio, click the Compare To Portfolio button. What happens next depends on whether the holdings information matches.

**When Holdings Match** When downloaded holdings match the holdings recorded in your portfolio, Quicken displays a dialog telling you that your Quicken account and your brokerage holdings are in agreement. Click OK to dismiss it and continue working with Quicken.

**When Holdings Don't Match**     When downloaded holdings don't match the holdings recorded in your portfolio, the Adjust Holdings Amount dialog, which is shown next, appears. It lists the discrepancies and offers to create placeholder entries to adjust your Quicken account balance. Turn on the check boxes beside each security you want Quicken to adjust and click Accept. Quicken creates the placeholder entries in your Transaction List. Chapter 10 explains how you can enter share price information for placeholder entries.

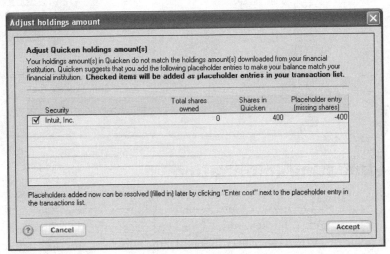

## Downloading Quotes, Headlines, and Alerts

Quicken enables you to download up-to-date stock quotes, news headlines, and alerts for the securities in your portfolio and on your Watch List. You set it up once and then update the information as often as desired. You can even download historical price information so you can review price trends for a security that only recently caught your eye.

Because the quote and headline download feature is built into Quicken, it doesn't rely on your brokerage firm for information. That means you can download quotes, headlines, and alerts even if your brokerage firm doesn't offer Transaction Download. All you need is an Internet connection.

### Setting Up the Download

Before you can get quotes online, you must set up the feature. Choose Edit | Preferences | Customize Online Updates. If necessary, click the Quotes tab in the Customize Online Updates dialog that appears, as shown next. Click to place a green check mark to the left of each security or index you want to download quotes, headlines, and alerts for. Then click OK.

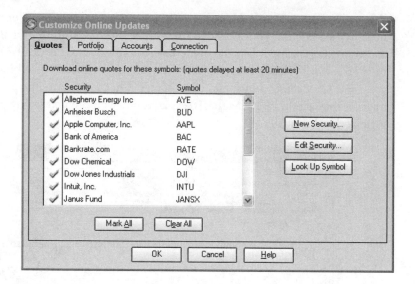

## Updating Information

You can update quotes and information any time you like. Choose Investing | Online Activities | Download Quotes. Quicken connects to the Internet and begins downloading information. While it works, a Quicken One Step Update Status dialog shows you what's going on. When the dialog disappears, the information is updated.

You can also update quotes using One Step Update, which I discuss in Chapter 7. It enables you to download quotes when you perform other tasks online.

## Viewing Downloaded Quotes and Headlines

You can view quotes and news headlines for a security in two places:

- **Security Detail View** window (see Figure 11-3), which I introduce in Chapter 10, displays quote information for individual securities. To open this window, choose Investing | Security Detail View.

- **Portfolio** window (see Figure 11-4), which I discuss in greater detail in Chapter 12, displays quotes and news headlines for all securities you own or watch. To display this window, choose Investing | Portfolio or press CTRL-U.

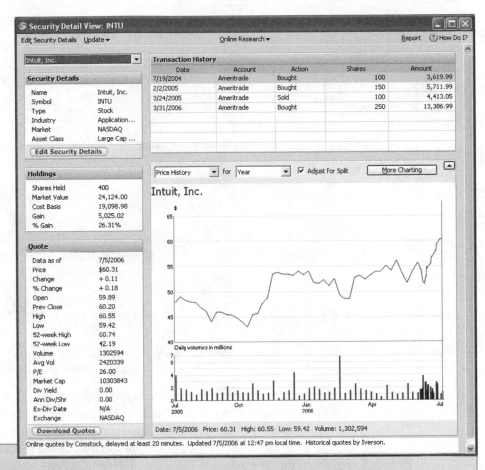

**Figure 11-3 • The Security Detail View window shows information about a security.**

## Viewing Stock Quotes

The Security Detail View window (see Figure 11-3) offers the most detailed quote information. You can find detailed information in the left side of the window. If you have been faithfully downloading quotes for your securities (or you have downloaded historical quotes, as discussed in the section titled "Downloading Historical Quote Information" later in this chapter), a chart of the price history appears in the body of the window. You can use the drop-down list in the top-left corner of the window to switch from one security to another.

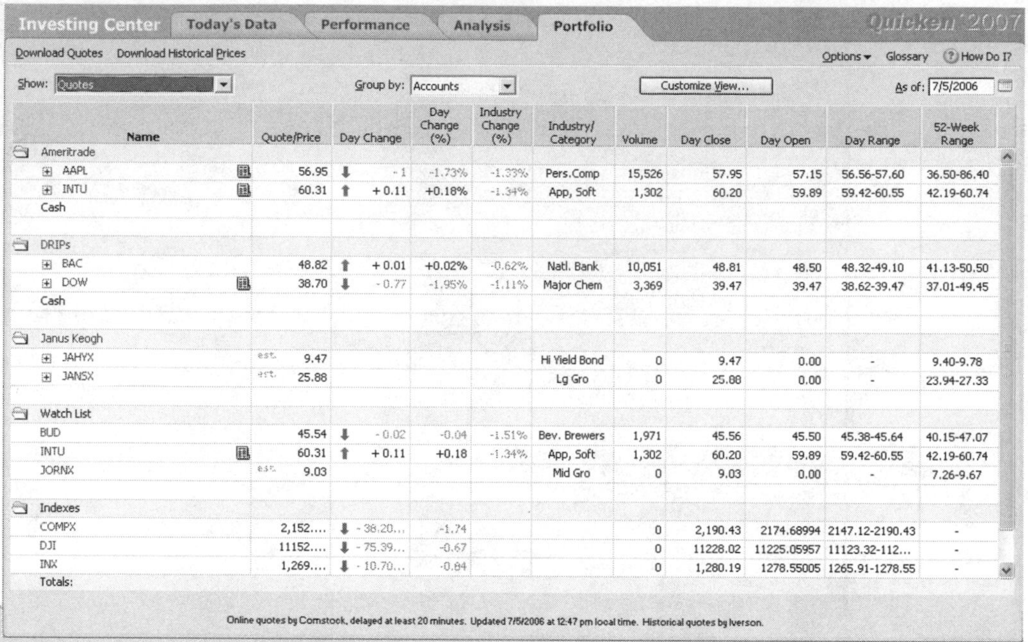


| Name | Quote/Price | Day Change | Day Change (%) | Industry Change (%) | Industry/ Category | Volume | Day Close | Day Open | Day Range | 52-Week Range |
|---|---|---|---|---|---|---|---|---|---|---|
| Ameritrade | | | | | | | | | | |
| AAPL | 56.95 | -1 | -1.73% | -1.33% | Pers.Comp | 15,526 | 57.95 | 57.15 | 56.56-57.60 | 36.50-86.40 |
| INTU | 60.31 | +0.11 | +0.18% | -1.34% | App, Soft | 1,302 | 60.20 | 59.89 | 59.42-60.55 | 42.19-60.74 |
| Cash | | | | | | | | | | |
| DRIPs | | | | | | | | | | |
| BAC | 48.82 | +0.01 | +0.02% | -0.62% | Natl. Bank | 10,051 | 48.81 | 48.50 | 48.32-49.10 | 41.13-50.50 |
| DOW | 38.70 | -0.77 | -1.95% | -1.11% | Major Chem | 3,369 | 39.47 | 39.47 | 38.62-39.47 | 37.01-49.45 |
| Cash | | | | | | | | | | |
| Janus Keogh | | | | | | | | | | |
| JAHYX | est. 9.47 | | | | Hi Yield Bond | 0 | 9.47 | 0.00 | - | 9.40-9.78 |
| JANSX | est. 25.88 | | | | Lg Gro | 0 | 25.88 | 0.00 | - | 23.94-27.33 |
| Watch List | | | | | | | | | | |
| BUD | 45.54 | -0.02 | -0.04 | -1.51% | Bev. Brewers | 1,971 | 45.56 | 45.50 | 45.38-45.64 | 40.15-47.07 |
| INTU | 60.31 | +0.11 | +0.18 | -1.34% | App, Soft | 1,302 | 60.20 | 59.89 | 59.42-60.55 | 42.19-60.74 |
| JORNX | est. 9.03 | | | | Mid Gro | 0 | 9.03 | 0.00 | - | 7.26-9.67 |
| Indexes | | | | | | | | | | |
| COMPX | 2,152.... | -38.20... | -1.74 | | | 0 | 2,190.43 | 2174.68994 | 2147.12-2190.43 | - |
| DJI | 11152.... | -75.39... | -0.67 | | | 0 | 11228.02 | 11225.05957 | 11123.32-112... | - |
| INX | 1,269.... | -10.70... | -0.84 | | | 0 | 1,280.19 | 1278.55005 | 1265.91-1278.55 | - |
| Totals: | | | | | | | | | | |



**Figure 11-4 • You can view quotes with the Quotes view in the Portfolio window.**

In the Portfolio window, downloaded quotes appear beside the security name or ticker symbol. Stock quotes are delayed 20 minutes or more during the trading day. Quotes for mutual funds are updated once a day by around 6:00 P.M. eastern time. Prior to that, you'll see the previous day's prices with *est* beside the price (short for *estimate*), indicating that the price has not been updated since the previous trading day. Choose Quotes from the Show drop-down list near the top of the window to see more quote details, as shown in Figure 11-4.

You can also view stock quotes by selecting the security in the Security Detail View window and choosing Edit Price History from the Update menu on the button bar. This displays the Price History window, which displays all of the recorded stock quotes for the security, as shown here. You can use buttons in this window's button bar to add, modify, or remove price information, as discussed in Chapter 12.

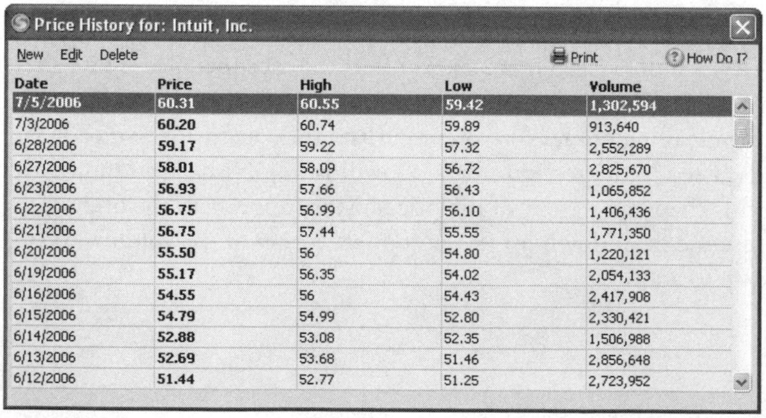


| Date | Price | High | Low | Volume |
|---|---|---|---|---|
| 7/5/2006 | 60.31 | 60.55 | 59.42 | 1,302,594 |
| 7/3/2006 | 60.20 | 60.74 | 59.89 | 913,640 |
| 6/28/2006 | 59.17 | 59.22 | 57.32 | 2,552,289 |
| 6/27/2006 | 58.01 | 58.09 | 56.72 | 2,825,670 |
| 6/23/2006 | 56.93 | 57.66 | 56.43 | 1,065,852 |
| 6/22/2006 | 56.75 | 56.99 | 56.10 | 1,406,436 |
| 6/21/2006 | 56.75 | 57.44 | 55.55 | 1,771,350 |
| 6/20/2006 | 55.50 | 56 | 54.80 | 1,220,121 |
| 6/19/2006 | 55.17 | 56.35 | 54.02 | 2,054,133 |
| 6/16/2006 | 54.55 | 56 | 54.43 | 2,417,908 |
| 6/15/2006 | 54.79 | 54.99 | 52.80 | 2,330,421 |
| 6/14/2006 | 52.88 | 53.08 | 52.35 | 1,506,988 |
| 6/13/2006 | 52.69 | 53.68 | 51.46 | 2,856,648 |
| 6/12/2006 | 51.44 | 52.77 | 51.25 | 2,723,952 |

## Viewing News Headlines

To view news headlines for a security, point to the newspaper icon that appears beside the ticker symbol for any security with news stories in the Portfolio window (refer to Figure 11-4). As shown next, a window pops up with links to recent news stories. When you click a link, Quicken uses its internal Web browser to connect to the Internet and display the news story.

# Downloading Historical Quote Information

Quicken enables you to download up to five years of historical quotes for any security you own or watch. Choose Investing | Online Activities | Download Historical Prices or click the Download Historical Prices button in the Portfolio View window's button bar. Quicken displays the Get Historical Prices dialog, as shown here:

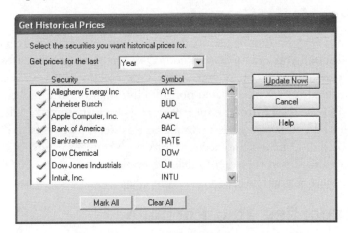

Choose a time period from the drop-down list at the top of the dialog. Your choices are Month, Year, Two Years, and Five Years. Make sure check marks appear beside all securities for which you want to get historical quotes. Then click the Update Now button. Quicken connects to the Internet and retrieves the information you requested. When it's done, it displays the One Step Update Summary window.

Click Close to dismiss the window. You can review the quotes that were downloaded in the Security Detail View window (refer to Figure 11-3).

## Downloading Asset Class Information

For each security you own or watch, you can include asset class information. This enables you to create accurate asset allocation reports and graphs. I explain how to enter asset class information manually in Chapter 10 and how you can use this information to diversify your portfolio to meet your investment goals in Chapter 12.

The trouble is, most mutual funds consist of many investments in a variety of asset classes. Manually looking up and entering this information is time-consuming and tedious. Fortunately, Quicken can download this information from the Internet and enter it for you.

Choose Investing | Online Activities | Download Asset Classes. Quicken displays the Download Security Asset Classes dialog, which looks and works very much like the Get Historical Prices dialog shown in the previous illustration. Make sure check marks appear beside all securities for which you want to download asset class information, and then click the Update Now button. Quicken connects to the Internet and retrieves the information you requested. When it's done, it displays the One Step Update Summary window. Click Close to dismiss the window. The asset classes are automatically entered for each security.

# Portfolio Export

The Portfolio Export feature enables you to track your portfolio's value on the Web. Although you can do this without Quicken by manually customizing and updating the default portfolio Web page at Quicken.com, it's a lot easier to have Quicken automatically send updated portfolio information to Quicken.com for you.

To use the Portfolio Export feature, you must register Quicken. (Quicken will remind you if you haven't completed this step.) The registration process sets up a private Quicken.com account for you to store your portfolio data. This same account is used for other Quicken.com features, including WebEntry and Bank Account Update, which I discuss in Chapter 6.

## Exporting Your Portfolio

In Quicken, choose Investing | Online Activities | Update Portfolio on Quicken.com. The Portfolio tab of the Customize Online Updates dialog appears, as shown next. If this dialog does not appear, you can display it by choosing Edit | Preferences | Customize Online Updates and then clicking the Portfolio tab in the dialog.

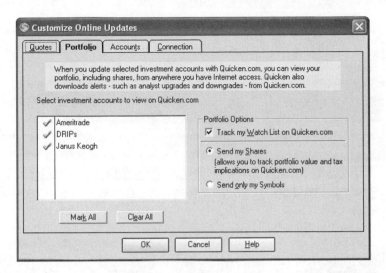

Click to place green check marks beside each account that you want to track on the Web. If you also want to track Watch List items on the Web, turn on the Track My Watch List On Quicken.com check box. Finally, select one of the upload options:

- **Send My Shares** exports the ticker symbols and the number of shares of each security you own for your portfolio. This enables you to track both prices and portfolio values.
- **Send Only My Symbols** exports just the ticker symbols for your portfolio. This enables you to track prices but not portfolio values.

When you're finished, click OK. Then click the Update button on the toolbar to display the One Step Update dialog. Make sure the check mark beside Update My Portfolio On Quicken.com is turned on, and then click Update Now. (I tell you more about using One Step Update in Chapter 7.)

A Quicken.com login dialog may appear. Use it to log in to Quicken.com and click the Update Now button. Quicken establishes a connection to the Internet and displays a status dialog while it updates information. When it's finished, it displays the One Step Update Summary window. You can click Close to dismiss it.

## Checking Your Portfolio on the Web

Once your portfolio has been updated, you can view it at any time from any computer with Web access. (Figure 11-5 shows an example.) Use a Web browser to navigate to http://www.quicken.com/investments/portfolio. (Or simply click the Investment Center - Portfolio link on the Quicken.com home page, http://www.quicken.com.) If prompted to log in, do so. The contents of your portfolio appear on the page.

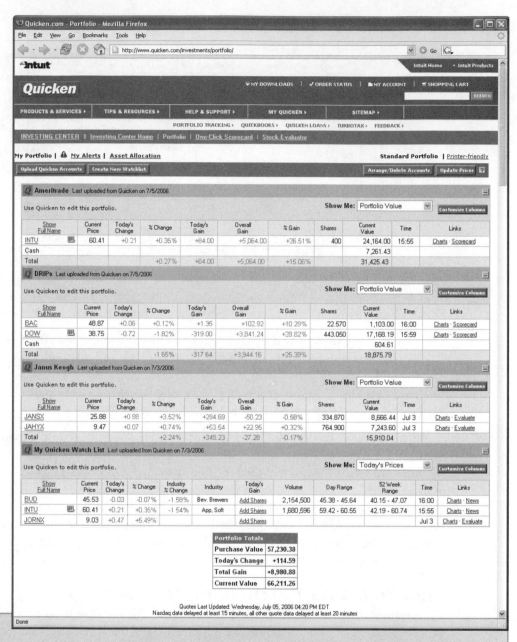

**Figure 11-5 •** Once your portfolio has been exported, you can view it on the Web from any computer—provided that you have logged into your private Quicken.com account.

# Using Online Research Tools

Quicken offers access to a number of research tools on Quicken.com. You can use these tools to find and learn about securities before you invest.

In this part of the chapter, I tell you a little about Quicken's online research tools so you can explore them on your own. I think you'll find them valuable resources for making wise investment decisions.

## Quote Lookup

The Quote Lookup feature enables you to look up stock ticker symbols. These symbols are required to use Quicken's Quotes, News, And Alerts Download feature as well as other features that obtain information about securities on the Web.

Choose Investing | Online Research Tools | Quote Lookup. Quicken displays the Quicken Ticker Search page in a Web browser window. Select a security type option, and then enter all or part of the security name in the edit box and click Search. Quicken displays all of the securities it found that matched the criteria you entered. You can note the ticker symbol or click underlined links in the Links column to get more information about the security.

## Multiple Security Charting

Quicken displays a chart of a security's prices in the Security Detail View window. This is a great way to see trends in a single security's values. But what if you want to see multiple charts? Or to see a popular index? That's where Multiple Security Charting comes in.

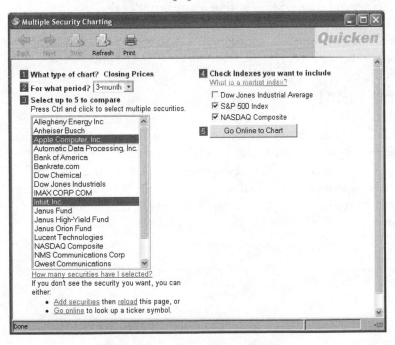

To begin, choose Investing | Online Research Tools | Multiple Security Charting. The Multiple Security Charting window, which is shown here, appears. Use it to set options and select securities for the charts you want to create. To select more than one security, hold down CTRL while clicking each security name. When you click the Go Online To Chart button, Quicken connects you to the Internet and displays a Yahoo! Finance page with the charts you requested.

## One-Click Scorecard

One-Click Scorecard instantly prepares reports that help you evaluate a security before you invest, using a variety of well-known analysis techniques and strategies.

To get started, choose Investing | Online Research Tools | One-Click Scorecard. Quicken connects to the Internet and displays the Getting Started page of the One-Click Scorecard on Quicken.com. Enter the ticker symbol for the security you want to evaluate and click Go. After a moment, Quicken displays the One-Click Scorecard recommended strategy report page for the security.

The report that appears automatically displays the results based on the recommended investing strategy for that type of investment. For example, the recommended strategy for a stock with strong growth and value characteristics is Robert Hagstrom's *The Warren Buffet Way.* You can change the strategy by choosing a different one from the drop-down list; just be aware that the strategy you choose may not be the best one for evaluating that security. Read through the report to learn more about the analysis. Pay close attention to the Next Steps area at the end of the report if you think you want to invest in the company.

## Security Evaluator

The Security Evaluator instantly prepares a detailed, six-report analysis of stocks that includes historical trends and industry comparisons. This information can help you determine whether a security's performance may meet your investing goals.

To get started, choose Investing | Online Research Tools | Evaluator. Quicken connects to the Internet and displays the Getting Started page of the Security Evaluator on Quicken.com. Enter the ticker symbol for the security you want to evaluate and click Go. After a moment, Quicken displays a detailed analysis page full of information for the security.

## Mutual Fund Finder

Quicken's Mutual Fund Finder enables you to search for mutual funds based on criteria you provide. To get started, choose Online | Online Research Tools | Mutual Fund Finder. Quicken connects to the Internet and displays the Screener Settings page of the Mutual Fund Screener on Yahoo! Finance. Click a link for one of the Preset Screens or enter search criteria and click the Find Funds button at the bottom of the page. The results appear in an Internet window. You can click a link in the More Info column of the list to learn more about a listed fund.

# Evaluating Your Position

## In This Chapter:

- *The Investing Center*
- *Investment alerts*
- *Investment analysis and reports*
- *The Portfolio window*
- *Asset Allocation Guide*
- *Portfolio Rebalancer*
- *Portfolio Analyzer*
- *Buy/Sell Preview*
- *Capital Gains Estimator*

A s you enter transactions into Quicken Personal Finance Software—whether manually or automatically via transaction download—Quicken builds a portrait of your investment portfolio and performance. If you're serious about investing, you can use this information to evaluate your investing position and fine-tune your portfolio to diversify and maximize returns.

Quicken's Investing Center offers a wide range of tools—including reports, graphs, alerts, analysis tools, and reference materials—that you can use to evaluate and strengthen your investment positions. This chapter takes a closer look at the features that can make you a better investor.

## Chapter 12

# The Investing Center

The Investing Center window should be your first stop for evaluating your investment position. Each of its four tabs includes snapshots with calculated information and links to more information on Quicken and Quicken.com features. Because the Investing Center always displays the most recent information it has, its windows are most useful immediately after downloading quotes, news, headlines, and alerts, as discussed in Chapter 11.

To open the Investing Center window, click the Investing Center button in the Account Bar. One of the Investing Center's four tabs appears. Click the tab for the window you want to view.

In this part of the chapter, I take you on a guided tour of Quicken's Investing Center window so you know exactly how you can use it to monitor your investments.

## Today's Data

The Today's Data tab, which is shown in Figure 12-1, offers snapshots with general information about your investment accounts and investments, as of the current date.

### Investment Alerts

Investment alerts are downloaded automatically with quotes and news headlines, as discussed in Chapter 11. They appear in the Investment Alerts area near the top of the window. You can click a link within an alert to view additional information either in your Quicken data file or on the Web.

There are ten investment alerts:

- **Price And Volume** consists of three alerts. Price alerts notify you when a security's price rises above or falls below values you specify. Volume alerts notify you when the sales volume of a security exceeds a value you specify. News alerts notify you when news stories are available for a security. You must set options for these alerts on Quicken.com.
- **Download Quotes Reminder** reminds you to download quotes from Quicken.com.
- **Maturity Date Reminder** reminds you when a CD or bond reaches its maturity date.
- **Stocks Ratings And Analysis** notifies you when ratings and analysis information becomes available for stocks you track.
- **Mutual Funds Ratings And Analysis** notifies you when ratings and analysis information becomes available for mutual funds you track.
- **Tax Implications On Sale** notifies you of your tax implications when you sell a security.

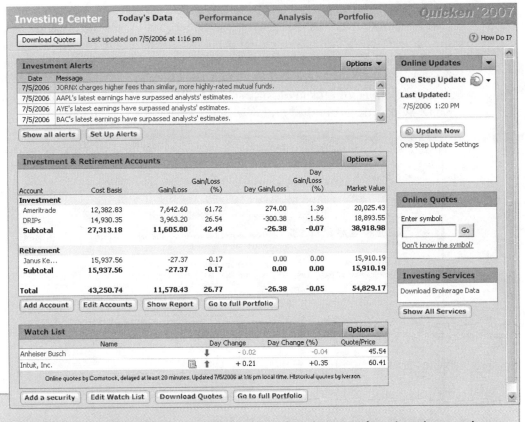

**Figure 12-1 • The Today's Data tab displays information about your investment accounts as of the current date.**

- **Cap. Gains For The Year** notifies you if you exceed your capital gains limit for the year.
- **Tax Efficient Investments** provides you with information about investments that are more tax efficient than those you already have.
- **Mutual Fund Distributions** provides you with information about mutual fund distributions.
- **Securities Holding Period** provides you with information about holding periods for securities you own.

The alerts I find most useful are Price And Volume, Maturity Date Reminder, Stocks Ratings And Analysis, and Cap. Gains For The Year. These alerts give me timely information that I need to know without subjecting me to information overload.

**Setting Up Alerts**   To set up investment alerts, click the Set Up Alerts button in the Investment Alerts area. Quicken displays the Setup tab of the Alerts Center window, shown next, which I discuss in greater detail in Chapter 9. On the left side of the window, click the name of an alert you want to set, and then set options for the alert in the right side of the window. (You must set some alerts, such as the Price And Volume alert, on Quicken.com.) You can disable an alert by removing the check mark beside its name. When you are finished making changes, click OK to save them.

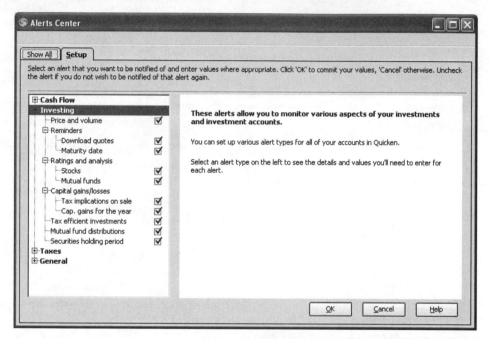

**Deleting Alerts**   To remove an alert from the Investment Alerts area, select the alert and choose Delete from the Options button on the Investment Alerts area button bar. Select an option in the Delete Alerts dialog that appears (shown here) and click OK. You can also use the Delete All command on the Options menu to delete all alerts in the Investment Alerts area.

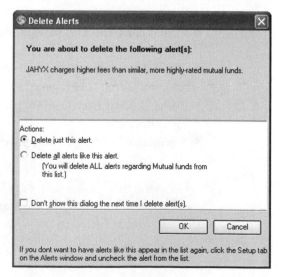

## Investment & Retirement Accounts

The Investment & Retirement Accounts snapshot lists all of your investment accounts, including those for retirement, along with their current market values. (Market value is determined by the most recently downloaded or entered security values.) You can click the name of an account to view its register.

## Watch List

The Watch List snapshot lists all of the securities on your Watch List, along with the most recently entered or downloaded quotes. Click a security's symbol to open the Security Detail View window for it. Two icons beside a ticker symbol display alerts and news headlines for a security when you point to them. The Options menu on the Watch List snapshot's button bar offers commands for working with securities and your Watch List.

## Online Updates

Online Updates offers links and buttons to update your investing information by downloading transactions and quotes and updating your Quicken.com portfolio. It also provides the date and time of your most recent online update. I discuss these features in Chapter 11.

## Online Quotes

Online Quotes offers a quick and easy way to request a quote from within Quicken. Enter the ticker symbol in the box and click Go. Quicken connects to the Internet and displays the security's quote information from Quicken.com in an Internet window.

## Investing Services

The Investing Services area offers links that you can use to learn more about various Quicken services for investors.

# Performance

The Performance tab of the Investing Center (see Figure 12-2) displays graphs and tables of information about your investment performance as well as links to tools within Quicken and on Quicken.com for helping you achieve your investing goals. You can customize many of the snapshots that appear in the Performance tab using commands on the snapshot's Options menu. You can further customize the Performance tab window by selecting one of the Show Accounts options: All, Investment, Retirement, or Multiple Accounts.

## Growth Of $10,000

The Growth Of $10,000 chart illustrates how an investment of $10,000 in your portfolio has grown over the past year. You can turn on check boxes beside popular investment indexes to compare your investment performance to one or more indexes, as shown in Figure 12-2.

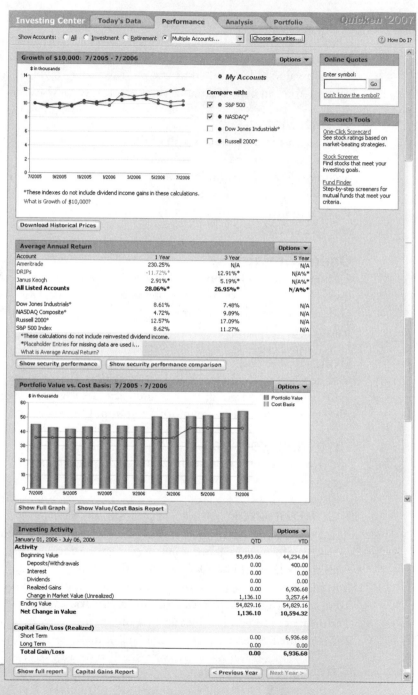

**Figure 12-2 • The Performance tab of the Investing Center shows you, at a glance, how your investments are doing.**

## Average Annual Return

The Average Annual Return displays the one-year, three-year, and five-year return on each of your investment accounts.

## Portfolio Value Vs. Cost Basis

The Portfolio Value Vs. Cost Basis graph uses a line graph and a bar graph to illustrate your portfolio's cost basis—what you've invested—and its market value. Ideally, you want the tops of the beige bars to appear above the line with the orange points.

## Investing Activity

Investing Activity provides quarter-to-date (QTD) and year-to-date (YTD) summaries of your investment values and transactions as well as capital gains information.

## Online Quotes

Online Quotes offers a quick and easy way to request a quote from within Quicken. Enter the ticker symbol in the box and click Go. Quicken connects to the Internet and displays the security's quote information from Quicken.com in an Internet window.

## Research Tools

Research Tools offers links to some of the online research tools I discuss in Chapter 11. Click a link to access that tool.

# Analysis

The Analysis tab of the Investing Center (see Figure 12-3) displays a number of customizable graphs of your investment data, along with a few snapshots with links to other features. Each of the graphs that appear in the Analysis tab can be customized using commands on the graph's Options menu. Buttons beneath each chart enable you to go to a full-sized graph in a report window or view a related report. You can further customize the Analysis tab window by selecting one of the Show Accounts options: All, Investment, Retirement, or Multiple Accounts.

## Asset Allocation

Asset Allocation, which I cover in detail later in this chapter, refers to the way your investment dollars are distributed among different types of investments. It's a measure of how well your portfolio is diversified.

The Asset Allocation graph displays two pie charts: Actual Allocation and Target Allocation. Actual Allocation indicates your portfolio's current diversification. Target Allocation is the allocation you set up with Quicken's Portfolio Rebalancer, which is discussed later in this chapter in the section titled "Using the Portfolio Rebalancer." If you have not yet used the Portfolio Rebalancer, the Target Allocation pie won't have any slices.

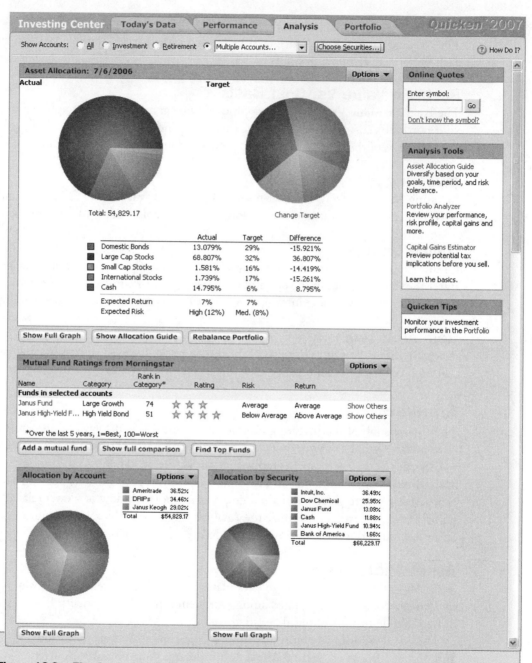

Figure 12-3 • The Analysis tab of the Investing Center displays analytical graphs of your investments.

## Mutual Fund Ratings From Morningstar

Quicken displays up-to-date ratings from Morningstar, an investment research organization that rates mutual funds based on a variety of criteria. Ratings for mutual funds you track in Quicken are automatically downloaded with asset class and related information. The more stars, the higher the rating.

## Allocation By Account

The Allocation By Account chart indicates how your portfolio's market value is distributed among your Quicken investing accounts.

## Allocation By Security

The Allocation By Security chart indicates how your portfolio's market value is distributed among different securities. This is a measure of diversification. The more pie slices and the more even the slices, the better your portfolio is diversified among securities.

## Online Quotes

Online Quotes offers a quick and easy way to request a quote from within Quicken. Enter the ticker symbol in the box and click Go. Quicken connects to the Internet and displays the security's quote information from Quicken.com in an Internet window.

## Analysis Tools

The Analysis Tools area offers links to Quicken features to help you manage and analyze your portfolio. I cover each of these features later in this chapter.

## Quicken Tips

The Quicken Tips area offers links to more information that can help you save time and get the most out of using Quicken.

# Portfolio

The Portfolio tab of the Investing Center (see Figure 12-4) displays all of your investments in one place. Information can be viewed in a wide variety of ways to show you exactly what you need to see to understand the performance, value, or components of your portfolio.

You can open the Portfolio window by clicking the Portfolio tab in the Investing Center, by choosing Investing | Portfolio, or by pressing CTRL-U.

| Investing Center | Today's Data | Performance | Analysis | **Portfolio** | | | | Quicken 2007 |

Download Quotes  Download Historical Prices                                          Options ▾  Glossary  (?) How Do I?

Show: [Value ▼]        Group by: [Accounts ▼]        [Customize View...]        As of: [7/6/2006]

| Name | Quote/Price | Shares | Market Value | Cost Basis | Gain/Loss | Gain/Loss (%) | Day Gain/Loss | Day Change | Day Change (%) |
|---|---|---|---|---|---|---|---|---|---|
| Ameritrade | | | 20,003.43 | 12,382.83 | 7,620.60 | 61.54 | -22.00 | | |
| ⊞ Apple Computer, Inc. | 56.25 | -200 | -11,250.00 | -13,977.58 | 2,727.58 | 19.51 | 150.00 | ↓ -0.75 | -1.32% |
| ⊞ Intuit, Inc. | 59.98 | 400 | 23,992.00 | 19,098.98 | 4,893.02 | 25.62 | -172.00 | ↓ -0.43 | -0.71% |
| Cash | | | 7,261.43 | 7,261.43 | | | | | |
| | | | | | | | | | |
| DRIPs | | | 18,719.25 | 14,930.35 | 3,788.90 | 25.38 | -174.30 | | |
| ⊞ Bank of America | 48.98 | 22.5693 | 1,105.44 | 1,000.00 | 105.44 | 10.54 | 2.93 | ↑ +0.13 | +0.27% |
| ⊞ Dow Chemical | 38.39 | 443.0634 | 17,009.20 | 13,325.74 | 3,683.46 | 27.64 | -177.23 | ↓ -0.40 | -1.03% |
| Cash | | | 604.61 | 604.61 | | | | | |
| | | | | | | | | | |
| Janus Keogh | | | 15,805.43 | 15,937.56 | -132.13 | -0.83 | 0.00 | | |
| ⊞ Janus Fund | est. 25.59 avg cost | 334.874 | 8,569.43 | 8,716.18 | -146.75 | -1.68 | 0.00 | | |
| ⊞ Janus High-Yield Fund | est. 9.46 avg cost | 764.905 | 7,236.00 | 7,221.38 | 14.62 | 0.20 | 0.00 | | |
| | | | | | | | | | |
| Watch List | | | | | | | | | |
| Anheiser Busch | 45.61 | | | | | | | ↑ +0.07 | +0.15 |
| Intuit, Inc. | 59.98 | | | | | | | ↓ -0.43 | -0.71 |
| | | | | | | | | | |
| Indexes | | | | | | | | | |
| Dow Jones Industrials | 11230.82031 | | | | | | | ↑ +73.5... | +0.66 |
| NASDAQ Composite | 2,160.17993 | | | | | | | ↑ +6.43... | +0.30 |
| Russell 2000 | 722.22998 | | | | | | | ↑ +2.38 | +0.33 |
| S&P 500 Index | 1,275.67004 | | | | | | | ↑ +4.76... | +0.37 |
| Totals: | | | 54,528.11 | 43,250.74 | 11,277.37 | 26.07 | -196.30 | | |

Online quotes by Comstock, delayed at least 20 minutes. Updated 7/6/2006 at 11:00 am local time. Historical quotes by Iverson.

**Figure 12-4 • The Portfolio tab of the Investing Center shows details for all of your investments in one place.**

## Using Portfolio View Options

You can quickly customize the Portfolio window's view by using the Show, Group By, and As Of options right beneath the button bar. There are many view combinations—far too many to illustrate in this book. Here's a brief overview so you can explore these options on your own.

**Show Options**    The Show drop-down list enables you to specify the view that should be used to display the information. Each of the nine predefined views can be customized with the Customize Current View dialog, shown later in this section. You can also customize nine "custom" views to make your own views of the data.

**Group By Options**    The Group By options enable you to select the order in which securities appear. The drop-down list offers seven options: Accounts, Industry, Security, Security Type, Investing Goal, Asset Class, and Sector. These options correspond to information entered as part of a security's definition, either manually when you add the security to Quicken or automatically when you download asset class information. I explain how to add securities to Quicken in Chapter 10 and how to download security information in Chapter 11.

**Portfolio Date**    You can use the As Of box to set the date for which you want to view the portfolio. For example, suppose you want to see what your portfolio looked like a month ago, before a particularly volatile market period. Enter that date in the text box. Or you can click the calendar button beside the text box to display a calendar of dates, and then click the date you want to display. The view changes to show your portfolio as of the date you specified.

## Customizing a View

Quicken offers an incredible amount of flexibility when it comes to displaying information in the Portfolio window. Not only does it come with nine preconfigured views that you can choose from the Show drop-down list, but it enables you to create nine additional custom views. You can customize any of these views.

To customize a view, begin by using the Show drop-down list to choose the view you want to customize. Then click the Customize View button. The Customize Current View dialog appears, as shown next. Set options as desired in the dialog and click OK to change the view.

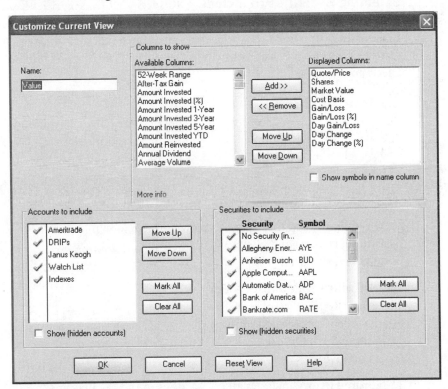

**Changing the View Name**    To change the name of the view, enter a new name in the Name box.

**Selecting Columns to Show**   To display a column of information, select it in the Available Columns list and click the Add button beside it. To hide a column of information, select it in the Displayed Columns list and click the Remove button. You can change the order in which columns appear by selecting a column name in the Displayed Columns list and using the Move Up or Move Down buttons to change its order in the list.

**Displaying Symbols Rather Than Names**   To display a security's ticker symbol rather than its name, turn on the Show Symbols In Name Column check box.

**Selecting Accounts to Include**   To specify which accounts should appear, toggle the green check marks to the left of the account name in the Accounts To Include list. Only those accounts that are checked will appear. You can change the order in which accounts appear by selecting an account name in the Accounts To Include list and clicking the Move Up or Move Down buttons. To include hidden accounts in the Accounts To Include list, turn on the Show (Hidden Accounts) check box.

**Selecting Securities to Include**   To specify which securities should appear, toggle the green check marks to the left of the security name in the Securities To Include list. Only those securities that are checked will appear. To include hidden securities in the Securities To Include list, turn on the Show (Hidden Securities) check box.

## Setting Portfolio View Options

Quicken also enables you to specify the period for return calculations and the tax rate used in the Portfolio window. Setting these options enables you to fine-tune the way Quicken makes Portfolio window calculations.

Choose Preferences from the Options menu on the Portfolio window's button bar (refer to Figure 12-4). Use the Portfolio View Options dialog that appears (shown here) to set options and click OK. Your options are as follows:

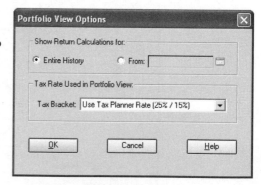

**Show Return Calculations For**

The Show Return Calculations For area offers two options for determining the period for which Quicken calculates the return on investment:

- **Entire History** includes all transactions in the calculations.
- **From** enables you to enter a starting date for calculations. All transactions between that starting date and the current date are included in the calculations.

**Tax Rate Used In Portfolio View**    Use the Tax Bracket drop-down list to choose tax rates that should be used in tax calculations for capital gains. If you are utilizing Quicken's Tax Planner, which I cover in Chapter 20, choose Use Tax Planner Rate. Otherwise, choose the rates that are appropriate for your financial situation.

## Tracking Security Values

As the individual tabs within the Investing Center illustrate, Quicken can automatically do all the math to tell you what your investments are worth—*if* you take the time to enter the per-share prices of each of your securities.

When you record transactions, Quicken automatically records the security price. It uses the most recently entered price as an estimate to calculate the current value of the investment. You can see this in the Portfolio window (see Figure 12-4)—those gray *est.* characters indicate that the price is an estimate. The *est.* characters appear if the current date is on a weekend or holiday or if you haven't entered or downloaded the current day's prices. Of course, the Portfolio window and all of Quicken's investing reports and charts are a lot more valuable with up-to-date security price information and a history of prices.

You can enter price information in two ways: manually (the hard way) and automatically (the easy way). I show you how to enter security prices manually in this chapter; to learn how to enter prices automatically via Internet download, consult Chapter 11.

### Manually Entering Security Prices

Manually entering security prices isn't difficult—it's just time-consuming. And the more securities you track, the more time-consuming it is. But without an Internet connection, this may be the only way you can enter prices into Quicken.

If you track more than one or two securities and want to update price information more often than once a week, skip the rest of this section. You don't want to enter security prices manually. Trust me. It's an extremely tedious task. Quicken's ability to download stock prices directly from the Internet—even five-year price histories—can save you tons of time and prevent data entry errors. And best of all, it's free. All you need is an Internet connection. Learn about setting up an Internet connection in Chapter 4 and about downloading quotes in Chapter 11.

To enter a security's price manually, start by displaying the Security Detail View window, which I discuss in Chapters 10 and 11. Use the drop-down list at the top-left corner of the window to select or display the security for which you want to enter price information. Then choose Edit Price History from the Update button on the button bar. The Price History window for the security appears, as shown next, showing all the price information stored within the Quicken data file for the security.

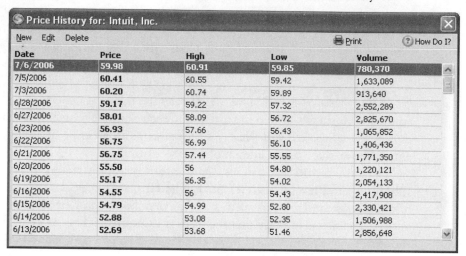

| Date | Price | High | Low | Volume |
|---|---|---|---|---|
| 7/6/2006 | 59.98 | 60.91 | 59.85 | 780,370 |
| 7/5/2006 | 60.41 | 60.55 | 59.42 | 1,633,089 |
| 7/3/2006 | 60.20 | 60.74 | 59.89 | 913,640 |
| 6/28/2006 | 59.17 | 59.22 | 57.32 | 2,552,289 |
| 6/27/2006 | 58.01 | 58.09 | 56.72 | 2,825,670 |
| 6/23/2006 | 56.93 | 57.66 | 56.43 | 1,065,852 |
| 6/22/2006 | 56.75 | 56.99 | 56.10 | 1,406,436 |
| 6/21/2006 | 56.75 | 57.44 | 55.55 | 1,771,350 |
| 6/20/2006 | 55.50 | 56 | 54.80 | 1,220,121 |
| 6/19/2006 | 55.17 | 56.35 | 54.02 | 2,054,133 |
| 6/16/2006 | 54.55 | 56 | 54.43 | 2,417,908 |
| 6/15/2006 | 54.79 | 54.99 | 52.80 | 2,330,421 |
| 6/14/2006 | 52.88 | 53.08 | 52.35 | 1,506,988 |
| 6/13/2006 | 52.69 | 53.68 | 51.46 | 2,856,648 |

You can use buttons on the window's button bar to add, edit, delete, and print the price history:

- **New** displays the New Price dialog. Use it to enter the date and closing price for the security. If you're really dedicated to entering data manually, you can even enter the daily high, low, and volume.
- **Edit** displays the Edit Price dialog for the currently selected price. This dialog looks and works just like the New Price dialog.
- **Delete** removes the selected price. When you click this button, a confirmation dialog appears. You must click OK to delete the price.
- **Print** prints the price list.
- **How Do I?** displays the Quicken Help window, which contains a list of topics about working with the Price History window.

## Viewing Market Values and Performance

Once you've entered price information for your securities, you can view their market value and performance information in the Portfolio window (see Figure 12-4) and Security Detail View window. Use options within the windows to modify the information that is displayed. I explain how earlier in this chapter and in Chapter 10.

## Investment Analysis Tools

In addition to the Quicken.com-based investment research tools discussed in Chapter 11, Quicken offers a number of built-in tools that can help you learn more about investing and analyze your investment portfolio.

In this part of the chapter, I introduce these analysis tools so you can explore them more fully on your own.

## Asset Allocation

Many investment gurus say that an investor's goals should determine his or her asset allocation. If you're not sure what your asset allocation should be, Quicken can help. It includes a wealth of information about asset allocation, including sample portfolios with their corresponding allocations. You can use this feature to learn what your target asset allocation should be to meet your investing goals. Then you can monitor your asset allocation and, if necessary, rebalance your portfolio to keep it in line with what it should be.

### Using the Asset Allocation Guide

The Asset Allocation Guide explains what asset allocation is, why it's important, and how Quicken can help monitor it in your portfolio. Choose Investing | Asset Allocation Guide. The Asset Allocation Guide window appears (see Figure 12-5).

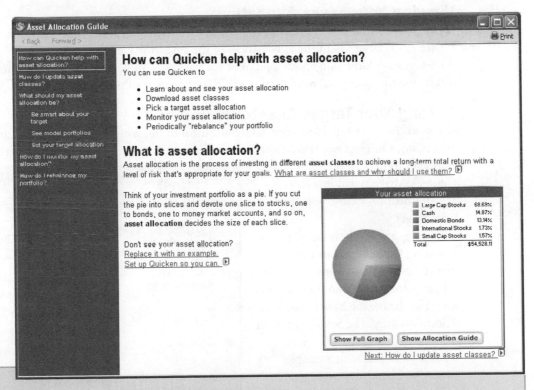

**Figure 12-5 • The Asset Allocation Guide explains what asset allocation is and how it can help you meet your investment goals.**

To take full advantage of this feature, read the information on the right side of the window. You can click links within the text or in the left column to learn more about specific topics. If you're new to asset allocation, you may find the See Model Portfolios link especially useful. It shows suggested asset allocations based on risk and returns for a number of portfolios.

## Monitoring Your Asset Allocation

To monitor the asset allocation of your portfolio, you must enter asset class information for each of your investments. You can do this in two ways:

- **Manually enter asset class information.** Although this isn't difficult for stocks, it can be time-consuming for investments that have an asset class mixture, such as mutual funds.
- **Download asset class information.** If you have a connection to the Internet, this is the best way to enter this information. With a few clicks, Quicken does all of the work in seconds. The information is complete and accurate. I explain how to download asset class information in Chapter 11.

## Viewing Your Asset Allocation

A pie chart of your asset allocation appears in the Asset Allocation Guide window (see Figure 12-5) as well as in the Analysis tab of the Investing Center (see Figure 12-3). To get more information about a piece of the pie, point to it. A yellow box appears, displaying the asset class, total market value, and percent of portfolio value.

## Setting Your Target Asset Allocation

If you know what you want your asset allocation to be, you can set up a target asset allocation. Quicken can then display your target in the pie chart beside the current asset allocation chart on the Investing Center's Analysis window so you can monitor how close you are to your target.

Display the Analysis tab of the Investing Center window (refer to Figure 12-3). Then choose Change Target Allocations from the Options menu in the button bar of the Asset Allocation area. The Set Target Asset Allocation dialog appears. Here's what it looks like with a sample allocation already entered.

Enter the desired percentages for each class of asset. When the total of all percentages equals 100, click OK

**Set Target Asset Allocation**

Set your target asset allocation.

| Asset Class | Percentage |
|---|---|
| Domestic Bonds | 29% |
| Global Bonds | 0% |
| Large Cap Stocks | 32% |
| Small Cap Stocks | 16% |
| International Stocks | 17% |
| Cash | 6% |
| Other | 0% |
| Unclassified | 0% |
| Total: | 100% |

[Must equal 100%]

OK / Cancel / Help

to save your settings. The Target chart in the Asset Allocation area of the Investing Center window reflects your settings (refer to Figure 12-3).

## Using the Portfolio Rebalancer

If your current asset allocation deviates from your target asset allocation, you may want to rebalance your portfolio. This means buying and selling investments to bring you closer to your target asset allocation.

Keep in mind that brokerage fees and capital gains impacts often are related to buying and selling securities. For this reason, you should carefully evaluate your investment situation to determine how you can minimize costs and capital gains while rebalancing your portfolio. If small adjustments are necessary to bring you to your target asset allocation, you may not find it worth the cost to make the changes. Use this information as a guideline only!

Quicken can tell you exactly how you must change your current asset allocation to meet your target asset allocation. Choose Investing | Portfolio Rebalancer. The Portfolio Rebalancer window, shown in Figure 12-6, appears. It provides instructions and shows you how much you must adjust each asset class to meet your targeted goals.

Here's an example. Figure 12-6 indicates that I need $8,649 more invested in domestic bonds and $20,006 less invested in large-cap stock. If I wanted to meet my target asset allocation, I could sell $8,600 worth of my large-cap stock investments and reinvest the funds in domestic bonds. This would change my asset allocation, bringing it closer to target, without changing the total value of my portfolio.

## Portfolio Analyzer

Quicken's Portfolio Analyzer enables you to look at your portfolio in a number of ways:

- **Performance** shows your portfolio's average annual rate of return, compared to market indexes like the Dow Jones Industrial Average and the S&P 500 index. It also shows your five best and worst performers, so you can see how individual securities are doing.

- **Holdings** lists your investment accounts and then shows a pie chart of your top ten holdings. Because most experts recommend that no single security take up more than 10 percent of your portfolio, you may find the percentage distribution helpful when considering diversification.

- **Asset Allocation** displays your current actual and target asset allocation so you can see how close you are to your target. I explain how to set up a target allocation earlier in this chapter.

- **Risk Profile** shows how "risky" your portfolio is when compared to the risk associated with specific classes of investments.

- **Tax Implications** summarizes your realized and unrealized YTD capital gains or losses. Capital gains and losses are broken down into three categories: short term, long term, and super long term.

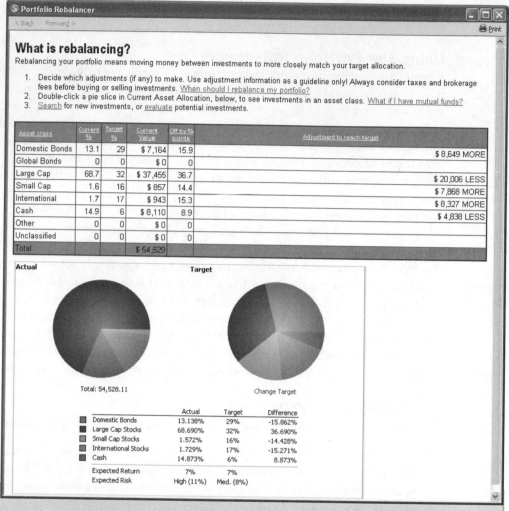

Figure 12-6 • The Portfolio Rebalancer window tells you what adjustments you need to make to bring your asset allocation closer to target.

What's great about the Portfolio Analyzer is that it provides tables and charts to show information about your portfolio, and then it explains everything in plain English so you know what the tables and charts mean. Using this feature regularly can really help you learn about the world of investing and how your portfolio measures up. To give it a try, choose Investing | Portfolio Analyzer.

## Buy/Sell Preview

Quicken Premier includes a feature called Buy/Sell Preview, which offers a quick and easy way to see the impact of a securities purchase or sale on your finances—including your taxes.

Choose Investing | Buy/Sell Preview. In the top half of the Buy/Sell Preview window that appears, enter information about the proposed purchase or sale. Quicken automatically enters the most recent price information for a security you own or watch, but you can override that amount if necessary. When you're finished setting options, click Calculate. Quicken displays its results in the bottom half of the window. Here are two examples—one for a purchase and the other for a sale:

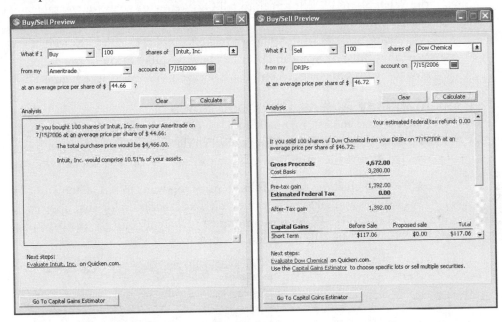

The Buy/Sell Preview feature works with Quicken's Tax Planner, which I discuss in Chapter 20, to calculate the net effect of a sale on your expected tax bill or refund. You can find this information in the window for a sale calculation.

## Capital Gains Estimator

Quicken's Capital Gains Estimator enables you to estimate capital gains or losses and their related tax implications *before* you sell a security. The information it provides can help you make an informed decision about which security to sell.

### Getting Started

Choose Investing | Capital Gains Estimator. The Capital Gains Estimator's welcome window appears.

Start by reading the information in the right side of the window. It explains what the Capital Gains Estimator does and offers links for learning more about specific terms and topics. Then click each of the links in the left side of the window, in turn, to step through the process of setting up the Capital Gains Estimator for your situation. You'll be prompted to name and choose a scenario, select taxable investment accounts to include, set your tax rate, and enter capital loss carryover information. When you enter complete and accurate information, Quicken can provide a more accurate indication of tax impacts.

## Deciding What to Sell

Quicken Premier users can tap into a feature in the Capital Gains Estimator that enables Quicken to help you decide which securities to sell. Follow instructions in the What Should I Sell? screen to tell Quicken your goals for the sale, and click the Search button at the bottom of the window.

A dialog appears while Quicken makes complex calculations to meet your goals. When it's finished, you can click the Show Results button in the dialog to display a scenario with Quicken's recommendation and the results (see Figure 12-7).

## Manually Adding Proposed Sales

If you prefer, you can manually indicate proposed sales in the Scenario window (refer to Figure 12-7). The Step 1 area shows all the securities you hold in the accounts you selected during the setup process. You can add a proposed sale in two ways:

- Double-click the name of the security you want to sell. Then enter the number of shares and sales price in the Add To Scenario dialog that appears, shown here, and click OK. If you have multiple purchase lots for the security, this automatically sells the oldest lots first.

**Add to Scenario**

Propose sale of:    Dow Chemical

Shares to Sell:    50

Sale Price:    46.72

If you don't want to sell the oldest shares first, click Cancel and select the specific lots you wish to sell.

[ OK ]    [ Cancel ]    [ Help ]

- If necessary, click the plus sign (+) to the left of the security that you want to sell to display the purchase lots. Then click the lot you want to sell. This enables you to specify exactly which lots are to be sold.

No matter which method you use, the sale is added to the Step 2 area of the window, which lists all of the proposed sales (see Figure 12-7).

To adjust the number of shares to be sold, click in the Shares To Sell field for the proposed sale (in the Step 2 area) and enter a new value. The value you enter must be less than or equal to the number of shares purchased in that lot.

You can set up proposed sales for up to three scenarios—just click the Scenario link on the left side of the window to see and set that scenario's options. You can mix and match any sales you like to reach your goal.

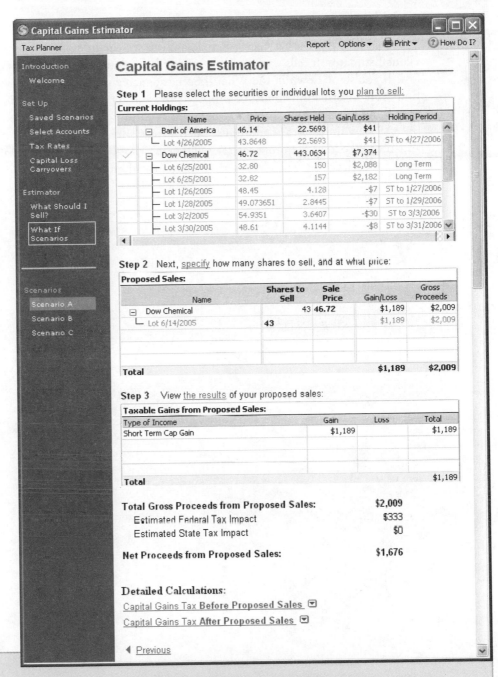

**Figure 12-7 • Quicken displays its recommendations as a scenario.**

## Reading the Results

When all information has been entered, you can see the true power of the Capital Gains Estimator. It tells you about the proceeds from the sales, as well as the gain or loss. If you scroll down in the What If Scenarios screen (refer to Figure 12-7), you'll find more information about the proposed sale and its tax implications in the Step 3 area, including the gross profit and net proceeds from proposed sales. You can click links to view the results of additional calculations, such as the tax situation before and after executing the proposed sales and gain or loss on the proposed sales. Do the same for each scenario to see how they compare—then make your selling decision.

# The Property & Debt Center

This part of the book explains how you can use the features of Quicken Personal Finance Software's Property & Debt Center to keep track of your property and loans. It starts with coverage of assets, such as a car and home, and the loans that you may have used to finance them. Then it moves on to some Quicken tools that can help you organize and keep track of important household information. Finally, it tells you how you can use the Property & Debt Center window and other Quicken features to keep tabs on expenses related to your assets and debt. This part of the book has three chapters:

**Chapter 13:**    Monitoring Assets and Loans

**Chapter 14:**    Managing Household Records

**Chapter 15:**    Keeping Tabs on Your Property and Debt

# Part Four

# Monitoring Assets and Loans

## In This Chapter:

- *Assets and liabilities defined*
- *Loan basics*
- *Setting up asset and loan accounts*
- *Tracking a loan*
- *Adjusting asset values*

Assets and loans (or liabilities) make up your net worth. Bank and investment accounts, which I cover in Chapters 5 and 10, are examples of assets. Credit card accounts, which I cover in Chapter 5, are examples of liabilities. But you may want to use Quicken Personal Finance Software to track other assets and liabilities, including a home, car, recreational vehicle, and related loans. By including these items in your Quicken data file, you can quickly and accurately calculate your net worth and financial fitness.

In this chapter, I explain how to set up asset and liability accounts to track your possessions and any outstanding loans you used to purchase them.

## The Basics

Before you begin, it's a good idea to have a clear understanding of what assets, liabilities, and loans are and how they work together in your Quicken data file.

## Assets and Liabilities

An *asset* is something you own. Common examples might be your house, car, camper, computer, television set, and patio furniture. Most assets have value—you can sell them for cash or trade them for another asset.

Although you can use Quicken to track every single asset you own in its own asset account, doing so would be cumbersome. Instead, you'll normally account for high-value assets in individual accounts and lower-value assets in a Home Inventory asset account. For example, you may create separate asset accounts for your home and your car but group personal possessions such as your computer, television, and stamp collection in a single Home Inventory asset account. This makes it easy to track all your assets, so you have accurate records for insurance and other purposes.

A *liability* is something you owe—often to buy one of your assets! For example, if you buy a house, chances are you'll use a mortgage to finance it. The mortgage, which is a loan that is secured by your home, is a liability. You can use Quicken to track all of your liabilities, so you know exactly how much you owe at any given time.

## Loans

A *loan* is a promise to pay money. Loans are commonly used to buy assets, although some folks often turn to debt consolidation loans to pay off other liabilities—I tell you more about that in Chapter 18.

Here's how it works. The lender gives the borrower money in exchange for the borrower's promise to pay it back. (The promise is usually in writing, with lots of signatures and initials.) The borrower normally pays back the loan to the lender with periodic payments that include interest on the loan balance or *principal*. The amount of the loan is reduced after each payment. The borrower incurs interest expense while the lender earns interest income.

While most people think of a loan as something you owe (a liability), a loan can also be something you own (an asset). For example, say you borrow money from your brother to buy a car. In your Quicken data file, the loan is related to a liability—money that you owe your brother. In your brother's Quicken data file, the loan is related to an asset—money that is due to him from you.

## Types of Loans

There are several types of loans, some of which are designed for specific purposes. Here's a quick summary of what's available, along with their pros and cons.

### Mortgage

A *mortgage* is a long-term loan secured by real estate. Most mortgages require a down payment on the property of 10 percent or higher. Monthly payments are based on the term of the loan and the interest rate applied to the principal. The interest you pay on a mortgage for a first or second home is tax deductible. If you fail to make mortgage payments, your house could be sold to pay back the mortgage.

A *balloon mortgage* is a special type of short-term mortgage. Rather than make monthly payments over the full typical mortgage term, at the end of the fifth, seventh, or tenth year, you pay the balance of the mortgage in one big "balloon" payment. Some balloon mortgages offer the option of refinancing when the balloon payment is due.

## Home Equity Loans or Lines of Credit

A *home equity loan* or *second mortgage* is a line of credit secured by the equity in your home—the difference between its market value and the amount of outstanding debt. Your equity rises when you make mortgage payments or property values increase. It declines when you borrow against your equity or property values decrease. A home equity loan lets you borrow against this equity.

A home equity loan has two benefits: interest rates are usually lower than other credit, and interest may be tax deductible. For these reasons, many people use home equity loans to pay off credit card debt; renovate their homes; or buy cars, boats, or other recreational vehicles. (I used a home equity line of credit in 1999 to buy a new Jeep. Not only did I get a low rate, but the interest I paid on the loan is tax deductible.) But, as with a mortgage, if you fail to pay a home equity reserve, your house could be sold to satisfy the debt.

## Reverse Equity Loans

A *reverse equity loan* provides people who own their homes in full with a regular monthly income. Instead of you paying the lender, the lender pays you. This type of loan is attractive to retirees who live on a fixed income. The loan is paid back when the home is sold—often after the death of the homeowner. (You can imagine how the next of kin feel about that.)

## Car Loans

A *car loan* is a loan secured by a vehicle such as a car, truck, or motor home. Normally, you make a down payment and use the loan to pay the balance of the car's purchase price. Monthly payments are based on the term of the loan and the interest rate applied to the principal. Interest on car loans is not tax deductible.

## Personal Loans

A *personal loan* is an unsecured loan—a loan that requires no collateral. Monthly payments are based on the term of the loan and the interest rate applied to the principal. You can use a personal loan for just about anything. Some people use them to pay off multiple smaller debts so they have only one monthly payment. Interest on personal loans is not tax deductible.

## Loan Considerations

When applying for a loan, a number of variables have a direct impact on what the loan costs you now and in the future. Ask about all of these things *before* applying for any loan. And be sure to check out the Loan Comparison and Mortgage Comparison worksheets available on the companion Web site for this book, www.marialanger.com/booksites/quicken.html.

### Interest Rate

The *interest rate* is the annual percentage applied to the loan principal. Several factors affect the interest rate you may be offered:

- **Your credit record** affects the interest rate offered, because a borrower with a good credit record can usually get a better rate than one with a bad credit record. Of course, if your credit record is really bad, you might not be able to borrow money at any rate.
- **The type of loan** affects the interest rate offered because, generally speaking, personal loans have the highest interest rates, whereas mortgages have the lowest. From highest to lowest between these two types are a used car loan, a new car loan, and a home equity reserve or line of credit.
- **The loan term** affects the interest rate offered, because the length of a loan can vary the interest within a specific loan type. For example, for car loans, the longer the term, the lower the rate.
- **The amount of the down payment** affects the interest rate offered, because the more money you put down on the purchase, the lower the rate may be.
- **Your location** affects the interest rate offered, because rates vary from one area of the country to another.
- **The lender** affects the interest rate offered, because rates also vary from one lender to another. Certain types of lenders have lower rates than others.

Two kinds of interest rates can apply to a loan:

- **Fixed rate** applies the same rate to the principal throughout the loan term.
- **Variable rate** applies a different rate to the loan throughout the loan term. For example, the loan may start with one rate and, each year, switch to a different rate. The rate is usually established by adding a certain number of percentage points to a national index, such as treasury bill rates. A cap limits the amount the rate can change. Mortgages with this type of rate are referred to as *adjustable rate mortgages,* or *ARMs.*

Although ARMs usually offer a lower initial interest rate than fixed-rate mortgages, you should consider the overall economic conditions before deciding on one. For example, when we purchased our first home, in the mid-1980s when interest rates were high, we selected an ARM. When interest rates dropped, so did the rate on our mortgage. If we'd selected a fixed-rate mortgage when we bought that home, we would have had to refinance to get the same savings. Rates were much lower when we bought our current home in the late 1990s, so we selected a fixed rate to protect us from possible rate increases in the future. Last year, we refinanced to lock in at an even lower rate to reduce our monthly payments and interest expenses.

## Term

A loan's *term* is the period of time between the loan date and the date payment is due in full. Loan terms vary depending on the type of loan:

- Mortgage loan and home equity reserve loan terms are typically 10, 15, 20, or 30 years.
- Balloon mortgage loan terms are typically 5, 7, or 10 years.
- Car loan terms are typically 3, 4, or 5 years.

## Down Payment

A *down payment* is an up-front payment toward the purchase of a home or car. Most mortgages require at least 10 percent down; 20 percent down is preferred.

Keep in mind that if you make only a 10 percent down payment on a home, you may be required to pay for the cost of private mortgage insurance (PMI). This protects the lender from loss if you fail to pay your mortgage, but it increases your monthly mortgage payments.

## Application Fees

Most lenders require you to pay an application fee to process your loan application. This usually includes the cost of obtaining a property appraisal and credit report. These fees are usually not refundable—even if you are turned down.

## Mortgage Closing Costs

In addition to the application fee and down payment, many other costs are involved in securing a mortgage and purchasing a home. These are known as *closing costs*. The Real Estate Settlement Procedures Act of 1974 requires that your lender provide a Good Faith Estimate of closing costs. This document summarizes all of the costs of closing on a home based on the mortgage the lender is offering.

Here's a brief list of the types of costs you may encounter. Because they vary from lender to lender, they could be a deciding factor when shopping for a mortgage. Note that most of these fees are not negotiable.

- **Origination fee** covers the administrative costs of processing a loan.
- **Discount or "points"** is a fee based on a percentage rate applied to the loan amount. For example, 1 point on a $150,000 mortgage is $1,500.

- **Appraisal fee** covers the cost of a market-value appraisal of the property by a licensed, certified appraiser.
- **Credit report fee** covers the cost of obtaining a credit history of the prospective borrower(s) to determine credit worthiness.
- **Underwriting fee** covers the cost of underwriting the loan. This is the process of determining loan risks and establishing terms and conditions.
- **Document preparation fee** covers the cost of preparing legal and other documents required to process the loan.
- **Title insurance fee** covers the cost of title insurance, which protects the lender and buyer against loss due to disputes over ownership and possession of the property.
- **Recording fee** covers the cost of entering the sale of a property into public records.
- **Prepaid items** are taxes, insurance, and assessments paid in advance of their due dates. These expenses are not paid to the lender but are due at the closing date.

## Tips for Minimizing Loan Expenses

Borrowing money costs money. It's as simple as that. But you can do some things to minimize the cost of a loan.

**Shop for the lowest rate.**    This may seem like a no-brainer, but a surprising number of people simply go to a local bank and accept whatever terms they are offered. You don't have to use a local bank to borrow money for a home, car, or other major purchase. Check the financial pages of your local newspaper or the Quicken Loans page on Quicken.com. And if you're shopping for a car, keep an eye out for low-interest financing deals. Sometimes, you can save a lot of money in interest by buying when the time is right. For example, suppose you have a choice of two five-year car loans for $20,000—one at 5.5 percent and the other at 7.5 percent. Over the course of five years, you'll pay $1,124 less if you go with the lower rate. That can buy a lot of gas—even at today's fuel prices.

**Minimize the loan term.**    The shorter the loan term, the less interest you'll pay over the life of the loan. The savings can be quite substantial. For example, suppose you have a choice of two loan terms for a $150,000, 5.5 percent mortgage: 15 years or 30 years. If you choose the 15-year mortgage, you'll pay $70,613 in interest, but if you choose the 30-year mortgage, you'll pay a whopping $156,606 in interest—nearly $86,000 more! Neither option is appealing, but the shorter-term mortgage is certainly easier to swallow. The drawback? The monthly payment for the 15-year mortgage is $1,226, while the payment for the 30-year mortgage is only $852. Obviously, your monthly spending budget will weigh heavily into the decision.

**Maximize the down payment.**    The less you borrow, the less you'll pay in interest—and the less your monthly payments will be. Take the loan term example just shown. Suppose your budget won't allow you to go with the shorter-term loan—you just can't make those monthly payments. But if you cashed in an IRA worth $20,000 and put that toward the down payment (talk to your tax advisor; you may be able to do this without penalty for the purchase of a first home), you could knock $163 per month off the 15-year loan's monthly payment, which might be enough to fit it into your budget—and save another $9,400 in interest!

**Make extra loan payments.**    If you can't go for a shorter-term loan, consider making extra payments toward the loan's principal. Take another look at the 30-year mortgage example just shown. If you pay an additional $100 per month (increasing your monthly payment to $952), you can save more than $39,888 in interest and pay off the loan more than six years early! Or perhaps you get a generous holiday bonus each year. If you put $1,000 of that bonus toward the mortgage each January as an extra payment, you can save $36,121 in interest and pay off the loan five years early!

**Clean up your credit before applying for a loan.**    Loan terms vary based on credit history. To get the best deal, your credit should be as clean as possible. If you think there might be problems in your credit report, get a copy—you can learn how by choosing Property & Debt | Quicken Services | Free Credit Report And Score. Then do what you need to get things cleaned up.

When evaluating the dollar impact of different loan deals, use Quicken's Loan Calculator. It'll make complex loan payment calculations for you. I explain how to use Quicken's financial calculators, including the Loan Calculator and Refinance Calculator, in Chapter 17.

# Setting Up Accounts

To track an asset or liability with Quicken, you must set up an appropriate account. All transactions related to the asset or liability will be recorded in the account's register.

In this section, I tell you about the types of accounts you can use to track your assets and liabilities, and explain how to set up each type of account.

## Choosing the Right Account

Quicken offers four property and loan account types for tracking assets and liabilities.

- **House (With Or Without Mortgage)**    A house account is used for recording the value of a house, condominium, or other real estate. When you create a house account, Quicken asks whether there is a mortgage on the property. If so, you can have Quicken create a related liability account for you or associate the house account with an existing liability account. This makes it possible to set up both your house asset account and mortgage liability account at the same time.
- **Vehicle (With Or Without Loan)**    A vehicle account is similar to a house account, but it's designed for vehicles, including cars, trucks, and recreational

vehicles. Quicken asks if there is a loan on the vehicle; if so, it can create a related liability account or link to an existing liability account.

- **Asset** An asset account is for recording the value of other assets, such as personal property. For example, my Quicken data file includes asset accounts for my horses, my art and antiques, and my personal possessions.
- **Liability** A liability account is for recording money you owe to others. As mentioned earlier, when you create a house or vehicle account, Quicken can automatically create a corresponding liability account for you. You can create a liability account to record other debts that are not related to the purchase of a specific asset.

## Creating Asset and Liability Accounts

You create asset and liability accounts with the Account Setup dialog, which walks you through the process of creating the account. Quicken offers a number of ways to open this dialog for an asset or liability account. Here are two suggestions:

- Click the Add Account button in the Property & Debt Accounts area of the Property & Debt Center window. In the Quicken Account Setup dialog that appears (shown next), select the option for the type of account you want to create and click Next.

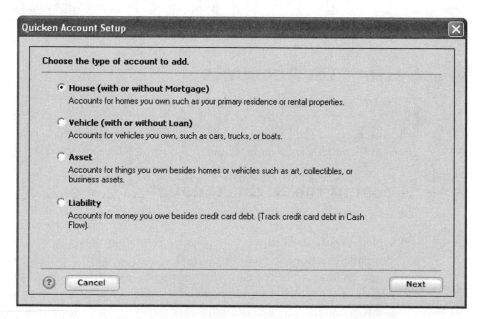

- Choose Property & Debt | Property & Debt Accounts | Add Account. In the Quicken Account Setup dialog that appears (just shown), select the option for the type of account you want to create and click Next.

Chapter 3 explains how to use the Quicken Account Setup dialog to create new Quicken accounts. In this section, I provide information about the kinds of data you'll have to enter to create asset and liability accounts.

## Account Name and Other Information

Give the account a name that clearly identifies the asset or liability. For example, if you have two cars and plan to track them in separate asset accounts, consider naming the account with the make and model of the car. *Jeep Wrangler* and *Chevy Pickup* do a better job identifying the cars than *Car 1* and *Car 2*. When creating a liability account, you may want to include the word *mortgage* or *loan* in the account name so you don't confuse it with a related asset.

For a vehicle account, Quicken will also ask for the make, model, and year of the car. Quicken stores this information in the Account Details dialog for the asset. (You can view and edit this information after the account has been created; simply click the Edit Account Details button in the Overview tab of the asset's account register.)

## Starting Point Information

For house and vehicle accounts, Quicken prompts you to enter information about the asset's purchase, including the acquisition date and purchase price. You can find this information on your original purchase receipts. Quicken also asks for an estimate of the current value. For a house, this number will (hopefully) be higher than the purchase price; for a car, this number will probably be lower. This is the amount that will appear as the asset account balance.

For assets and liabilities, Quicken prompts you for a starting date and value (asset) or amount owed (liability). If you don't know how much to enter now, you can leave it set to zero and enter a value when you know what to enter. I explain how to adjust asset values later in this chapter.

## Optional Tax Information

For asset and liability accounts, you can click a Tax button to enter tax schedule information for transfers in and out of the account. This is completely optional and, in most cases, unnecessary. I explain how to set up Quicken accounts and categories to simplify tax preparation in Chapter 19.

## Related Mortgage or Loan

When creating a house or vehicle account, Quicken asks whether there is a related mortgage or loan. You have three options:

- **Yes, Create A Liability Account For Me.** This option tells Quicken that there is a loan and that it should create a liability account.
- **There Is A Mortgage/Loan And I'm Already Tracking It In Quicken.** This option enables you to select an existing liability account to link to the loan.

- **The House/Vehicle Is Paid For, So I Don't Need A Liability Account.** This option tells Quicken that there is no loan so no liability account is necessary. (Lucky you!)

### Loan Information

If you indicated that Quicken should create a liability account for a house or vehicle, it automatically displays the Edit Loan dialog, which you can use to enter information about the loan. If you set up a liability account, Quicken asks if you want to set up an amortized loan to be associated with the liability. I explain how to set up a loan later in this chapter in the section "Setting Up a Loan."

## The Account Register

When you're finished setting up an asset or liability account (and related loans and loan payments, if applicable), Quicken automatically displays the account's register. Figure 13-1, shown later in the chapter in the section "Recording Other Asset Transactions," shows what a house account might look like. The first transaction, dated 10/15/1997, shows the opening balance, which is the amount paid for the house. The second transaction, dated 6/16/2006, shows an adjustment automatically made by Quicken to increase the account's balance based on my estimate of its worth on the day I created the account.

All transactions that affect an asset or liability account's balance appear in the account register. I tell you more about using account registers for asset and liability accounts later in this chapter in the section "Recording Other Asset Transactions."

## Tracking a Loan

Quicken makes it easy to track the principal, interest, and payments for a loan. Once you set up a loan and corresponding liability or asset accounts, you can make payments with Quicken using QuickFill (see Chapter 7), scheduled transactions (see Chapter 7), or online payments (see Chapter 6). The Loan feature keeps track of all the details so you don't have to.

Before I explain how to use the Loan feature, let me take a moment to make something clear. A loan is not the same as an asset or liability account. A loan, in Quicken, is information that Quicken uses to calculate the amount of interest and principal due for each payment of an amortized loan, such as a mortgage or car loan. A loan must be associated with an asset account (if you are a lender) or a liability account (if you are a borrower), as well as an income or expense category to record interest income or expense. Loan transactions are recorded in the associated asset or liability account—not in Quicken's loan records. It's possible to delete a loan without losing any transaction data, as I explain later in this section. But you can't delete an asset or liability account that has a loan associated with it unless the loan is deleted first.

## Setting Up a Loan

You can set up a loan in three ways:

- Create a house, vehicle, or liability account with a related mortgage or loan as discussed earlier in this chapter. Quicken automatically prompts you for loan information.
- Click the Add Loan button in the Loan Accounts Summary area of the Property & Debt Center window.
- Choose Property & Debt | Loans or press CTRL-H to display the View Loans window (shown later in this chapter). Then click New in the window's button bar.

The method you use determines what dialogs and prompts appear. For example, if you create a loan when you create a house account, Quicken displays the Edit Loan dialog that summarizes all loan information in two screens. If you create a loan by clicking the New button in the View Loans window, Quicken displays the Loan Setup dialog with EasyStep screens that walk you through the loan creation process. It doesn't matter which method you use; the information you need to enter is basically the same. Here's what you can expect.

**Type of Loan**    The Loan Setup dialog starts by prompting you for a loan type. You have two options:

- **Borrow Money** is for loans for which you're borrowing money from a lender, such as a car loan, mortgage, or personal loan. Quicken uses a liability account to record the loan.
- **Lend Money** is for loans for which you're the lender. Quicken uses an asset account to record the money owed from the borrower.

**Loan Account**    The Loan Setup dialog prompts you to enter the account for the loan. Again, you have two options:

- **New Account** enables you to set up a brand-new account for the loan. Be sure to enter a name for the account.
- **Existing Account** enables you to select one of your existing liability accounts for the loan. This option is available only if you have already created a liability account that isn't already linked to a loan.

**Loan Details**    No matter how you create the loan, you'll be prompted for information about the loan creation, amount, and payments. It's important to be accurate; get the numbers directly from a loan statement or agreement if possible.

Quicken can calculate some of the values—such as the loan balance and monthly payments—for you. It does this automatically based on your answers to questions in the Set Up Loan dialog. If you're using the Edit Loan dialog, select the Calculate option in the Payment area. When you click Done, Quicken displays a dialog telling you that it has calculated the values. Click OK to return to the Edit Loan dialog to see the calculated amount. Keep in mind, however, that Quicken's calculated amounts may not exactly match those calculated by your bank or finance company.

When you've finished entering loan information in the Setup Loan dialog, a series of Summary tab windows display entered and calculated values. Here's what the Edit Loan dialog screens look like for a $20,000, five-year car loan started on August 15, 2003; these windows are virtually identical to the last two screens that appear in the Loan Setup dialog when you create a loan from the View Loans window:

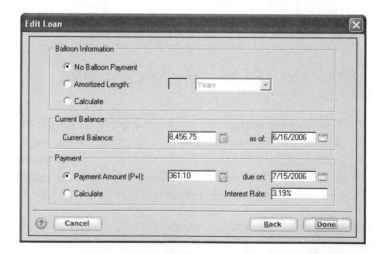

## Setting Up Payments

When you set up a loan, Quicken automatically prompts you to set up payment information by displaying the Edit Loan Payment (or Set Up Loan Payment) dialog:

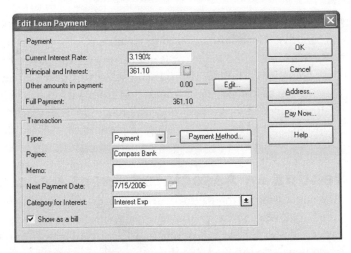

Enter information in this dialog to set up the payment. If the total payment should include additional amounts for property taxes, insurance, or other escrow items, click the Edit button. This displays the Split Transaction window, which you can use to enter categories, memos, and amounts to be added to the payment.

In the Transaction area of the dialog, you can specify the type and method for the transaction. For type, three options appear on the drop-down list:

- **Payment** is a transaction recorded in your account register only. You must manually write and mail a check for payment. This is covered in Chapter 5.
- **Print Check** is a transaction recorded in the Write Checks dialog and account register. You can use the Print Check command to print the check, and then you can mail it for payment. This is also covered in Chapter 5.
- **Online Pmt** creates a payment instruction to be processed by your financial institution for use with online payment. This is covered in Chapter 6. This option appears only if at least one of your bank accounts is enabled for Quicken's online payment feature.

To indicate the method of payment, click the Payment Method button. The Select Payment Method dialog, shown here, appears. This dialog offers three Payment Type options:

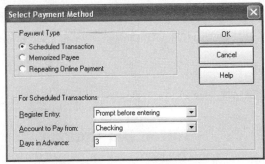

- **Scheduled Transaction** is a transaction scheduled for the future. If you select this option, you must also choose options and enter values to specify how Quicken should enter the transaction, which account should be used to pay, and how many days in advance it should be entered and paid. All this is covered in Chapter 7.

- **Memorized Payee** is a transaction memorized for use with QuickFill or Quicken's Calendar. This is also covered in Chapter 7.
- **Repeating Online Payment** is a recurring online payment instruction processed by your financial institution. If you select this option, you must also select a repeating online payment transaction from a drop-down list. If you have not already created a transaction to link to this loan payment, select one of the other options and return to this dialog after you have created the required transaction. Consult Chapter 6 for complete instructions.

## Creating an Associated Asset Account

At the conclusion of the payment setup process, Quicken may display a dialog asking if you want to create an asset to go with the loan. This enables you to set up an asset account for the full purchase price of your new home or car. Click Yes to create a new account; click No if you have already created one. I discussed creating an asset account earlier in this chapter in the section titled "Creating Asset and Liability Accounts."

## Reviewing Loan Information

The View Loans window displays information about your loans, as shown next. You can open this window by choosing Property & Debt | Loans or by pressing CTRL-H.

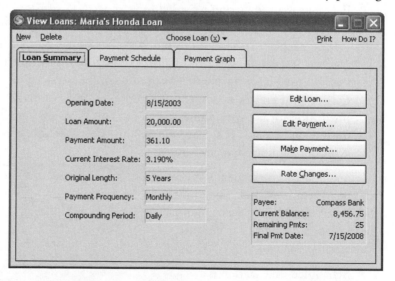

## Button Bar Options

The View Loans window's button bar offers options for working with loans:

- **New** enables you to create a new loan. I explained how this option works earlier in this chapter.

- **Delete** removes the currently displayed loan. If you click this button, a dialog appears, asking if you want to save the associated account for your records. If you click Yes, Quicken removes the loan information but keeps the liability account and all of its transactions. If you click No, Quicken deletes the loan information and the liability account. This causes any related transactions in other accounts—such as payments made from your checking account—to be uncategorized. (I recommend that you click Yes. You can always hide the account if you don't want to see it; I explain how in Chapter 3.)

- **Choose Loan** displays a menu of your current loans. Use it to choose the loan you want to display in the window.

- **Print** prints a loan payment schedule for the currently displayed loan. The printout includes all of the information in the Payment Schedule tab of the View Loans window, which is shown and discussed momentarily.

- **How Do I?** provides instructions for working with the View Loans window.

## Window Tabs

The tabs along the top of the window's information area enable you to view various pieces of information about a loan.

**Loan Summary**    Loan Summary, shown earlier, summarizes the loan information.

**Payment Schedule**    Payment Schedule, shown next, displays a schedule of past and future payments. You can turn on the Show Running Totals check box to display cumulative totals, rather than individual payment information.

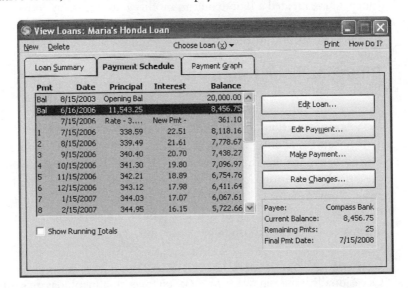

**Payment Graph**   Payment Graph, shown next, displays a graph of the loan payments. Where the two lines meet indicates the point at which you start paying more toward the loan principal than for interest. You can click a position on a graph line to display its value.

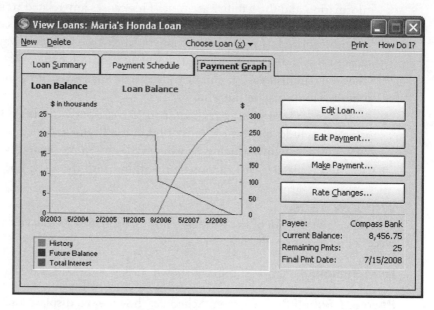

# Modifying Loan Information

Once you've created a loan, you can modify it as necessary to record corrections, changes in the interest rate, or changes in payment methods. You can do all these things with buttons in the View Loans window.

## Changing Loan Information

If you discover a discrepancy between the loan information in the View Loans window and information on statements or loan agreement papers, you can change the loan information in Quicken.

If necessary, choose the loan account's name from the Choose Loan menu in the button bar to display the information for the loan you want to modify. Then click the Edit Loan button. A pair of Edit Loan windows enables you to change just about any information for the loan. Modify values and select different options as desired. Click Done in the last window to save your changes. Quicken automatically makes any necessary entries to update the account.

## Changing Payment Information

Occasionally, you may want to make changes to a loan's payment information. For example, suppose the real estate taxes on your property are reduced (you can always hope!) and the resulting escrow amount, which is included in the payment, changes. Or suppose you decide to switch payment method from a scheduled transaction to a repeating online payment.

If necessary, choose the loan account's name from the Choose Loan menu in the button bar to display the information for the loan payment you want to modify. Then click the Edit Payment button. The Edit Loan Payment dialog, shown earlier, appears. Make changes as desired and click OK. Quicken updates the payment information with your changes.

## Changing the Interest Rate

If you have an adjustable rate mortgage, you'll periodically have to adjust the rate for the loan within Quicken to match the rate charged by the lender.

If necessary, choose the loan account's name from the Choose Loan menu in the button bar to display the information for the loan whose rate you want to change. Then click the Rate Changes button. The Loan Rate Changes window appears. It lists all the loan rates throughout the history of the loan:

**Loan Rate Changes**

New   Edit   Delete                                    Print   Close   How Do I?

| Date | Rate | Principal and Interest |
|------|------|------------------------|
| 7/1/2003 | 5.250% | 166.04 |
| 10/1/2003 | 5.50% | 171.28 |
| 3/1/2004 | 5.650% | 175.07 |
| 9/1/2005 | 6.50% | 194.93 |
| 7/4/2006 | 7.0% | 199.59 |

To insert a rate change, click New in the window's button bar. The Insert An Interest Rate Change dialog appears, as shown here:

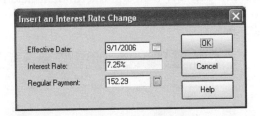

**Insert an Interest Rate Change**

Effective Date:    9/1/2006            OK

Interest Rate:     7.25%               Cancel

Regular Payment:   152.29             Help

Enter the effective date and new rate in the appropriate text boxes. Quicken automatically calculates the new loan payment. When you click OK, the rate appears in the Loan Rate Changes window. Click the Close button to dismiss the window. Quicken recalculates the loan payment schedule for you.

## Making a Loan Payment

Although it's usually more convenient to set up a loan payment as a scheduled transaction or repeating online payment instruction, as discussed earlier, you can also use the View Loans window to make a loan payment. This method is especially useful for making extra loan payments—payments in addition to your normal periodic payments.

If necessary, choose the loan account's name from the Choose Loan menu in the button bar to display the information for the loan for which you want to make a payment. Then click the Make Payment button. A Loan Payment dialog appears, asking whether you are making a regularly scheduled payment or an extra payment. Click the appropriate button.

### Making a Regular Loan Payment

If you click the Regular button, the Make Regular Payment dialog, which is shown next, appears. Set options to specify the bank account from which the payment should be made, the type of transaction, the payee information, the date, and a memo for the transaction. If the Type Of Transaction drop-down list is set to Payment, you can enter a check number in the Number box or use one of the options on the Number drop-down list to set a number option. The Category and Amount are already set using values calculated by Quicken—you shouldn't have to change them. Click OK to enter the transaction.

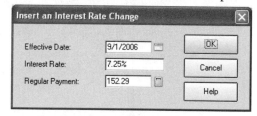

### Making an Extra Loan Payment

If you click the Extra button, the Make Extra Payment dialog appears. As you can see in the following illustration, it's almost identical to the Make Regular Payment dialog, with two differences: the loan account is automatically set as the transfer account in the Category field and the Amount field is left blank. Set options in the dialog to specify payment information, including the amount. Then click OK to enter the transaction.

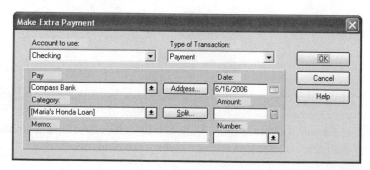

# Recording Other Asset Transactions

Part of tracking assets is keeping track of their current values and modifying account balances when necessary. Like a bank or investment account, which I discuss in Chapters 5 and 10, activity for an asset account appears in its account register.

As usual, Quicken offers several ways to open an asset account's register:

- Click the name of the account in the Property & Debt Accounts area of the Account Bar or the Property & Debt Center.
- Choose the name of the account from the Property & Debt Accounts submenu under the Property & Debt menu.
- Double-click the name of the account in the Account List window.

The account register, which is shown in Figure 13-1, appears in the Property & Debt Center. You can use button bar buttons to work with the register and its entries:

- **Delete** removes the currently selected transaction.
- **Find** enables you to search for transactions in the window. I discuss searching for transactions in Chapter 5.
- **Transfer** enables you to create a transfer transaction. I cover transfers in Chapter 5, too.
- **Update Balance** enables you to create a transaction to update the value of the asset. I discuss this option later in this section.
- **View** displays a menu of options for sorting and filtering the register window's contents.

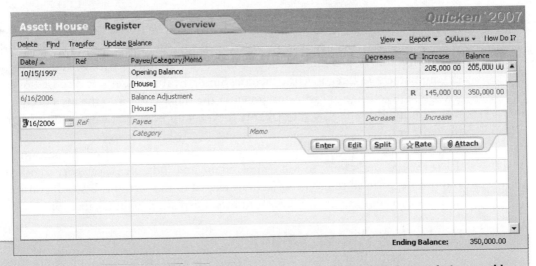

Figure 13-1 • The account register for a newly created asset account shows what you paid for the asset, as well as the estimated market value as of the account creation date.

- **Report** is a menu that offers a variety of reporting options for account information.
- **Options** is a menu that offers a variety of options for changing the view of the window.
- **How Do I?** provides instructions for completing tasks with the account register window.

In this section, I explain how you can record changes in asset values due to acquisitions and disposals, improvements, market values, and depreciation.

## Adding and Disposing of Assets

The most obvious change in an asset's value occurs when you add or remove part of the asset. For example, I have a single asset account in which I record the value of my horses and related equipment. When I buy a new saddle, it increases the value of the account. Similarly, when I sell one of my horses, it decreases the value of the account.

In many instances, when you add or dispose of an asset, money is exchanged. In that case, recording the transaction is easy: simply use the appropriate bank account register to record the purchase or sale and use the asset account as a transfer account in the Category field. Here's what the purchase of a new saddle might look like in my checking account:

| 6/2/2006 | 5178 | Double D. Western World | 1,124 96 | | 2,851 54 |
| | | [Horses & Tack]   New saddle | | | |

And here's the same transaction in my Horses & Tack asset account:

| 6/2/2006 | | Double D. Western World | | 1,124 96 | 9,624 96 |
| | | [Checking]   New saddle | | | |

If the asset was acquired without an exchange of cash, you can enter the transaction directly into the asset account, using the Gift Received category (or a similar category of your choice) to categorize the income. Similarly, if the asset was disposed of without an exchange of cash, you can enter the transaction into the asset account register using the Gifts Given or Charity (or other appropriate category) to categorize the write-off.

If you have completely disposed of the asset and no longer need the account, don't delete the account! Doing so will remove all income and expense category transactions and uncategorize all transfer transactions related to the account. Instead, consider hiding the account to get it off account lists. I explain how in Chapter 3.

## Updating Asset Values

A variety of situations can change the value of a single asset. The type of situation will determine how the value is adjusted. Here are three common examples.

## Recording Improvements

Certain home-related expenditures can be considered improvements that increase the value of your home. It's important that you keep track of improvements because they raise the property's tax basis, thus reducing the amount of capital gains you may have to record (and pay tax on) when you sell the house. Your tax advisor can help you determine which expenditures can be capitalized as home improvements.

Since most home improvements involve an expenditure, use the appropriate cash flow account register to record the transaction. Be sure to enter the appropriate asset account (House, Condo, Land, and so on) as a transfer account in the Category field. Here's what a home improvement transaction might look like in my checking account:

| 6/10/2006 | 5240 | Dan The Man Home Improvements | 3,200 00 | | 5,318 87 |
| | | [House]          New Deck | | | |

And here's the same transaction in my House asset account:

| 6/10/2006 | | Dan The Man Home Improvements | | 3,200 00 | 338,200 00 |
| | | [House Checking]   New Deck | | | |

## Adjusting for Market Value

Real estate, vehicles, and other large-ticket item assets are also affected by market values. Generally speaking, real estate values go up, vehicle values go down, and other item values can vary either way depending on what they are.

To adjust for market value, click the Update Balance button in the button bar of the account register for the asset you want to adjust. The Update Account Balance dialog, which is shown next, appears. Use this dialog to enter the date and market value for the asset. Then select a category or transfer account to record the gain or loss of value.

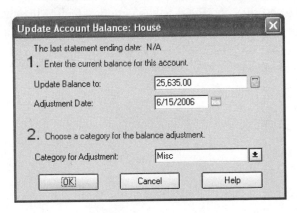

When you click OK, the entry is added to the account register as a reconciled transaction:

| 6/15/2006 | Balance Adjustment | 9,547 | 24 | R | | 25,635 | 00 |
|-----------|--------------------|-------|----|----|----|--------|----|
| | Misc | | | | | | |

If you don't want the adjustment to affect any category or account other than the asset, choose the same asset account as a transfer account. When you click OK, a dialog will warn you that you are trying to record a transfer into the same account. Click OK again. You can see an example of an adjustment like this in Figure 13-1.

## Recording Depreciation

Depreciation is a calculated reduction in the value of an asset. Depreciation expense can be calculated using a variety of acceptable methods, including straight line, sum of the year's digits, and declining balance. Normally, it reduces the asset's value regularly, with monthly, quarterly, or annual adjustments.

Depreciation is commonly applied to property used for business purposes, since depreciation expense on those assets may be tax deductible. If you think depreciation on an asset you own may be tax deductible, use Quicken to track the depreciation expense. Otherwise, depreciation probably isn't worth the extra effort it requires to track.

To record depreciation, create an entry in the asset account that reduces the value by the amount of the depreciation. Use a Depreciation expense category to record the expense. The transaction might look something like this:

| 6/1/2006 | Depreciation | 200 | 00 | | 24,363 | 17 |
|----------|-------------------|-----|----|----|--------|----|
| | Auto:Depreciation | | | | | |

Keep in mind that you can set up monthly, quarterly, or annual depreciation transactions as scheduled transactions. This automates the process of recording them when they are due. I tell you about scheduled transactions in Chapter 7.

# Managing Household Records

## Chapter 14

## In This Chapter:

- *Tracking the value of personal possessions*
- *Organizing emergency records*

When most people think of assets, they think of homes, cars, and other big-ticket items. But personal possessions—such as the furniture and electronics equipment in your home, the bicycle and golf clubs in your garage, and the stamp collection on the shelf in your hall closet—are also part of your assets. Quicken Home Inventory makes it easy to record and track the value of these things. Similarly, Quicken's Emergency Records Organizer enables you to keep track of information that's good to have on hand, especially in the event of an emergency. Together, these Quicken features help you keep your household records manageable.

In this chapter, I explain how to use Quicken Home Inventory and the Emergency Records Organizer to create detailed records of your belongings and other important information.

## Quicken Home Inventory Manager

If you like the features of Quicken Home Inventory but want even more features and flexibility, check out Quicken Home Inventory Manager, a separate software package from Intuit. With Quicken Home Inventory Manager, you can track all of your family possessions by owner or beneficiary, mark items sold or donated, and even include photographs of items. Best of all, the software works with Quicken, so there's no need to duplicate data entry or maintain two separate databases.

You can learn more about Quicken Home Inventory Manager on the Quicken Web site, www.quicken.com.

# Quicken Home Inventory

Quicken Home Inventory is a separate program that comes with Quicken Personal Finance Software. You can open it from within Quicken, enter or edit information about the things in your home, and then update your Quicken data file with item valuations. You can also use Quicken Home Inventory to keep track of your insurance policies and any insurance claims you might make.

Quicken Home Inventory is excellent for providing detailed information about your possessions. This information is extremely valuable in the event of a burglary, fire, or other loss when you need to provide details to the police and/or insurance company. Enter this information and print reports to keep in a safe place. Then, once a year or so—or right after a big yard sale—update the entries and prepare a fresh report so your printed files are up-to-date. Don't get carried away! Although you can use Quicken Home Inventory to track every possession in every room, from the ceiling lamp to the carpeting, entering that kind of detail isn't really necessary. Instead, enter the most valuable items, the ones that would be most difficult or costly to replace. This will save you time while enabling you to record your most important possessions.

## Entering Basic Information

To start, choose Property & Debt | Quicken Home Inventory. The Quicken Home Inventory program starts and appears onscreen, over your Quicken program window (see Figure 14-1). You can use this List View window to add or modify summary information about each inventory item.

To add an item to the home inventory, begin by choosing a home location from the drop-down list near the top of the window. Click New at the bottom of the window or click anywhere in the first empty line to start a new line. Then enter basic information about the item on the line and press ENTER.

A quick way to enter a standard item is to choose the item category and then double-click one of the suggested items in the list on the right side of the window. Modify the values if necessary and press ENTER.

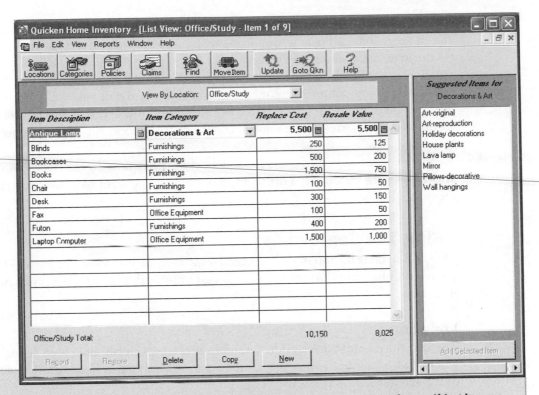

**Figure 14-1 •** Quicken Home Inventory enables you to report the value of everything in your home, room by room.

## Adding Details

To add details about an item, select it and then click the icon beside it in the Item Description column. Use the Detail View window (shown here) to enter more information about the item, such as its make and model, its serial number, and its purchase date.

Clicking the Receipts & Records button displays the Receipts And Records dialog. You can toggle check boxes in this dialog to indicate the types of records you have for the item and to enter information about where those records can be found.

Clicking the Resale Value History button displays the Resale Value History dialog, which you can use to record changes in the item's resale value. Click the New button in this dialog to create a new value entry. You may find this feature useful for keeping track of the value of collectible items, especially those you hold as "investments."

When you're finished adding item details, click the Return To List View button at the top of the window. If a dialog appears asking if you want to record changes to the item, click Yes.

## Using the Toolbar

The toolbar along the top of the Quicken Home Inventory window (see Figure 14-1) offers a number of options you can use to customize and work with the program and its data.

### Locations

The Locations button displays the Locations dialog, which is shown here. It enables you to add, modify, or remove names for rooms in your home. It also displays a list of entered items by location.

### Categories

The Categories button displays the Categories dialog, shown next, which enables you to add, modify, or remove names for categories of items. It also displays a list of entered items by category.

A quick note here: Don't confuse "categories" in Quicken Home Inventory with "categories" in Quicken. The two terms are used differently. Quicken Home Inventory categories have nothing to do with Quicken categories.

## Policies

The Policies button displays the Policies dialog, shown next, which enables you to add, modify, or remove information about insurance policies. It also displays a list of entered items by insurance policy. (You can set the insurance policy for an item in the Detail View window, shown earlier.)

When you click the dialog's New button to create a new policy or Edit button to edit an existing policy, the New Policy or Edit Policy dialog appears. Use it to enter details about the policy, including the contact information for making changes or claims. If you enter a Coverage dollar amount, Quicken displays the amount in the Policies dialog, along with the difference between the Coverage amount and the value of insured items. A negative number indicates that you don't have enough insurance to cover all items.

## Claims

The Claims button displays the Insurance Claims dialog, which lists any claims you have entered into Quicken Home Inventory.

To create a new claim, click the New button in the dialog. A new Claim Instructions dialog appears, with information about creating a claim. Read the instructions and click OK to dismiss it. Then fill out the fields in the New Claim dialog to enter details about the claim. You can click the Items button to display a list of all items entered in Quicken Home Inventory for the policy you selected. Then select each item you want to include in your claim and click OK.

When you're finished entering information in the New Claim dialog, click OK. A new dialog appears, asking if you want to create a report showing the claim information. Click Yes to create the report onscreen, and then click Print to print it and Close to return to the Quicken Home Inventory List View window.

## Find

The Find button displays the Find Item dialog, which you can use to search for inventory items. Enter search criteria in the Search For box, and then toggle check boxes in the Search In area to determine where the text should be matched. When you click Find All, Quicken Home Inventory displays a list of all items that matched the search criteria.

## Move Item

The Move Item button enables you to change the location of an item. Click the button to display the Move Item dialog, shown next. Choose a location from the Current Location drop-down list to view a list of items in that location. Select the item(s) you want to move in the Items list, and then select the location you want to move it to in the Move To This Location list. Click the Move button to change the item's location. (I wish it were this easy to move a refrigerator from the kitchen to the garage!)

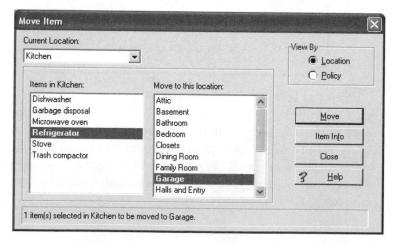

You can repeat this process for each item you want to move. When you're finished, click Close.

## Update

The Update button updates the home inventory information in Quicken to reflect any changes you made while working with Quicken Home Inventory. I explain how this works a little later in this chapter in the section titled "Updating Quicken Information."

## Goto Qkn

The Goto Qkn (go to Quicken) button switches you back to Quicken without closing Quicken Home Inventory. You can use the Windows task bar or choose Property & Debt | Quicken Home Inventory to return to Quicken Home Inventory.

## Help

The Help button changes the mouse pointer into a help pointer—a pointer with a question mark. Click the item you want to learn more about. A window appears with information. You can click the window's close button to dismiss it when you're finished reading it.

## Printing Home Inventory Reports

The Reports menu in the Quicken Home Inventory program window offers a number of basic reports you can use to print inventory information, as shown next. This is extremely useful when applying for homeowner or home office insurance, especially when the insurance company requires detailed information about certain types of belongings.

To create a report, choose its name from the menu. The report appears onscreen—Figure 14-2 shows an example. You can use the View drop-down list to change the way information is presented in the report, and click the Preview button to see exactly what it will look like when printed. When you're ready to print the report, click the Print button. Click the Close button to close the report and return to Quicken Home Inventory's List View window.

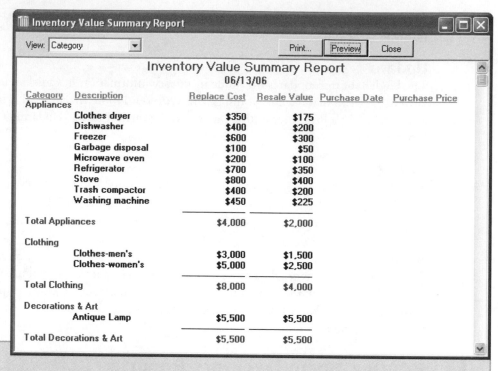

**Figure 14-2 • A Quicken Home Inventory report can provide information about all of the items you entered in your home inventory.**

## Updating Quicken Information

When you've finished entering or modifying information in Quicken Home Inventory, click the Update button on its toolbar. A small dialog appears, asking you whether you want to send inventory data to the Home Inventory account in your Quicken data file. Click Yes. Then choose File | Exit to close Quicken Home Inventory.

When you switch back to Quicken, you'll see a Home Inventory account—even if you didn't create one—with a balance corresponding to the resale value of home inventory items, as shown here. When you open the account, Quicken Home Inventory automatically launches, enabling you to add or update information.

| Property & Debt Accounts | Options ▼ |
|---|---|
| Account | Ending Balance |
| **Property (Assets)** | |
| Holiday Savings | 1,250.00 |
| Home Inventory | 20,075.00 |
| Honda S2000 | 25,635.00 |
| Horses & Tack | 9,624.96 |
| House | 338,200.00 |
| Jeep | 21,550.00 |
| Office Condo | 72,000.00 |
| **Subtotal** | **488,334.96** |

# Emergency Records Organizer

The Emergency Records Organizer (ERO) enables you to track personal, financial, and legal information that may come in handy in the event of an emergency. It consists of a number of forms you can fill in with information. You can enter as much or as little information as you like. You can go into great detail on subjects that are important to you and completely ignore others. You can update and print the information at any time. It's this flexibility—and the fact that all information can be stored in one place—that makes the ERO a useful tool.

To open the ERO, choose Property & Debt | Emergency Records Organizer. Its main window, which provides an introduction to its features, appears. Read what's in the window or click the Getting Started link to learn more.

## Creating and Updating Records

To create or modify ERO records, click the ERO's Create/Update Records tab to display the entry window, which is shown in Figure 14-3. The window has three parts: the area drop-down list, the topic list, and the entry form.

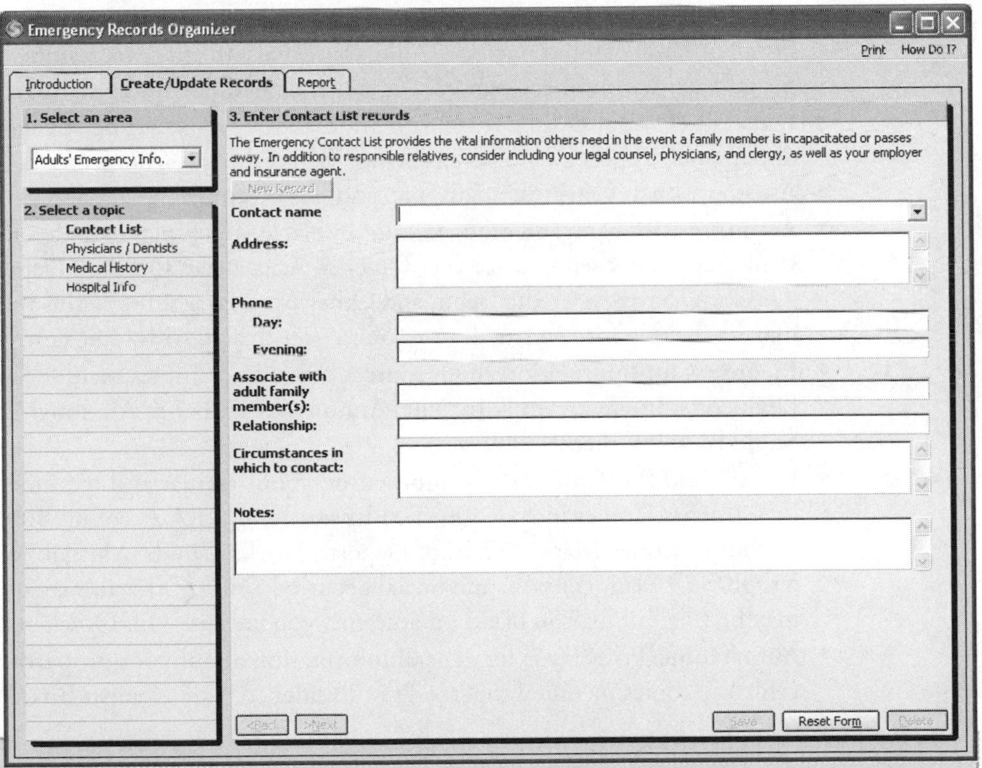

**Figure 14-3 • Use the main entry window of the Emergency Records Organizer to add records.**

To enter the information you want to organize, follow the steps as they appear in the window, and then click Save. You can then click New Record to add another record for the same area and topic or repeat the steps to add records for other areas or topics.

## Areas and Topics

The ERO offers 11 different areas of information, each with its own set of topics:

- **Adults' Emergency Info** is information you may need in the event of an adult's health-related emergency. Topics include Contact List (refer to Figure 14-3), Physicians/Dentists, Medical History, and Hospital Information.

- **Children's Emergency Info** is information you may need in the event of a child's health-related emergency. Topics include Contact List, Physicians/Dentists, Medical History, and Hospital Information.

- **Adults' Important Info** is important information about the adults in your home or family. Topics include Summary (birth date, Social Security number, driver's license number, and so on), Residence, Employment/Business, Business Partners, Education, Marriage Info, and Military Record.

- **Children's Important Info** is important information about the children in your home or family. Topics include Child's Summary (birth date, school, grade, and Social Security number), School, Caretaker, Schedules, and Guardian.

- **Personal & Legal Docs** is for information about important personal and legal documents. Topics include Will, Living Will, Funeral Arrangements, Powers of Attorney, Birth Certificate, Passport, and Tax Records.

- **Accounts** is for bank and other account information. Topics include Quicken Bank Acct., Quicken Credit Acct., Quicken Asset Acct., Quicken Liability Acct., Checking, Savings, Credit/Debit, and Other Accounts. Some of this information may be filled in for you based on accounts you created with Quicken.

- **Income** is for information about sources of income. Topics include Salary, Dividends, Interest, Rental Income, Annuity, Trust Fund, Alimony, Child Support, and Other.

- **Invest. And Retirement** is for information about regular and retirement investments. Topics include Quicken Invest. Acct., IRA Account, 401(k) Account, Money Market, Cert. of Deposit, Stocks, Bonds, Mutual Funds, Keogh/SEP Plan, Pension, and Social Security. Some of this information may be filled in for you based on accounts you created with Quicken.

- **Auto/Home/Property** is for general information about your property and vehicles. Topics include Property, Prev. Residence, Safe Deposit Box, Post

Office Box, Safe, Alarm Information, Storage, Pets, Automobile, Motorcycle, and Recreational.

- **Insurance** is for insurance information. Topics include Life Insurance, Medical Insurance, Dental Insurance, Auto Insurance, Property Insurance, Disability Insurance, and Other Insurance.
- **Mortgage/Loans** is for information about loans. Topics include Mortgage, Personal Loans, Auto Loans, and School Loans.

At this point, you might be wondering about the wisdom of keeping all kinds of important—and often private—information in one place. After all, the burglar who took your stamp collection and fax machine could also take your computer. Fortunately, you can back up and password-protect your Quicken data file. I show you how in Appendix A.

## Entry Form

The entry form that appears when you choose an area and select a topic (see Figure 14-3) varies with the area and topic. Each form offers labeled text boxes for entering appropriate information. You can enter as much information as you like and skip over as many fields as you like. You won't get an error message for entering "wrong" information.

When you've finished filling in a form for a topic, click the Save button in the entry form part of the window. Then, to create a new record in the same area, click the New Record button and fill in a fresh form. You can view and edit other records at any time by clicking the Back or Next button.

When a topic has one or more records stored for it, a green check mark appears to the left of the topic name. This makes it easy to locate completed records.

## Printing Reports

The ERO includes its own reporting feature, which makes it easy to generate reports for a variety of purposes based on the information you entered. You can give printed reports to people who may need them and lock others up in a secure place for when you need them.

Click the Report tab on the ERO window to display the report options (see Figure 14-4). You can select a report from the drop-down list at the top of the window and preview it in the area below. Then click the Print button on the button bar to print the currently selected report. It's as simple as that.

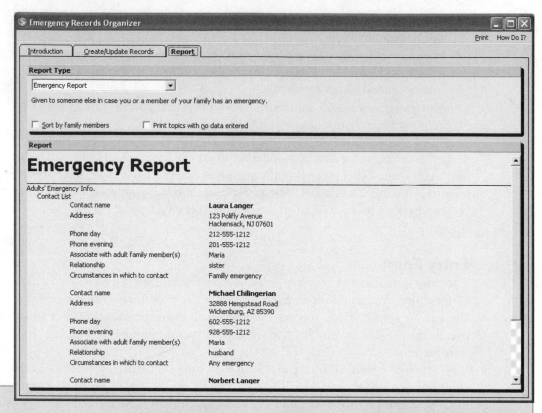

**Figure 14-4 • The Report tab of the ERO window enables you to select predefined reports to view onscreen or print.**

Here's a quick list of the reports so you know what's available:

- **Emergency Report** (shown in Figure 14-4) is to give to someone in case of a family emergency.
- **Caretaker Report** is for someone taking care of your home or pet while you are away.
- **Survivor's Report** is for your lawyer or heirs in the event of your death.
- **Summary Of Records Entered Report** lists the areas, topics, and record names you've entered in the ERO. It does not provide any detailed information.
- **Detail Report** lists everything you've entered into the ERO. As the name implies, it provides detail and can be used as a kind of master list.

# Keeping Tabs on Your Property and Debt

## Chapter 15

## In This Chapter:

- *The Property & Debt Center*
- *Property and debt alerts*
- *Asset and liability account details*
- *Reports and graphs*

When you create asset and liability accounts and enter related transactions into Quicken, as discussed in the previous two chapters, Quicken summarizes your entries and calculates balances. It displays this information in a number of places: the Account Bar, the Property & Debt Center, account registers and overviews, and reports and graphs. You can consult Quicken's calculated balances and totals at any time to learn about your equity and the expenses associated with your debt and automobile.

In this chapter, I explain how to use Quicken's reporting features to keep tabs on your property and debt. As you'll learn in these pages, a wealth of information about your net worth is just a mouse click away.

## The Property & Debt Center

Asset and liability accounts are part of Quicken's Property & Debt Center. You can open the Property & Debt Center by clicking its button on the Account Bar or by choosing Property & Debt | Go To Property & Debt Center. Figure 15-1 shows what the Property & Debt Center might look like.

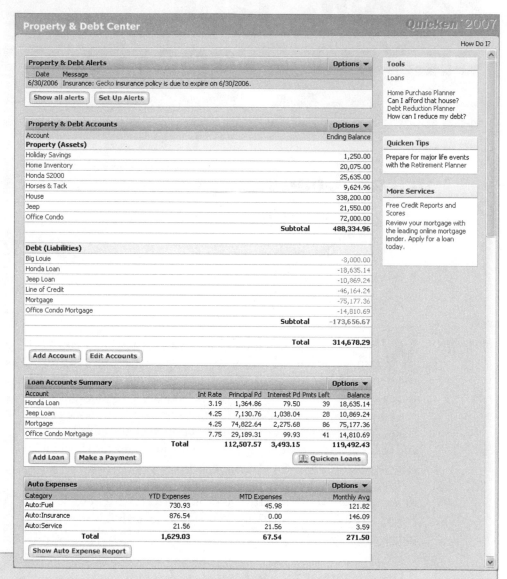

**Figure 15-1 • The Property & Debt Center displays information about assets and liabilities.**

This part of the chapter takes a closer look at the Property & Debt Center, so you know exactly what you can find there and how you can customize it for your own use.

## Account Balances

The Property & Debt Accounts area (refer to Figure 15-1) lists all of your asset and liability accounts and displays each account's ending balance. You can click the name of an account to view its account register or overview—I tell you about those windows later in this chapter in the section titled "Account Details."

One of the nice things about the Property & Debt Accounts area is that it separates assets from liabilities and provides subtotals for each. The total at the bottom is the net of the two. If this is a negative number, your finances are in some serious trouble.

The Options pop-up menu at the top of the Property & Debt Accounts area and two buttons at the bottom of the area offer several options for working with accounts:

- **Add An Account** (menu option) and **Add Account** (button) display the Quicken Account Setup dialog, which you can use to create an asset or liability account. I explain how to create accounts in Chapter 3 and provide details specific to asset and liability accounts in Chapter 13.
- **Reconcile An Account** (menu option) displays a dialog you can use to choose any of your accounts and perform a reconciliation. I explain how to reconcile accounts in Chapter 8.
- **Get Transactions Online** (menu option) displays the One Step Update dialog, which you can use to download transactions from your financial institution. I explain how to use One Step Update in Chapter 7 and how to download cash flow account transactions in Chapter 6.
- **Set Up Alerts** (menu option) displays the Setup tab of the Alerts Center window, so you can set up alerts. I explain how to set up property- and debt-related alerts later in this chapter in the section titled "Alerts."
- **View Account List** (menu option) and **Edit Accounts** (button) display the View Accounts tab of the Account List window, which you can use to view and manage accounts. The Account List is covered in detail in Chapter 3.

## Loan Accounts Summary

The Loan Accounts Summary (refer to Figure 15-1) lists all of your amortized loans—the ones you set up in the View Loans dialog, as instructed in Chapter 13. It includes several columns of information for each loan:

- **Account** is the name of the account. You can click the account name to view its register or overview, which I discuss later in this chapter.
- **Int Rate** is the current interest rate.
- **Principal Pd** is the total of the payments made toward the loan balance.
- **Interest Pd** is the total of the interest paid for the loan.
- **Pmts Left** is the number of payments left on the loan. This does not take into consideration any extra payments you may have made that will reduce the loan term.
- **Balance** is the ending balance for the account.

The Principal Pd, Interest Pd, and Balance columns contain information calculated by Quicken based on transactions entered in your Quicken data file. It's important to note that the Interest Pd column totals only the amount of interest entered in Quicken. If you set up an existing loan for which payments (including interest) had already been made, Quicken does not include principal or interest already paid on the loan in the totals.

The Options pop-up menu at the top of the Loan Accounts Summary area and three buttons at the bottom of the area offer several loan-related options:

- **Set Up A New Loan** (menu option) and **Add Loan** (button) display the Loan Setup dialog, so you can create a new loan. I explain how to use this dialog in Chapter 13.
- **Make A Payment** (menu option and button) displays the Loan Summary tab of the View Loans window. To make a payment on a loan, choose the loan name from the Choose Loan pop-up menu and then click the Make Payment button. I explain how to use the View Loans window and make payments in Chapter 13.
- **Plan To Reduce My Debt** (menu option) displays the Debt Reduction dialog, which you can use to develop a debt reduction plan. I cover this planning feature in Chapter 18.
- **Quicken Loans** (button) displays information about Quicken Loans, one of the services available through Quicken.

## Auto Expenses

The Auto Expenses area, at the bottom of the Property & Debt Center (refer to Figure 15-1), offers a customizable summary of expenses related to your automobile. There are four columns of information:

- **Category** is the full name of the category (including subcategory, if applicable) of expense.
- **YTD Expenses** is the total year-to-date amount for that category.
- **MTD Expenses** is the total month-to-date amount for that category.
- **Monthly Avg** is the monthly average expenditure for that category.

You can customize the Auto Expenses report by choosing Customize This Report from its Options pop-up menu. The Customize Auto Expenses Component dialog appears. It has three tabs: Accounts, Categories (shown next), and Classes. Click a tab, and then toggle check marks next to account or category names to include them in or exclude them from the report. By default, the report includes all accounts and just the Auto category (with its subcategories). But you can make the report include anything you like. When you're finished making changes, click OK to save them. The Auto Expenses area refreshes to reflect your changes.

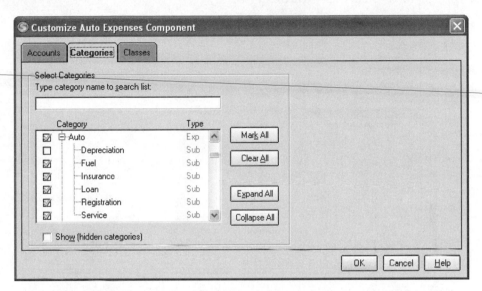

Clicking the Show Auto Expense Report button at the bottom of the Auto Expenses area displays a report window containing the Auto Expenses report. I explain how to work with and customize reports in Chapter 9.

## Alerts
Property and debt alerts appear right at the top of the Property & Debt Center (refer to Figure 15-1). This area displays any alerts you have created for your assets or liabilities, when it's time to alert you.

### Setting Up Property and Debt Alerts
To set up an alert, begin by clicking the Setup Alerts button in the Property & Debt Alerts area. The Setup tab of the Alerts Center window appears. Click the name of the alert you want to set on the left side of the window to display its options on the right. Figure 15-2 shows what the Insurance Reappraisal alert settings might look like with two alerts already set.

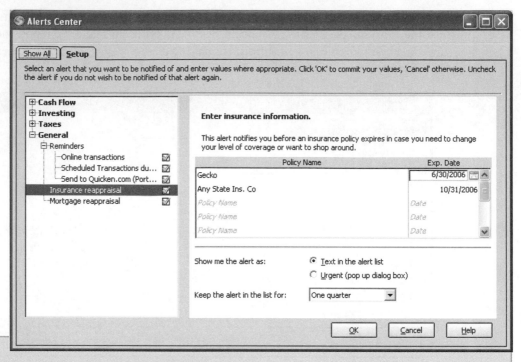

**Figure 15-2 • Use the Setup tab of the Alerts Center window to set up alerts, such as the Insurance Reappraisal alert shown here.**

Two alerts apply to property and debt:

- **Insurance Reappraisal** (see Figure 15-2) notifies you before an insurance policy expires so you can either reevaluate coverage or shop for a new policy.
- **Mortgage Reappraisal** notifies you before a mortgage changes from variable to fixed (or fixed to variable) so you can consider refinancing. Even if your mortgage doesn't convert, you can use this alert to remind you periodically to check for better mortgage deals.

Both alerts work pretty much the same way. For each alert, enter a name and date in the far right column. Select one of the options at the bottom of the window to indicate how you want the alert to appear: as text in the alert list (refer to Figure 15-1) or as a pop-up dialog that appears when you start Quicken. Finally, use the drop-down list to specify the length of time the alert should remain in the list and click Apply.

Repeat this process for each alert you want to set. When you're finished, click OK.

## Working with Property and Debt Alerts

The Options pop-up menu at the top of the Property & Debt Alerts area and two buttons at the bottom of the area offer several options for working with alerts:

- **Show All Alerts** (menu option and button) displays the Show All tab of the Alerts Center window, so you can see all alerts set up in Quicken.
- **Set Up Alerts** (menu option and button) displays the Setup Alerts tab of the Alerts Center window, so you can add an alert.
- **Delete** and **Delete All** (menu options) display the Delete Alert(s) dialog, which you can use to delete either the selected alert (and all alerts like it) or all alerts.

## Account Details

To learn more about the transactions and balances for a specific account, you can view account details in the Register and Overview windows. Click the name of an account (other than a Home Inventory account, as discussed in Chapter 14) in the Account Bar or Property & Debt Center to open these windows—click a tab at the top of the window to display the one you want (refer to Figures 15-3 and 15-4).

### Register

An account's Register window (see Figure 15-3) lists all transactions entered into that account, as well as the ending balance. As I explain in Chapter 13, you can enter transactions directly into the register. Other transactions—such as principal payments for a mortgage or other loan—are automatically calculated and entered by Quicken.

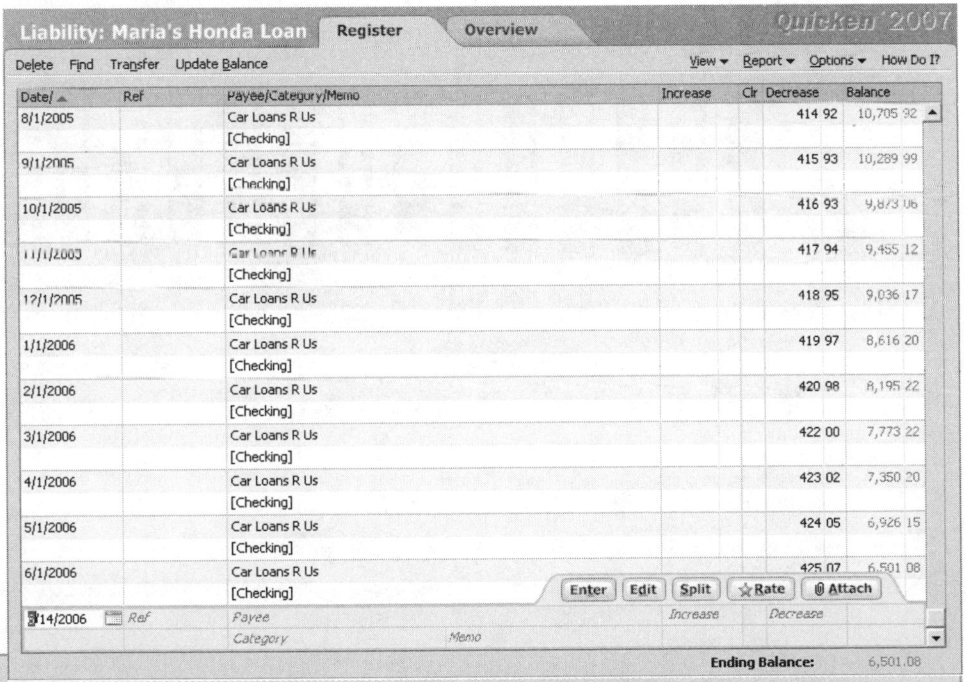

**Figure 15-3** • **Here's an example of the register window for a car loan.**

## Overview

An account's Overview window (see Figure 15-4) is split into four different areas of information about the account: Account Attributes, Account Status, Account Balance (or Equity, for assets with associated loans), and Account Attachments.

### Account Attributes

The Account Attributes area provides basic information about the account, including its name and description and whether it can be viewed on Quicken.com.

The Options menu at the top of the area offers several related commands:

- **Create A New Account** displays the Quicken Account Setup dialog, which enables you to create any kind of Quicken account. I explain how to create accounts in Chapter 3.

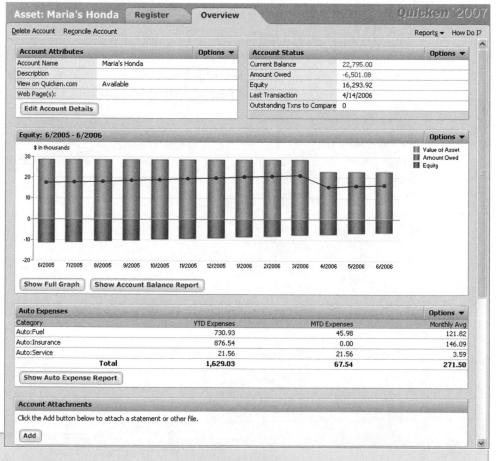

Figure 15-4 • Here's the Overview tab for a vehicle account.

- **View/Edit Comments** displays the Account Comments dialog, which you can use to enter comments about the account.
- **Set Tax Attributes** displays the Tax Schedule Information dialog, which you can use to choose tax return schedules and lines to associate with transfers in and out of the account. I explain how this feature works in Chapter 19.
- **Set Web Pages** displays the Set Web Pages dialog. You can use this dialog to enter the web addresses (or URLs) for up to three web pages related to the account; the addresses you enter appear as clickable links in the Account Attributes area. For example, you can include a link to your mortgage company's Home page or Login page in the Account Attributes area of your mortgage account so you can quickly jump to that page when working with Quicken.
- **Browse Web Pages** displays a submenu that lists the web pages you entered in the Set Web Pages dialog. Choose an option to launch Quicken's built-in browser and view that page on the Internet.

Clicking the Edit Account Details button at the bottom of the Account Attributes area displays the Account Details window, which you can use to enter general information about the account. The fields that appear in this dialog vary depending on the type of account that is displayed. The following illustration shows what it looks like for the account shown in Figure 15-3.

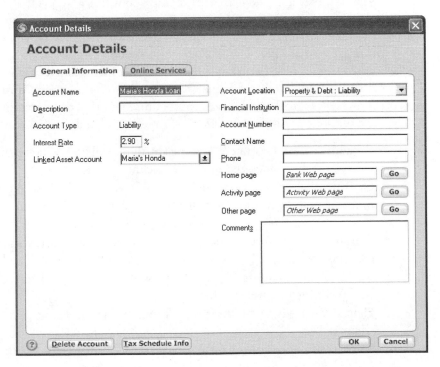

## Account Status

The Account Status area provides information about the status of the account, including balance, linked account, and equity information. You can click underlined text in the Account Status area to view the details behind linked information or perform reconciliations.

The Options pop-up menu offers three related commands:

- **Update My Account Balance** displays the Update Account Balance dialog, which you can use to change the balance of the account. I explain how to modify an account's balance with this dialog in Chapter 13.
- **Manage My Loans** displays the View Loans dialog, which you can use to add, modify, or delete loans. I explain how this dialog works in Chapter 13, too.
- **View All My Accounts** displays the View Accounts tab of the Account List window, which I cover in Chapter 3.

## Account Balance or Equity

The Account Balance or Equity area (refer to Figure 15-4) displays a graphical representation of the balance of the account. (This area is labeled Equity for any asset with an associated loan, such as the automobile in Figure 15-4; it is labeled Account Balance for any other asset or any liability.) You can click a column to see its exact value.

What's interesting (and extremely useful) about this graph is that if the account is linked to another account, both accounts are displayed on the graph, and your equity—the difference between what an asset is worth and what you still owe on its loan—is charted as a line. Figure 15-4 shows a good example. Although the Overview window is for an asset (a car), it shows the value of the related liability (a car loan). See how the Equity line and Value Of Asset column go down in April 2006? That's because the car's market value was updated that month, thus decreasing both.

The Options pop-up menu offers a number of related commands:

- **Customize This Graph** displays the Customize dialog, which you can use to change the date range and categories included in the graph.
- **Go To A Full Screen View Of This Graph** displays the Account Balance graph in its own report window, with a tab for its corresponding report. I tell you about creating reports and graphs next in this chapter and in Chapter 9.
- **Report My Net Worth** displays an Account Balance report, with a tab for its corresponding graph. I discuss reports and graphs in this chapter and in Chapter 9.
- **View All My Accounts** displays the View Accounts tab of the Account List window, which I cover in Chapter 3.
- **Help Reduce My Debt** displays the Debt Reduction dialog, which I discuss in Chapter 18.
- **Forecast My Future Account Balances** starts Quicken's forecasting feature, which I discuss in detail in Chapter 18.

## Account Attachments

The Account Attachments area lists all file attachments to the account. I explain how to attach files to an account in Chapter 5.

# Reports and Graphs

The information you enter in Property & Debt Center accounts appears on two reports and their corresponding graphs: Account Balances and Net Worth. These reports provide the same information with slight differences in the order and wording of the presentation.

## Creating Reports

To create a report, choose its name from the appropriate submenu—in this case, Net Worth & Balances—under the Reports menu. Quicken makes its calculations and displays the report (see Figure 15-5) in a report window.

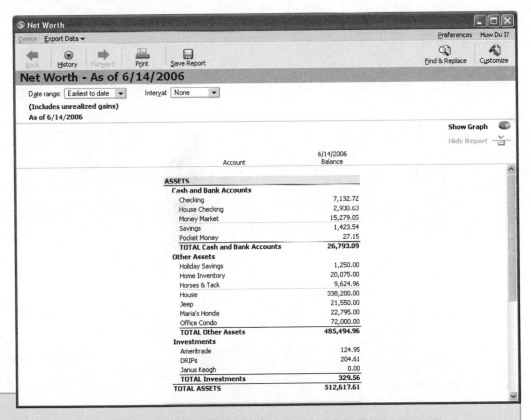

**Figure 15-5 • A Net Worth report summarizes the balances in all of your accounts.**

## Working with the Report Window

The report window works the same for the Account Balances and Net Worth reports as it does for any other Quicken report. I explain how to use buttons and other options in the report window to customize reports, create subreports, and save reports in Chapter 9; consult that chapter for details.

# The Planning Center

This part of the book tells you about Quicken Personal Planning Software's planning features, which you can use to plan for your retirement, major purchases, and other life events. It covers Quicken's built-in financial calculators, as well as features that can help you save money and make your dreams come true. Its three chapters are:

Part Five

# Planning for the Future

## Chapter 16

## In This Chapter:

- *Quicken planning overview*
- *Life event planners*
- *Playing "what if"*

To many people, the future is an unknown, a mystery. After all, who can say what will happen tomorrow, next year, or ten years from now? But if you think about your future, you can usually come up with a few events that you can plan for: your marriage, the purchase of a new home, the birth of your children (and their education years later), and your retirement. (These are just examples—everyone's life runs a different course.) These events, as well as many unforeseen events, all have one thing in common: they affect your finances. In this chapter, I tell you about planning for future events and how tools within Quicken Personal Finance Software and on Quicken.com can help.

## Planning for Retirement

Throughout your life, you work and earn money to pay your bills, buy the things you and your family need or want, and help your kids get started with their own lives. But there comes a day when it's time to retire. Those regular paychecks stop coming, and you find yourself relying on the money you put away for retirement.

Retirement planning is one of the most important financial planning jobs facing individuals and couples. In this section, I tell you about the importance of planning, and offer some planning steps and a word of advice based on personal experience.

## The Importance of Planning

Retired people live on fixed incomes. That's not a problem—*if* the income is fixed high enough to support a comfortable lifestyle. You can help ensure that there's enough money to finance your retirement years by planning and saving now.

Poor retirement planning can lead to catastrophic results—imagine running out of money when you turn 75. Or having to make a lifestyle change when you're 65 to accommodate a much lower income.

Planning is even more important these days as longevity increases. People are living longer than ever. Your retirement dollars may need to support you for 20 years or more, at a time when the cost of living will likely be much higher than it is today.

With proper planning, it's possible to properly finance your retirement years without putting a strain on your working years. By closely monitoring the status of your retirement funds, periodically adjusting your plan, and acting accordingly, your retirement years can be the golden years they're supposed to be.

## Planning Steps

Retirement planning is much more than deciding to put $2,000 in an IRA every year. It requires careful consideration of what you have, what you'll need, and how you can make those two numbers the same.

### Assess What You Have

Take a good look at your current financial situation. What tax-deferred retirement savings do you already have? A pension? An IRA? Something else? What regular savings do you have? What taxable investments do you have? The numbers you come up with will form the basis of your final retirement funds—like a seed you'll grow.

Be sure to consider property that can be liquidated to contribute to retirement savings. For example, if you currently live in a large home to accommodate your family, you may eventually want to live in a smaller home. The proceeds from the sale of your current home may exceed the cost of your retirement home. Also consider any income-generating property that may continue to generate income in your retirement years or can be liquidated to contribute to retirement savings.

### Determine What You'll Need

What you'll need depends on many things. One simple calculation suggests you'll need 80 percent of your current gross income to maintain your current lifestyle in your retirement years. You may find a calculation like this handy if retirement is still many years in the future and you don't really know what things will cost.

Time is an important factor in calculating the total amount you should have saved by retirement day. Ask yourself two questions:

- **How long do you have to save?** Take your current age and subtract it from the age at which you plan to retire. That's the number of years you have left to save.
- **How long will you be in retirement?** Take the age at which you plan to retire and subtract it from the current life expectancy for someone of your age and gender. That's the number of years you have to save for.

Doing this math tells me that I have only 18 years left to save for a 28-year retirement. I'm glad I've been saving!

## Develop an Action Plan

Once you know how much you need, it's time to think seriously about how you can save it. This requires putting money away in one or more savings or investment accounts. I tell you about your options a little later in this chapter.

## Stick to the Plan!

The most important part of any plan is sticking to it. For example, if you plan to save $5,000 a year, don't think you can just save $2,000 this year and make up the $3,000 next year. There are two reasons: First, you can't "make up" the interest lost on the $3,000 you didn't save this year, and second, you're kidding yourself if you think you'll manage to put away $8,000 next year.

If you consider deviating from your plan, just think about the alternative: making ends meet with a burger-flipping job in the local fast food joint when you're 68 years old.

## Don't Wait! Act Now!

I remember when I first began thinking about retirement. I was 30 or 31 and had been self-employed for about three years. I didn't have a pension or 401(k) plan with my former employer. I didn't have much saved. I had only $2,000 in an IRA. Up until that point, I never worried about retirement—but one day something just clicked, and retirement became something to think about.

I've done a lot of retirement planning and saving since then. While I admit that I don't have a perfect plan (yet), I've certainly come a long way in ten years. But when I consider how much more I could have saved if I'd begun five years earlier, I could kick myself for waiting.

See for yourself. Table 16-1 shows how $2,500, $5,000, and $7,500 per-year contributions to a tax-deferred retirement account earning 5 percent a year can grow. (These calculations do not take into consideration tax benefits or inflation.)

| Savings at Age 62 | | | | |
|---|---|---|---|---|
| Start Age | Years of Saving | $2,500/year | $5,000/year | $7,500/year |
| 60 | 2 | $5,125 | $10,250 | $15,375 |
| 50 | 12 | $39,793 | $79,586 | $119,378 |
| 40 | 22 | $96,263 | $192,526 | $288,789 |
| 30 | 32 | $188,247 | $376,494 | $564,741 |
| 20 | 42 | $338,079 | $676,159 | $1,014,238 |

**Table 16-1 • Regular Savings Can Make Your Money Grow**

## Getting Started with the Quicken Planner

The Planning Center—which is really the Planning tab of the Financial Overview window (refer to Figure 16-1, later in this chapter)—offers access to all of Quicken's built-in planning features, including the Quicken Planner's main plan assumptions and individual financial planners. Once you have set up your plan, the Planning Center provides an up-to-date view of how well your plan is working.

Here's how it works. You start by entering plan assumptions, which include information about you, your current finances, and your tax rate. Quicken makes calculations based on what you entered to display plan results. As you continue working with Quicken, entering transactions that affect your finances, Quicken updates the result of the plan. It also takes into consideration your entries in any of Quicken's other planners, such as the College Planner or Special Purchase Planner.

I won't lie to you: setting up Quicken Planner assumptions can be time-consuming. But I think that the benefit of using this feature far outweighs the cost (in time) of setting it up. This is especially true if you're settled down and raising a family—Quicken can help you plan for the major events of your life so you're prepared for them. If you don't have the time to set up the Quicken Planner now, make time in the future.

In this section, I explain how to set assumptions for the Quicken Planner and how to view the results of your plan in the Planning Center.

### Setting Plan Assumptions

The easiest way to see what plan assumptions need to be made is to view the Plan Assumptions area of the Planning tab of the Financial Overview window. Choose Planning | Go To Planning Center. When you first start out, the Plan Assumptions area may look like the illustration here:

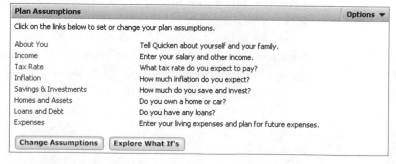

To set details for an assumption category, click its link. This displays a dialog you can use to enter information. Here's a look at each category.

## About You

Clicking the About You link displays the About You dialog, which is shown next. Its fields are pretty self-explanatory, so I won't go into much detail. (After all, you should be able to figure out how to enter your name and date of birth!) When you're finished entering information in the dialog, click Done to save it.

Here are some less obvious things to consider when entering data into the About You dialog.

**Include Spouse**   If you turn on the Include Spouse check box, you can enter information into the Spouse column of the dialog. If you don't have a spouse or don't want to include him or her in your plan, leave that check box turned off.

**Life Expectancy**   You can either enter what you think might be your life expectancy or click the Calculate button to display the Calculate Life Expectancy dialog. Set options in the dialog, and Quicken tells you how long you may live. Of course, this is an estimate based on current research into life expectancy; you may or may not live to reach the age Quicken suggests.

**Children and Dependents**   To enter information about children or other dependents, click the New button at the bottom of the dialog. This displays the Add Child/Dependent dialog, in which you can enter the name and date of birth for a dependent. When you click OK, the person's name and age are added to the list. Repeat this process for each child or dependent you need to add. Once a child or dependent has been added, you can select his or her name and click the Edit button to change information about him or her (although I can't see why a name or birth date would change), click the Delete button to remove him or her permanently from the plan, or turn on the Exclude From Plan check box so Quicken doesn't use him or her in its calculations.

## Income

Clicking the Income link displays the Income dialog, which is organized into three separate tabs of information. This is where you enter salary, retirement benefits, and other income information for you and your spouse.

**Salary**    The Salary tab, which is shown here, enables you to record information about current and future salary and self-employment income.

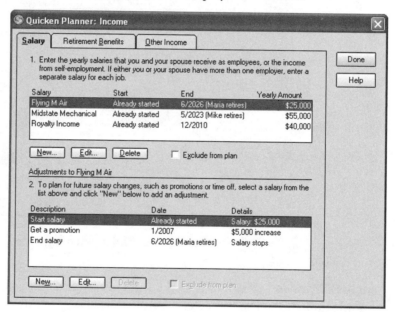

To add an income item, click the New button to display the Add Salary dialog. Then set options to enter information about the income item. As you can see in the following illustration, the Add Salary dialog is extremely flexible, enabling you to enter start and end dates for a salary—which is useful for income from seasonal employment. If you don't need to enter specific dates, choose Already Started from the When Does This Salary Start drop-down list and one of the retirement options from the When Does This Salary End drop-down list. When you click OK, the item is added to the list.

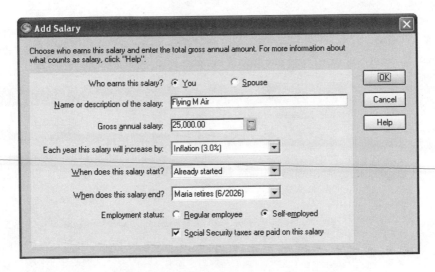

For each item you add, Quicken automatically includes adjustments that specify when the item begins and ends. But you can add other adjustments if you know about changes that will occur in the future. Select the item in the top half of the dialog, and then click the New button at the bottom of the dialog. Enter information in the Add Salary Adjustment dialog that appears (shown next) and click OK. The information is added to the bottom half of the Salary tab of the Income dialog.

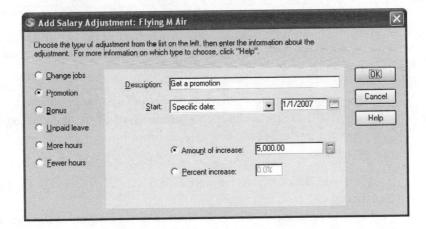

On the Salary tab, you can select any of the salary or adjustment items and click the Edit or Delete button to change or remove it. You can also select an item and turn on the Exclude From Plan check box to exclude its information from the Quicken Planner.

**Retirement Benefits**   The Retirement Benefits tab, which is shown next, enables you to enter information about Social Security or pension benefits you are currently receiving or to estimate future benefits.

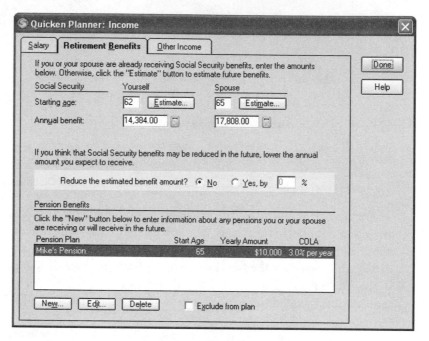

To estimate future Social Security benefits, enter the age at which you expect to begin collecting benefits and click the Estimate button. The Estimate Social Security Benefits dialog appears. You have two options:

- **Use Rough Estimate** enables you to select a salary range option to estimate benefits.
- **Use Mail-In Estimate From SS Administration** enables you to enter the amount provided by the Social Security Administration on your annual Social Security Statement.

When you click OK, the amount is automatically entered in the Retirement Benefits tab.

To add a pension, click the New button at the bottom of the Retirement Benefits tab of the Income dialog. This displays the Add Pension dialog, which is shown next. Enter information about the pension and click OK to add it to the Retirement Benefits tab. In that tab, you can select the pension and click Edit or Delete to change or remove it, or select it and turn on the Exclude From Plan check box to exclude it from the Quicken Planner's calculations.

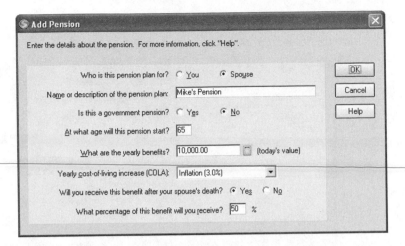

**Other Income**    The Other Income tab, shown next, enables you to enter income from other sources, such as gifts, child support, and inheritances. Don't use this tab to enter income from investments or rental properties; the Quicken Planner provides other places to enter this information.

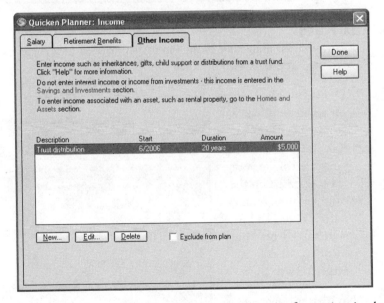

To enter an income item, click the New button. Enter information in the Add Other Income dialog, which is shown next. An interesting option in this dialog is the ability to specify how the money will be used: either saved and invested or used to pay expenses. The option you select determines how this income is used in the plan. If you're not sure what to select, leave it set to the default option. When you click OK, the item is added to the Other Income tab's list. You can edit, delete, or exclude the item from the plan as desired.

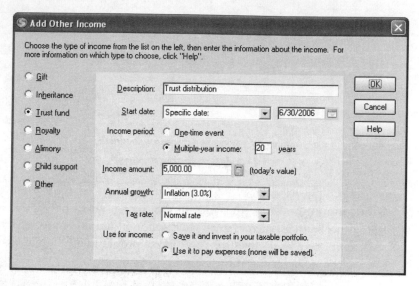

## Tax Rate

Clicking the Tax Rate link in the Plan Assumptions area displays the Average Tax Rate dialog. You have two options:

- **Demographic Average**, shown next, enables you to estimate your tax rate based on where you live and what your income is.
- **Tax Returns** enables you to estimate your tax rate based on the total income, total federal taxes, and total state taxes from your most recent tax returns.

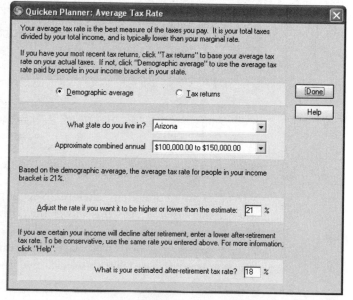

No matter how you estimate the tax rate, you can adjust it by entering a preferred value. You can also enter an estimate of your post-retirement tax rate, which may be lower.

## Inflation

Clicking the Inflation link displays the Estimated Inflation dialog, which includes a graphic depiction of the inflation trend from 1927 through 2001. Quicken suggests an inflation rate of 3 percent, but you can enter any rate you think is correct in the text box. Click Done to save your estimate.

## Savings & Investments

Clicking the Savings & Investments link displays the Savings And Investments dialog, which is organized into three tabs. Use this dialog to enter information about current bank and investment accounts, as well as contributions you or your spouse makes regularly to accounts and the return you expect to earn on your investments.

**Savings**   The Savings tab, which is shown next, lists all of the bank accounts you have set up in Quicken, along with their current balances.

If you have omitted any accounts from Quicken, now is a good time to add them if you want them to be part of your plan. Click the New button to display the Add New Account dialog; I explain how to use this dialog to create new accounts in Chapter 3.

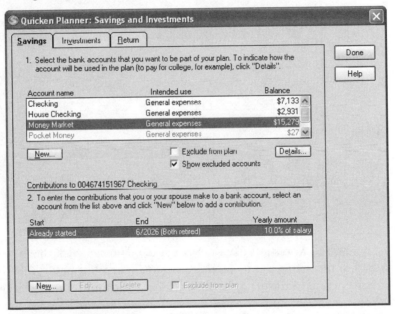

Quicken automatically assumes that each bank account will be used for General expenses. You can change this assumption by selecting an account and clicking the Details button. Choose a new purpose from the drop-down list in the Account Details dialog that appears and click OK. You'll find that until you use Quicken's other planners, General expenses is the only offered option. But if you use another planner—for example, the College Planner—an option for that planner's expense appears in the drop-down list.

If you or your spouse makes regular contributions to one of your bank accounts, you can enter information about that contribution in the dialog. In the top half of the dialog, select the account that receives the contribution. Then click the New button at the bottom of the dialog. Use the Add Contribution dialog that appears to indicate how much you contribute. The dialog will walk you through the process of entering information based on whether the contribution is a percentage of a salary or a base amount that increases each year.

**Investments**  The Investments tab, which is shown next, lists all of the investment accounts you have set up in Quicken, along with their current market values. Remember, since market value is determined by security prices, the market value is only as up-to-date as the most recently entered or downloaded security prices.

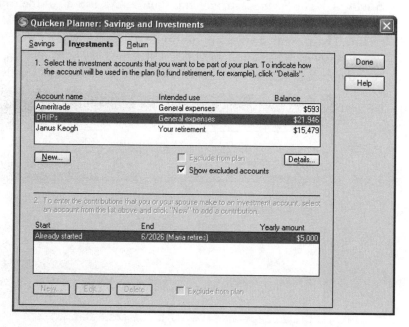

This tab works just like the Savings tab. You can click the New button in the top half of the dialog to add another investment account or click the New button in the bottom half of the dialog to enter regular contribution information for any selected investment account. You can also specify the intended use for any account by selecting the account name and clicking the Details button.

**Return**  The Return tab, shown next, enables you to specify your expected rates of return for preretirement and postretirement investments. If you turn on the check box near the top of the dialog, additional text boxes appear, enabling you to enter different rates of return for taxable and tax-deferred investments. At the bottom of the dialog, you can enter the percentage of the taxable return that is subject to taxes. This is normally 100 percent, but for your situation, the percentage may be different.

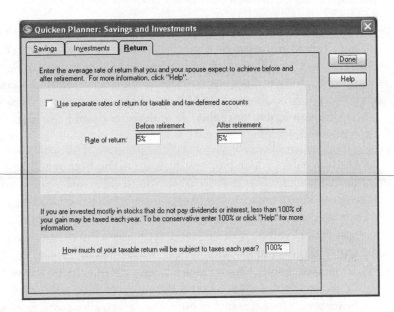

## Homes and Assets

Clicking the Homes And Assets link displays the Homes And Assets dialog, which is organized into two tabs. This is where you can enter information about currently owned assets and assets you plan to purchase in the future.

**Asset Accounts**    The Asset Accounts tab, which is shown next, lists all of the asset accounts you have created in Quicken, including accounts for your home, vehicle, home inventory, and other assets. If you have additional assets that have not yet been entered in Quicken and you want to include them in your plan, click the New button and use the Add New Account dialog that appears to create the new account; I explain how in Chapter 3.

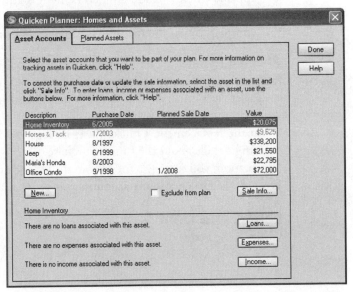

If you plan to sell an asset, you can enter selling information for it. Select the asset in the top half of the dialog, and then click the Sale Info button. A series of dialogs prompts you for information about the asset's purchase and sale date and price, as well as other information that affects how much money you can expect to receive and pay taxes on. This information is then added to your plan.

Three buttons at the bottom of the dialog enable you to associate loans, expenses, and income with a selected asset. This is especially important when working with assets you plan to sell, since the sale of the asset should also end associated debt, expenses, and income.

- **Loans** enables you to link existing loans to the asset or add new loans, including home equity loans. It also enables you to enter information about planned loans—for example, if you plan to use a home equity loan to build an addition on your house sometime next year. You can also enter information about planned payoffs—perhaps you're expecting a big trust fund check (lucky you!) and plan to use it to pay off your house.

- **Expenses** enables you to enter property tax information as well as other expenses related to the asset. For a home, this might include association fees, homeowner's insurance, and estimated maintenance and utility costs. For a car, this might include registration, fuel, service, and insurance. For each expense you add, Quicken prompts you for information about the expense, including how you expect to pay for it—with money in a specific bank account or with a loan. It even enables you to set up a monthly savings target to pay for the item.

- **Income** enables you to enter information about income you expect to earn from the asset. This is especially useful if you own rental property. The dialog that appears when you add an income item is almost the same as the Add Other Income dialog, shown earlier in this chapter. It even allows you to specify how you plan to use the income: for investment or to pay expenses.

**Planned Assets**     The Planned Assets tab enables you to enter information about any assets you plan to purchase in the future. For example, suppose you indicated in the Asset Accounts tab that you plan to sell your home or car on a specific date. If you plan to replace it with another home or car, this is where you'd enter information about the replacement. Quicken uses dialogs that walk you through the process of entering details about the future purchase. Once you've entered planned asset information, you can select the asset in the list and add loans, expenses, and income for it, as well as choose the accounts you plan to use to pay for it.

## Loans and Debt

Clicking the Loans And Debt link in the Plan Assumptions area displays the Loans And Debt dialog, which is organized into three tabs. This is where you enter information about current and planned loans, as well as information from your debt reduction plan.

**Loan Accounts**    The Loan Accounts tab, which is shown next, displays information about current loans. This information comes from loans you have set up within Quicken. To add another loan that isn't already recorded in Quicken, click the New button to display the Loan Setup dialog, which I cover in Chapter 13. If you plan to pay off a loan before its last payment date, you can click the Payoff button to enter future payoff information.

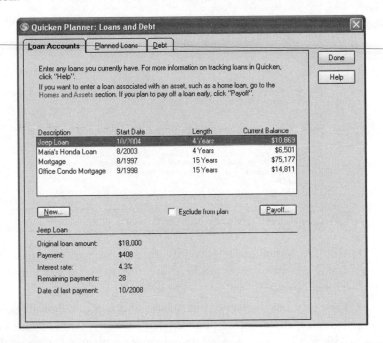

**Planned Loans**    The Planned Loans tab enables you to enter information about loans you plan to make in the future. This does not include any loans you may have already planned in the Homes And Assets dialog discussed earlier. Instead, this is for loans that are not associated with any particular asset, such as a personal loan you plan to pay for flying lessons or a really special vacation.

**Debt**    The Debt tab includes information from the Debt Reduction Planner, which I cover in detail in Chapter 18. If you have credit card and other debt, it's a good idea to complete the Debt Reduction Planner as part of your overall planning strategy.

## Expenses

Clicking the Expenses link displays the Expenses dialog, which is organized into four tabs. This is where you enter information about your living expenses, as well as any adjustments to expenses, and the expenses for college or other special events.

**Living Expenses**   The Living Expenses tab, which is shown next, enables you to enter your estimated living expenses using one of two techniques:

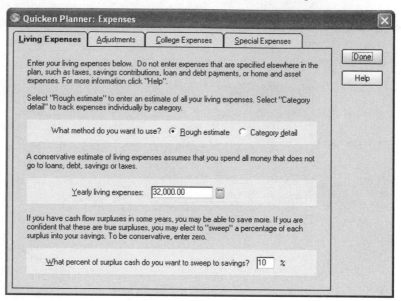

- **Rough Estimate** enables you to enter an estimate of your annual living expenses. Using this technique is quicker, but it may not be as accurate as using the Category Detail option.

- **Category Detail** enables you to have Quicken calculate an estimate of your annual living expenses based on transactions already entered in your Quicken data file. This technique is more accurate than Rough Estimate, especially if you have been using Quicken for a while and have a good history of transactions. If you select this method, you can click the Details button that appears in the middle of the dialog to display the Living Expense Category Detail dialog. Toggle check marks in the list of categories to include or exclude specific categories and enter monthly amounts as desired. When you click OK, Quicken annualizes the amounts and enters them in the Living Expenses tab.

One thing to keep in mind here: don't include expenses that you may have already included for an asset. For example, if you included car insurance expenses in the Homes And Assets dialog as an expense associated with an automobile, don't include them again here. Doing so would duplicate the expense and overstate your annual expenses.

At the bottom of the dialog, you can enter a percentage of surplus cash—cash left over after paying living expenses—that you want to put into savings.

**Adjustments**   The Adjustments tab enables you to enter any adjustments to your expenses that are related to planned changes in your life. For example, perhaps you plan to hire a nanny to take care of your child while you go back to work. You can add this planned expense as an adjustment for a predefined period of time. When you click the New button in the Adjustments tab, the Add Living Expense Adjustment dialog appears. The illustration here shows how it might look if I sent my dependent, Alex (okay, so he's just a parrot), to speech school for a few years.

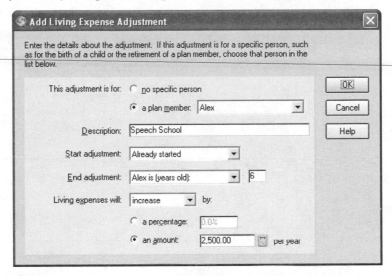

**College Expenses**    The College Expenses tab enables you to plan for the education of your children—or yourself! Clicking the New button in this tab displays the Add College Expense dialog, shown next, which walks you through the process of entering expected college expenses for a plan member. You'll have to do a little homework to come up with realistic estimates of college costs, including tuition, room, board, books, and supplies. Remember, if you underestimate expenses, your plan won't be accurate. The dialog also prompts you for information about expected financial aid, student loans, and student contributions to cover all sources of financing. If you have a college fund—such as an educational IRA— already set up for the college expense, you can associate it with the expense to indicate how it will be paid for.

**Special Expenses**   The Special Expenses tab, which is shown next, includes any expenses you may have already added in the Homes And Assets dialog and enables you to enter other one-time or annual expenses you expect to incur. Use this for items like a vacation, wedding, or large purchase. When you click the New button, Quicken prompts you for information about the expense, including the amount and how you expect to finance it.

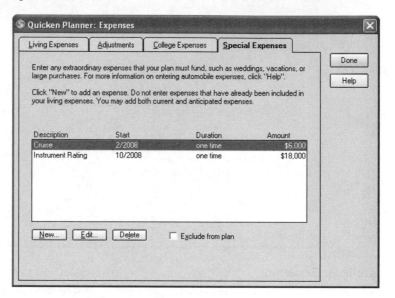

# Reviewing and Changing Assumptions

You can review and modify your plan assumptions at any time. Quicken offers a number of ways to do this.

## The Plan Assumptions Area

Once you enter assumptions into the Quicken Planner, a brief summary of the assumptions appears in the Plan Assumptions area in the Planning tab of the Financial Overview window (see Figure 16-1). To open this window, choose Planning | Go To Planning Center.

You can click links in the Plan Assumption area to open the same dialogs discussed earlier in this chapter. Review and change plan assumptions as desired and click Done in the dialog to save them.

## The Planning Assumptions Window

A better way to review plan assumptions is in the Planning Assumptions window (see Figure 16-2). To open this window, choose Planning | Planning Assumptions, or click the Change Assumptions button in the Plan Assumptions or Plan: Results area of the Planning tab of the Financial Overview window.

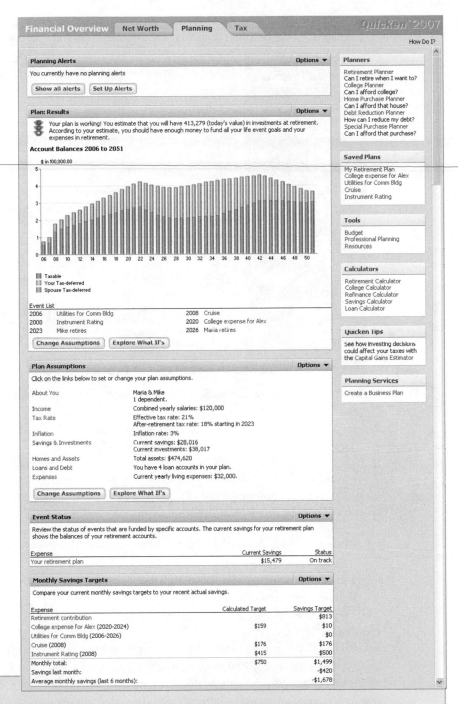

**Figure 16-1 • The Planning tab of the Financial Overview window displays plan details and results.**

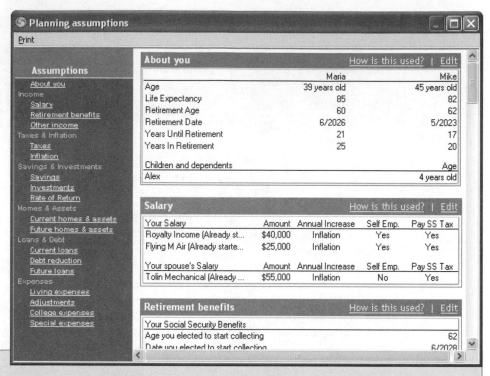

**Figure 16-2 • The Planning Assumptions window displays details about your Quicken Plan assumptions.**

You can use links on the left side of the window to navigate quickly from one category of assumption to another. The details appear in the main part of the window. Each category of assumption offers two links:

• **How Is This Used?** explains how the information in that category of assumption is used in the plan.
• **Edit** enables you to edit the assumptions for that category, using the same dialogs discussed earlier in this chapter.

## Saved Plans

The Saved Plans area of the Financial Overview window's Planning tab (see Figure 16-1) lists individual plans you have added to the Quicken Planner, whether with the various Assumptions dialogs or with individual planners. Click a link to open the associated planner and change data as desired. I discuss Quicken's planners later in this chapter in the section "Using Quicken's Planners."

## Planners

As I discuss later in this chapter in the section titled "Using Quicken's Planners," each individual planner can also be used to add assumptions to your plan. Follow the instructions within the planner to enter data, and the data is added to the Quicken Planner's data.

## Viewing Plan Results

When Quicken has enough data about your assumptions to calculate plan results, it displays them graphically in the Plan: Results area of the Financial Overview window's Planning tab (see Figure 16-1).

The top of the Plan: Results area tells you whether your plan is working and how much you should have in investments at retirement. Amounts are in today's dollars; to view them in future dollars, choose Show Amounts In Future Value from the Options pop-up menu at the top right of the area.

The graph beneath this summary shows your taxable and tax-deferred savings. The ideal shape of this graph shows a steady increase until the year you retire, and then a gradual decrease. You can click a column to display a yellow box with the exact value in it. Plan results change automatically based on a variety of changes within your Quicken data file:

- When the account balances referred to in the plan change, the plan changes accordingly.
- When you change plan assumptions, the plan changes accordingly.
- When you use Quicken's planners to plan for major purchases, college, retirement, and other events that affect your finances, the plan changes to include these events.
- When you play "what if" with assumptions and save the changes as your plan, the plan changes accordingly. I tell you about playing "what if" a little later in this chapter in the section "Playing 'What If.'"

## Viewing Event Status and Savings Targets

Quicken also keeps track of your progress toward certain events and savings targets. It displays this information in the Planning tab of the Financial Overview window (refer to Figure 16-1):

- **Event Status** displays information about events in your plan that are funded with specific accounts.
- **Monthly Savings Targets** displays information about your savings toward events in your plan.

Clicking a link for an expense displays the summary area of the appropriate planner. As discussed next, you can use the planner to review and modify event information.

# Using Quicken's Planners

Quicken's planners offer another way to add financial planning information to Quicken. Rather than enter general assumptions, most planners concentrate on specific events or goals, such as buying a home or sending a child to college. Unlike the plan assumptions dialogs discussed earlier in this chapter, the individual planners provide more information about the event or item you are planning for.

In this part of the chapter, I introduce the individual planners and give you an idea of how their interface works. You can then explore each of the planners on your own.

## A Look at the Planners

Quicken includes five planners, all of which can be accessed through commands on the Planning menu or via links in the Planning tab of the Financial Overview window:

- **Retirement Planner** is the most comprehensive planner. It looks at all of your current financial information, as well as the results of other planners, to help you plan for retirement. It basically reviews all data entered for Quicken Planner assumptions, as discussed earlier in this chapter.

- **College Planner** helps you plan for your children's college education. It gathers the same information you could enter for a new college expense in the College Expenses tab of the Expenses dialog.

- **Home Purchase Planner** helps you plan for the purchase of a new home. It gathers the same information you could enter for a new home in the Planned Assets tab of the Homes And Assets dialog.

- **Debt Reduction Planner** helps you save money while getting out of debt as quickly as possible. I cover this planner in detail in Chapter 18.

- **Special Purchase Planner** helps you plan for special purchases, such as vacations, vehicles, and other large expenditures. It gathers the same information you could enter for major expenditures in the Special Expenses tab of the Expenses dialog.

All of these planners work pretty much the same way. You enter information about your current financial situation or let Quicken enter the information for you based on account balances and category transactions. Then you tell the planner a little about the event you're planning for. For example, the College Planner needs to know how old your children are now and when you expect them to go to college. It also needs to know how much you expect their education to cost. When you enter all this information into Quicken, it performs calculations and shows you results. Planning information is saved within your Quicken data file so you can view or update it at any time.

## Adding Plan Details with Quicken's Planners

You can add details to the assumptions of your financial plan by using Quicken's planners to add specific events to the plan. The information you enter into these plans becomes part of your overall financial plan, thus changing the plan results. When you use any of these planners to create plans, each individual plan appears in the Planning tab of the Financial Overview window and on submenus that appear on the Planning menu. This makes it easy to view and change plans.

Here's a look at four of Quicken's planners; the other one (the Debt Reduction Planner) is covered in Chapter 18.

### Retirement Planner

The Retirement Planner enables you to plan for your retirement. It is, by far, the most exhaustive planner, primarily because it requires all the information entered as plan assumptions. In fact, if you have already entered plan assumptions, you can go through the Retirement Planner very quickly; if not, it'll take you about 30 minutes to enter all the information it requires. (That information will be saved for use by other planners.)

To start, choose Planning | Retirement Planner or click the Retirement Planner link in the Planners area of the Planning tab of the Financial Overview window to display the My Retirement Plan window (see Figure 16-3). Read the information in the window, and then click the Next link to begin entering information. Follow the prompts that appear to open dialogs and enter data for a number of topics, many of which may already include information from plan assumptions or other planners. The items you complete are checked off in the navigation bar on the left side of the My Retirement Plan window; you can also click links for items there to complete them in any order you like.

When you have finished entering information, the Your Plan screen shows your financial plan. Subsequent windows enable you to check your plan for problems, play "what if" with your plan (as I discuss later in this chapter in the section "Playing 'What If'"), and view a summary of your plan.

### College Planner

The College Planner enables you to plan for a college education. It uses information already entered as plan assumptions as well as new information you enter about your child's college plans.

Choose Planning | College Planner or click the College Planner link in the Planners area of the Planning tab of the Financial Overview window to display the Can I Afford College? window. Read the information in the introduction screen and click the Next link to get started. Then follow the prompts to add or edit information about a dependent's college education.

When you have finished entering information in the planner windows, the Results screen shows your financial plan with your child's college education included. Subsequent

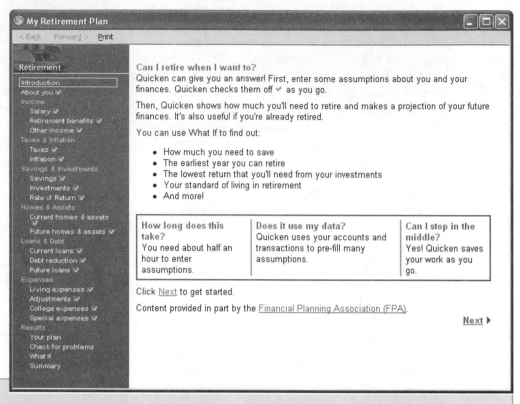

**Figure 16-3 • The Retirement Planner can help you determine whether you can retire when you want to.**

screens offer you a chance to play "what if" with your financial plan, summarize cost and funding information, and allow you to connect to the Internet for other resources, including college and financial aid information.

## Home Purchase Planner

The Home Purchase Planner enables you to plan for the purchase of a home—either a primary residence or a vacation home. Like the other planners, it prompts you for information about a specific event, but it also has built-in calculators to help you determine affordability so you can understand how a home would fit into your budget.

To get started, choose Planning | Home Purchase Planner or click the Home Purchase Planner link in the Planners area of the Planning tab of the Financial Overview window to display the Can I Afford That House? window. Read the information on the introduction screen and click the Next link. Then follow the prompts to enter information about your finances (see Figure 16-4) and the proposed purchase. In some cases, you can get information from your Quicken data file and from the Internet by

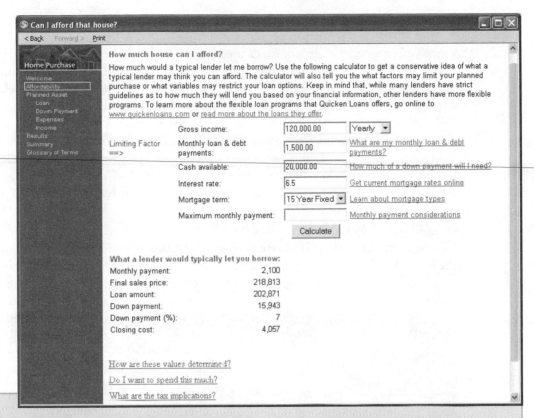

**Figure 16-4 • The Home Purchase Planner even helps you determine whether you can afford to buy a home.**

clicking links within the window. When you're finished entering information, the planner displays its results. Subsequent screens summarize the information and display a glossary of terms you should know when purchasing a home.

## Special Purchase Planner

The Special Purchase Planner enables you to plan for a major purchase, such as a new car or recreational vehicle or a costly vacation. It uses information already entered as plan assumptions as well as new information you enter about the special purchase.

Choose Planning | Special Purchase Planner or click the Special Purchase Planner link in the Planners area of the Planning tab of the Financial Overview window to display the Can I Afford This Purchase? window. Read the information in the window and follow the prompts that appear to enter all information about the purchase. When you are finished, the Results window shows your financial plan with the planned purchase included. The Resources window provides links to other resources within Quicken and on Quicken.com to learn more about purchasing big-ticket items.

# Playing "What If"

Once you've entered assumptions, created plans for specific events, and viewed your plan results, you might wonder how a change in one or more assumptions would affect the plan. You can use the "What If" Event Scenarios feature to see how the changes would affect the plan without changing the plan itself.

Here's an example. Say you've been offered a job in another state. The job pays about the same salary that you make now, but you can move to a town where your living expenses would be greatly reduced. You can see how the job change would affect your financial plans for the future by playing "what if" to modify existing assumptions, and then see the old and new plan results side by side.

## Setting "What If" Options

Choose Planning | "What If" Event Scenarios or click the Explore What If's button in the Plan: Results area. The What If window, which is shown in Figure 16-5, appears. The first time you use it, it displays the account balances shown in your plan results.

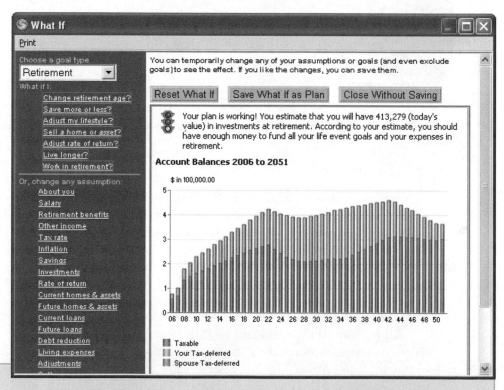

**Figure 16-5 • You can use the What If window to play "what if" with your financial plans.**

Choose a goal option from the drop-down list at the top left of the window. Then click appropriate links on the left side of the window to open dialogs to change assumptions.

In our example, you might use the following links:

- Click Current Homes & Assets to add proposed sale information about your current home.
- Click Current Loans to record the proposed payoff of your mortgage when you sell your current home.
- Click Future Homes & Assets to add proposed purchase information about your new home and its associated mortgage.
- Click Adjustments to add a proposed adjustment for the reduced living expenses when you move to your new home.

Get the idea? Each time you make a change, the Plan Comparison chart changes. Here's what it might look like for our example:

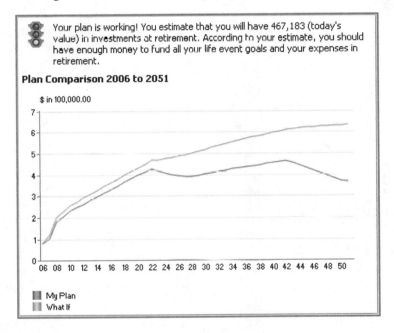

## Using "What If" Results

When you've finished changing assumptions and viewing results, you can click one of the three buttons at the top of the What If window:

- **Reset What If** clears all the assumptions you changed while playing "what if." This enables you to start over.

- **Save What If As Plan** saves the assumptions you changed while playing "what if" as your actual financial plan. When the window closes, you'll see the results in the Planning tab of the Financial Overview window change accordingly.
- **Close Without Saving** simply closes the window so you can continue working with Quicken. Your settings are not saved.

# Using Financial Calculators

**Chapter 17**

Sometimes, the hardest part about financial planning is making the calculations you need quickly, to determine the feasibility of a potential plan. For example, suppose you're thinking about refinancing your home because you can now get an interest rate that's lower than the rate you locked into six years ago. You know your monthly payment can decrease, but you're not sure if you'll save enough money to cover the fees involved in the refinancing. The calculations seem complex and you're not sure what to do. That's where one of Quicken Personal Finance Software's financial calculators—the Refinance Calculator—can help. It can take raw data about your current mortgage and the one you're considering, and crunch the numbers in a flash to tell you whether it's worthwhile to take the next step.

In this chapter, I tell you about each of Quicken's financial calculators. I'm sure you'll find them handy tools for making the quick calculations you need to start the decision-making process with your financial plans.

# A Look at Quicken's Financial Calculators

Quicken includes five financial calculators you can use to make quick financial calculations: the Retirement Calculator, the College Calculator, the Refinance Calculator, the Investment Savings Calculator, and the Loan Calculator. These calculators make complex calculations simple.

## How the Calculators Work

All five of the financial calculators share the same basic interface. But although they are similar in appearance, each is designed for a specific purpose. It's important that you use the correct calculator to get the job done.

In most instances, you begin by telling the calculator what part of the formula you want to calculate. For example, when calculating a loan, you can calculate the loan amount or the periodic payment. Then you enter values and set other options in the calculator's dialog to give Quicken the information it needs to make its calculations. Clicking a Calculate button completes the process. Quicken is fast; the results appear as soon as you click Calculate—if not sooner.

## Accessing the Financial Calculators

All of Quicken's financial calculators can be opened at least two ways:

- Choose the name of the calculator from the Financial Calculators submenu under the Planning menu:

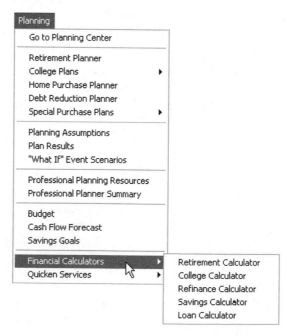

- Click the name of the calculator in the Calculators area of the Planning Center.

| Calculators |
| --- |
| Retirement Calculator |
| College Calculator |
| Refinance Calculator |
| Savings Calculator |
| Loan Calculator |

# Using the Financial Calculators

Ready to give Quicken's financial calculators a try? The rest of this chapter provides some detailed instructions for using each of them.

## Retirement Calculator

The Retirement Calculator can help you calculate some of the numbers you need to plan for your retirement. To open it, choose Planning | Financial Calculators | Retirement Calculator, or click the Retirement Calculator link in the Calculators area of the Planning Center. The Retirement Calculator appears:

**Retirement Calculator**

Retirement Information

| | |
| --- | --- |
| Current savings: | 150,000.00 |
| Annual yield: | 6.000% |
| Annual contribution: | 15,000.00 |
| Current age: | 44 |
| Retirement age: | 60 |
| Withdraw until age: | 85 |
| Other income (SSI, etc.): | 30,000.00 |
| Annual income after taxes: | 52,425.80 |

Inflation

Predicted inflation: 3.000%

☐ Inflate contributions
☑ Annual income in today's $

Calculate For

○ Current savings
○ Annual contribution
◉ Annual retirement income

Tax Information

◉ Tax sheltered investment
○ Non-sheltered investment

Current tax rate: 28.000%
Retirement tax rate: 15.000%

Done
Help
Calculate
Schedule...

To develop a complete retirement plan, use the Retirement Planner in the Planning Center.

Select a Calculate For option, and then enter or select values and options throughout the dialog. Most options are pretty straightforward and easy to understand. When you're finished, click the Calculate button to see the results.

Here's a closer look at the options in the Retirement Calculator.

## Calculate For

The Calculate For option affects which value is calculated by Quicken:

- **Current Savings** calculates the amount of money you should currently have saved based on the values you enter.
- **Annual Contribution** calculates the minimum amount you should contribute to a retirement account based on the values you enter.

- **Annual Retirement Income** calculates the annual amount of retirement income you'll have based on the values you enter.

## Retirement Information

Retirement Information options enable you to enter the values Quicken should use in its calculations. The values you must enter vary depending on the Calculate For option you select.

## Tax Information

Tax Information options enable you to indicate whether your retirement savings are in a tax-sheltered investment or a non-sheltered investment. If you select the Non-Sheltered Investment option, you can enter your current tax rate and Quicken will automatically calculate the effect of taxes on your investment income. By experimenting with this feature, you can clearly see why it's a good idea to use tax-sheltered or tax-deferred investments whenever possible.

## Inflation

Inflation options make complex calculations to account for the effect of inflation on your savings dollars. To use this feature, enter an inflation rate in the Predicted Inflation box, and then toggle check marks for the two options below it:

- **Inflate Contributions** makes calculations assuming that the annual contributions will rise with the inflation rate.
- **Annual Income In Today's $** makes calculations assuming that the Annual Income After Taxes entry is in today's dollars and not inflated.

## Schedule

Clicking the Schedule button displays a printable list of deposits made and income withdrawn, with a running balance total. Here's what it looks like with the calculations shown earlier:

Deposit Schedule

Print                                                                Close    How Do I?

This deposit schedule assumes that your retirement income keeps pace with a 3% annual inflation rate. Note that income is in future, pre-tax dollars.

| Age | Deposit | Income | Balance |
|---|---|---|---|
| 0 | 0.00 | 0.00 | 150,000.00 |
| 44 | 15,000.00 | 0.00 | 174,000.00 |
| 45 | 15,000.00 | 0.00 | 199,440.00 |
| 46 | 15,000.00 | 0.00 | 226,406.40 |
| 47 | 15,000.00 | 0.00 | 254,990.78 |
| 48 | 15,000.00 | 0.00 | 285,290.23 |
| 49 | 15,000.00 | 0.00 | 317,407.64 |
| 50 | 15,000.00 | 0.00 | 351,452.10 |
| 51 | 15,000.00 | 0.00 | 387,539.23 |
| 52 | 15,000.00 | 0.00 | 425,791.58 |
| 53 | 15,000.00 | 0.00 | 466,339.08 |

## College Calculator

The College Calculator enables you to calculate savings for the cost of a college education. Choose Planning | Financial Calculators | College Calculator or click the College Calculator link in the Calculators area of the Planning Center. The College Calculator, shown here, appears.

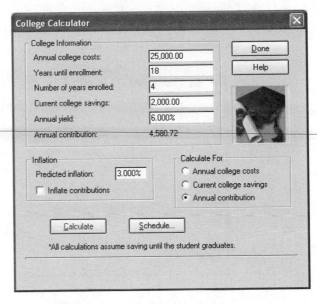

Select a Calculate For option, and then enter or select values and options throughout the dialog. Most options are pretty straightforward and easy to understand. When you click Calculate, Quicken calculates the results.

Here's a look at the options in the College Calculator.

## Calculate For

The Calculate For option affects which value is calculated by Quicken:

- **Annual College Costs** calculates the annual tuition you'll be able to afford based on the values you enter.
- **Current College Savings** calculates the amount of money you should currently have saved based on the values you enter.
- **Annual Contribution** calculates the minimum amount you should contribute to college savings based on the values you enter.

## College Information

The College Information area is where you enter the values Quicken should use in its calculations. The values you must enter vary depending on the Calculate For option you select.

## Inflation

Inflation options make complex calculations to account for the effect of inflation on your savings dollars. To use this feature, enter an inflation rate in the Predicted Inflation box. You can then toggle the Inflate Contributions check box, which makes calculations assuming that the annual contributions will rise with the inflation rate. Quicken automatically inflates the amount of tuition no matter how you set the Inflate Contributions check box.

## Schedule

Clicking the Schedule button displays a printable list of deposits made and money withdrawn for tuition, with a running balance total. Here's what it looks like with the calculations shown earlier:

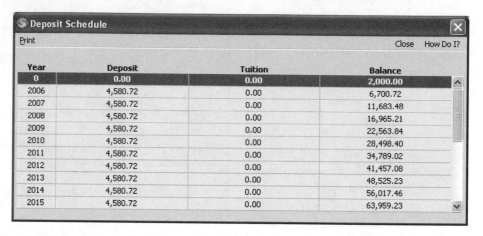

# Refinance Calculator

If you own a home and are thinking about refinancing, you can try the Refinance Calculator to see whether refinancing will really save you money and, if so, how much. Choose Planning | Financial Calculators | Refinance Calculator or click the Refinance Calculator link in the Calculators area of the Planning Center. The Refinance Calculator, shown next, appears.

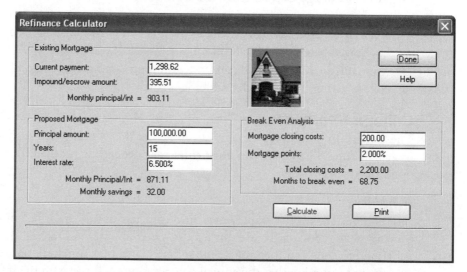

Enter values for your current mortgage and proposed mortgage in the text boxes to calculate your monthly savings with the new mortgage. Here's a closer look at the entries.

## Existing Mortgage

Existing Mortgage options enable you to enter your current total monthly mortgage payment and the amount of that payment that is applied to property taxes and other escrow items. Quicken automatically calculates the amount of principal and interest for each payment. If you already know the principal and interest amount, you can enter that in the Current Payment box and leave the Impound/Escrow Amount box empty. The result is the same.

## Proposed Mortgage

Proposed Mortgage options enable you to enter information about the mortgage that you are considering to replace your current mortgage. The Principal Amount may be the balance on your current mortgage, but it could be more or less depending on whether you want to refinance for more or less money. (Refinancing often offers a good opportunity to exchange equity for cash.)

## Break Even Analysis

Break Even Analysis options are optional. If you enter the closing costs and points for the proposed mortgage, Quicken will automatically calculate how long it will take to cover those costs based on your monthly savings. As you can see in the previous illustration, it will take 68.75 months for the savings to pay for the closing costs and points on the new mortgage.

## Print

Clicking the Print button displays the Print dialog, which you can use to print the results of your calculations.

# Investment Savings Calculator

The Investment Savings Calculator enables you to calculate savings annuities— periodic payments to a savings account or investment. Choose Planning | Financial Calculators | Savings Calculator or click the Savings Calculator link in the Calculators area of the Planning Center. The Investment Savings Calculator appears, as shown here.

Select a Calculate For option, and then enter or select values and options throughout the dialog. Most options are pretty straightforward and easy to understand. When you click Calculate, Quicken displays the results.

Here's a closer look at each of the entry options.

## Calculate For

The Calculate For option affects which value is calculated by Quicken:

- **Opening Savings Balance** calculates the amount of money you should currently have saved based on the values you enter.
- **Regular Contribution** calculates the minimum amount you should regularly contribute to savings based on the values you enter.
- **Ending Savings Balance** calculates the total amount saved at the end of the savings period based on the values you enter.

## Savings Information

Savings Information enables you to enter values for Quicken to use in its calculations. The option you choose from the Number Of drop-down list will determine how interest is compounded; in most cases, you'll probably set this to Months.

## Inflation

Inflation options make complex calculations to account for the effect of inflation on your savings dollars. To use this feature, enter an inflation rate in the Predicted Inflation box, and then toggle check boxes for the two options below it:

- **Inflate Contributions** makes calculations assuming that the annual contributions will rise with the inflation rate.
- **Ending Balance In Today's $** makes calculations assuming that the Ending Savings Balance is in today's dollars and not inflated.

When you click Calculate, Quicken displays the results. You can click the Schedule button to see a printable list of deposits, with a running balance total.

## Schedule

Clicking the Schedule button displays a printable list of deposits made, with a running balance total. Here is what it looks like with the calculations shown earlier:

**Deposit Schedule**

Print                                      Close   How Do I?

The effect of 3.0% annual inflation over the period of 10 years will make $35,315.83 worth $26,278.29 in terms of today's purchasing power.

| Number | Deposit | Total |
|--------|---------|-------|
| 0 | 0.00 | 5,000.00 |
| 1 | 2,000.00 | 7,300.00 |
| 2 | 2,000.00 | 9,738.00 |
| 3 | 2,000.00 | 12,322.28 |
| 4 | 2,000.00 | 15,061.62 |
| 5 | 2,000.00 | 17,965.31 |
| 6 | 2,000.00 | 21,043.23 |
| 7 | 2,000.00 | 24,305.83 |
| 8 | 2,000.00 | 27,764.18 |
| 9 | 2,000.00 | 31,430.03 |
| 10 | 2,000.00 | 35,315.83 |

## Loan Calculator

Quicken's Loan Calculator can quickly calculate the principal or periodic payment for a loan. Choose Planning | Financial Calculators | Loan Calculator or click the Loan Calculator link in the Calculators area of the Planning Center. The Loan Calculator appears, as shown here.

Select one of the Calculate For options, enter information in the remainder of the dialog, and click Calculate. Getting the answer is a lot quicker and easier with the Loan Calculator than using one of those loan books or building an Excel spreadsheet to do the job.

Here's a look at the Loan Calculator options.

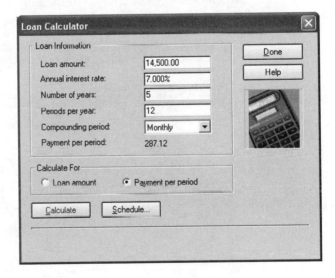

**Loan Calculator**

Loan Information

Loan amount:            14,500.00
Annual interest rate:   7.000%
Number of years:        5
Periods per year:       12
Compounding period:     Monthly
Payment per period:     287.12

Done
Help

Calculate For
○ Loan amount    ● Payment per period

Calculate    Schedule...

## Calculate For

The Calculate For options determine what Quicken calculates:

- **Loan Amount** enables you to calculate the amount of a loan based on specific periodic payments.
- **Payment Per Period** enables you to calculate the periodic loan payment based on the loan amount.

## Loan Information

Loan Information options enable you to enter values for Quicken to use in its calculations. The information you must enter varies depending on the Calculate For option you select. Be sure to set the Periods Per Year and Compounding Period options correctly; an incorrect entry will misstate the results.

## Schedule

Clicking the Schedule button displays a printable amortization table that lists the payment number, the amount of the principal and interest paid at each payment, and the ending balance for the loan:

**Approximate Future Payment Schedule**

Print                                           Close   How Do I?

| Pmt | Principal | Interest | Balance |
|---|---|---|---|
| | | 7.0% | 14,500.00 |
| 1 | 202.54 | 84.58 | 14,297.46 |
| 2 | 203.72 | 83.40 | 14,093.74 |
| 3 | 204.91 | 82.21 | 13,888.83 |
| 4 | 206.10 | 81.02 | 13,682.73 |
| 5 | 207.30 | 79.82 | 13,475.43 |
| 6 | 208.51 | 78.61 | 13,266.92 |
| 7 | 209.73 | 77.39 | 13,057.19 |
| 8 | 210.95 | 76.17 | 12,846.24 |
| 9 | 212.18 | 74.94 | 12,634.06 |
| 10 | 213.42 | 73.70 | 12,420.64 |
| 11 | 214.67 | 72.45 | 12,205.97 |
| 12 | 215.92 | 71.20 | 11,990.05 |
| 13 | 217.18 | 69.94 | 11,772.87 |

# Reducing Debt and Saving Money

## Chapter 18

## In This Chapter:

- *Reducing debt*
- *Budgeting and forecasting*
- *Setting up savings goals*

The best way to prepare for life events is to build up your savings. Saving money is an important part of financial management. Savings enable you to take vacations and make major purchases without increasing debt, help your kids through college, handle emergencies, and have a comfortable retirement.

In this chapter, I tell you about saving money and how tools within Quicken Personal Finance Software can help. If you're in debt and can't even think about saving until you dig your way out, this chapter can help you, too. It starts by covering Quicken tools for reducing your debt.

## Reducing Your Debt

Consumer credit is a huge industry. It's easy to get credit cards—sometimes too easy. And it's a lot easier to pay for something with a piece of plastic than with cold, hard cash. The "buy now, pay later" attitude has become an acceptable way of life. It's no wonder that many Americans are deeply in debt.

Those credit card bills can add up, however. And paying just the minimum payment on each one only helps the credit card company keep you in debt—and paying interest—as long as possible. I've been there, so I know. Unfortunately, it took two experiences to set me straight. I hope you can learn your lesson the first time.

**371**

If you're in debt, don't skip this part of the chapter. It'll help you dig yourself out of debt so you can build a solid financial future.

## Take Control

It's not easy to save money if most of your income is spent paying credit card bills and loan payments. If you're heavily in debt, you might even be having trouble keeping up with all your payments. But don't despair. There is hope! Here are a few simple things you can do to dig yourself out of debt.

### Breaking the Pattern

Your first step to reducing debt must be to break the pattern of spending that got you where you are. For most people, that means cutting up credit cards. After all, it's tough to use a credit card if you can't hand it to a cashier at the checkout counter.

Before you take out the scissors, however, read this: You don't have to cut up *all* of your credit cards. Leave yourself one or two major credit cards for emergencies, such as car trouble or unexpected visits to the doctor. The cards that should go are the store and gas credit cards. They can increase your debt, but they can be used in only a few places.

Here's the logic behind this strategy. If you have 15 credit cards, each with a credit limit of $2,000, you can get yourself into $30,000 of debt. The minimum monthly payment for each card may be $50. That's $750 a month in minimum credit card payments. If you have only two credit cards, each with a credit limit of $2,000, you can get yourself into only $4,000 of debt. Your monthly minimum payment may be only $100. This reduces your monthly obligation, enabling you to pay more than the minimum so you can further reduce your debt.

### Reducing Your Credit Limits

Sure, it's a real temptation to use your credit cards to spend just a little more every month—especially when you're not even close to your credit limit. But high credit limits are a trap. The credit card company or bank flatters you by offering to lend you more money. What they're really doing is setting you up so you'll owe them more—and pay them more in monthly finance and interest fees.

The next time your credit card company tells you they've raised your credit limit, do yourself a favor: call them up and tell them to reduce it right back to where it was—or lower!

### Shopping for Cards with Better Interest Rates

Yes, it's nice to have a credit card with your picture on it. Or one that's gold, platinum, or titanium. Or one with your college, team, club, or association name on it. A friend of mine who breeds horses showed off a new Visa card with a picture of a horse on it. She told me it was her favorite. I asked her what the interest rate was, and she didn't know.

The purpose of a credit card is to purchase things on credit. When you maintain a balance on the account, you pay interest on it. The balance and interest rate determine how much it costs you to have that special picture or name on a plastic card in your wallet. Is it worth 19.8 percent a year? Or 21 percent? Not to me!

Here's a reality-check exercise: Gather together all of your credit card bills for the most recent month. Now add up all the monthly finance fees and interest charges. Multiply that number by 12. The result is an approximation of what you pay in credit card interest each year. Now imagine how nice it would be to have that money in your hands the next time you go on vacation or need a down payment on a new car or home.

Low-interest credit cards are widely available. Sometimes you don't even have to look for them—offers arrive in the mail all the time. They promise low rates—usually under 10 percent a year. But you must read these offers carefully before you apply for one of these cards. Most offer the low rates for a short, introductory period—usually no longer than 6 or 12 months. (I once got one that offered 0 percent for the first 25 days. Big deal.) Some offer the low rate only on new purchases, while others offer the low rate only on balance transfers or cash advances. Be sure to find out what the rate is after the introductory period.

Here are two strategies for using a low-interest card:

- Consolidate your debt by transferring the balances of other credit cards to the new card. For this strategy, select a card that offers a low rate on balance transfers. When you transfer the balances, be sure to cut up the old cards so you don't use them to add more to your debt.
- Make purchases with the low-interest card. Make the new card your emergency credit card. Be sure to cut up your old emergency card so you don't wind up using both of them.

And if you really like that special picture or name on the card in your wallet, call the credit card company and ask if they can give you a better interest rate. In many instances, they can—especially when you tell them you want to close your account.

## Consolidating Your Debt

Consolidating your debt is one of the best ways to dig yourself out. By combining balances into one debt, whether through balance transfers to a single credit card or a debt consolidation loan, you're better able to pay off the balances without causing financial hardship. This is sometimes the only option when things have gotten completely out of control and you can't meet your debt obligations.

If you own a home, consider a home equity loan to consolidate your debt. The interest rate is usually lower than any credit card or debt consolidation loan, and the interest may be tax deductible. I tell you more about home equity loans in Chapter 13.

## Using Charge Cards, Not Credit Cards

There's a difference between a credit card and a charge card:

- **Credit cards** enable you to buy things on credit. If each month you pay less than what you owe, you are charged interest on your account balance. Most major "credit cards" are true credit cards. MasterCard, Visa, and Discover are three examples. Most store "charge cards" are also credit cards.
- **Charge cards** enable you to buy things on credit, too. But when the bill comes, you're expected to pay the entire balance. You don't have to pay any interest, but if you don't pay the entire balance on time, you may have to pay late fees and finance charges. American Express is an example of a charge card.

The benefit of charge cards is that they make it impossible to get into serious debt. How can you owe the charge card company money if you must pay the balance in full every month? Using these cards prevents you from overspending. Every time you use the card to make a purchase, a little accountant in the back of your head should be adding the charge to a running total. You should stop spending when that total reaches the limit of your ability to pay.

Chapters 5 and 6 explain how you can use Quicken to track credit and charge card balances manually or online. If you use Quicken to keep track of expenditures, you won't need that little accountant in the back of your head.

If you don't want an American Express card (for whatever reason), use another major credit card as a charge card. Just pay the entire balance each time you get a bill. If you don't carry a balance, you won't be charged interest.

## If You Can't Stop Spending, Get Help

Many people who are deeply in debt may have a spending problem. They can't resist buying that fifth pair of running shoes or that trendy new outdoor furniture. They don't *need* the things they buy, but they buy them anyway. There's nothing wrong with that if your income can support your spending habits, but if your net worth is less than $0, it's a real problem—one that might require counseling to resolve.

The next time you make a purchase, stop for a moment and think about what you're buying. Is it something you need? Something you can use? Something you can justify spending the money on? If you can't answer yes to any of these questions, don't buy it. If you have to buy it anyway, it's time to seek professional help.

## Living Debt-Free

It is possible to live debt-free—and you don't have to be rich to do it. Just stop relying on credit to make your purchases and spend only what you can afford to spend.

Imagine how great it would feel to be completely debt free. It's worth a try, isn't it?

## Using the Debt Reduction Planner

Quicken's Debt Reduction Planner is a tool for helping you reduce your debt. You enter information about your financial situation, and Quicken develops a debt reduction plan for you. The Debt Reduction Planner is thorough, easy to use, and an excellent tool for teaching people how they can get out of debt as quickly as possible, saving hundreds (if not thousands) of dollars in interest charges.

### What Does This Mean to You?
### The Debt Reduction Planner

If you're in serious debt—actually having trouble making ends meet because you can't seem to get any of your debts paid down—a pair of scissors, a telephone, and the Debt Reduction Planner are probably your three best tools for getting things under control.

First, use the scissors to cut up most, if not all, of your credit cards. Next, use the telephone to call your credit card companies and try to get your interest rates reduced. (The worst they can do is say no.) Then use the Debt Reduction Planner to come up with a solid plan for reducing your debt.

Here's what the Debt Reduction Planner can do that you might not be able to do on your own:

- Objectively look at your debts and organize them by interest rate. The debts that cost you the most are the ones that are paid off first, thus saving you money.
- Show you the benefit of using some of your savings to reduce the balances on your most costly debt.
- Help you set up spending limits, with alarms, for the categories on which you spend too much money.
- Create an itemized plan based on real numbers that you can follow to reduce your debt.
- Show you, in dollars and cents, how much money you can save and how quickly you can become debt-free, by following the plan.

Don't dread the daily mail and its package of bills. Use the Debt Reduction Planner to get things under control.

Note that the Debt Reduction Planner works best when you track all of your debt—including credit card debt—using Quicken accounts. That means setting up accounts for your credit cards rather than simply tracking monthly payments as bills paid. I tell you more about the two different ways to track credit cards in Chapters 2 and 5.

To get started, choose Planning | Debt Reduction Planner or click the Debt Reduction Planner link in the Planners area of the Planning Center. If you have explored this feature before, the Debt Reduction window appears with a chart showing the information you previously entered (refer to Figure 18-1 later in this chapter). If you have never used it before, the Debt Reduction dialog appears, enabling you to create a new debt reduction plan.

### Creating a New Debt Reduction Plan

If necessary, click the New Plan button on the button bar of the Debt Reduction window. If a dialog warns that you will overwrite your current plan, click Yes. The Debt Reduction dialog appears, displaying its Welcome screen. Insert your Quicken CD in your CD-ROM drive and click Next to continue. An introductory movie plays, telling you what the Debt Reduction Planner can do for you. (If you don't have your Quicken CD-ROM available, you can skip the movie. But I do recommend viewing it the first time you use the Debt Reduction Planner.) When the movie has finished, click Next to begin.

## Entering Debt Information

When you click Next after viewing the movie, the Debts tab of the window appears. It should look something like this:

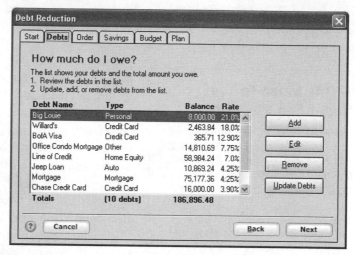

This tab lists all of your current debts, as they are recorded in Quicken. Use the buttons to the right of the list to modify the list:

- If the debt list is not up-to-date or complete, click the Update Debts button to import current debt information from your Quicken data file.

- To add a debt that you do not track in Quicken, click the Add button. The Edit Debt Reduction dialog, shown next, appears. Use it to enter information about the debt and click OK to add it to the list.

- To modify information about a debt, select it and click the Edit button to display the Edit Debt Reduction dialog shown next. Make changes as desired and click OK to save the changes.

- To remove a debt from the list, select it and click the Remove button. In the confirmation dialog that appears, click Yes. This removes the debt from the Debt Reduction Planner but does not remove it from your Quicken data file. You may want to use this feature to remove a long-term debt, such as a mortgage, so you can concentrate on higher interest, short-term debt, such as credit cards and personal loans.

When the debt list shows all of your debts, click Next to continue.

If required information is missing from one or more debts, Quicken will tell you and then display the Edit Debt Reduction dialog for each debt so you can update the information. You must complete this process before you can continue.

Next, Quicken tells you about your current debt situation, including your total debt, your total monthly payments, and a projection of when you will be debt-free based on the debt information you provided. Click Next to continue.

## Setting the Order of Debts

The Order tab of the Debt Reduction dialog begins with some information about the order in which debts are paid off. Click Next to continue. Quicken puts your debts in the order of cost, with the highest at the top. It might look something like this:

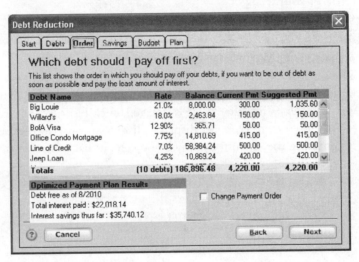

This tab sets the debt payoff order so that the most expensive debt is paid off first, thus saving you interest charges. The Suggested Pmt column offers a suggested payment amount; following the suggestion makes it possible to pay off the debts faster without increasing your total monthly payments. If desired, you can turn on the Change Payment Order check box to change the order in which debts are paid off—this, however, will cost you more and increase the payoff time.

If you turn on the Change Payment Order check box and click the Next button, the dialog changes to enable you to change the order of debts. Click a debt to select it, and then click Move Up or Move Down to change its location in the list. When you've finished, click Next.

## Using Savings to Pay Off Debt

The Savings tab begins by playing a movie that tells you why you might want to use savings and investments to pay off your debt. Listen carefully—the movie is full of good information! When the movie is finished, click Next.

Quicken summarizes your current savings and investments, and enables you to specify how much of your savings should be applied to your debt, as shown here.

Enter a value in the text box and click the Recalculate button. The Results area shows the effect of your change. Click Next to continue.

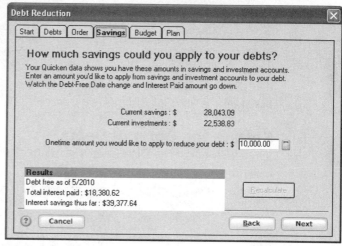

## Adjusting Your Budget

The Budget tab offers options for helping you reduce your spending, which can, in turn, help you reduce your debt. It begins by displaying a movie with tips and instructions. When the movie is finished, click Next to continue.

As shown next, Quicken displays a list of your top four expenses, with text boxes for entering the amount by which you can cut back on each one every month.

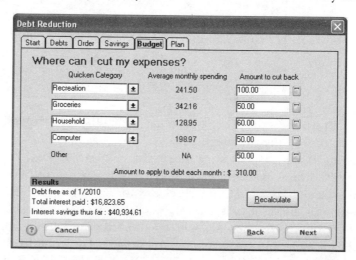

Enter the amounts by which you can cut back for the categories that appear or for different categories you select from the drop-down lists. Quicken automatically suggests that you apply the savings to the debt, thus adjusting the Results area for your entries. Click Next to continue.

## Reviewing the Plan

The Plan tab, shown here, displays your custom debt reduction action plan:

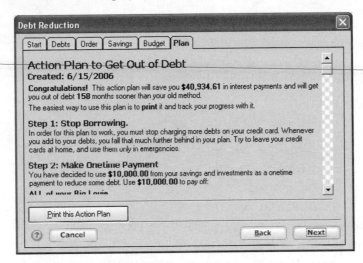

Scroll through the debt reduction plan to see what it recommends. Better yet, click the Print This Action Plan button to print a copy you can refer to throughout the coming months. Click Next to continue.

Next, Quicken offers to track your debt reduction plan for you. You can toggle the settings for two different check boxes to enable this feature:

- **Alert Me If I Fall Behind** tells Quicken to alert you if you fall behind on debt reduction and to include your debt in budgeting and forecasting models. (I tell you about Planning Center alerts, budgeting, and forecasting later in this chapter.)
- **Set Up Scheduled Transactions For My Monthly Payments** tells Quicken to schedule transactions for the monthly payments included in your debt reduction plan. This makes it impossible for you to forget about debt reduction payments. (I tell you about scheduling payments in Chapter 7.)

Turn on the check box for each option that you want to enable, and then click Next. Quicken provides a bit more information about reducing debt. Click Done.

## Viewing the Debt Reduction Plan Results

When you click Done in the final screen of the Debt Reduction dialog, the Debt Reduction window appears (see Figure 18-1). It uses a graph to compare debt reduction using your current method (the blue line) with that of your new debt reduction plan (the green line).

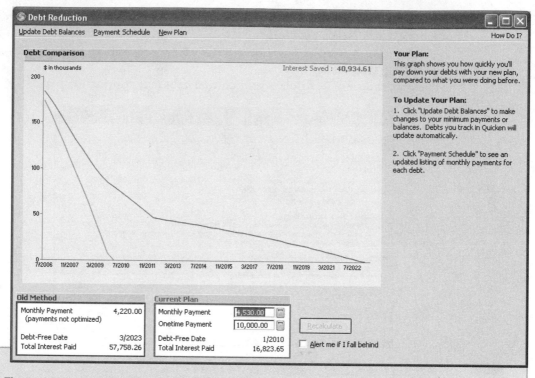

**Figure 18-1 • The Debt Reduction Plan window clearly illustrates how quickly you can get out of debt and save interest costs by using Quicken's plan.**

To see the results of your plan on a month-to-month basis, click the Payment Schedule button at the top of the Debt Reduction window. The Debt Reduction Payment Schedule dialog, shown here, appears. It lists the payments you should make for each month, according to the plan and your account balances at month-end.

## Modifying the Plan

Once you have a debt reduction plan, you can modify it in a number of ways.

- Click the Update Debt Balances button on the button bar to import the current balances of your debt into the Debt Reduction Planner.
- Enter new values in the Current Plan area at the bottom of the Debt Reduction window.
- Click the New Plan button on the button bar to create a new plan from scratch.

No matter which method you choose, Quicken will automatically revise the graph and other information to reflect your changes.

# Budgeting and Forecasting

When money is tight or you're interested in meeting financial goals, it's time to create a budget and monitor your spending. But if you're serious about managing your money, you might want to create a budget *before* you need one. While Quicken's categories give you a clear understanding of where money comes from and where it goes, budgets enable you to set up predefined amounts for each category, thus helping you to control spending.

Budgets also make it easier to create forecasts of your future financial position. This makes it possible to see how much cash will be available at a future date—before the holidays, for summer vacation, or for the day you plan to put down a deposit on a new car.

In this part of the chapter, I tell you how to create a budget and use it to monitor your spending habits. I also explain how to create a forecast so you can glimpse your financial future.

## Budgeting

The idea behind a budget is to determine expected income amounts and specify maximum amounts for expenditures. This helps prevent you from spending more than you earn. It also enables you to control your spending in certain categories. For example, say you realize that you go out for dinner a lot more often than you should. You can set a budget for the Dining category and track your spending to make sure you don't exceed the budget. You'll eat at home more often and save money.

In this section, I explain how to set up a budget and use it to keep track of your spending. I think you'll agree that budgeting is a great way to keep spending under control.

### Organizing Categories into Groups

Budgets are based on transactions recorded for categories and subcategories. (That's why it's important to categorize all your transactions—and not to the Misc category!) Quicken also enables you to organize categories by category groups. Although you don't have to use the Groups feature when creating your budget—it's entirely optional—grouping similar categories together can simplify your budget.

You can see the group to which each category is assigned in the Group column of the Category List window (see Figure 18-2). Choose Tools | Category List to display it. If the Group column does not appear in your list, choose Show Category Group from the window's Options menu to display it. (You might also find it helpful to hide the Description column, as shown in Figure 18-2, by choosing Show Description from the window's Options menu.)

**The Default Groups**   By default, Quicken includes several category groups that it assigns to the categories it creates when you first set up your Quicken data file:

- **Income** is for earned income, such as your salary, and miscellaneous income items, such as interest, dividends, and gifts received.
- **Discretionary** is for expenses you can avoid (or at least minimize), such as entertainment, subscriptions, and vacation.
- **Mandatory Expenses** are expenses you can't avoid, such as fuel for your car, groceries, rent, and insurance.

In addition, if your Quicken data file includes business-related categories, Quicken includes Business Income and Business Expenses groups to track the income and expenses from your business.

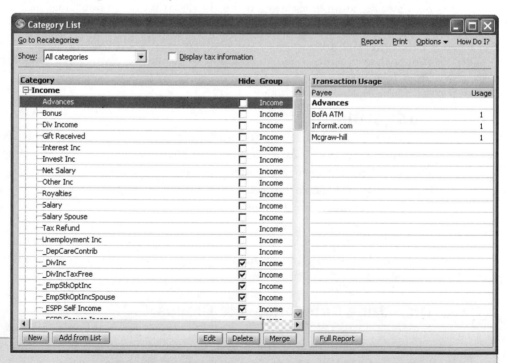

**Figure 18-2 • The Category List window displays all categories and the names of the groups to which they are assigned.**

**Assigning a Group to a Category**  You can assign a group to a category when you create or edit the category. In the Category List window (see Figure 18-2), either click New or select an existing category and click Edit. The Set Up Category or Edit Category dialog, shown here, appears. Click the arrow next to the Group box to display the Group drop-down list, which is shown here, and choose a group. When you click OK, the group you chose is assigned to the category.

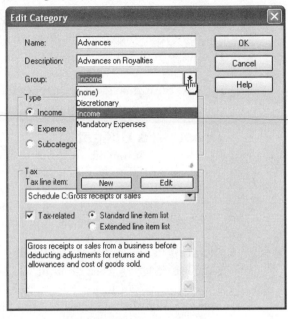

**Assigning Groups to Multiple Categories**  You can also assign groups to multiple categories at once. In the Category List window (see Figure 18-2), choose Assign Category Groups from the Options menu on the button bar. The Assign Category Groups dialog, which is shown next, appears. Select a category name from the Category Name list, select a group name from the Category Group List, and click the Assign Category To Group button. Repeat this process for each category for which you want to assign a group. When you are finished, click OK.

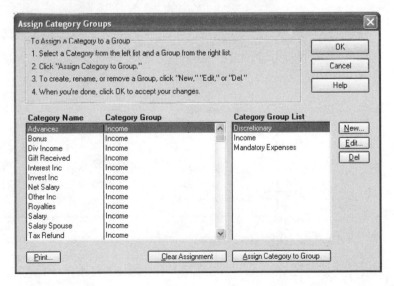

**Modifying the Category Group List**   You're not stuck with the group names built into Quicken. You can add new group names or modify existing group names:

- In the Set Up Category or Edit Category dialog (shown earlier), choose New or Edit from the Group drop-down list. Then use the dialog that appears to add, modify, or remove a group name.
- In the Assign Category Groups dialog (shown earlier), click the New, Edit, or Del button beside the Category Group List to add a new group or modify or remove a selected group.

## Creating a Budget

Quicken can automatically generate a budget for you based on past transactions. You can edit the budget it creates to meet your needs. Or you can create a budget from scratch.

To start creating a budget, choose Planning | Budget. The Setup tab of the Budget window, which is shown in Figure 18-3, appears.

**Creating a Budget Automatically**   The quickest and easiest way to create a budget is to let Quicken do it for you based on your income and expenditures. For Quicken to create an accurate budget, however, you must have several months' worth of transactions in your Quicken data file. Otherwise, the budget may not reflect all regular income and expenses.

Select the Automatic option in the Setup tab of the Budget window (refer to Figure 18-3) and click Create Budget. The Create Budget: Automatic dialog, which is shown here, appears. Use this dialog to set options for the budget.

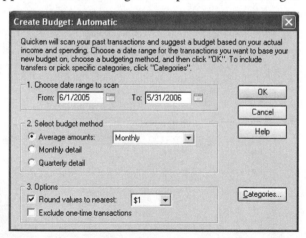

In the date range area, enter the starting and ending dates for the transactions on which you want to base the budget. Whenever possible, the date range should be the most recent 12-month period. But if you have less than 12 months' worth of data, enter the date range for the period for which you have data.

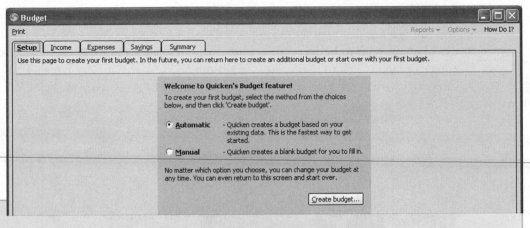

**Figure 18-3 • The Setup tab of the Budget window offers options to create a budget.**

Next, select a budget method option:

- **Average Amounts** enters monthly averages based on the period in the date range. If you select this option, choose a frequency from the drop-down list.
- **Monthly Detail** copies the total values for each month to the corresponding month in the budget.
- **Quarterly Detail** copies the total values for each quarter to the corresponding quarter in the budget.

If you're not sure which to select, consider this advice: Select Monthly Detail or Quarterly Detail if you have a full year of transactions (or close to it) and you have seasonal income (such as a teaching job) or expenses (such as a vacation home). Select Average if you have less than six months of transactions or don't have seasonal income or expenses.

Toggle check boxes in the Options area as desired:

- **Round Values To Nearest** enables you to round calculated values to the nearest $1, $10, or $100. If you enable this option, choose a value from the drop-down list beside it.
- **Exclude One-Time Transactions** tells Quicken not to consider one-time transactions when creating the budget. For example, suppose you made a single large payment to a furniture company to buy living room furniture. If that transaction is considered for budgeting purposes, Quicken will automatically assume that you make payments like that every year and include it in the budget. (Of course, you can always edit a budget to exclude such items after the budget has been created.)

Clicking the Categories button displays the Choose Categories dialog, shown here. You can use this dialog to select specific categories to budget. You may find this useful if you want to budget only certain categories, such as dining, clothing, and entertainment. Click to toggle the check boxes beside each category name. The categories with check marks will be included in the budget when you click OK.

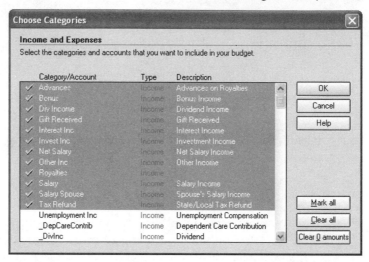

When you click OK in the Create Budget: Automatic dialog, Quicken displays a dialog telling you that the new budget has been created. Click OK to dismiss this dialog. The Income tab of the Budget window appears next.

**Creating a Budget Manually**     If you prefer, you can create a budget from scratch. This is more time-consuming, but it forces you to look at each category carefully to estimate future expenses.

Select the Manual option in the Setup tab of the Budget window (refer to Figure 18-3) and click Create Budget. A dialog appears with instructions for completing your budget. Click OK to dismiss the dialog. The Income tab of the Budget window appears next.

## Completing a Budget

Once you have created a budget, you can fine-tune it to set the categories and amounts that should appear. If you created your budget automatically, this is a matter of reviewing budget income, expense, and savings items and making changes you deem necessary. If you created a budget manually, however, you must manually add categories and set amounts for each one. You do this in the Income, Expenses, and Savings tabs of the Budget window. Because these windows all look and work pretty much the same way, only one is illustrated: the Expenses tab, which is shown in Figure 18-4.

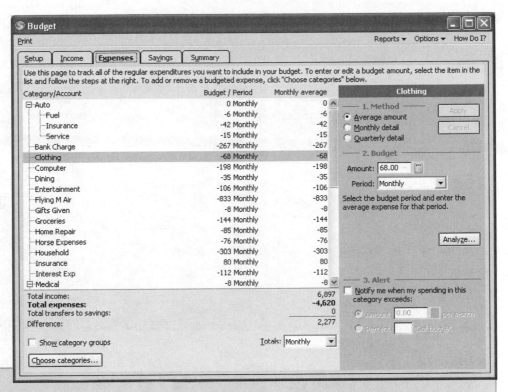

**Figure 18-4 • Here's an example of the Expenses tab of the Budget window, with several expense categories entered.**

**Adding a Category**   To add a category, click the Choose Categories button at the bottom of the Budget window. This displays the Choose Categories dialog shown earlier. Click to place a check mark beside each category you want to include in the budget.

By default, when you create a budget automatically, Quicken includes only the categories for which transactions exist. When you create a budget manually, Quicken does not include any categories at all; all categories must be added manually.

**Setting a Budget Item's Options**   You can modify the budget for a category or other item by modifying its settings on the right side of the Budget window. Click the item name in the Budget window to select it, and then make changes as desired and click Apply.

• Change the budget method to enter budget amounts as averages, monthly details, or quarterly details. As shown in the following illustration, the Budget options change depending on the method you select:

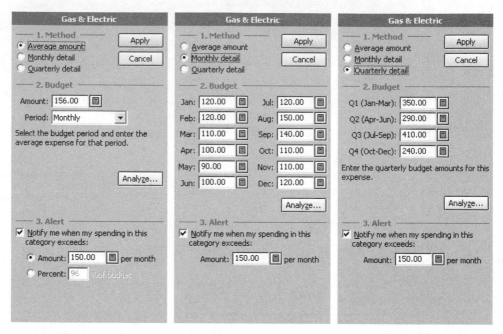

• Change the budget amount by entering values in each of the amount boxes in the Budget area. If you selected the Average Amount method, you can also choose a frequency from the Period drop-down list.

Set up an alert for a category by turning on the Notify Me check box in the Alert area and entering an amount or percent in one of the two text boxes below it. (This option appears for Expense categories only.) If your monthly spending exceeds the amount you specified, Quicken displays a dialog to tell you.

**Adding a Savings Transfer**  The Savings tab of the Budget window enables you to add budgeted transfers to investment or savings accounts. Click the Choose Accounts button at the bottom of the window and use the dialog that appears to select the accounts you want to transfer money to. Then set Budget options for the account as instructed in the preceding section.

**Analyzing Actual Category Amounts**  Clicking the Analyze button in the Budget window displays a column chart, like the one shown on the next page, of actual expenditures for the selected category. This helps you visualize the actual pattern of income, expense, or savings.

**Viewing Amounts by Category Group**   To organize categories by group, turn on the Show Category Groups check box at the bottom of the Budget window. A dialog may appear, telling you that some category groups contain both income and expense items; click OK to dismiss it. The view changes to sort categories by group, as shown in Figure 18-5, and the separate

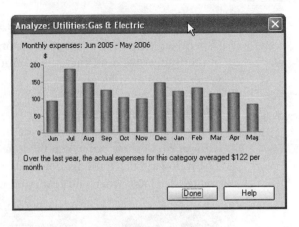

Income, Expenses, and Savings tabs are replaced by a single Budget tab. To return to the default view, turn off the Show Category Groups check box and choose Separate View from the Options menu on the window's button bar.

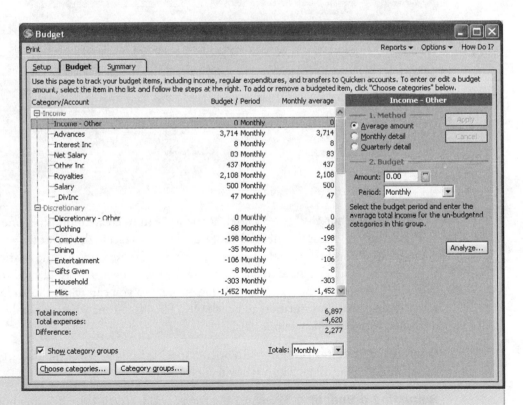

**Figure 18-5 • You can view a budget's categories by group.**

## Viewing a Completed Budget

When you're finished setting options in the Income, Expenses, and Savings tabs of the Budget window, click the Summary tab. This displays the budget summary, which is shown in Figure 18-6.

## Working with Budgets

Here are a few additional things you might want to do with Quicken's budgeting feature. All of these things can be done from the Setup tab of the Budget window. The following illustrations show what the tab looks like when you've created one budget (left) and when you've created multiple budgets (right):

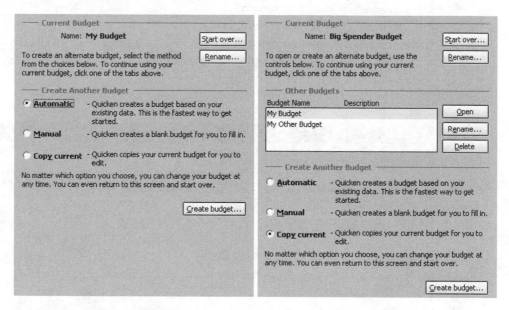

**Creating Another Budget**   Quicken enables you to create more than one budget. In the Setup tab, select the method you want to use to create the new budget and click Create Budget. If you selected Automatic, the Create Budget: Automatic dialog that appears includes a place to enter a name for the budget. If you selected Manual or Copy Current, the Budget Name dialog appears so you can name the budget. Enter the requested information and click OK. Then fine-tune your new budget as discussed earlier in this section.

**Opening a Specific Budget**   To open a specific budget, select the budget name in the middle part of the Setup tab and click Open.

**Renaming a Budget**   To rename the current budget, click the Rename button in the top part of the Setup tab. To rename another budget, select the budget name and

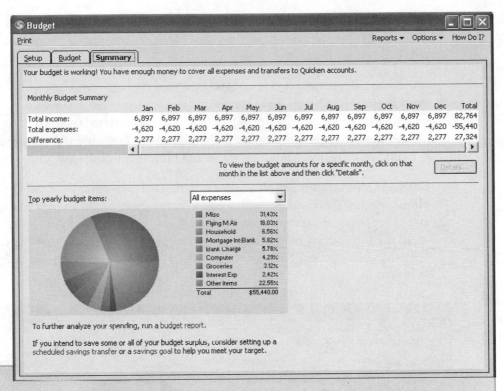

**Figure 18-6 • The Summary tab of the Budget window summarizes your budget information.**

click the Rename button in the middle part of the Setup tab. Enter a name and description in the Rename Budget dialog that appears and click OK.

**Deleting a Budget**    To delete a budget, select the budget name and click the Delete button in the middle part of the Setup tab. Click Yes in the confirmation dialog that appears. You cannot delete the currently open budget.

## Comparing a Budget to Actual Transactions

Once you have created a budget you can live with, it's a good idea to periodically compare your actual income and expenditures to budgeted amounts. Quicken lets you do this in a number of different ways.

There's one important thing to keep in mind when comparing budgeted amounts to actual results: make sure your comparison is for the period for which you have recorded data. For example, don't view a year-to-date (YTD) budget report if you began entering data into Quicken in March. Instead, customize the report to show actual transactions beginning in March. I provide details about creating and customizing reports and graphs in Chapter 9.

**Budget Reports and Graphs**    The Reports menu on the button bar in the Budget window offers two reports and one graph for comparing budgeted amounts to actual results:

- **Budget Report** displays actual and budgeted transactions. Figure 18-7 shows a budget report with YTD amounts.
- **Monthly Budget Report** displays the actual and budgeted transactions by month.
- **Monthly Budget Graph** graphically displays the favorable and unfavorable differences between monthly actual and budgeted income amounts.

**Budget Comparison Graphs**    You can display budget graphs in the Quicken Home window. This feature enables you to keep an eye on the budget categories and groups that interest you most.

To use this feature, switch to the Quicken Home window and customize it as instructed in Appendix B. The following items or snapshots provide budget information:

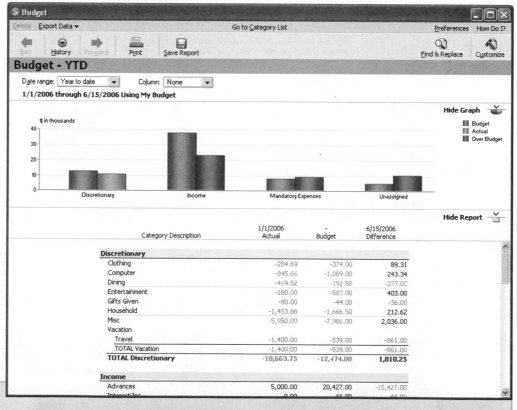

**Figure 18-7 • A budget report compares actual to budgeted amounts.**

- **Budget** displays a chart that compares your actual to budgeted income and expenses.
- **Budget Goal Progress** tracks spending for a single category's budget. This helps you monitor spending for a specific category that's important to you.
- **Budgeted Categories** compares actual category amounts with your budget.
- **Budgeted Net Income** displays a chart that compares your budgeted to actual net income.
- **Category Group Budget** tracks progress against your budget by category group.

You can customize any of the graphs by right-clicking them and choosing the Customize This Chart or Customize This Graph command from the context menu that appears. I explain how to customize reports and graphs in Chapter 9.

## Forecasting

Forecasting uses known and estimated transactions to provide a general overview of your future financial situation. This "crystal ball" can help you spot potential cash flow problems (or surpluses) so you can prepare for them.

### Creating a Forecast

A forecast without data is like a crystal ball that's full of fog—it doesn't show you much. To get a clear picture, you need to enter data about future transactions by creating a forecast.

To create a forecast, begin by opening the Cash Flow Forecast window. Choose Planning | Cash Flow Forecast. If you have not yet created a forecast, the Automatically Create Forecast dialog, which is shown here, appears. If you have already created a forecast and want to create a new one, choose Options | Update Forecast on the Cash Flow Forecast window's button bar.

How you proceed depends on the kind of data you use—budget data or register data.

### Creating a Forecast with Budget
**Data**    To create a forecast with budget data, enter beginning and ending dates for which you have a budget. This will normally be the current year. Click the Advanced button to display the Advanced AutoCreate dialog, shown here. Select Create Both in the top part of the dialog and From Budget Data in the bottom part of the dialog. Click Done to save your settings, and then click OK in the Automatically Create Forecast dialog to create the forecast. Figure 18-8, shown later in the chapter, illustrates a forecast based on a budget.

**Creating a Forecast with Register Data**    To create a forecast based on register data, enter beginning and ending dates for which you have register data. The time span should cover at least six months; for best results, it should cover a full year. Click the Advanced button to display the Advanced AutoCreate dialog. Select Create Both in the top part of the dialog and From Register Data in the bottom part of the dialog. Click Done to save your settings, and then click OK in the Automatically Create Forecast dialog to create the forecast.

## Entering Income and Expense Items

Once you've created a forecast, you can fine-tune it by entering or modifying known or estimated events. Click the Income Items or Expense Items button in the Cash Flow Forecast window (see Figure 18-8). The Forecast Income Items or Forecast Expense Items window appears, as shown next; use this window to add, modify, or delete items.

| Forecast Expense Items | | | |
|---|---|---|---|
| **Expense Item** | **Amount** | **Frequency** | **Date** |
| Known items | | | |
| APS - Arizona Public Se... | 139.12 | Monthly | 7/12/2006 |
| Bank of America | 1,016.10 | Monthly | 6/28/2006 |
| Bank of America - Line ... | 500.00 | Monthly | 7/12/2006 |
| CableAmerica{026-144... | 39.95 | Monthly | 7/5/2006 |
| Capital One | 750.00 | Monthly | 6/18/2006 |
| Car Loans R Us | 441.83 | Monthly | 7/1/2006 |
| Compass Bank | 361.09 | Monthly | 6/27/2006 |
| Countrywide Home Lo... | 714.16 | Monthly | 7/5/2006 |
| Dish Network | 65.96 | Monthly | 7/10/2006 |
| Frontier Village Condo ... | 85.00 | Monthly | 7/1/2006 |
| Qwest | 100.00 | Monthly | 7/1/2006 |
| Qwest Residential | 60.00 | Monthly | 6/30/2006 |
| Sickles Sanitation, Inc. | 34.00 | Monthly | 7/14/2006 |
| Saguaro Theater | 180.00 | Quarterly | 7/8/2006 |
| Estimated items | | | |
| Auto:Fuel | 6.00 | Monthly | Average |
| Auto:Insurance | 42.00 | Monthly | Average |
| Average Monthly Expense: | | | -8,323.81 |

Buttons: Done, Help, Show: Income Items / Expense Items, New, Edit, Delete

- To display either income or expense items, select one of the Show options.
- To edit an item, click it to select it and enter a new value.
- To add, modify, or remove items, click the New, Edit, or Delete button.

When you click New or Edit, the Create New Income/Expense Item or Edit Income/ Expense Item dialog appears, as shown here. Use this dialog to enter or edit information for a forecast item. The exact name of the dialog varies, depending on how you're using it, but the options are the same.

Start by selecting the Income or Expense option to determine the

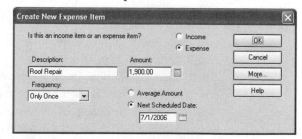

type of item you are creating. Then fill in the remaining fields with information

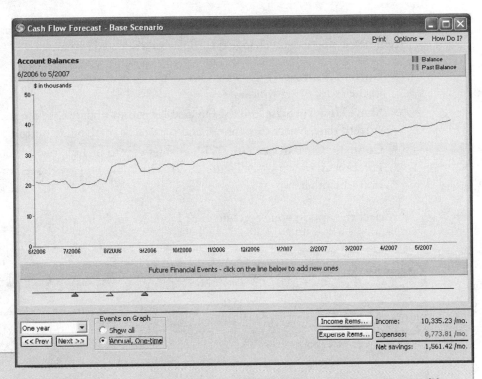

**Figure 18-8 • This forecast was based on budgeted expenditures for the current year with some additional known events.**

about the item. You can click More to select a category for the item and set the total number of entries for a recurring item. When you're finished, click OK.

## Working with Scenarios

When you create a single forecast, you create a forecast for the *base scenario*. Just as you can have multiple budgets, you can also have multiple forecast scenarios.

**Creating a New Scenario**     To create a new scenario, choose Manage Scenarios from the Options menu on the Cash Flow Forecast window's button bar. The Manage Forecast Scenarios dialog, which is shown here, appears. Click New to display a dialog in which you can enter a scenario name and choose to copy the existing scenario. When you click OK, the new scenario's name appears as the selected scenario on the Scenario Data drop-down list.

**Changing a Scenario's Display**    The Display Options in the Manage Forecast Scenarios dialog let you change the display of a selected scenario:

- **Current Scenario Only**, which is the default option, displays only one scenario in the Forecasting window.
- **Show How Forecast Looked On** enables you to update the scenario for the current date. Select this option, and then click the Update button.
- **Compare Current Scenario With** enables you to include two scenarios in the Forecasting window (see Figure 18-9). This makes it easy to see how one differs from the other.

Select the option you want and click Done to apply it.

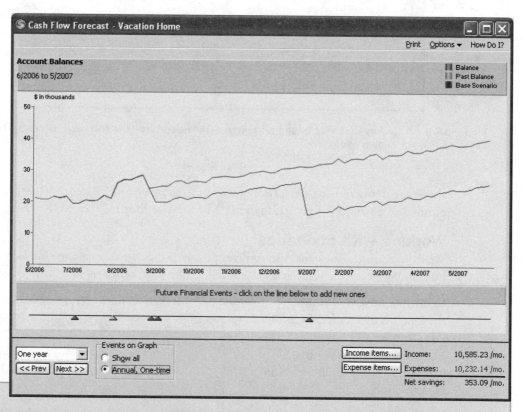

**Figure 18-9 • By including two scenarios in the Cash Flow Forecast window, you can see how they compare.**

## Saving Money

Remember when you got your first piggy bank? It may not have looked like a pig, but it had a slot for slipping in coins and, if you were lucky, a removable rubber plug on the bottom that made it easy to get the coins out when you needed them. Whoever gave you the bank was trying to teach you your first financial management lesson: save money.

As an adult, things are a little more complex. In this section, I explain why you should save, provide some saving strategies, and tell you about the types of savings accounts that make your old piggy bank obsolete.

## Why Save?

Most people save money so there's money to spend when they need it. Others save for a particular purpose. Still others save because they have so much they can't spend it all. (We should all have such problems!) Here's a closer look at why saving makes sense.

### Saving for "Rainy Days"

When people say they are "saving for a rainy day," they probably aren't talking about the weather. They're talking about bad times or emergencies—situations when they'll need extra cash.

For example, suppose the family car needs a new transmission. Or your beloved dog needs eye surgery. Or your daughter manages to break her violin three days before the big recital. In the "rainy day" scheme of things, these might be light drizzles. But your savings can help keep you dry.

Here are a few other examples. Suppose your employer goes bankrupt and closes up shop. Or after a three-martini lunch with a customer, you get back to the office, tell your boss what you really think of him, and quit on the spot. Or after being poked one too many times in the butt by a bull, you find it impossible to continue your career as a rodeo clown. If your paychecks stop coming, do you have enough savings to support yourself or your family until you can get another source of income? On the "rainy day" scale, this could be a torrential downpour. Your savings can be a good umbrella.

### Saving for a Goal

Planning for your future often includes planning for events that affect your life—and your wallet. Saving money for specific events can help make these events memorable for what they are, rather than what they cost.

For example, take a recently engaged couple, Sally and Joe. They plan to marry within a year and buy a house right away. Within five years, they plan to have their first child. That's when Sally will leave her job to start the more demanding job of mother and homemaker. They hope their children will go to college someday, and they want to help cover the expenses. They also want to be able to help pay for their children's weddings. Eventually, they'll retire. And throughout their lives, they want to be able to take annual family vacations, buy a new car every six years or so, and get season tickets for the Arizona Diamondbacks.

All of these things are major events in Sally and Joe's lives. Saving in advance for each of these events will make them possible—without going into debt.

## Saving for Peace of Mind

Some people save money because events in their lives showed them the importance of having savings. Children who lived through the Depression or bad financial times for their families grew up to be adults who understand the value of money and try hard to keep some available. They don't want to repeat the hard times they went through. Having healthy savings accounts gives them peace of mind.

# Saving Strategies

There are two main ways to save: when you can or regularly.

## Saving When You Can

When money is tight, saving can be difficult. People who are serious about saving, however, will force themselves to save as much as possible when they can. Saving when you can is better than not saving at all.

## Saving Regularly

A better way to save money is to save a set amount periodically. For example, save $25 every week or $200 every month. Timing this with your paycheck makes sense; you can make a split deposit for the check. A savings like this is called an *annuity*, and you'd be surprised at how quickly the money can accumulate. Table 18-1 shows some examples based on a 4.5 percent annual interest rate.

# Types of Savings Accounts

There are different types of savings accounts, each with its own benefits and drawbacks. Here's a quick look at them.

Keep in mind that all the accounts discussed in this chapter (except where noted) should be insured by the FDIC (Federal Deposit Insurance Corporation). This organization covers savings deposits up to $100,000 per entity (person or company) per bank, thus protecting you from loss in the event of a bank failure.

**Standard Savings Accounts**   All banks offer savings accounts, and most accommodate any balance. Savings accounts pay interest on your balance and allow you to deposit or withdraw funds at any time.

| | Weekly Contributions | | | | Monthly Contributions | | | | |
|---|---|---|---|---|---|---|---|---|---|
| Month | $25 | $50 | $75 | $100 | $50 | $100 | $200 | $300 | $400 |
| 1 | $100 | $200 | $300 | $401 | $50 | $100 | $200 | $300 | $400 |
| 2 | $226 | $452 | $677 | $903 | $100 | $200 | $401 | $601 | $801 |
| 3 | $327 | $653 | $980 | $1,307 | $151 | $301 | $602 | $903 | $1,205 |
| 4 | $428 | $856 | $1,284 | $1,712 | $201 | $402 | $805 | $1,207 | $1,609 |
| 5 | $555 | $1,110 | $1,665 | $2,220 | $252 | $504 | $1,008 | $1,511 | $2,015 |
| 6 | $657 | $1,314 | $1,971 | $2,628 | $303 | $606 | $1,211 | $1,817 | $2,423 |
| 7 | $759 | $1,519 | $2,278 | $3,038 | $354 | $708 | $1,416 | $2,124 | $2,832 |
| 8 | $888 | $1,776 | $2,664 | $3,552 | $405 | $811 | $1,621 | $2,432 | $3,242 |
| 9 | $991 | $1,982 | $2,974 | $3,965 | $457 | $914 | $1,827 | $2,741 | $3,654 |
| 10 | $1,095 | $2,190 | $3,284 | $4,379 | $509 | $1,017 | $2,034 | $3,051 | $4,068 |
| 11 | $1,225 | $2,449 | $3,674 | $4,899 | $560 | $1,121 | $2,242 | $3,363 | $4,483 |
| 12 | $1,329 | $2,658 | $3,987 | $5,316 | $613 | $1,225 | $2,450 | $3,675 | $4,900 |

**Table 18-1 • Your Savings Can Grow over Time**

**Holiday Clubs**    A "holiday club" account is a savings account into which you make regular, equal deposits, usually on a weekly basis. Many banks offer these accounts, along with an option to withdraw the deposit funds automatically from your regular savings or checking account. The money stays in the account, earning interest until the club ends in October or November. The idea behind these accounts is to provide you with cash for the holidays, but there are variations on this theme, such as vacation club accounts that end in May or June.

**Credit Union Payroll Savings**    A bank isn't the only place where you can open a savings account. If your company has a credit union, it also offers a number of accounts. These accounts often offer the option of payroll savings deductions. This is a great feature for people who have trouble saving money, because the money comes out of their paychecks before they see (and can spend) it. It's as if the money never existed, when in reality it's accumulating in an interest-bearing account. In case you're wondering, the withdrawn funds are included in your taxable income.

**Certificates of Deposit**    A certificate of deposit, or CD, is an account, normally with a bank, that requires you to keep the money on deposit for a specific length of time. As a reward for your patience, your earnings are based on a higher, fixed-interest rate than what is available for a regular savings account. The longer the term of the deposit and the more money deposited, the higher the rate. At the CD's maturity date, you can "roll over" the deposit to a new account that may have a different interest rate, or you can take back the cash. If you withdraw the money before the

CD's maturity date, you pay a penalty, which can sometimes exceed the amount of the interest earned.

**Money Market Accounts**    A money market account is actually a form of investment, but it should be included here because many banks offer it. It has a higher rate of return than a regular savings account but is not insured by the FDIC. It is considered a conservative investment and can be treated just like a savings account for depositing money. There may, however, be restrictions on the number of withdrawals you can make each month.

**Interest-Bearing Checking Accounts**    Many banks offer interest-bearing checking accounts. They usually have minimum balance requirements, however, forcing you to keep a certain amount of money in the account at all times. Although it's nice to earn money on checking account funds, the interest rate is usually so low that it's better to have a regular checking account and keep your savings in a savings account or money market account.

### What Does This Mean to You? Savings Goals

Kind of sounds silly, doesn't it? Using Quicken to transfer money from your checking account to another account that doesn't even exist.

But don't laugh—the Savings Goals feature really works. I used a technique similar to this with a paper check register years ago, before I started using Quicken. I simply deducted $50 or $100 from the account balance, thus giving the illusion that I had less money in the account than I really did. This helped me save money by making me think twice about writing a check for something I really didn't need. More important, however, is that it prevented me from bouncing checks in the days when I kept a dangerously low checking account balance.

Give it a try and see for yourself!

## Using Savings Goals

Quicken's Savings Goals feature helps you save money by "hiding" funds in an account. You set up a savings goal and make contributions to it using the Savings Goals window. Although the money never leaves the source bank account, it is deducted in the account register, thus reducing the account balance in Quicken. If you can't see the money in your account, you're less likely to spend it.

## Getting Started

Open the Savings Goals window by choosing Planning | Savings Goals. Here's what the window looks like with one savings goal already created:

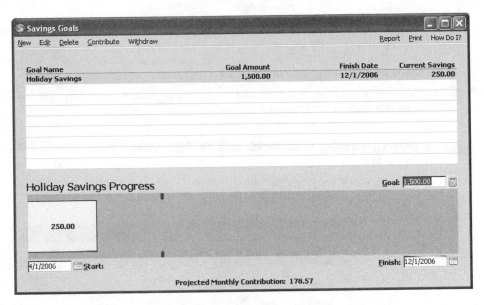

The top half of the Savings Goals window lists the savings goals you have created with Quicken. The bottom half shows the progress for the selected goal. You can use button bar options to work with window contents:

- **New** enables you to create a savings goal.
- **Edit** enables you to modify the selected savings goal.
- **Delete** removes the selected savings goal.
- **Contribute** enables you to contribute funds from a Quicken account to the selected savings goal.
- **Withdraw** enables you to remove funds from a savings goal and return them to a Quicken account.
- **Report** creates a report of the activity for savings goals.
- **Print** prints a report of savings goal details.
- **How Do I?** provides instructions for performing specific tasks with the Savings Goals window.

## Creating a Savings Goal

To create a savings goal, click New on the button bar in the Savings Goals window. The Create New Savings Goal dialog, which is shown here, appears.

Enter the information for your savings goal in the text boxes. The name of the savings goal cannot be the same as any Quicken category or account. For the Finish Date, enter the date by which you want to have the money saved. For example, if you're using a savings goal to plan for a vacation, the Finish Date should be shortly before the date you want to start the vacation. When you've finished, click OK to add the savings goal to the list in the Savings Goals window.

## Contributing Funds to a Savings Goal

To contribute funds to a savings goal, select the savings goal in the Savings Goals window and click the Contribute button on the button bar. The Contribute To Goal dialog, shown here, appears:

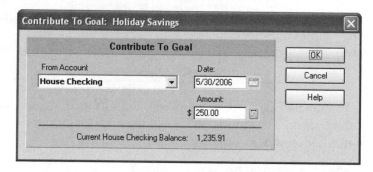

Select the account from which you want to transfer the money from the drop-down list. The balance of the account appears in the bottom of the dialog. Then enter the amount of the transfer in the Amount box. By default, Quicken suggests the projected monthly contribution amount, but you can enter any amount you like. When you've finished, click OK.

As shown in the next illustration, Quicken creates an entry in the account register of the account from which the money was contributed. It also updates the progress bar and information in the Savings Goals dialog.

When you create a savings goal, Quicken creates an asset account to record the goal's transactions and balance. To automate contributions to the goal, you can create a scheduled transaction to transfer money periodically from one of your bank accounts to the savings goal asset account. I tell you about scheduled transactions in Chapter 7.

## Meeting Your Goal

Once you have met your savings goal, you can either withdraw the funds from the savings goal so they appear in a Quicken account or delete the savings goal to put the money back where it came from.

**Withdrawing Money**    In the Savings Goals window, select the savings goal from which you want to withdraw money. Click the Withdraw button on the button bar. The Withdraw From Goal dialog (shown here), which works much like the Contribute To Goal dialog, appears. Use it to remove funds from the savings goal and put them back into the account from which they were contributed.

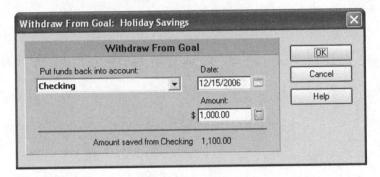

**Deleting a Savings Goal**    In the Savings Goals window, select the savings goal you want to delete and click the Delete button on the button bar. A dialog appears, asking if you want to keep the savings goal account for your records:

- Click Yes to transfer the funds back to the original account(s) and keep the savings goal account.
- Click No to transfer funds back to the original account(s) and delete the savings goal account.

# The Tax Center

This part of the book explores the features of Quicken Personal Finance Software's Tax Center, which can make tax preparation quicker and easier, enable you to plan for tax time, and even help you save money on your income taxes. Its two chapters are:

Part Six

# Simplifying Tax Preparation

## Chapter 19

## In This Chapter:

- *Including tax information in accounts and categories*
- *Tax reports*
- *Online tax tools*
- *TurboTax*

Tax time is no fun. It can force you to spend hours sifting through financial records and filling out complex forms. When you're done with the hard part, you may be rewarded with the knowledge that you can expect a refund. But it is more likely that your reward will be the privilege of writing a check to the federal, state, or local government—or worse yet, all three.

Fortunately, Quicken Personal Finance Software can help. Its reporting features can save you time. By using the tax tools that are part of Quicken or available on Quicken.com, the next tax season may be a little less stressful. In this chapter, I show you how.

## Tax Information in Accounts and Categories

As discussed briefly in Chapter 3, Quicken accounts and categories can include information that will help you at tax time. In this section, I explain how you can set it up.

## Including Tax Information in Accounts

You enter an account's tax information in the Tax Schedule Information dialog for the account. Choose Tools | Account List or press CTRL-A to display the Account List window. Select the name of the account in the View Accounts tab and click the Edit button on the button bar. In the General Information tab of the Account Details dialog that appears, click the Tax Schedule Info button. The Tax Schedule Information dialog, shown here, appears:

Use the Transfers In and Transfers Out drop-down lists to map account activity to specific lines on tax return forms and schedules. If the account has tax-deferred or tax-exempt status, be sure to turn on the Tax-Deferred Or Tax-Exempt Account check box. When you're finished, click OK. Repeat this process for all accounts for which you want to enter tax information.

Keep in mind that if you use the Paycheck Set Up feature to account for all payroll deductions, including retirement plan contributions, you shouldn't have to change the settings for any of your accounts. (That's another good reason to set up your regular paychecks in Quicken.) I explain how to set up a paycheck in Quicken in Chapter 7.

## Including Tax Information in Categories

You can enter tax line item information for Quicken categories in two ways:

- Enter tax line item information for a single category in the Edit Category dialog.
- Match multiple categories to tax line items with the Tax Line Item Assignment pane.

Quicken automatically sets tax information for many of the categories it creates. You can see which categories are tax-related and which tax form lines have been assigned to them in the Category List window. Concentrate on the categories without tax assignments; some of these may require tax information, depending on your situation.

## What Does This Mean to You? Entering Tax Information in Quicken

I know what you're saying! More entry stuff! Ick!

Stop whining! This is one Quicken setup task that can save you hours of time and maybe even a bunch of money. You see, by including tax information in Quicken accounts and categories, you make it possible for Quicken to do several things for you:

- Prepare tax reports that summarize information by tax category or schedule. You can take these tax reports to your tax preparation guy and make it a lot easier for him to do your taxes. He'll be so appreciative that he'll knock a few bucks off his bill and take you to lunch. (Okay, so he might not take you to lunch, especially during tax time when he's really busy.)
- Display tax information in the Tax Center window, which shows an up-to-date summary of your tax situation. Knowing how you stand now will help prevent surprises at tax time.
- Save time using the Tax Planner, a Quicken feature that can import information from your Quicken data file based on tax information you enter. Do a little work here and save a bunch of work there. I tell you about the Tax Planner in Chapter 20.
- Distinguish between taxable and nontaxable investments so you can create accurate reports on capital gains, interest, and dividends. You wouldn't want to include tax-exempt income with taxable income when preparing your tax returns, would you?
- Use TurboTax to prepare your tax return based on information imported right from your Quicken data file. With the money you save on doing your returns yourself, you can buy yourself lunch. I tell you a little more about using TurboTax with Quicken in the section "TurboTax" later in this chapter.

See? By spending a few minutes setting up tax information for your accounts and categories, you can save time and money at tax time, and know your tax situation all year long.

You can also enter tax information when you first create a category. The Set Up Category dialog looks and works much like the Edit Category dialog (shown a bit later). I tell you more about the Set Up Category dialog in Chapter 3.

## Using the Edit Category Dialog

The Edit Category dialog, shown next, is handy when you need to set up tax information for just one or two categories. Choose Tools | Category List to open the Category List window. Select the category for which you want to enter tax information. Then click the Edit button to display the Edit Category dialog:

If the category's transactions should be included on your tax return as either income or a deductible expense, turn on the Tax-Related check box. Then use the Tax Line Item drop-down list to choose the form or schedule and line for the item. (You can expand this list by selecting the Extended Line Item List option.) A description of the tax line item you chose appears at the bottom of the dialog. Click OK. Repeat this process for all categories that should be included on your tax return.

## Using the Tax Line Item Assignments Pane

The Tax Line Item Assignments pane offers a quick and easy way to set tax information for multiple categories all in one place. Choose Tax | Tax Line Item Assignment. The Category List window appears, with the Tax Line Item Assignments pane on the right side of the window (see Figure 19-1). Use this area to assign tax line information to Quicken categories.

To assign a tax line item to a category, select the category on the left side of the window. Then use the Tax Item drop-down list to choose the form or schedule and line for the item. (You can expand this list by selecting the Extended List option.) A description of the tax line item you chose appears on the right side of the Tax Line Item Assignments pane. Repeat this process for all categories that should be included on your tax return.

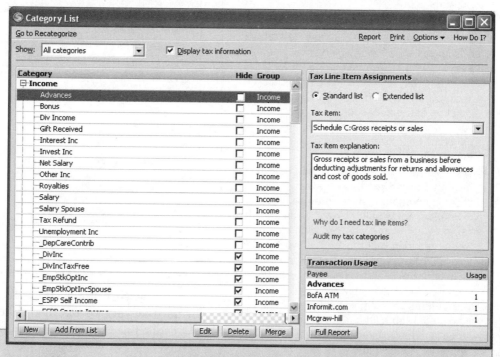

**Figure 19-1 • The Tax Line Item Assignments pane appears on the right side of the Category List window.**

It is not necessary to match all categories—just the ones that should appear on your tax return. You'll find that the tax-related categories automatically created by Quicken—such as Charity—have already been assigned tax lines. When you've finished, you can close the Category List window. The information is recorded for each category.

## Auditing Your Tax Line Assignments

Quicken can "audit" the tax line information associated with categories and tell you where there may be problems with the assignments. This feature helps ensure that you have properly set up your categories to take advantage of Quicken's tax features.

Choose Tax | Tax Category Audit or click the Audit link in the Tax Line Item Assignments pane (refer to Figure 19-1). Quicken quickly reviews all your categories. If it finds potential problems, it displays them in the Tax Category Audit window (see Figure 19-2).

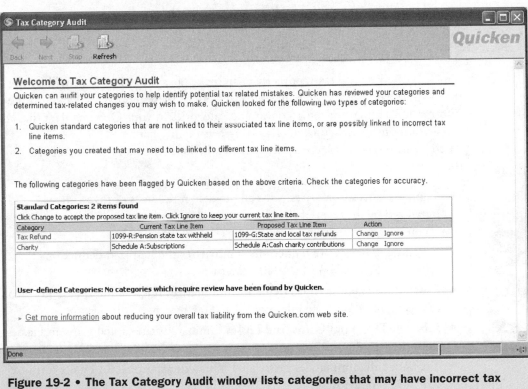

**Figure 19-2** • **The Tax Category Audit window lists categories that may have incorrect tax line assignments.**

You have three choices for working with the items Quicken finds:

- To accept Quicken's suggested correction for the category, click the Change link in the Action column on the category's line. Then click OK in the Edit Selected Tax Audit Category dialog that appears. (This dialog looks and works just like the Edit Category dialog, shown earlier in this chapter.)
- To ignore the possible problem, click the Ignore link in the Action column on the category's line.
- To change the tax line assignment manually, click the category name link and make the desired changes in the Edit Selected Tax Audit Category dialog that appears, and then click OK. (This dialog looks and works just like the Edit Category dialog shown earlier in this chapter.)

If Quicken doesn't find any problems with your categories, it displays a dialog that tells you so. Keep in mind, however, that this doesn't necessarily mean that your tax line assignments are error-free. You should review them the old-fashioned way—by looking them over yourself—before relying on them.

## Tax Reports

Quicken offers several tax reports that can make tax time easier by providing the information you need to prepare your taxes. All of these reports are based on the tax information settings for the accounts and categories in your Quicken data file. You can learn more about Quicken's reporting feature in Chapter 9.

To create a report, select Reports | Tax and choose the name of the report from the submenu:

- **Capital Gains** summarizes gains and losses on the sales of investments, organized by the term of the investment (short or long) and the investment account.
- **Schedule A-Itemized Deductions** summarizes the itemized deductions that appear on Schedule A of a 1040 tax return.
- **Schedule B-Interest And Dividends** summarizes interest and dividends income that is reported on Schedule B of a 1040 tax return.
- **Schedule D-Capital Gains And Losses** summarizes the capital gains and losses from the sale of investments that is reported on Schedule D of a 1040 tax return.
- **Tax Schedule** summarizes tax-related transactions, organized by tax form or schedule and line item.
- **Tax Summary** summarizes tax-related transactions, organized by category and date.

## Online Tax Tools

The Online Tax Tools submenu under the Tax menu offers access to a number of tax-related features and information sources on the TurboTax.com Web site that can help you with your taxes. All you need to take advantage of these features is an Internet connection.

Here's a quick look at the online tax tools. The next time you're thinking about taxes, be sure to check these out.

**Tax Calculators**    The Tax Calculators command displays the Tax Tools page on TurboTax.com, where you can find dozens of tools for making tax and other financial calculations. Just click a link on the page to work with the calculator.

**Common Tax Questions**    The Common Tax Questions command displays the Getting Ready page on TurboTax.com. This page includes dozens of links to tax-related topics.

**Tax Forms**    The Tax Forms command displays the Tax Forms page on TurboTax.com, which offers links to various categories of tax forms. Click a link to display additional information and links to forms. When you click a form link, Quicken downloads the form as an Acrobat PDF file that appears in either a web browser window or an Adobe Acrobat Reader window. (You must have the freely distributed Adobe Acrobat Reader software to open and use these forms.) Print the form to fill it out manually.

**Federal Tax Publications**    The Federal Tax Publications command displays the IRS Publications page on TurboTax.com. This page is full of links to IRS publications available on the Web. You'll find these publications extremely helpful when trying to figure out tax laws—provided you can understand the publications!

## TurboTax

If you're tired of paying a tax preparer to fill out your tax return for you, but you're not quite confident enough about your tax knowledge to prepare your own return manually, it's time to check out TurboTax tax-preparation software. It's the best way to simplify tax preparation.

Intuit offers two versions of TurboTax for Windows PC users. You can learn more about both of them by choosing Tax | Quicken Services | TurboTax Software.

**TurboTax Deluxe Software**    TurboTax Deluxe is software that works seamlessly with Quicken to prepare your taxes. Just follow the instructions in this chapter to set up your accounts and categories with tax information. Then import your Quicken data into TurboTax. You can go through an easy interview process to make sure you haven't left anything out—much like the interview you might go through with a paid tax preparer. TurboTax calculates the bottom line and enables you to either print your returns or file them electronically.

**TurboTax for the Web**    TurboTax for the Web enables you to fill out your tax forms online, using the same kind of interview process you'd find in TurboTax Deluxe. When you're finished preparing your return, you can print out the forms or file electronically.

# Planning for Tax Time

## Chapter 20

## In This Chapter:

- *Tax planning basics*
- *Tax Planner*
- *Tax Withholding Estimator*
- *Tax Center*
- *Deduction Finder*
- *Itemized Deduction Estimator*

Surprises can make life interesting. But not all surprises are good ones. Consider the surprise you may get one April when your tax preparer announces that you'll have to write a rather large check to your Uncle Sam and his friends in your state revenue department.

Quicken Personal Finance Software's tax planning features, like the Tax Planner and Tax Withholding Estimator, can help you avoid nasty surprises. Other built-in tax tools, like the Deduction Finder, Itemized Deduction Estimator, and Tax-Exempt Investment Yield Comparison, can save you money and help you make smarter financial decisions. All these features can be found in the Tax Center, which is full of snapshots to help you monitor your tax situation. In this chapter, I tell you all about Quicken's tax planning and monitoring features.

## Planning to Avoid Surprises

One of the best reasons to think about taxes before tax time is to avoid surprises on April 15. Knowing what you'll owe before you owe it can help ensure that you pay just the right amount of taxes up front—through proper deductions or estimated tax payments—so you don't get hit with a big tax bill or tax refund.

You may think of a big tax refund as a gift from Uncle Sam. Well, it isn't. It's your money that Uncle Sam has been using, interest free, for months. When you overpay your taxes, you're giving up money that you could be using to reduce interest-bearing debt or earn interest or investment income. Make sure you don't overpay taxes throughout the year so you can keep your money where it'll do *you* the most good.

Quicken offers two built-in tax planning tools that you can use to keep track of your tax situation throughout the year. The Tax Planner helps you estimate your federal income tax bill for the 2006 and 2007 tax years. The Tax Withholding Estimator helps you determine whether your withholding taxes are correctly calculated. Finally, the Tax Center summarizes your tax situation with a number of useful snapshots. Here's a closer look at each of these features.

### Using the Tax Planner

Quicken's Tax Planner includes features from Intuit's TurboTax product to help you estimate your federal income tax bill for the 2006 and 2007 tax years. While this can help you avoid surprises, it can also help you see how various changes to income and expenses can affect your estimated tax bill.

#### Opening the Quicken Tax Planner Window

To open the Tax Planner, choose Tax | Tax Planner. The first time you open the Tax Planner, it may display a dialog that offers to import TurboTax data into Quicken for tax planning purposes. If you click Yes, follow the instructions that appear onscreen to complete the import. If you click No, or when the import process is complete, the Tax Planner window with introductory information appears. Read this information to get a clear understanding of what the Tax Planner can do for you and how it works.

#### Viewing the Tax Planner Summary

To see what data is already entered in the Tax Planner, click the Tax Planner Summary link in the navigation bar on the left side of the Tax Planner window. A summary of all data, as well as the calculated tax implications, appears as shown in Figure 20-1.

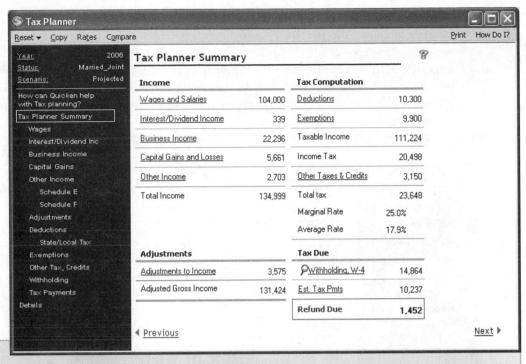

**Figure 20-1 • The Tax Planner Summary screen displays a summary of all information stored in the Tax Planner.**

## Entering Tax Planner Data

Data can be entered into the Tax Planner from three different sources:

- **TurboTax** data can be imported into Quicken. In the main Quicken application window, choose File | Import | TurboTax. Then use the dialog that appears to locate and import your TurboTax data. This information can be used to project current-year amounts in the Tax Planner.

- **User Entered** data can override any automatic entries. Use this to enter data that isn't entered any other way or has not yet been entered into Quicken—such as expected year-end bonuses or tax-deductible expenses.

- **Quicken Data** can be automatically entered into the Tax Planner. This works only if you have properly set up your tax-related Quicken categories with appropriate tax return line items, as discussed in Chapter 19.

Here's how it works. Click a link in the navigation bar on the left side of the Tax Planner window or in the Tax Planner Summary screen (refer to Figure 20-1) to view a specific type of income or expense. Then click a link within the window for a specific item. Details for the item appear in the bottom of the window, as shown in Figure 20-2. (You may have to click the Show Details link to expand the window and show the details.) If desired, change the source option and, if necessary, enter an amount.

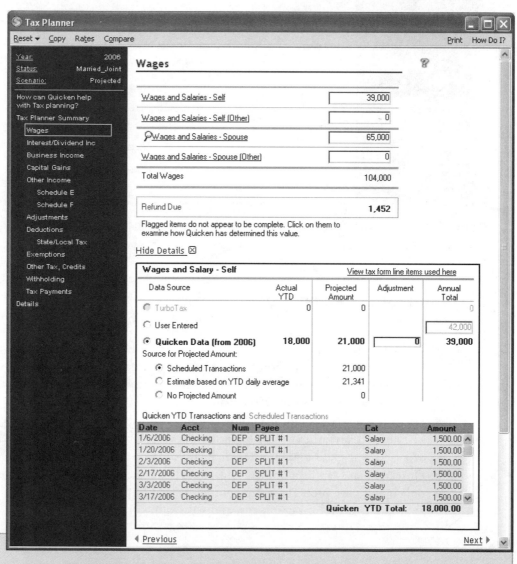

**Figure 20-2 • You can enter additional information into the Tax Planner.**

The options you can choose from vary depending on whether TurboTax data is available or the item has transactions recorded in Quicken. For example, in Figure 20-2, TurboTax data is not available, but transactions have been entered in Quicken. You can either select the User Entered option and enter a value in the Annual Total column or select the Quicken Data option and enter an adjusting value in the Adjustment column. This makes it easy to manually override any automatic source entries.

Repeat this process for any Tax Planner items you want to check or change. The Tax Planner automatically recalculates the impact of your changes.

To reset values quickly to amounts automatically entered by Quicken, choose Reset To Quicken Default Values from the Reset menu on the Tax Planner's button bar.

## Using Scenarios

The Scenarios feature of the Tax Planner enables you to enter data for multiple scenarios—a "what if" capability that you can use to see tax impacts based on various changes in entry data. For example, suppose you're planning to get married and want to see the impact of the additional income and deductions related to your new spouse. You can use a scenario to see the tax impact without changing your Projected scenario.

To use this feature, click the Scenario link in the navigation bar on the left side of the Tax Planner window (refer to Figure 20-1 or 20-2). The Tax Planner Options screen, which is shown next, appears. Choose a different scenario from the Scenarios drop-down list. If Quicken asks whether you want to copy the current scenario to the scenario you chose, click Yes if that other scenario hasn't been set up yet. Choose options from the Tax Year and Filing Status drop-down lists to set the scenario options. Then click the Next link at the bottom of the window to return to the Tax Planner Summary window. If necessary, change the values in the new scenario.

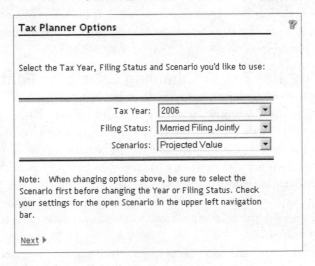

To compare one scenario to another, click the Compare button in the Tax Planner window's button bar. A Tax Scenario Comparisons dialog like the one shown next appears, showing the results of each scenario's calculations. When you're finished viewing the comparative information, click OK to dismiss the dialog.

**Tax Scenario Comparisons**

| | Projected | Scenario 1 | Scenario 2 | Scenario 3 |
|---|---|---|---|---|
| Filing Status | Married-Joint | Married-Sep | Qual. Widow | Single |
| Tax Year | 2006 | 2006 | 2006 | 2005 |
| Adjusted Gross Income | 133,424 | 68,424 | 68,424 | 0 |
| Deductions and Exemptions | 16,900 | 8,450 | 13,600 | 0 |
| Taxable Income | 116,524 | 59,974 | 54,824 | 0 |
| Total Tax | 24,973 | 14,278 | 10,195 | 0 |
| Marginal, Avg. Tax Rates | 25.0%  18.7% | 25.0%  20.8% | 15.0%  14.9% | 0.0%  0.0% |

OK    Help

## Finishing Up

When you're finished using the Tax Planner, click the close button on the button bar or switch to another window. This saves the information you entered and updates the Projected Tax calculations in the Tax Center. (I tell you about the Tax Center window later in this chapter in the section "The Tax Center.")

## Tax Withholding Estimator

Quicken's Tax Withholding Estimator feature helps you determine whether your W-4 form has been correctly completed. It does this by comparing your estimated tax bill from the Tax Planner to the amount of withholding tax deducted from your paychecks.

### Using the Tax Withholding Estimator Feature

To get started, choose Tax | Tax Withholding Estimator. The Am I Under Or Over Withholding? window appears, as shown in Figure 20-3.

Read the information and follow the instructions in the middle column of the window. You'll be prompted to enter information related to withholding taxes. The instructions are clear and easy to follow, so I won't repeat them here. Each time you enter data and click the Adjust Tax Projection button, the Projected Refund Due or Projected Tax Due amount in the lower-right corner of the window changes. Your goal is to get the amount as close to zero as possible, which you can do by adjusting the number of W-4 allowances and additional withholding per pay period.

(Although I tell you that your goal is to get the Projected Tax Due amount as close to zero as possible, a *Quicken 2002 The Official Guide* reader had a problem

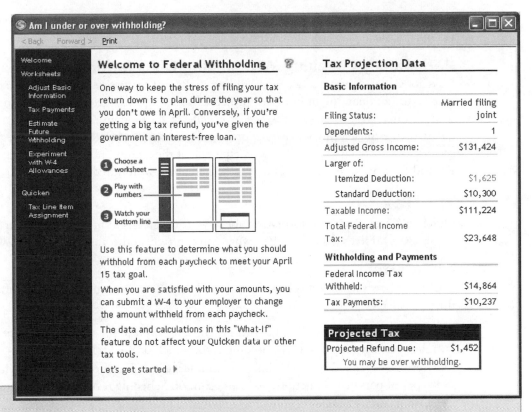

**Figure 20-3 • Use the Tax Withholding Estimator to determine whether your federal withholding taxes are correct.**

with my advice. He pointed out that your goal should be to pay as little taxes as possible throughout the year without getting an underpayment penalty on April 15. His logic is to hold onto your money as long as you can. While his strategy is good and legal—remember, if there's no penalty, you couldn't have done anything wrong—I personally don't like to write a check on April 15, so I aim for zero. It's your choice.)

None of the entries you make in the Tax Withholding Estimator feature will affect your Quicken data or any other tax planning feature within Quicken, so don't be afraid to experiment.

## Acting on the Results of Tax Withholding Estimator Calculations

What do you do with this information once you have it? Well, suppose your work with the Tax Withholding Estimator feature tells you that you should change your W-4 allowances from 2 to 3 to avoid overpaying federal withholding taxes. You can act on this information by completing a new W-4 form at work. This will decrease the amount of withholding tax in each paycheck. The result is that you reduce your tax overpayment and potential refund.

### Periodically Checking Withholding Calculations

It's a good idea to use the Tax Withholding Estimator feature periodically to make sure actual amounts are in line with projections throughout the year. (I recommend using it once every three months or so.) Whenever possible, use actual values rather than estimates in your calculations. And be sure to act on the results of the calculations by filing a new W-4 form, especially if the amount of your Projected Refund Due or Projected Tax Due is greater than a few hundred dollars.

## The Tax Center

Quicken summarizes all information about your tax situation in the Tax Center (see Figure 20-4). Here's a quick look at what you can find in the Tax Center window.

### Tax Alerts

The Tax Alerts snapshot displays alerts related to your tax situation. Quicken offers three tax alerts:

- **Over/Under Withholding** (shown next) enables you to set a threshold value to alert you if your payroll withholding is too much or not enough.
- **Itemized Deductions** (Schedule A Reminder) displays information about the types of personal deductions you can claim on Schedule A of your tax return.
- **Important Tax Dates** notifies you in advance of tax calendar events, such as estimated tax due dates and extension deadlines.

To set tax alerts, click the Set Up Alerts button at the bottom of the Tax Alerts snapshot. Then use the Setup tab of the Alerts Center window that appears (shown here) to set alert options. I tell you more about setting alerts in Chapter 9.

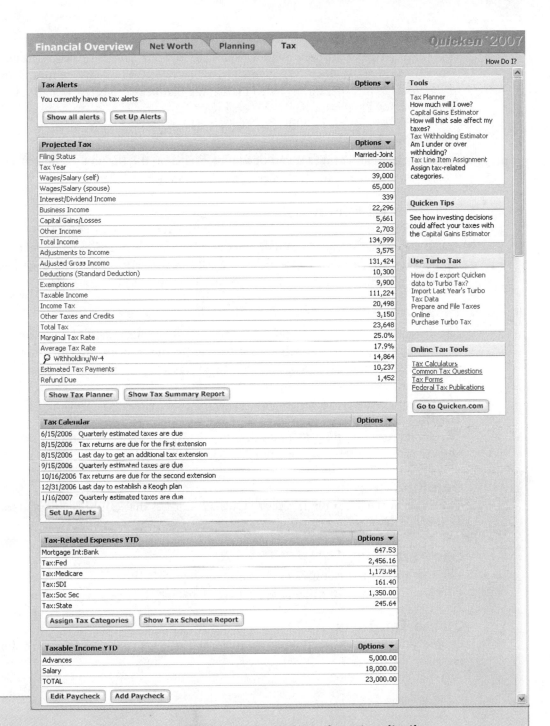

**Figure 20-4 • The Tax Center window is full of snapshots of your tax situation.**

### Projected Tax

The Projected Tax snapshot provides a summary of your upcoming projected tax return, including the amount that you'll have to pay or get back as a refund. The information in this snapshot is based on the Tax Planner's Projected scenario. I discuss the Tax Planner earlier in this chapter.

### Tax Calendar

The Tax Calendar lists recent and upcoming events on the IRS tax calendar. You can use the Options menu to set up alerts or visit an online tax calendar.

### Tax-Related Expenses YTD

The Tax-Related Expenses YTD snapshot summarizes all of your year-to-date tax-related expenses. Quicken automatically calculates this information based on the transactions you enter throughout the year. All expense categories that are marked "tax-related" and have transactions appear in this snapshot.

### Taxable Income YTD

The Taxable Income YTD snapshot summarizes all of your year-to-date tax-related income. Quicken calculates these totals based on the transactions you enter throughout the year. All income categories that are marked "tax-related" and have transactions appear in this snapshot.

### Tools

The Tools area offers links to a number of Quicken tax-related features. I discuss all of these features in this chapter and in Chapters 12 and 19.

### Quicken Tips

The Quicken Tips area offers links to Quicken features that can help you plan for or minimize taxes.

### Use TurboTax

The Use TurboTax area provides links for working with TurboTax tax preparation software. I tell you a little about TurboTax in Chapter 19.

### Online Tax Tools

Online Tax Tools provides links to tax tools on TurboTax.com. I discuss the online tax tools in Chapter 19.

# Minimizing Taxes by Maximizing Deductions

One way to minimize taxes is to maximize your deductions. While Quicken can't help you spend money on tax-deductible items—that's up to you—it can help you identify expenses that may be tax deductible, so you don't forget to include them on your tax returns.

Quicken offers two features to help maximize your deductions. Deduction Finder asks you questions about expenditures to determine whether they may be tax deductible. Itemized Deduction Estimator helps make sure you don't forget about commonly overlooked itemized deductions.

## Deduction Finder

The Deduction Finder uses another TurboTax feature to help you learn which expenses are deductible. Its question-and-answer interface gathers information from you and then provides information about the deductibility of items based on your answers.

### Working with the Deduction Finder Window

To open the Deduction Finder, choose Tax | Deduction Finder. An Introduction dialog may appear. Read its contents to learn more about Deduction Finder and then click OK. Figure 20-5 shows what the Deductions tab of the Deduction Finder window says about the expenses I incur for maintaining an office.

You can use button bar options to work with the Deduction Finder window:

- **See Introduction** displays the Introduction window, so you can learn more about how Deduction Finder works.
- **Clear Checkmarks** removes the check marks from items for which you have already answered questions.
- **Print** prints a summary of deduction information about all the deductions for which you have answered questions.
- **How Do I?** provides instructions for completing tasks within the Deduction Finder window.

### Finding Deductions

As you can see in Figure 20-5, the Deductions tab of the Deduction Finder window uses clearly numbered steps to walk you through the process of selecting deduction types and deductions and then answering questions. It's easy to use. You don't have to answer questions about all the deductions—only the deductions you think may

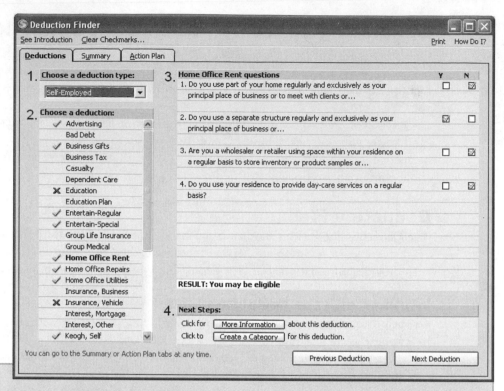

**Figure 20-5 • The Deduction Finder helps you identify expenses that may be tax deductible.**

apply to you. When you've finished answering questions about a deduction, the result appears near the bottom of the window. You can then move on to another deduction.

The Summary tab of the window, shown next, summarizes the number of deductions available in each category, the number for which you answered questions, and the number for which you may be eligible to take deductions based on your answers to the questions.

| Deduction types | # Available | # Answered | # Eligible |
| --- | --- | --- | --- |
| Employee type | 28 | 0 | 0 |
| Homeowner type | 5 | 2 | 2 |
| Individual type | 26 | 5 | 4 |
| Investor type | 7 | 2 | 1 |
| Medical type | 11 | 1 | 1 |
| Self-Employed type | 33 | 14 | 12 |

When you've finished answering questions, you can click the Action Plan tab to get more information about the deductions and the things you need to do to claim them. Although you can read the Action Plan information onscreen, if you answered many questions, you may want to use the Print button on the button bar to print the information for reference.

## Itemized Deduction Estimator

The Itemized Deduction Estimator feature helps make sure you don't overlook any itemized deductions—the deductions on Schedule A of your tax return—that you might qualify for. It does this by guiding you through a review of deduction ideas and providing the information you need to know whether you may qualify.

To get started, choose Tax | Itemized Deduction Estimator. The How Can I Maximize My Deductions? window appears, as shown in Figure 20-6.

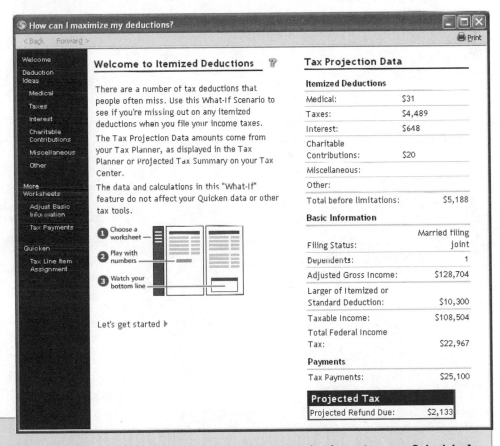

**Figure 20-6 • With the Itemized Deduction Estimator, you won't miss out on any Schedule A deductions.**

Read the information and follow the instructions in the middle column of the window. You'll be prompted to enter information related to itemized deductions for medical expenses, taxes paid, interest paid, charitable contributions, and other items. The instructions are clear and easy to follow. Each time you enter information and click the Calculate Total button, the Projected Refund Due or Projected Tax Due amount in the lower-right corner of the window changes. Your goal is to get a Projected Refund Due amount as high as possible or a Projected Tax Due amount as low as possible.

Again, none of the entries you make in the Itemized Deduction Estimator feature will affect your Quicken data or any other tax planning feature within Quicken. Experiment as much as you like.

# Appendixes

This part of the book provides some additional information you may find helpful when using Quicken Personal Finance Software. These two appendixes explain how to work with Quicken data files and how to customize Quicken.

# Part Seven

# Managing Quicken Files

## In This Appendix:

- *Creating and opening data files*
- *Backing up and restoring data files*
- *Performing other file management tasks*
- *Password-protecting Quicken data*

All the data you enter in Quicken Personal Finance Software is stored in a Quicken data file. This file includes all account and category setup information, transactions, and other data you have entered into Quicken.

Technically speaking, your Quicken data file consists of a number of files with the same name and different extensions. Manipulating these files without using Quicken's built-in file management tools can cause errors.

Commands under Quicken's File menu enable you to perform a number of file management tasks, including creating, opening, backing up, restoring, exporting, renaming, deleting, and password-protecting data files. In this appendix, I cover all of these tasks.

## Working with Multiple Data Files

Chances are, you won't need more than one Quicken data file—the one that's created as part of the Quicken Express Setup process, covered in Chapter 2. But just in case you do, here's how you can create and open another one.

**Appendix A**

## Creating a Data File

Start by choosing File | New. A dialog appears, asking whether you want to create a new Quicken file or a new Quicken account. (Some users confuse the two and try to use the File menu's New command to create a new account. I tell you the correct way to create an account in Chapters 2 and 3.) Select New Quicken File and click OK.

A Create Quicken File dialog, like the one shown next, appears. Use it to enter a name for the data file. Although you can also change the default directory location, it's easier to find the data file if it's in the C:\Documents and Settings\\*yourname*\My Documents\Quicken\ subdirectory with other Quicken data files. Click OK.

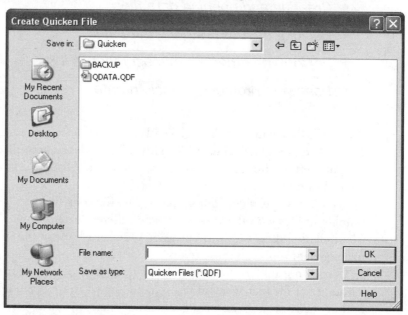

Quicken Express Setup appears next. It walks you through the process of specifying information about yourself and your finances for a basic Quicken setup. I explain how to use Quicken Express Setup in Chapter 2; turn to that chapter if you need help.

## Opening a Different Data File

If you have more than one Quicken data file, it's important that you enter transactions into the right one. You can see which data file is currently open by looking at the file name in the application window's title bar.

To open a different data file, choose File | Open, or press CTRL-O, and use the standard Open dialog that appears to select and open a different file. Only one Quicken data file can be open at a time.

# Backing Up Your Quicken Data File

Imagine this: You set up Quicken to track all of your finances, and you record transactions regularly so the Quicken data file is always up-to-date. Then one evening, when you start your computer to surf the Net, you find that your hard drive has died. Not only have your plans for the evening been ruined, but your Quicken data file is also a casualty of your hard drive's untimely death.

If you back up your Quicken data as regularly as you update its information, the loss of your Quicken data file would be a minor inconvenience, rather than a catastrophe. In this section, I explain how to back up your Quicken data file and how to restore it if the original file is lost or damaged.

## Backing Up to Disk

Quicken makes it difficult to forget backing up. Every third time you exit the Quicken program, it displays the Quicken Backup dialog, shown here, which prompts you to back up your data file. Click the Backup button to display the Quicken Backup dialog.

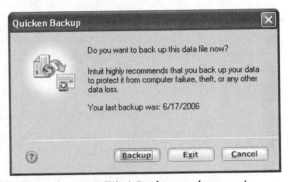

You can also begin the backup process by choosing File | Backup or by pressing CTRL-B at any time while using Quicken. This displays the Quicken Backup dialog for the currently open Quicken data file:

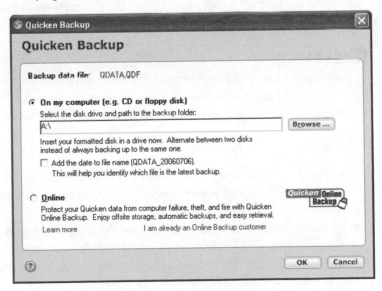

Select one of the backup location options:

- **On My Computer** enables you to back up to another disk, either on your computer or on one that's accessible via a network. If you select this option, you can use the Browse button to locate and select a backup disk and directory. As the dialog recommends, it's a good idea to alternate between two disks for backup purposes. This means you'll always have two versions backed up, in case one version is bad. It's a good idea to choose a backup location other than your hard disk, such as a floppy disk (for very small data files) or CD-R disc. (Backing up to your hard disk defeats the purpose of backing up!) If you want to automatically append the current date to the backup file name, turn on the Add The Date To File Name check box. (These instructions assume you have selected On My Computer.)

- **Online** enables you to back up to a server on the Internet, using Quicken's Online Backup service, which is available for a nominal fee. You can learn more about this service by selecting Online and then clicking OK to display the Quicken Services window for the Quicken Online Backup service.

After selecting On My Computer and indicating a backup directory in the Quicken Backup dialog, click OK. Your Quicken data file disappears momentarily and a small window tells you that Quicken is backing up your data. When the backup is complete, the data file's windows reappear and a dialog informs you that the file was backed up successfully. Click OK to dismiss the dialog.

If your Quicken data file is too large to fit on the disk you indicated in the Quicken Backup dialog, Quicken will prompt you to insert additional formatted disks until the backup is complete. Follow the instructions that appear onscreen to complete the backup.

## Restoring

In the event of loss or damage to your data file, you can restore from the most recent backup. Start Quicken and then choose a backup file from the Restore Backup File submenu under the File menu. This submenu includes all backups you have created with Quicken.

When you choose the backup file, one of two things may happen:

- If the file has the same name as the Quicken data file currently in use, a dialog appears, asking if you want to overwrite the file in use. To replace the current file with the backup copy, click OK.
- If the file has the same name as another Quicken data file in the Quicken directory in your My Documents folder, a dialog appears, warning you that you will overwrite the existing file. If you're sure you want to restore the backup and overwrite the existing file with the same name, click OK.

Quicken restores the file from the backup copy. It places a copy of the restored file in the Quicken directory in your My Documents folder on your hard disk, displaying a status window as it works. When it has finished, it displays a dialog telling you that the file has been restored successfully. Click OK.

## Moving a Quicken Data File Between Two Computers

Intuit's Technical Support staff is often asked how to move a Quicken data file from one computer to another. In fact, this question is so common that Intuit asked me to address it in this book.

The best way to move a data file from one computer to another is with the Backup and Restore Backup File commands. Begin by opening the file with Quicken on the computer on which it resides. Then follow the instructions in this appendix to back up the file to removable media, such as a floppy disk or CD-R disc, or to a network drive (preferably one that the other computer is connected to). Then fire up Quicken on the other computer and follow the restoring instructions in this appendix to restore the backup copy. When you're finished, the Quicken data file is ready to use on the new computer.

It's important to remember that once you begin making changes to the file on the new computer, the file on the old computer will no longer be up-to-date. That means that if you want to use the file on the old computer again, you need to complete the backup and restore process to move the file back to that computer. As you can imagine, if you often move the file from one computer to another and back, it can be difficult to keep track of which version of the file is the most up-to-date.

Although you can make your Quicken data file "portable" by keeping it on removable media so you can access it from any computer, neither Intuit nor I recommend doing so. Removable media is more susceptible to data loss and damage than an internal or networked hard disk. Quicken users have reported numerous problems using this technique; don't add your own problems to the list.

## Other File Management Tasks

The File Operations submenu under Quicken's File menu enables you to perform several other tasks with Quicken data files. Here's a quick summary of each command, with tips for when you may find them useful.

### Copying the Current Data File

The Copy command enables you to copy the current data file to a different disk or save a copy with a different name. When you choose File | File Operations | Copy, the Copy File dialog, shown next, appears. Use it to enter a pathname for the copy and specify which transactions should be included. Click OK to make the copy.

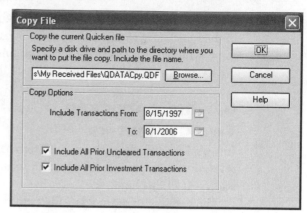

When the copy is finished, a dialog asks if you want to continue working with the original data file or the new copy. Select the appropriate option and click OK to continue working with Quicken.

## Deleting a Data File

The Delete command enables you to delete a data file. When you choose File | File Operations | Delete, the Delete Quicken File dialog, which looks a lot like the Create Quicken File dialog shown earlier in this appendix, appears. Use it to locate and select the data file you want to delete. When you click OK, another dialog appears, asking you to confirm that you want to delete the file. You must type in **yes** to delete the file.

Remember, deleting a Quicken data file permanently deletes all of its data. Use this command with care!

## Renaming a Data File

The Rename command enables you to rename a data file. This is the best way to rename a data file and the only method you should use. Renaming files in Windows could cause information to be lost.

When you choose File | File Operations | Rename, the Rename Quicken File dialog, shown here, appears. Use it to select the file you want to rename and enter a new name. When you click OK, Quicken changes the name of the main data file you selected and all of its support files.

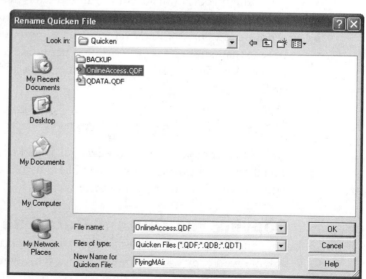

## Checking the Integrity of a Data File

The Validate command enables you to check the integrity of a Quicken data file. This command is particularly useful if you believe that a file has been damaged.

When you choose File | File Operations | Validate, the Validate Quicken File dialog appears. It looks very much like the Create Quicken File dialog illustrated earlier in this appendix. Use it to locate and select the file you want to validate. When you click OK, Quicken checks the data file's integrity. It then displays a dialog that tells you whether the file has any problems.

Sometimes you can repair a damaged file by simply opening it in Quicken. Use the Open command as discussed near the beginning of this appendix. If Quicken can't open the file, it tells you. That's when it's time to reach for that backup file. You *did* make one recently, didn't you?

## Making a Year-End Copy of a Data File

The Year-End Copy command creates two special copies of your data file. Choose File | File Operations | Year-End Copy to display the Year-End Copy dialog, shown here, and set options for the two files.

## Current Data File

The Current Data File section allows you to set options for the file you will continue working with in Quicken:

**Do Nothing. My Current Data File Will Remain Unchanged.**   This option simply saves a copy of the current data file as is.

**I Only Want Transactions In My Current Data File Starting With This Date.** This option enables you to enter a starting date for the files in the data file you will continue to use. For example, if you enter 1/1/2006, all transactions prior to that date will be removed from the data file. This option reduces the size of your data file, which makes it easier to back up and may help Quicken operate quicker and more efficiently.

### Archive File

The Archive File section allows you to set options for creating an archive copy of the file. An *archive* is a copy of older transactions saved in a separate file. You can set two options:

- Enter a complete path (or use the Browse button to enter a path) for the archive file.
- Enter the date for the last transaction to be included in the file. For example, if you enter 12/31/2005, the archive file will include all transactions in the current file, up to and including those transactions entered on 12/31/2005.

### Creating the Files

When you click OK in the Year-End Copy dialog, Quicken creates the two files. It then displays a dialog that enables you to select the file you want to work with: the Current File or the Archive File. Select the appropriate option (normally Current File) and click OK to continue working with Quicken.

# Password-Protecting Quicken Data

Quicken offers two types of password protection for your data: file passwords and transaction passwords. In this section, I tell you how these options work.

## Protecting a Data File

When you password-protect a data file, the file cannot be opened without the password. This is the ultimate in protection—it prevents unauthorized users from even seeing your data.

### Setting Up the Password

Choose File | Passwords | File to display the Quicken File Password dialog, which is shown here. Enter the same password in each text box and click OK.

## Opening a Password-Protected Data File

When you open a data file that is password-
protected, the Quicken Password dialog,
which is shown here, appears. You must enter
your password correctly and then click OK
to open the file.

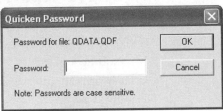

## Changing or Removing
## a Password

Choose File | Passwords | File to display the Quicken File Password dialog. Enter the
current password in the Old Password box, and then enter the same new password in
the two boxes beneath it. (To remove a password, leave the two bottom boxes empty.)
Click OK.

# Protecting Existing Transactions

When you password-protect existing transactions, the transactions cannot be
modified unless the password is properly entered. This prevents unauthorized or
accidental alterations to data.

## Setting Up the Password

Choose File | Passwords | Transaction
to display the Password To Modify
Existing Transactions dialog, shown
here. Enter the same password in the
top two text boxes. Then enter a date
before which the transactions cannot
be modified and click OK.

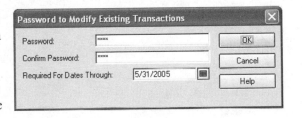

## Modifying a Password-Protected Transaction

When you attempt to modify a transaction
that is protected with a password, the
Quicken Password dialog, shown here,
appears. You must enter your password
correctly and then click OK to modify the
transaction.

## Changing or Removing a Password

Choose File | Passwords | Transaction to display the Change Transaction Password
dialog. Enter the current password in the Old Password box, and then enter the same
new password in the two boxes beneath it. (To remove a password, leave the two
bottom boxes empty.) Click OK.

## Password Tips

Here are a few things to keep in mind when working with passwords:

- Passwords can be up to 16 characters in length and can contain any character, including a space.
- Passwords are case sensitive. That means, for example, that *PassWord* is not the same as *password*.
- If you forget your password, you will not be able to access the data file. Write your password down and keep it in a safe place—but not on a sticky note attached to your computer monitor.

Your data file is only as secure as you make it. Quicken's password protection can help prevent unauthorized access to your Quicken data files.

# Customizing Quicken

## In This Appendix:

- *Customizing the Quicken Home window*
- *Customizing the toolbar*
- *Setting Quicken preferences*

Once you've worked with Quicken Personal Finance Software for a while, you may want to fine-tune the way it looks and works to best suit your needs. Some customization options—like selecting securities for online quotes and selecting accounts to synchronize with Quicken.com—are an integral part of using Quicken. Most of these options are discussed elsewhere in this book. Other customization options—like customizing the toolbar and setting Web Connect—are less commonly used. In this appendix, I explain all the customization options available for Quicken and provide cross-references to other chapters in the book where you can learn more about the features they work with.

 ## Customizing Quicken's Interface

Quicken offers a number of ways to customize its interface to best meet your needs. In this part of the appendix, I explain how to customize the Quicken Home window and toolbar.

### Customizing the Quicken Home Window

As discussed in Chapter 1, the Quicken Home window appears when you start Quicken. It displays a number of snapshots full of information about your finances and links to Quicken features.

**Appendix B**

**441**

Although you cannot customize the default Quicken Home window, you can create new views of the window and customize them. This makes it possible to include only the information you think is important in the window.

## Creating a New View

By creating multiple views, you can make several versions of the Quicken Home window, each with a specific set of information. You can then quickly switch from one view to another to see the information you want.

In the Quicken Home window, click the Create New View button on the button bar (or, if a second view already exists and is displayed, choose Create A New View from the Customize menu on the button bar). The Customize View dialog appears:

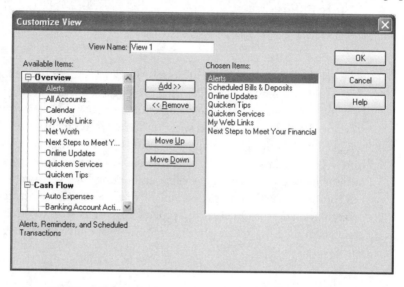

Enter a name for the view in the View Name box. Then follow the instructions in the next section to add items to the view and click OK. A new Quicken Home window view is created to your specifications and appears onscreen.

## Modifying the Current View

You can modify the current view with the Customize View dialog, shown previously. If it's not showing, choose Customize This View from the Customize menu on the button bar. Make changes as desired and click OK to save them.

**Adding an Item**    Items are organized by type in the Available Items list, making it easy to find the one you want. To add an item to the view, select it in the Available Items list and click Add. Its name appears in the Chosen Items list. You can include up to 16 items in the Quicken Home window.

**Removing an Item**    To remove an item from the view, select it in the Chosen Items list and click Remove.

**Rearranging Items**    To rearrange the order of items in the Chosen Items list, select an item and click Move Up or Move Down. Repeat this process until the items appear in the order you want.

## Switching from One View to Another

If you have created more than one view for the Quicken Home window, each view has its own tab at the top of the Quicken Home window, as shown here. To switch from one view to another, simply click its tab.

## Deleting a View

To delete a view, begin by switching to the view you want to delete. Then choose Delete This View from the Customize menu on the button bar. Click Yes in the confirmation dialog that appears. The view is deleted, and another view takes its place. You cannot delete the Home view.

## Customizing the Toolbar

The toolbar is a row of buttons along the top of the screen, just beneath the menu bar. These buttons offer quick access to Quicken features.

You can customize the toolbar by adding, removing, or rearranging buttons, or by changing the display options for toolbar buttons. You can do all this with the Customize Toolbar dialog, which is shown next. To open this dialog, choose Edit | Customize Tool Bar.

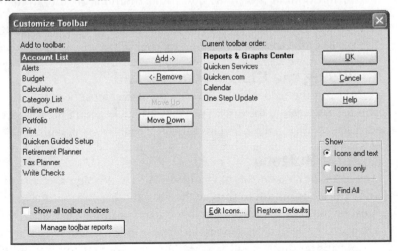

To customize the toolbar, make changes in this dialog and click OK. The toolbar is redrawn to your specifications.

## Adding Buttons

To add a button, select it in the Add To Toolbar list and click Add. Its name appears in the Current Toolbar Order list. If you want more items to choose from, turn on the Show All Toolbar Choices check box. The list expands to show at least five times as many items.

You can include as many buttons as you like on the toolbar. If the toolbar includes more buttons than can fit within the Quicken application window, a More button appears on the toolbar. Click this button to display a menu of buttons; choose the name of the button you want.

## Adding Saved Reports to the Toolbar

To add a saved report to the toolbar, click the Manage Toolbar Reports button. Then turn on the In Toolbar check box beside each saved report you want to add to the toolbar. Click OK to save your changes. I tell you more about the Manage Toolbar Reports dialog in Chapter 9.

## Removing Buttons

To remove a button, select it in the Current Toolbar Order list and click Remove. Its name is removed from the list.

## Rearranging Buttons

You can rearrange the order of buttons in the toolbar by changing their order in the Current Toolbar Order list. Simply select a button that you want to move and click Move Up or Move Down to change its position in the list.

## Changing the Appearance of Buttons

Two Show options determine how toolbar buttons are displayed:

- **Icons And Text** displays both the toolbar button and its label.
- **Icons Only** displays just the toolbar icon. When you point to an icon, its label appears.

## Including the Global Search Field

Turning on the Find All check box displays the global Search field in the toolbar. You can use this feature to search your entire Quicken data file for specific transactions, as discussed in Chapter 5. This feature is enabled by default.

## Editing Buttons

You can modify a button to change its label and assign a keyboard shortcut. Click the Edit Icons button to display the Edit Toolbar Button dialog. Then change the label or shortcut key for the toolbar button's command. Click OK to save your change. The label change does not appear in the Current Toolbar Order list, but it does appear on the toolbar when you save your customization settings.

### Restoring the Default Toolbar

To restore the toolbar back to its "factory settings," click the Restore Defaults button in the Customize Toolbar dialog. Then click OK in the confirmation dialog that appears. The buttons return to the way they appear throughout this book.

## Setting Preferences

The Preferences submenu under the Edit menu gives you access to dialogs for changing Quicken preference settings. In this section, I review all of the options you can change and tell you where you can learn more about the features they control.

## Quicken Program Preferences

As the name suggests, Quicken Program preferences control Quicken's general appearance and operations. To access these options, choose Edit | Preferences | Quicken Program. The Quicken Preferences dialog appears. It lists a variety of preference categories, each of which is discussed next.

### Startup

Startup preferences enable you to specify what should appear when you start Quicken. Use the drop-down list to select Quicken Home (the default setting), one of Quicken's Centers, or one of your accounts.

### Setup

Setup preferences enable you to set a number of general Quicken configuration options. Four groups of preference settings appear.

**Setup**   Setup options, which are illustrated next, control basic Quicken operations:

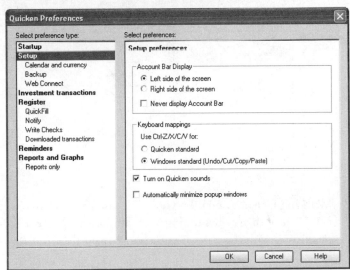

- **Account Bar Display** lets you position the Account Bar on either the left (default) or right side of the screen. Turning on the Never Display Account Bar check box hides the Account Bar from view. I tell you more about the Account Bar and how to customize it in Chapters 1 and 3.

- **Keyboard Mappings** enables you to change what certain standard Windows keyboard shortcuts do. In most Windows programs, the CTRL-Z, CTRL-X, CTRL-C, and CTRL-V shortcut keys perform commands on the Edit menu. Because these commands have limited use within Quicken, you can map several Quicken-specific commands to these keys. Select the option as shown in Table B-1 for the mapping you want.

- **Turn On Quicken Sounds** turns on Quicken sound effects. You may want to turn this check box off if you use Quicken in an environment where its sounds might annoy the people around you.

- **Automatically Minimize Popup Windows** automatically minimizes a Quicken window—such as a report window or the Category List window—to the Quicken task bar when you click outside that window. (This is the window behavior in previous versions of Quicken.) With this option turned off, you can have multiple Quicken windows open at once and can manually minimize each one. I tell you more about Quicken's windows in Chapter 1.

**Calendar and Currency**    The folks at Intuit realize that not everyone manages their finances on a calendar year basis or in U.S. dollars alone. The Calendar And Currency options, which are shown next, enable you to customize these settings for the way you use Quicken:

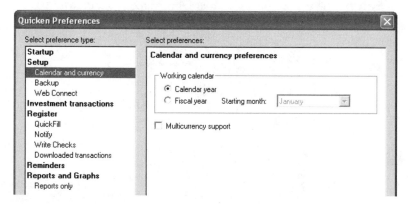

- **Working Calendar** enables you to choose between two options: Calendar Year is a 12-month year beginning with January, and Fiscal Year is a 12-month year beginning with the month you choose from the drop-down list.

| Keystroke | Quicken Standard | Undo/Cut/Copy/Paste (Windows Standard) |
|-----------|------------------|----------------------------------------|
| CTRL-Z | QuickZoom a report amount | Edit I Undo |
| CTRL-X | Edit I Transaction I Go To Matching Transfer | Edit I Cut |
| CTRL-C | Tools I Category List | Edit I Copy |
| CTRL-V | Edit I Transaction I Void Transaction | Edit I Paste |

**Table B-1 • Keyboard Mapping Options**

- **Multicurrency Support** assigns a "home" currency to all of your current data, placing a currency symbol beside every amount. You can then enter amounts in other currencies by entering the appropriate currency symbol. You can confirm the default currency in the Windows Regional Settings control panel. It is not necessary to set this option unless you plan to work with multiple currencies in one Quicken data file.

**Backup**    The Backup options, illustrated next, enable you to customize the way Quicken's Automatic Backup feature works:

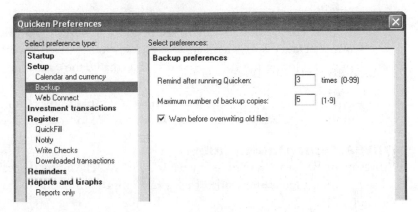

- **Remind After Running Quicken** *NN* **Times** enables you to specify how often you should be reminded to back up your Quicken data file. The lower the value in this text box, the more often Quicken reminds you to back up. Keep the value low if you don't regularly back up Quicken data with other files. I tell you how to back up your data in Appendix A.
- **Maximum Number Of Backup Copies** is the number of backup copies Quicken should keep. The higher the value in this text box, the more backup copies of your Quicken data are saved. This enables you to go back further if you discover a problem with your current Quicken data file. I tell you more about backing up data in Appendix A.

- **Warn Before Overwriting Old Files** tells Quicken to display a warning before it overwrites old backup files with new ones.

**Web Connect**    The Web Connect options, shown next, enable you to customize the way Quicken's Web Connect feature works. Web Connect, as discussed in Chapter 6, is an alternative method for downloading transaction information from your financial institution into your Quicken data file.

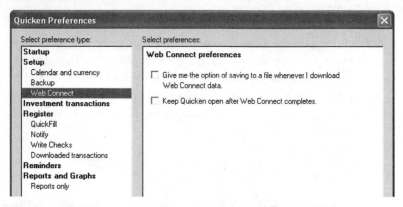

- **Give Me The Option Of Saving To A File Whenever I Download Web Connect Data** displays a dialog that enables you to save the downloaded Web Connect information to a file on disk. Normally, the data is imported directly into the appropriate account in your Quicken data file.
- **Keep Quicken Open After Web Connect Completes** tells Quicken to keep running after Web Connect completes a download from the Web.

## Investment Transactions

Investment Transactions options (shown next) let you customize the way the Investment Transaction list looks and works. I tell you about the Investment Transaction list in Chapter 10.

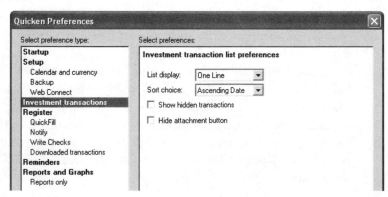

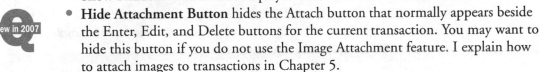

- **List Display** determines whether transactions should appear with one or two lines in the list.
- **Sort Choice** determines whether transactions should be sorted in ascending or descending order by date.
- **Show Hidden Transactions** displays hidden transactions in the list.
- **Hide Attachment Button** hides the Attach button that normally appears beside the Enter, Edit, and Delete buttons for the current transaction. You may want to hide this button if you do not use the Image Attachment feature. I explain how to attach images to transactions in Chapter 5.

## Register

Register preferences enable you to fine-tune the way the account register works. Four groups of settings appear. I discuss account register windows throughout this book, but I provide details for using them in Chapter 5.

**Register**    Register options, shown next, affect the way the transactions you enter appear in the account register window. I discuss using the register window in detail in Chapter 5.

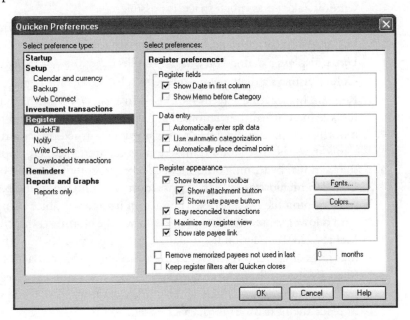

- **Show Date In First Column** displays the transaction date in the first column of the register.
- **Show Memo Before Category** displays the Memo field above the Category field.

- **Automatically Enter Split Data** turns the OK button in the Split Transaction window into an Enter button for entering the transaction.
- **Use Automatic Categorization** uses the Automatic Categorization feature to "guess" which category should be assigned to a transaction based on a database of company names and keywords stored within Quicken.
- **Automatically Place Decimal Point** automatically enters a decimal point two places to the left when using Quicken's built-in calculator. For example, if you enter 1543 in the calculator, Quicken enters 15.43.
- **Show Transaction Toolbar** adds the Enter, Edit, and Split buttons to the currently selected transaction.
- **Show Attachment Button** displays the attachment button, which looks like a paper clip.

- **Show Rate Payee Button** displays the Rate button in the toolbar for the current transaction.
- **Gray Reconciled Transactions** displays all reconciled transactions with gray characters rather than black characters.
- **Maximize My Register View** makes the register part of the Quicken application window take up as much space as possible.

- **Show Rate Payee Link** displays the Rate Your Payees On Zipingo link at the bottom-right corner of account register windows.
- **Fonts** displays a dialog you can use to select the font for register windows.
- **Colors** displays a dialog you can use to select colors for register windows.
- **Remove Memorized Payees Not Used In Last *NN* Months** tells Quicken to remove memorized transactions that have not been used within the number of months you specify. By default, this feature is turned off; as a result, Quicken remembers the first 2,000 transactions you enter and then stops remembering transactions. By turning on this check box and entering a value of **6** (for example), Quicken memorizes only the transactions you entered in the past six months, thus keeping the Memorized Transaction list manageable. Using this feature with a lower value (for example, **3**) can weed one-time transactions out of the Memorized Transaction list. Changing this option does not affect transactions that have already been entered. I discuss memorized transactions in Chapter 7.
- **Keep Register Filters After Quicken Closes** remembers any register filter settings you may have made when you close Quicken so those settings are in place the next time you start Quicken.

**QuickFill**    QuickFill options, which are shown next, allow you to fine-tune the way Quicken's QuickFill feature works. I tell you more about QuickFill in Chapter 7.

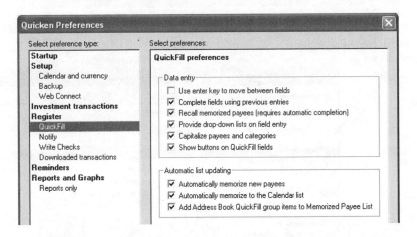

- **Use Enter Key To Move Between Fields** enables you to use both the ENTER and TAB keys to move from field to field when entering data.
- **Complete Fields Using Previous Entries** enters transaction information using the information from previous entries.
- **Recall Memorized Payees** uses memorized payees to fill in QuickFill entries. This option is not available if the Complete Fields Using Previous Entries option is disabled.
- **Provide Drop-Down Lists On Field Entry** automatically displays the drop-down list when you advance to a field with a list.
- **Capitalize Payees And Categories** automatically makes the first letter of each word in a payee name or category uppercase.
- **Show Buttons On QuickFill Fields** displays drop-down list buttons on fields for which you can use QuickFill.
- **Automatically Memorize New Payees** tells Quicken to automatically enter all transactions for a new payee to the Memorized Transaction list.
- **Automatically Memorize To The Calendar List** tells Quicken to automatically add memorized transactions to the Memorized Transaction list in the Calendar window. This option is turned on by default. The Financial Calendar is covered in Chapter 7; you can display the Memorized Transaction list by choosing Show Memorized Transaction List from the Options menu on the Calendar's button bar.
- **Add Address Book QuickFill Group Items To Memorized Payee List** tells Quicken to add entries from the Financial Address Book to the Memorized Payee list so they automatically fill in address fields when writing checks.

**Notify**   Notify options, shown next, affect the way you are notified about problems when you enter transactions in the register:

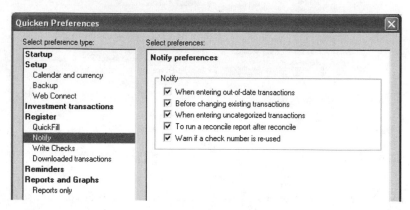

- **When Entering Out-Of-Date Transactions** warns you when you try to record a transaction for a date more than a year from the current date.
- **Before Changing Existing Transactions** warns you when you try to modify a previously entered transaction.
- **When Entering Uncategorized Transactions** warns you when you try to record a transaction without assigning a category to it.
- **To Run A Reconcile Report After Reconcile** asks if you want to display a Reconcile report when you complete an account reconciliation.
- **Warn If A Check Number Is Re-used** warns you if you assign a check number that was already assigned in another transaction.

**Write Checks**   Write Checks options, shown here, affect the way the checks you enter with the Write Checks window appear when printed:

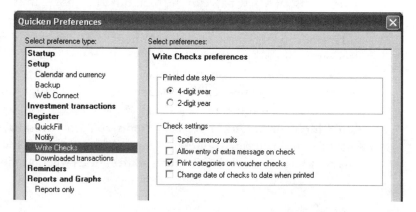

- **Printed Date Style** enables you to select a four-digit or two-digit date style.
- **Spell Currency Units** tells Quicken to spell out the currency amount in the second Amount field.
- **Allow Entry Of Extra Message On Check** displays an additional text box for a message in the Write Checks window. The message you enter is printed on the check in a place where it cannot be seen if the check is mailed in a window envelope.
- **Print Categories On Voucher Checks** prints category information, including splits and classes, on the voucher part of voucher checks. This option affects only voucher-style checks.
- **Change Date Of Checks To Date When Printed** automatically prints the print date, rather than the transaction date, on each check.

**Downloaded Transactions**    Downloaded Transactions options, which are shown next, control the way Quicken handles transactions downloaded into Quicken from your financial institution:

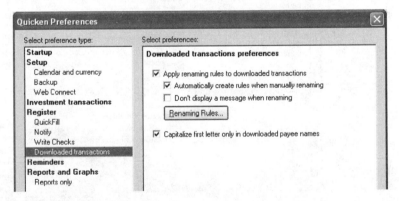

- **Apply Renaming Rules To Downloaded Transactions** turns on Quicken's new renaming feature, which I discuss in Chapter 6.
- **Automatically Create Rules When Manually Renaming** tells Quicken to create renaming rules automatically based on transactions you rename manually.
- **Don't Display a Message When Renaming** tells Quicken to rename transactions without displaying a dialog telling you that it has done so.
- **Renaming Rules** displays the Renaming Rules For Downloaded Transactions dialog, which you can use to create, modify, and remove renaming rules.
- **Capitalize First Letter Only In Downloaded Payee Names** capitalizes just the first letter of a payee name for a downloaded transaction.

## Reminders

Reminder preferences enable you to set the lead time for calendar notes to appear in Alerts snapshots. This does not affect the lead time for scheduled transactions. Select a lead time period from the drop-down list; timing options range from Last Week to Next 14 Days. I tell you about alerts in Chapter 7.

## Reports and Graphs

Reports And Graphs preferences include two categories of options for creating reports and graphs. I tell you about creating reports and graphs in Chapter 9.

**Reports And Graphs Preferences**   Reports And Graphs options, shown next, enable you to set default options for creating reports and graphs:

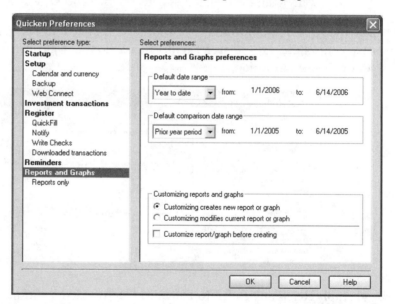

- **Default Date Range** and **Default Comparison Date Range** enable you to specify a default range for regular and comparison reports. Choose an option from each drop-down list. If you choose Custom, you can enter exact dates.
- **Customizing Reports And Graphs** options determine how reports and graphs are customized and what happens when they are. **Customizing Creates New Report Or Graph**, which is the default setting, creates a subreport based on the report you customize. **Customizing Modifies Current Report Or Graph** changes the report you customize without creating a subreport.
- **Customize Report/Graph Before Creating** tells Quicken to offer to customize a report or graph when you choose its name from a submenu under the Reports menu.

**Reports Only**    This group of options, which is shown next, applies only to reports:

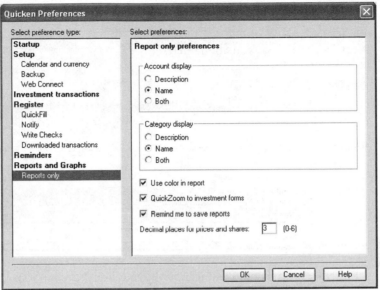

- **Account Display** and **Category Display** enable you to set what you want to display for each account or category listed in the report: Description, Name, or Both.
- **Use Color In Report** tells Quicken to use color when displaying report titles and negative numbers.
- **QuickZoom To Investment Forms** tells Quicken to display the investment form for a specific investment when you double-click it in an investment report. With this check box turned off, Quicken displays the investment register transaction entry instead.
- **Remind Me To Save Reports** tells Quicken to ask whether you want to save a customized report when you close the report window.
- **Decimal Places For Prices And Shares** enables you to specify the number of decimal places to display for per share security prices and number of shares in investment reports.

## Customize Online Update Options

You can customize One Step Update options in the Connection tab of the Customize Online Updates dialog, shown next. (Other options in this dialog are covered in Chapters 6 and 11.) Choose Edit | Preferences | Customize Online Updates and click the Connection tab.

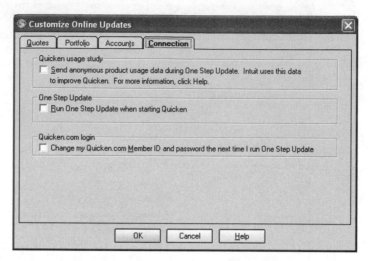

- **Send Anonymous Product Usage Data During One Step Update** sends information about the way you use Quicken to the product development team at Intuit. This helps them understand how users like you utilize Quicken's features so they can improve Quicken.
- **Run One Step Update When Starting Quicken** automatically starts the One Step Update procedure when you start Quicken. You might find this feature useful if you always run One Step Update as part of a Quicken work session.
- **Change My Quicken.com Member ID And Password The Next Time I Run One Step Update** instructs Quicken to display the Quicken.com login screen when you connect to Quicken.com. With this option turned off, Quicken can automatically enter your saved login information if, when you registered with Quicken.com, you selected the option to save your login information and are connecting with the same computer. This check box is disabled until you set up a Quicken.com login by registering your copy of Quicken online. I tell you about registering Quicken in Chapter 1.

# Index

## I

asset and liability account listings on, 320–321

Auto Expenses area of, 322–323

Loan Accounts Summary on, 321–322

opening, 319–320

Options pop-up menu on, 321, 324–325, 328

Overview window of, 326–329

viewing account details in Register window, 325

## Q

Quicken

about, 3

accessing on the Web, 59

adding features to, 18

built-in Internet links in, 51

converting existing data file, 8

exiting, 18

importing TurboTax data to, 417

installing, 5–6

interface for, 9–13

launching built-in browser, 327

Online Backup service, 434

onscreen help, 16–17

preparing data files as new use, 6–7

registering, 8–9

setting reminders in, 147

setup preferences, 445–446

starting, 6, 445

switching from Quicken Home Inventory to, 313

tasks handled by, 4

turning sound on/off, 446

types of accounts in, 32–33

updates for, 6

upgrading and converting data for, 8

versions of, 4–5

*See also* user interface

Quicken Account Setup dialog. *See* Account Setup dialog

Quicken Backup dialog, 433

Quicken Basic, 4

Quicken Bill Pay

about, 60, 62

costs of, 109

Online Payment vs., 109

setting up, 111–112

Quicken.com

about, 13, 59

built-in browser in, 13, 327

checking exported portfolio information from, 257–258

finding participating financial institutions, 60–62

illustrated, 14

navigating on Web sites from, 58

One Step Update with, 168

testing Internet connections by visiting, 54–55

types of user support on, 57

updating bank accounts in, 106, 138–140

Web surfing from, 57

WebEntry, 106, 135–138

Quicken Deluxe, 4

Quicken Express Setup, 19–30

account creation with, 20

Add My Deposits And Other Income window, 25–26

Add Regular Bills And Expenses window, 26–27

additional data file setup tasks, 30

automatic launching of, 21

connecting accounts to bank, 23–24

entering personal information, 21–22

finishing processes in, 28–30

No, I Do Not Want To Connect option, 24

**S**